W9-AMP-855

Make My Day

ALSO BY J. HOBERMAN

Film After Film (Or, What Became of 21st Century Cinema?)
Found Illusions I: An Army of Phantoms: American Movies and the Making of the Cold War
Rituals of Rented Island: Object Theater, Loft Performances, and the New Psychodrama—Manhattan, 1970–1980 (with Jay Sanders)
Entertaining America: Jews, Movies and Broadcasting (with Jeffrey Shandler)
The Magic Hour: Film at Fin de Siècle
Found Illusions II: The Dream Life: Movies, Media, and the Mythology of the Sixties
On Jack Smith's Flaming Creatures (and Other Secret-flix of Cinemaroc)
The Red Atlantis: Communist Culture in the Absence of Communism
42nd Street
Bridge of Light: Yiddish Film Between Two Worlds
Vulgar Modernism: Writing on Film and Other Media
Midnight Movies (with Jonathan Rosenbaum)
Dennis Hopper: From Method to Madness
Home Made Movies: Twenty Years of American 8mm & Super-8 Films

Make My Day

MOVIE CULTURE IN THE AGE OF REAGAN

J. Hoberman

THE
NEW
PRESS

NEW YORK
LONDON

Requests for permission to reproduce selections from this book should be mailed
to: Permissions Department, The New Press, 120 Wall Street, 31st floor, New York,
NY 10005.

Published in the United States by The New Press, New York, 2019
Distributed by Two Rivers Distribution

ISBN 978-1-62097-100-0 (ebook)

LIBRARY OF CONGRESS CATALOGING-IN-PUBLICATION DATA

Names: Hoberman, J., author.
Title: Make my day : movie culture in the age of Reagan / J. Hoberman.
Description: New York : The New Press, 2019. | Includes bibliographical
    references and index.
Identifiers: LCCN 2019001037 | ISBN 9781595580061 (hc : alk. paper)
Subjects: LCSH: Motion pictures—United States—History—20th century. |
    Motion pictures—Political aspects—United States. | United
    States—Politics and government—1981-1989.
Classification: LCC PN1993.5.U6 H565 2019 | DDC 791.430973—dc23
LC record available at https://lccn.loc.gov/2019001037

The New Press publishes books that promote and enrich public discussion and
understanding of the issues vital to our democracy and to a more equitable
world. These books are made possible by the enthusiasm of our readers; the
support of a committed group of donors, large and small; the collaboration of our
many partners in the independent media and the not-for-profit sector; booksellers,
who often hand-sell New Press books; librarians; and above all by our authors.

www.thenewpress.com

Book design and composition by Westchester Publishing Services
This book was set in Minion Pro

Printed in the United States of America

10   9   8   7   6   5   4   3   2   1

For Julian, Izidore, Caleb, and Elena in hope that their generation will help America find a just future

CONTENTS

PREFACE

Make My Day: Movie Culture in the Age of Reagan completes a trilogy begun with *The Dream Life: Movies, Media, and the Mythology of the Sixties* (2003) and, albeit flashing back to the 1940s and 1950s, continued in *An Army of Phantoms: American Movies and the Making of the Cold War* (2011).

These can be read in chronological order, the order in which they were written, or independently. In any case, I see them as one book, titled *Found Illusions*, and cherish the hope, however utopian, that they might someday be published with a common index. Readers of the first two books will see certain ideas come to fruition in the third; readers of *Make My Day* will find much that is prefigured in the earlier books.

Although *Found Illusions* was conceived long ago, I began writing *Make My Day* during the presidency of Barack Obama and finished it under that of Donald Trump. His presence casts a shadow over the entire book although I do not explicitly acknowledge it until the epilogue.

Because I began in the middle of the story, I did not anticipate the obvious, namely that the villainous Ronald Reagan would eventually be my protagonist. Reagan is the lone American politician, save South Carolina senator Strom Thurmond, whose career spanned four decades (although only half of them were spent holding or seeking public office), the duration of the Cold War. I believe that Frank Sinatra and Jerry Lewis, both Reagan buddies, may be the only other American pop stars with comparable longevity.

Many individuals figure in two of the three books, but the only other people, besides Ronald and Nancy Reagan, who are even marginally present in all three are JFK, Richard Nixon, Bill Clinton, George W. Bush, Martin Luther King, Norman Mailer, Tom Wolfe, Ayn Rand, John Ford, John Huston, John Wayne, Marilyn Monroe, Henry Fonda, Marlon Brando, Dennis Hopper, Elvis, and the fictional Davy Crockett—which probably says as much about my sense of the period as it does about the period itself.

All three volumes reference Disneyland and the film critics Andrew Sarris and Pauline Kael. That the latter became more prominent as *Found*

Illusions continued came as a surprise to me, in that my critical disagreements with Kael are profound. The conclusion I draw is that she was the Cold War's preeminent sociological film critic—a characterization she would surely have rejected, although it's worth noting that by the mid-1970s, sociological analysis of Hollywood movies had become commonplace. The philosopher Jacques Ellul, author of *Propaganda: The Formation of Men's Attitudes*, is also cited throughout.

Make My Day is not a work of film criticism. Nor is it strictly speaking a history. I see it rather as a chronicle in which political events and Hollywood movies are folded into each other to illuminate what, writing in 1960, Mailer termed America's "dream life." Consequently I have discussed many movies that I dislike, often at some length, and omitted or minimized some that I admire. *The Next Voice You Hear, High Noon, On the Waterfront, A Face in the Crowd, Bonnie and Clyde, Dirty Harry, Jaws,* and *Ghostbusters* are not to my mind the greatest movies of their era. Rather, they are among the richest political allegories. Similarly, I have concentrated on certain genres—action films and science fiction—which lend themselves most obviously to political readings. (Westerns, so crucial to *The Dream Life* and *An Army of Phantoms*, were all but played out in the period covered by *Make My Day*.) Virtually all movies discussed could have viewed by Reagan—or actually were.

I believe that to some degree every movie is a documentary of its own making and I am particularly interested in how movies were received in their own time. Box office grosses aside, it is not easy to gauge initial reception. For that reason, I have relied on contemporary reviews—both from mainstream and from sectarian sources—to provide some sense of how they were taken by journalists and professional filmgoers. In writing *Make My Day*, I could not ignore the fact that, throughout the 1980s, I myself was one such professional, reviewing movies for the *Village Voice*, a publication that allowed me an extraordinary amount of freedom to write what and how I wanted.

Rather than paraphrase my articles and columns, I have excerpted them, sometimes in annotated form. Consequently *Make My Day* is a good deal more personal than its predecessors—not least for the strong opinions I then expressed on Ronald Reagan, candidate and president.

—J. Hoberman
New York City, December 2018

Make My Day

INTRODUCTION:
THE DEPARTMENT OF AMUSEMENT

Film is forever.

—RONALD REAGAN, March 31, 1981

Two months and ten days after his inauguration as president and on the afternoon of the 53rd Academy Awards ceremony, Ronald Reagan was struck and wounded by the last of six shots fired by John Hinckley Jr., a deranged fan obsessed with the 1976 movie *Taxi Driver* and its star Jodie Foster.

The Oscars were delayed for twenty-four hours but, on the night of March 31, even as the president lay recuperating in George Washington University Hospital, his image addressed the American people. After an introduction by the evening's host, Johnny Carson, who noted that Reagan had asked for a TV in his hospital room so that he might watch the show, a screen descended on the stage of the Dorothy Chandler Pavilion.

Speaking from the White House, where he had been recorded several weeks earlier, the president—a member of the Academy until his election—then welcomed, on behalf of himself and his wife, herself a film actress as Nancy Davis, those fellow citizens "eagerly awaiting" the presentation of the awards:

> It's surely no state secret that Nancy and I share your interest in the results of this year's balloting. We're not alone; the miracle of American technology links us with millions of moviegoers around the world. It is the motion picture that shows us all not only how we look and sound but—more important—how we feel. When it achieves its most noble intent, film reveals that people everywhere share common dreams and emotions.

Reagan's brief speech, which came an inch from being delivered beyond the grave, was followed by a tribute to the year's departed movie stars that included Steve McQueen, Peter Sellers, and Mae West, ending with a tap-dance finale, suggests a sense of cinema as collective fantasy and shared national narrative.*

Call it a political unconscious, a social imaginary, or simply America's dream life—the place where, as Greek tragedies addressed the Athenian polity's primal conflicts, Hollywood scenarios and movie stars articulated the public's inchoate yearnings. Norman Mailer used the term in his account of the 1960 Democratic National Convention that nominated John F. Kennedy, predicting that the American landscape would be overwhelmed by the "subterranean river of untapped, ferocious, lonely, and romantic desires, that concentration of ecstasy and violence which is the dream life of the nation."

Throughout the Reagan presidency, that Dream Life would be more channeled—which is to say more rational in its irrationality.

Stand Up and Cheer! (1934)

Politicians within a democracy and the makers of mass culture share a common mission, namely to project scenarios that will attract the largest possible audience—or perhaps, using a word derived from the Latin "hold together," entertain them.

Why entertain entertainment? Film theorist Richard Dyer suggests that "entertainment" is essentially compensatory—it not only offers "the image of 'something better' to escape into" but also "something we want deeply that our day-to-day lives don't provide." (That something, crucially, may be something we didn't know we even wanted.) Entertainment is utopian, although, as Dyer points out, its appeal is largely to the emotions, presenting "what utopia would feel like rather than how it would be organized."

---

* Jack Valenti, president of the Motion Picture Association of America, made the request for this special appearance in early February, less than two weeks into the Reagan presidency, telling Michael Deaver, White House deputy chief of staff and Reagan's prime image adviser, that "as you well know, the American film dominates the world, enticing audiences in more than 120 countries. It may well be the most wanted U.S. export!"

Dyer's entertainment paradigm is the Hollywood musical. The paradigm of that paradigm is the 1934 Hollywood musical, *Stand Up and Cheer!* Directed by Hamilton MacFadden, this Fox Film production, based on a story idea by the popular humorist and social commentator Will Rogers and best remembered for introducing audiences to six-year-old Shirley Temple, exemplifies the virtual utopia Dyer describes. A manifesto as well as a musical, the command in its title demands action. Not for the last time Hollywood would acknowledge an actual problem and propose itself as the solution. See, for example, *The Next Voice You Hear*, the 1950 MGM production, stolidly directed by William Wellman, in which God takes to the radio to address the American people, ensuring that everyone receives the same divine message.

Stand Up and Cheer! opens with a helicopter landing on the White House lawn. Warner Baxter, who distinguished himself the previous year in the Warner Bros. musical *42nd Street* (released to coincide with Franklin D. Roosevelt's inauguration and promoted as "a New Deal in Entertainment"), emerges as Lawrence Cromwell, "the world's recognized authority on feminine beauty and charm," drafted by the president of the United States (coyly unidentified) to head a new amalgam of the movie industry and the National Recovery Administration called the Department of Amusement.

Although set at a moment of crisis, *Stand Up and Cheer!* has relatively little conflict. As a child, Shirley Dugan (Shirley Temple) needs a waiver, easily acquired, to continue working as her father's dance partner, while Cromwell must prevail over a cabal of evil businessmen who, obscurely profiting from the Depression, attempt to thwart the Department of Amusement with a campaign of ridicule: "It shouldn't be hard to make them see the hand of the devil in Cromwell's national nonsense," one sneers, articulating a widespread attitude regarding Hollywood.

Needless to say, the broom of Cromwell's "national nonsense" easily sweeps these straw men into history's dustbin. The first instance of federalized amusement is a mega-production that begins with a burly worker bursting through a facsimile of a newspaper front page to declare "I'm Laughing," and it goes on to visualize what political theorist Benedict Anderson calls an "imagined community." Everyone in America—welders, blacksmiths, hillbilly farmers, street sweepers, cops, chorines, railroad engineers—unites in the struggle against self-pity. There are Irish mothers and Jewish seamstresses, and in the shadowy conclusion, the white actress Tess Gardella performs in burnt cork under the name Aunt Jemima for an apparently African American congregation.

Together they sing a song of mildly coercive good cheer:

> I'm laughin' and I have nothing to laugh about,
> But if I can laugh and sing and shout—brother, so can you!

Entertainment is inscribed throughout the movie. After a half-dozen more numbers, including a vision of total mobilization provocatively titled "We're Out of the Red," *Stand Up and Cheer!* concludes by proclaiming its own success. A providential messenger arrives: "Mr. Cromwell, I have great news for you—the Depression is over!" Cromwell's visceral metaphors of social organization have cured the malaise.

If entertainment is a form of organized feelings, Dyer identifies five issues it addresses: the condition of scarcity is replaced by the spectacle of abundance, that of exhaustion by energy, dreariness by intensity, manipulation by transparency (meaning "honesty"), and fragmentation by community. I would propose two other relevant binary oppositions: anxiety versus reassurance and constraint versus freedom. For entertainment is also an ideology. As the concept of freedom is to America, so entertainment is to Hollywood.

Some took *Stand Up and Cheer!* to be a blatant advertisement for Roosevelt's New Deal. "The gist of this preposterous [National Recovery Act] propaganda musical is that the depression is a purely mental state," the future *Daily Worker* film critic David Platt declared in the leftist journal *New Theatre*. "Mass campaigns of musical enlightenment are forthwith organized against poverty and misery. An insatiable longing for tap-dancing and mammy songs is created in the army of unemployed and hungry workers"— which is one way to describe the movie's utopian premise or the social function of entertainment. Indeed, *Stand Up and Cheer!*—that is to say the Department of Amusement—produced Shirley Temple who, by mid-1936, was the biggest star in Hollywood, the savior of her studio, 20th Century Fox, the seventh-highest-paid person in America and the president's rival as a national icon.*

---

* *Stand Up and Cheer!* also features a powerful appearance by a representative of another powerless group—thirty-two-year-old Stepin Fetchit, then the best-known and most

The Department of Amusement anticipates Hollywood's subsequent mobilization: its World War II contributions (through the intervention of a Ministry of Truth, Justice and the American Way, acting in concert with the Office of War Information) and its role in a cosmic struggle (under the pressure of the FBI, the CIA, the House Committee on Un-American Activities, and the Department of Defense). In this later phase, the adversary was not the Great Depression but an Implacable Alien Other.

It's not impossible that the mass-produced idea of *Stand Up and Cheer!*, originally released scarcely more than a year into the New Deal, impressed itself upon a twenty-three-year-old Des Moines sportscaster named Ronald "Dutch" Reagan. And even if it did not, the movie is nevertheless a material manifestation of an idea that would inform the consciousness of that generation of Americans to which Ronald Reagan belonged.*

The Dream Life would never be more transparent.

"Where Were You in '62" (or August 1973)?

Stand Up and Cheer! cheerfully anticipates the nightmare scenario of Elia Kazan and Budd Schulberg's 1957 film *A Face in the Crowd*—in which an unscrupulous television personality becomes a political force—suggesting that movie stars and media personalities might nominate themselves for a leading role in American democracy.

Liberated from their studios as a result of the movie industry's post–World War II reorganization, confident that their images might change the world, the newly powerful movie stars imagined themselves on the stage of history,

---

successful African American actor in Hollywood. Both Temple and Fetchit are exploited, but if Fetchit's grotesque routines, excised from most versions of the film in circulation, are excruciating theater of embarrassment, Temple's remain profoundly utopian. More than any other child star, she had the capacity to embody joy. For her, work was play. "Shirley doesn't really work in the act," her father in the film explains, circumnavigating child labor laws.

* Reagan was not only a movie fan but an ardent New Dealer whose father John Edward "Jack" Reagan was then employed by the Works Progress Administration in Dixon, Illinois. Although the historical record is sketchy and the future president vague with regard to the nature of his father's WPA job, Reagan biographer Anne Edwards maintains that "the days of Jack's government employment were, perhaps, the finest of his life, more exciting and fulfilling than any previous experience."

playing Hollywood Freedom Fighters, Righteous Outlaws, and Legal Vigilantes.

Writing in the mid-1950s, movie critic Pauline Kael called the youth rebellion embodied in juvenile delinquency films like *The Wild One* (1953), *The Blackboard Jungle* (1955), and *Rebel Without a Cause* (1955) "a movement so nihilistic it doesn't even have a program" and "its only leader is a movie star: Marlon Brando." Her analysis proved prophetic. Kirk Douglas produced *Spartacus*; John Wayne countered with *The Alamo*—both timed to open during the 1960 presidential campaign that resulted in the election of America's first movie-star president, John F. Kennedy. Five years and another campaign later, Wayne regarded himself as a president's rival, producing *The Green Berets* (1968) in order to show Lyndon Johnson how the Vietnam War should be presented—and won.

At the same time, Warren Beatty (a young actor who had declined the opportunity to play the young JFK in *PT 109*) addressed himself to America's internal state with *Bonnie and Clyde* (1967)—a movie that was not only exceedingly violent but, steeped in movie-ness, this was the first Hollywood film to project the past as the "movie" past, in part by showing its wildly contemporary protagonists at the cinema, happily enjoying *Gold Diggers of 1933*.

That sense of the past was similarly embodied in California's newly elected governor, the former radio broadcaster, Hollywood activist, and TV personality Ronald Reagan. Having grown up in the Department of Amusement, Reagan instinctively understood how a president (or a friendly neighbor or John Wayne) is supposed to act. A politician who built a career as a professional image addressed an audience supremely responsive to these images. It was as if he had been summoned out of the past to fabricate the future.

"How much more nostalgia can America take?" *Time* magazine asked in May 1971, nearly seven years into America's involvement in Vietnam and four months after Ronald Reagan's second inauguration as California governor, even as the counterculture's last Righteous Outlaws—Sweet Sweetback (Melvin Van Peebles), El Topo (Alejandro Jodorowsky), and Billy Jack (Tom Laughlin)—were storming the nation's movie screens, freak flags high.

The real questions were: How can a nation be understood as nostalgic? And what accounts for *Time*'s confidence in diagnosing this presumed universal condition?

The word "nostalgia" derives from the Greek term for homesickness; it connotes a place that once was or perhaps a movie once seen. "Without question, the most popular pastime of the year is looking back," *Time* declared, connecting this cultural homesickness to the movies, and the movies to their pre-1945 Golden Era. "Sometimes it seems as if half the country would like to be dancing cheek to cheek with Fred Astaire and Ginger Rogers. The other half yearns to join Humphrey Bogart and Ingrid Bergman on a back-lot *Casablanca*."

Where this left the audience for *Billy Jack*, the year's second-highest-grossing movie, or Melvin Van Peeble's immensely profitable *Sweet Sweetback's Baadasssss Song*, let alone the midnight movie blockbuster *El Topo*, is unclear. Perhaps all movies are in some sense *Casablanca*, carrying within themselves an implanted memory of better, more innocent, more entertaining times. The Department of Amusement has a part to play. For thanks to cinema and television, the past had become a collection of images, readily evoked by outmoded styles of consumption, discarded fashions, and obsolete attitudes. An audience might brainwash itself: In its reactionary celebration of dated movies, *Time* had intuited that nostalgia for an imaginary past would soon become a political tool.

George Lucas's *American Graffiti* (1973) was the product of a miserable, score-settling period. Richard Nixon had begun withdrawing American troops from Vietnam, but 330,000 still remained in January 1971. The month of March began with the Weather Underground detonating a bomb in a Capitol building toilet and ended with judgement passed on the two arch-criminals of December 1969: two days after Lieutenant William Calley was found guilty of murdering twenty-two Vietnamese civilians at My Lai and sentenced to life in prison, while the longest murder trial in American history concluded with Charles Manson convicted of first-degree murder and condemned to death.

In late April, in advance of a demonstration estimated by organizers as half a million strong, Vietnam veterans protested the war by dumping over seven hundred medals on the steps of the U.S. Capitol building. It was that spring that Lucas's first feature, the dystopian science fiction film *THX 1138*, was shown at the Cannes Film Festival and Lucas first contemplated making a movie about his adolescence. Reacting to the cultural malaise he blamed on the endless War in Vietnam as well as the negative response to *THX 1138*, he decided "it was time to make a movie where people felt better coming out of the theater than when they went in. It had become depressing to go to the movies." Entertainment, neglecting its social function, needed to be reformed.

With some exceptions (the films noir of the 1940s and 1950s, the American new wave films of the late 1960s and early 1970s), feel-bad entertainments (which typically concern protagonists defeated by forces beyond their control) have been immeasurably rarer than feel-good entertainments— unambiguous examples of what the French philosopher Jacques Ellul calls "sociological propaganda."*

The summer of 1971 was a season of pessimistic, druggy hippie Westerns and crypto-Westerns: *McCabe and Mrs. Miller, Two-Lane Blacktop, The Hired Hand, Doc*, and *The Last Movie*. Released in November, Don McLean's song "American Pie" went to number one for four weeks in early 1972, installing on the national soundtrack a lengthy, cryptic dirge about "the day the music died," apparently an allegory about the origins and end of rock 'n' roll. The mass audience fractured. A full-scale reinterpretation of twentieth-century American history from the viewpoint of white ethnic immigrants, Francis Ford Coppola's *The Godfather*—perhaps Hollywood's last truly universal entertainment until the 1984 reelection of Ronald Reagan—opened on March 24, 1972, in the midst of a presidential campaign that ended with Richard Nixon's overwhelming victory. The counterculture suffered a mortal blow, although the youth audience, however disillusioned, remained.

The end of the epoch known as the Sixties may be dated to August 1973, the first Watergate summer, with the premiere of *American Graffiti*. Advertised with the question "Where were you in '62?," Lucas had made the movie primarily to periodize the early 1960s, a time that by comparison with the chaos that would follow was readily folded back into the supposedly innocent epoch known as the Fifties. He also suggested a way in which history might be subsumed by the history of style, the myth of a generation, and the collective Dream Life that a nation lived through its mass media.

---

* As opposed to political propaganda, Ellul defines the sociological sort as the ubiquitous form of social bonding advanced by the forces we call the media, an often spontaneous or half-conscious form of ideological conditioning provided not only by movies and television but advertising, educational institutions, newspaper editorials, political speeches, public opinion polls, patriotic pageants, and anything using the phrase "way of life"—or, in the American context, the "American Dream."

Born in 1944 in Modesto, a city in California's Central Valley some seventy miles south of Sacramento, George Lucas Jr. grew up in the 1950s. His father was a successful self-made businessman and a conservative Republican, a contemporary of and most likely an enthusiastic supporter of Ronald Reagan.

Lucas's biographer Dale Pollock compares George Jr.'s childhood to a sitcom idyll, citing the popular family comedy *Leave It to Beaver* (CBS, 1957–58; ABC, 1958–63). The Lucas family bought a television in 1954; eleven-year-old George (like Reagan) was present for Disneyland's opening day, July 17, 1955, and with his family, made an annual pilgrimage for some years thereafter. In the fall of 1957, George journeyed to San Francisco to see Elvis Presley at the Civic Auditorium.

His was an American life. A boyhood friend recalled that the teenaged Lucas used to come home from school, play his rock 'n' roll records, read comic books, eat Hershey bars, and drink Coke. A few years later, he cultivated a mildly greaser or hoody image. Obsessed with cars, George spent almost every night of high school driving up and down Modesto's Tenth and Eleventh Streets, the "strip" subsequently designated the Modesto Historic Cruise Route, partaking in what Tom Wolfe would breathlessly call the "American Teenage Drive-In Life"—"Superkid" Saturday nights at "the big high-school drive-in, with the huge streamlined sculpted pastel display sign with streaming streamlined superslick A-22 italic script, floodlights, clamp-on trays, car-hop girls in floppy blue slacks, hamburgers in some kind of tissuey wax paper . . ."*

After two years at Modesto Junior College, Lucas transferred to the University of Southern California in the fall of 1964 (the same semester that saw Lyndon Johnson's landslide election and the birth of the Free Speech movement at the Berkeley campus of the University of California). He was now engrossed in filmmaking, "too busy to get into drugs"—although by his own description he was at least passively political, supporting the civil rights struggle, protesting the war in Vietnam, and maintaining a general antiauthoritarian stance. He learned to edit, not altogether happily, on U.S. Information

---

* Wolfe's "Superkids," as he described them in *The Electric Kool-Aid Acid Test*, were a few years older than Lucas, although his account of their myths ("not Hercules, Orpheus, Ulysses, and Aeneas—but Superman, Captain Marvel, Batman, The Human Torch, The Sub-Mariner, Captain America, Plastic Man, The Flash") is predictive of Lucas's chef d'oeuvre, *Star Wars*.

Agency projects, including a documentary of Lyndon Johnson's 1966 trip to the Far East.

Lucas was a star at USC. His student film *THX 1138*, a bleak vision of a computer-driven asexual world, attracted the attention of Francis Ford Coppola, whom he met in 1967 while an intern on Coppola's production of *Finian's Rainbow*. In 1969, Coppola helped facilitate the transformation of *THX 1138* into a low-budget feature. Released in 1971, the film was a commercial failure and Lucas decided to next make a movie about his life as a Superkid. The script for *American Graffiti* was passed around Hollywood for a year before Coppola once again intervened to place the movie at Universal, the last production made by the studio's "youth" unit that, headed by Ned Tanen, underwrote Dennis Hopper's *The Last Movie*, among other flops.

American Graffiti was shot in twenty-eight days for less than a million dollars; still, feeling burned by Tanen's previous productions, the Universal brass instinctively disliked the film and, however well it tested with audiences, considered it unreleasable. Lucas's instincts, however, were impeccable. The third top-grossing film of 1973, *American Graffiti* ultimately returned close to $100 million as one of the most profitable investments in Universal history.

The movie is a total immersion in an imagined past. Nostalgia is everywhere inscribed. The movie is set at the end of summer. The music is not that of 1962 but rather consists of Fifties songs that would then have been considered "oldies." John (Paul Le Mat), the champion drag racer and the closest character that the movie has to a greaser, is a romantic figure—an obsolete James Dean type who gallantly protects a young girl, paraphrases "American Pie" by complaining that "rock 'n' roll has been going downhill since Buddy Holly died," and mourns that "the whole strip is shrinking." Soon to leave for college, his buddy Curt (Richard Dreyfuss) tells him that "we are going to remember the good times," while Terry, the nerdiest member of the clique (Charles Martin Smith), maintains, "You'll always be number one, John. You're the greatest." (Terry, as we learn in the final titles, is the one who goes missing in Vietnam—a loser to the end.)

However nostalgic, *American Graffiti* has certain science-fiction elements—it's a bridge between *THX 1138* and *Star Wars*, imbuing the Teenage Drive-In Life with a chrome-and-neon jukebox look. As predicated as it is on automobiles, the movie is a ballet *mécanique*. All the kids are on wheels—

even the waitresses at the drive-in burger joint are on roller skates. You are what you drive. The most melancholy scene is set in an automobile graveyard.

There is also the quality of a universal mind meld. To be fully alive in *American Graffiti* is to be in a moving car, listening—along with everyone else—to the rock 'n' roll disc jockey Wolfman Jack on the radio. It is a secular version of the divine broadcasts that animate *The Next Voice You Hear,* wherein God addresses Cold War anxieties by endorsing the American way of life. Radio is an invisible force that serves to unite the movie's teenaged protagonists, providing anthems, dramatizing emotions, and defining their world: "The Wolfman is everywhere," someone says.

Playing a steady diet of oldies, the DJ demiurge serves to construct a generation or rather the illusion of one. Pauline Kael, who reviewed *American Graffiti* in the *New Yorker,* called the movie "fake folk art." Audiences, she wrote, respond "as a peer group when they laugh at the picture and say, 'That's just what it was like.'" But for whom? "Not for women, not for blacks or Orientals or Puerto Ricans, not for homosexuals, not for the poor. Only for white middle-class boys whose memories have turned into pop."*

The quintessential Kennedy-era film, *The Manchurian Candidate* (1962) had introduced the idea of implanted memory. *American Graffiti,* however, *was* cinema as implanted memory. (A bit less than a decade later, this would be one of the themes of the great science-fiction romance *Blade Runner,* as it was stock in trade for the president, Ronald Reagan.)

Recognizing that *American Graffiti* had inaugurated a "new aesthetic discourse," the literary theorist Frederic Jameson saw the film as a key postmodernist text that sought to embody the "mesmerizing lost reality of the Eisenhower era," which, at least for Americans, would be "the privileged lost object of desire"—not just for its presumed notion of a prosperous, politically stable Pax Americana but for the "first naïve innocence" of a youthful counterculture.

Ronald Reagan, who, in his role as a corporate spokesman, had lived in General Electric's House of the Future and served as a master of ceremonies

---

* Michael Schultz's 1976 jukebox musical *Car Wash,* set largely in a Los Angeles car wash and populated mainly by socially marginal African Americans, may be taken as an anti–*American Graffiti*—a self-aware compensatory entertainment that critiques the fantasies created for and by a radio-defined community.

for the opening of Disneyland, was one manifestation of the Fifties, but the reinvention of the decade was well underway when he became president. Released in late 1971, *The Last Picture Show*, directed by Peter Bogdanovich from Larry McMurtry's novel, was a straw in the wind—a hyperreal version of a 1950s Hollywood movie that the French philosopher Jean Baudrillard claims to have momentarily mistaken for the real thing. But the Fifties revival achieved material form in 1973 with *American Graffiti* and reached its apotheosis five years later with the film *Grease*, the number-one grossing movie of 1978, adapted from a play billed as a "New Fifties Rock 'n' Roll Musical" that was first staged in Chicago's Kingston Mines Theater in 1971.

In June 1972, with *The Godfather* in release, *Grease* an off-Broadway hit, and *American Graffiti* in postproduction, *Life* magazine cited "the practically instant revival" of "the Nifty Fifties," an era of innocent sexuality and iconic personalities (Ike, Elvis, Marilyn). "In the grand sweep of American history, the 1950s were one of the blandest decades ever," *Newsweek* explained in October 1972. "But now a revival of those very same quiet years is swirling across the nation like a runaway Hula-Hoop." The cause, the writer opined, was the political dominance of Richard Nixon, "a fifties hero" as, the following June, the *New York Times Magazine* described the president in *its* Fifties nostalgia piece—"nostalgia" being the media term by which the media ponders its own history.

Not long before *American Graffiti* opened, with Nixon under fire, *Time* reported that, cognizant of the impending U.S. Bicentennial, Americans were "searching for the past, a simpler time, a hometown they may never have known." Lucas provided that imaginary hometown. Because the actual Modesto had grown too large to serve as a location, he had to use San Rafael and Petaluma to recreate his adolescent space as a theme park, or as his title suggests, an archeological excavation like Pompeii.

In 1982, Jameson identified *American Graffiti* and other nostalgia movies as "an alarming and pathological symptom of a society that has become incapable of dealing with time and history," noting that "we seem condemned to seek the historical past through our own pop images and stereotypes about that past, which itself remains forever out of reach."

But *American Graffiti* was not only a symptom but an idea that had become reality. "An idea bursts out of the darkness and can be formulated," as the pioneer media critic Siegfried Kracauer wrote of the spiritual forces that fill the social world. Long before Jameson's observation, Lucas's sentimental evocation of a lost folk community (what German sociology terms a "gemeinschaft") had inspired two television sitcoms, both produced by Gary Marshall and featuring actors who had appeared in *American Graffiti*. *Happy Days* (ABC, 1974–84) starred Ron Howard as high school student Richie Cunningham, while its spin-off *Laverne & Shirley* (ABC, 1976–83) featured Howard's *American Graffiti* girlfriend Cindy Williams and Gary Marshall's sister Penny as a pair of assembly-line "bottle-cappers" in a Milwaukee brewery.*

Writing on *Happy Days* in January 1974, a *New York Times* reviewer called the show a stale sandwich slathered with "the store-bought mayonnaise of nostalgia" and a backdrop of "standard time-machine gimmicks" (the use of old pop music and dated slang). An even more hostile piece published in the *Times* a month later characterized *Happy Days* as a sitcom based on Fifties sitcoms, noting that "the decade itself is presumed to be a sitcom." And yet, a teaser on the same page asked, "Are all reruns bad? Not according to some buffs who believe there are 'classics' among old TV programs," namely the most popular of Fifties sitcoms, *I Love Lucy*. Less than a year later, a *Times* headline would report, "Precolor TV Era Enjoying Revival."

Happy Days was not just inspired by Fifties sitcoms like *Father Knows Best*, it was the Fifties sitcom that should have been—analogous to the critic Donald Lyons's interpretation of Roman Polanski's neo-noir *Chinatown* (1974) as a "dream of what a 1937 [private eye] movie might have looked like with A-picture treatment and anachronistic technology," or to the hyperreal Fifties-style diners that began to populate American malls in the late 1970s. The show was set in suburban Milwaukee, a place the historian of television David Marc characterized as "a racially segregated, crime-free, culturally homogenous neighborhood of spacious single-family homes." The theme song, Bill Haley's once-incendiary anthem "Rock Around the Clock," was appropriated, by way of *American Graffiti*, from *The Blackboard Jungle*—a

---

* *American Graffiti* and *Happy Days* had something of a dialectical relationship. The series began as unsold pilot starring Howard, which aired in 1972 as a segment titled "Love and the Television Set" on ABC's anthology show *Love, American Style*. On the basis of the pilot, Lucas cast Howard as a lead in *American Graffiti*, causing ABC to take a renewed interest.

movie that, back in the real Fifties, the American ambassador to Italy had attempted to remove from the Venice Film Festival.

For two seasons, *Happy Days* focused on Richie and his friends. (According to Marc, the show's most striking divergence from the actual sitcoms of the Fifties was generational: the son, rather than the father, was the "point-of-view character.") After finishing number sixteen for the 1973–74 season, the show's ratings slipped; with brilliant results, however, Marshall decided to emphasize a hitherto minor character, the cool high school dropout and garage mechanic, biker Arthur Fonzarelli (Henry Winkler) aka Fonzie or the Fonz.

Powered by this domesticated, heavily merchandized, white ethnic version of Marlon Brando's nihilistic Wild One, now a part of the Cunningham family, *Happy Days* reigned as number one during the 1976–77 season, and then ranked number two, behind *Laverne & Shirley*, another white ethnic sitcom, in 1977–78 and number three in 1978–79. As *Happy Days* unseated the Norman Lear production *All in the Family* (CBS, 1971–79), ending that show's string of five straight number-one seasons, so the Fonz supplanted Archie Bunker as America's working-class hero.

Indeed, as the show slid back down in the ratings, Fonzie further marginalized Richie's dad in morphing from implicit threat to an omniscient guide to righteous American living. In the show's final season he becomes a schoolteacher, while Richie leaves for Hollywood just as Ron Howard—or years earlier, the young Ronald Reagan—did in real life.

Found Illusions

The original affinity of business and amusement is shown in the latter's special significance: to defend society.

—THEODOR ADORNO and MAX HORKHEIMER,
Dialectic of Enlightenment

There is a sense in which *American Graffiti* evoked the successful cultural revolution of 1956 (or at least its youth component) to efface the failed political revolution of 1968–70. Given the movie's focus on car culture, it is additionally poignant for appearing in 1973, the year of the OPEC oil embargo and the end of cheap gasoline. The ensuing recession brought a cycle of dystopian science-fiction films suggesting a new pessimistic vision of American history.

A ruptured narrative had to be restored. The so-called disaster films that inaugurated the return of movie special effects in the early 1970s would be succeeded by paradigms of Hollywood's conspicuous consumption—the *Star Wars* trilogy, the *Superman* movies, and the *Star Trek* series (and ultimately by the comic book superhero movies of the post-9/11 era). These blockbusters were typically kid's films, souped-up Fifties sci-fi, or Saturday afternoon serial adventures writ large—precisely the type of films once addressed to adolescents but that are now made for "children of all ages."

In their emphasis on special effects, such films asserted that the basis of cinematic power was not so much narrative as it was spectacle—and in the case of Steven Spielberg, to offer reassurance in the face of disaster. In his 1977 *Close Encounters of the Third Kind*, Spielberg employed the occult belief in extraterrestrial beings as a means to dispel certain rational contemporary fears—among them the instability of the nuclear family, mental illness, government manipulation—as well as the complexity of technological society and rationality itself. As suggested by Jacques Ellul, an abundance of information is paralyzing: "A surfeit of data, far from permitting people to make judgments and form opinions, prevents them from doing so. . . . The more the techniques of distributing information develop, the more the individual is shaped by such information."

When individuals sense a lack of control over their destinies, they may be attracted to demagogues or occultism (or both). As president, Ronald Reagan was fascinated by miraculous artifacts like the Shroud of Turin, believed in a spirit world, and had faith in biblical prophecy, including Armageddon. After the attempt on his life, Nancy Reagan, who was her husband's closest adviser, regularly sought the guidance of an astrologer.

The special effects blockbuster *Ghostbusters* was released at the start of Reagan's 1984 reelection campaign; coinciding with the period of his maximum popularity, it would be, for the remainder of his reign, the highest grossing-movie made by anyone other than George Lucas or Steven Spielberg. Does Reagan's appeal for the public during the summer of 1984 illuminate that of *Ghostbusters* or vice versa? Or are they rather manifestations of the same thing? The social forces that produced the Reagan presidency and the collective fantasies Reagan articulated or embodied are inscribed in *Ghostbusters*—along with certain antipodes that served to inoculate a viewer against questioning such fantasies.

Energy and intensity may be entertainment's most universal attributes, characteristic of even such dystopian social critiques as *A Face in the Crowd* (1957) or the horror film *Night of the Living Dead* (1968). There are also "feel bad" movies like *Taxi Driver* (1976) or *Blow Out* (1981) that would seem to verge on anti-entertainment. But in addition to their energy and intensity, these films emphasize transparency, which may include unpleasant truths as well as the possibility of an unhappy ending. So successfully cynical is *Ghostbusters* that there is even room for those not taken in. As the culture critic Fred Pfeil put it, Peter Venkman, the character played by Bill Murray, guarantees "a level of crass self-interest so low as to be resistant to any of the stereotypical roles that ensnare, delude and trivialize the film's secondary characters."

Entertainment may acknowledge an actual problem and propose itself as the solution. Thus, mirroring the president, *Ghostbusters* addressed an acute case of late–Cold War jitters that might be considered to have been a collective anxiety attack. Reagan both stoked fears by characterizing the Soviet Union as "an evil empire" on March 8, 1983, and attempted to ameliorate them when he announced his proposed Strategic Defense Initiative, popularly known as "Star Wars," fifteen days later. *Ghostbusters*, which was in development in 1983, would specifically celebrate what Venkman calls "the indispensable defense science of the next decade."

Considering that the boldly irrational president presented himself as the enemy of big government, it is significant that the indispensable defense science would also be a business: "The franchise rights alone will make us rich beyond our wildest dreams," Venkman exults. Public service is denigrated along with the academy. "I've worked in the private sector—they expect results," he jokes. Driving an ambulance, wearing paramilitary outfits, and wielding "unlicensed nuclear accelerators," the Ghostbusters are privatized disaster specialists, operating a freelance Department of Amusement.

Ghostbusters sets up Armageddon as its punchline but, as in *Stand Up and Cheer!*, the catastrophe is only a crisis of confidence. Thus, the movie parallels the psychic sleight of hand by which Lawrence Cromwell ended the Depression and President Reagan "saved" America from its psychosomatic ills.

The old Hollywood faded in the Sixties even as America's great imperial project, the War in Vietnam, proved disastrous. If the Sixties and early Seventies were, at least in part, periods of disillusionment, the late Seventies and Eighties brought a process of re-illusionment. Its agent was Ronald Reagan. His mandate wasn't simply to restore America's economy and sense of military superiority but also, even more crucially, its innocence.

Lyndon Johnson's war, Richard Nixon's crimes, and Jimmy Carter's willingness to reduce "America" to the level of common sense made Reagan not only possible but necessary—an idea fervently wished for burst out of the darkness (or off the TV screen). Like an old movie or TV rerun, Reagan reversed the flow of time and remade our days.

I

NASHVILLE CONTRA *JAWS*, 1975

June 1975, six weeks after *Time* magazine headlined the Fall of Saigon as "The Anatomy of a Debacle" and wondered "How Should Americans Feel?," brought two antithetical yet analogous movies: Robert Altman's *Nashville* and Steven Spielberg's *Jaws*.

Each in its way brilliantly modified the cycle of "disaster" films that had appeared during Richard Nixon's second term and were now, at the nadir of the nation's self-esteem, paralleled by the spectacular collapse of South Vietnam and the unprecedented Watergate drama.

The multi-star, mounting-doom, intersecting-narrative format of extravaganzas like Mark Robson's *Earthquake* and John Guillermin's *The Towering Inferno* (both 1974), produced by Irwin Allen, was, as the film critic Robin Wood then noted, elaborated and politicized in *Nashville*. But while *Nashville*, the movie widely regarded as Altman's masterpiece, deconstructed the disaster film, Spielberg's *Jaws* gave the cycle a new intensity and, perhaps, a second lease on life.

Cine-catastrophe was scarcely a new concept. It was only the movies, Susan Sontag observed in "The Imagination of Disaster" (first published in the October 1965 issue of *Commentary*), that allowed one to "participate in the fantasy of living through one's own death and more, the death of cities, the destruction of humanity itself."

Writing in the aftermath of the Watts insurrection, even as the folk-rock protest song "Eve of Destruction" entered the Top 40, Sontag argued that the Armageddon-minded science-fiction films that enlivened drive-in screens were not about science but disaster—the aesthetics of destruction, the beauty of wreaking havoc, the pleasure of making a mess, the pure spectacle of "melting tanks, flying bodies, crashing walls, awesome craters and fissures in the earth."

The aesthetics of destruction was globalized in the Sixties: after the profligate *Cleopatra* (1963) nearly wrecked an entire studio, 20th Century Fox, and more or less ended the Cold War PaxAmericanArama cycle of ancient-world spectaculars, Arthur Penn created the doomsday gangster film with *Bonnie and Clyde*, and Sam Peckinpah pioneered the disaster Western with *The Wild Bunch* (1969). Hollywood turned on Hollywood as *Myra Breckinridge* (1970) materialized and *The Last Movie* declared itself. *Night of the Living Dead*, the most apocalyptic horror movie ever made in America (originally released in 1968), achieved full cult status in early 1971 with a late-night run in Washington, DC, inexorably spreading to other cities and college towns throughout the year.*

Nor was that the only vivid representation of Judgment Day. The evangelical commentator Hal Lindsey's *The Late Great Planet Earth*, an interpretation of biblical prophecy that extrapolated from current Cold War events to predict an immanent worldwide catastrophe followed by the return of Jesus Christ, appeared as a mass-market paperback in February 1973 after running through twenty-six printings in its original edition. Lindsey's predictions for the 1970s included an increase in crime, civil unrest, unemployment, poverty, illiteracy, mental illness, and illegitimate births, as well as the greatest famines in world history, the election of open drug-addicts to public office, and the increasing dominance of astrology, Oriental religions, and satanic cults; by the end of the decade, his book went through another thirty-odd printings and sold some fifteen million copies.

From beyond the grave, the counterculture presented its own apocalyptic scenario. The Weather Underground's 150-page Marxist-Leninist manifesto *Prairie Fire*, clandestinely published in the summer of 1974, was the first salvo in a new bid for relevance. Naturally, it presented America as a disaster.

> This is a deathly culture. It beats its children and discards its old people, imprisons its rebels and drinks itself to death. It breeds and educates us to be

---

* In New York City, *Night of the Living Dead* ran continuously as a midnight attraction from May 1971 through the following February and then again for thirty-four weeks following Nixon's reelection to July 1973.

socially irresponsible, arrogant, ignorant, and anti-political. We are the most technologically advanced people in the world and the most politically and socially backward.

More hysterical and diffuse than *The Next Voice You Hear*, a warning was sounded in the land, although the direct stimulus for disaster films was, of course, neither Watergate nor the Cold War cosmic spectacle *When Worlds Collide* (1951), neither the Book of Daniel nor the collapse of the counterculture, but rather the over-performance of two earlier movies: *Airport* (1970), grossing over $45 million and for a time ranking number fourteen on *Variety*'s list of Hollywood's all-time moneymakers, and *The Poseidon Adventure* which, released shortly after Richard Nixon's reelection, took in nearly as much and proved the number one box-office attraction of 1973.

Once more, movies returned to their fairground origins to offer audiences the treat of spectacular cataclysms. But there was something else as well. "Use value in the reception of cultural commodities is replaced by exchange value," Theodor Adorno and Max Horkheimer observed in *Dialectic of Enlightenment*. "The consumer becomes the ideology of the pleasure industry." Beginning perhaps with *Bonnie and Clyde* and certainly since *The Godfather* provided a new and tragic myth of contemporary America's origins in 1972, there were must-see Movie-Events that everyone needed to attend in order to fully participate in American life and that, in Adorno and Horkheimer's phrase, would come to support "a model of the huge economic machinery which has always sustained the masses, whether at work or at leisure."

The disaster cycle gathered momentum along with the Watergate scandal, approaching its climax as the president resigned in August 1974. By then, *Time* had offered "A Preview of Coming Afflictions," reporting that Hollywood's "lemming-like race for the quintessential cataclysm" had spawned some thirteen disaster movies at various stages of production.

Earthquake, co-written by *The Godfather* author Mario Puzo; *The Towering Inferno*; Irwin Allen's spectacular follow-up to *The Poseidon Adventure*; and an *Airport* sequel were scheduled to open by Christmas—to be followed by movies whose major attractions were an avalanche, a tidal wave, a volcanic eruption, the explosion of the dirigible *Hindenburg*, a plague of killer bees, and an earthquake freeing a horde of giant, incendiary cockroaches to exit the center of the earth and overrun Los Angeles. (For the latter, veteran producer of exploitation films William Castle was planning "a floor-mounted windshield-wiper device that will softly brush across [the] moviegoer's feet and ankles at crucial moments.")

"There is absolutely no social criticism, of even the most implicit kind," Sontag had generalized regarding the "disaster" science-fiction films of the late '50s and early '60s. But movies like *The Towering Inferno* and *Earthquake* (the second and fifth top-grossing movies released in 1974) were scarcely perceived as anything else but social criticism. The explanation of the trend arrived almost before the trend itself.

Why were disaster films taken seriously? "Every couple of years, the American movie public is said to crave something. Now it's calamity, and already the wave of apocalyptic movies—which aren't even here yet—is being analyzed in terms of our necrophilia," wrote *New Yorker* film critic Pauline Kael shortly after *Time*'s piece and thus staking out the counter-pundit position that disaster films were nothing more than meaningless pseudo-events.

Necrophilia, however, was not the explanation offered by most commentators—although some did see apocalyptic movies appealing to a popular schadenfreude. Disaster films were more often discussed as reflections of the economic crisis (perceived as "natural" in capitalist society) precipitated by the OPEC oil embargo following the Yom Kippur war in late 1973. Alternately, they were manifestations of Watergate—as if Watergate were not the most entertaining disaster film of all. (Vietnam may have been too painfully obvious to mention; Kael evoked it in spite of herself when she characterized the directors of disaster movies as "commanders-in-chief in an idiot war.")*

Often, catastrophe arrived as punishment for some manifestation of the Orgy that was the Sixties. Both *The Poseidon Adventure* and *The Towering Inferno* heighten the thrill by arranging for disaster to strike in the midst of gala parties; in *Tidal Wave* (1973), the volcanic eruption that triggers the eponymous cataclysm is synchronized to the lovemaking of an unmarried couple on a targeted beach. Some disaster movies offered a populist critique by blaming the catastrophe on rapacious corporations; in most cases, the

---

* Vietnam was not yet a subject for the movies, but Watergate did coincide with a cycle of conspiratorial thrillers, including *Executive Action* (1973), *The Parallax View* (1974), *Chinatown* (1974), *The Conversation* (1974), and *Three Days of the Condor* (1975).

disaster was worsened by mendacious, greedy, corrupt, and inadequate leaders. Along with TV cop shows and vigilante films of Nixon II, disaster movies questioned the competence of America's managerial elite. Kael extended that elite to include the captains of America's film industry, specifically Universal (which also had *Airport '75*, *The Hindenburg*, and *Jaws* in the works): "The people who reduced Los Angeles to rubble in *Earthquake* must have worked off a lot of self-hatred: you can practically feel their pleasure as the freeways shake, the skyscrapers crumble, and the Hollywood dam cracks. . . . *Earthquake* is Universal's death wish for film art: these destruction orgies are the only way it knows to make money."

Still, it was the iron rule of disaster films that individuals were at fault, never the system itself, and the natural leader who emerged from the chaos was almost uniformly a white male in uniform (pilot, naval officer, policeman, fire chief, priest). Indeed, heroism under stress was practiced by nearly everyone except the top public officials who were typically upper-class and devious. Thus, like the Senate's televised Watergate hearings, disaster films offered the spectacle of all-star casts impersonating ordinary, middle-class people coping, as a group, with a limited Armageddon—that is, the total breakdown of institutions hubristically imagined to be safe. These ocean liners, airplanes, skyscrapers, theme parks, and cities were microcosms of America.

Despite their overt fatalism, the disaster films were fundamentally reassuring; they celebrated the inherent virtue of decent, everyday Middle Americans, linking their survival skills to traditional social roles and conventional moral values—a particularly Darwinian form of sociological propaganda. The notion of God's will may only be implicit, but the cataclysm effectively disciplines an overly permissive social order. On an interpersonal level, the reversals wrought by the disaster were often positive. (Reviewing *Earthquake* in the *New York Times*, Nora Sayre experienced a "sense of ritual cleansing.") As previously atomized individuals formed a community, class distinctions disappeared. Marriages were reinforced. Middle-class virtue prevailed.

With their abundant stars and intense special effects, disaster films were highly entertaining. They not only fostered a sense of community within their narratives but also, as acknowledged Movie-Events, for the audience and even the public at large—additionally comforting in that they revived the old-time movie religion. (In this sense, *Airport*—like the same year's *Love Story*—can be seen as the trial balloon for a return to proven Hollywood formulae). They were populated largely by Nixon-supporters and Reagan-peers, filled with familiar faces from the Pax Americana: Charlton Heston, William Holden, Dean Martin, Shelley Winters, Ava Gardner, Jennifer Jones, Myrna Loy, Dana Andrews, Gloria Swanson, Helen Hayes, Fred Astaire, James Stewart, hardy showbiz survivors all!*

It was the return of the ritual potlatch, tempting Hollywood's alienated audience with the promise of conspicuous consumption and spectacular effects. Nora Sayre whimsically deemed *Earthquake* an "awesome" advance toward the total cinema of *Brave New World*'s feelies (in which an on-screen kiss made the "facial erogenous zones" of six thousand spectators tingle with "an almost intolerable galvanic pleasure") but unsarcastically called *The Towering Inferno* "old-fashioned Hollywood make-believe at its painstaking best."

Thus, the disaster films brought PaxAmericanArama up to date. Not only were these movies more economically produced and rationally conceived (everything centered upon a single epic special effect), but they were also set in the present. Using the ahistoric direct address of *High Noon*, which in offering an obvious civics lesson had little to do with the old West and everything to do with the political situation of 1952, disaster films effectively denied that Americans had become permissive and jaded or that traditional values had broken down. They insisted, rather, that these values were intact and, unlike in the terrifying scenario proposed by *Night of the Living Dead*, enabled people to help each other through the crisis to guarantee society's survival.

In short, the cycle of disaster films successfully recuperated the apocalyptic visions of the Sixties. Indeed, as Herbert J. Gans would note in the journal *Social Policy*, disaster films "almost suggest that the 1960s never happened."†

---

* Disaster movies embodied the anonymous fan's ambivalent attitude toward stardom—a condition that incurred punishment as well as reverence. Irwin Allen told the *Hollywood Reporter* that *The Poseidon Adventure* was "a perfect set-up . . . a group of people who have never met before and who are thrown together in terrible circumstances. In the first six minutes, 1,400 people are killed and only the stars survive." *Earthquake* provides a perfect inoculation to this implicit absence of democracy: the trustworthy cop in *Earthquake* (George Kennedy) is suspended from the LAPD for injuring Zsa Zsa Gabor's hedges while pursuing a criminal in the line of duty.

† Like a low-level contagion, the cycle continued—with largely diminishing returns—for the remainder of the 1970s. In addition to *Meteor* and a belated sequel to *The Poseidon*

Watergate Unplugged

In their time, *Jaws* and *Nashville* were regarded as Watergate films and, indeed, both were in production as the Watergate disaster played its final act in the summer of 1974.

On May 2, three days after Richard Nixon had gone on TV to announce that he was turning over transcripts of forty-two White House tapes subpoenaed by the House Judiciary Committee, the *Jaws* shoot opened on Martha's Vineyard with a mainly male, no-star cast. The star was the shark or, rather, the three mechanical sharks—one for each profile and another for stunt work—that, run by pneumatic engines and launched by a sixty-five-foot catapult, were created by Robert Mattey, the former Disney special effects expert who had designed the submarine and giant squid for the 1956 hit *Twenty Thousand Leagues Under the Sea.*

Brought to Martha's Vineyard in pieces and cloaked in secrecy, Mattey's sharks took longer than expected to become fully operational, and *Jaws* was further delayed by poor weather conditions. Accounts of the production routinely refer to the movie itself as a catastrophe only barely avoided: "All over the picture shows signs of going down, like the *Titanic*."

In late June, a month when *Jaws* was still unable to shoot any water scenes, and while Nixon visited the Middle East and Soviet Union in a hapless attempt to, as the president wrote in his diary, "put the whole Watergate

---

Adventure, the last year of the decade saw two final transformations of the model: the socially responsible *China Syndrome*, immeasurably helped for its release at the time of the real-life disaster at Three Mile Island, and Francis Ford Coppola's multi-leveled disaster, *Apocalypse Now.*

Some of the purest examples appeared on television. The eponymous disaster in Irwin Allen's $2.5 million *Flood* (NBC, 11/24/76), promoted as the most expensive movie ever made for television, is immeasurably worsened in that it concerns the mayor of a small Ohio town who would rather protect local fishing rights than open the dam spill gates. The conflagration that decimates an Oregon forest in Allen's production *Fire!* (NBC, 5/8/77) similarly feeds on official "neglect." In another Allen extravaganza, *The Night the Bridge Fell Down* (produced in 1979 but not aired by NBC until February 28, 1983), amoral business concerns conspire with corrupt politicians to span the river at an unsafe spot. Allen claimed that the ideas for his movies came to him in dreams and linked his message to a religious revival. "I'm no Billy Sunday, but 25 years ago we allowed structural breakdowns to creep into our society. . . . Life has become cheaper, morals have changed."

The ultimate and most influential disaster telefilm was *The Day After* (ABC, 11/20/83), which depicted the effect of a nuclear exchange on a small town in Kansas.

business into perspective," Altman's cast and crew arrived in the city of Nashville. They were all put up at the same motel, with everyone expected to stick around for the entire ten-week shoot.

There is a sense in which *Nashville* represented a last bit of Sixties utopianism—the idea that a bunch of talented people might just hang out together in a colorful environment and, almost spontaneously, generate a movie. Even by Altman's previous standards, *Nashville* seemed a free-form composition. It surely helped that neophyte producer Jerry Weintraub's previous experience lay in managing tours, for Frank Sinatra and Elvis Presley among others, and packaging TV specials.

A number of key performers—including comedienne Lily Tomlin and singer Ronee Blakley—were making their movie debuts, but as a director of actors, Altman was famously permissive. His performers contributed much of their own material—dialogue as well as songs. Altman filmed Barbara Baxley's monologue on the Kennedy assassination without reading it first; he let Ronee Blakley completely rework her character's breakdown. When Julie Christie and Elliott Gould visited the set, Altman built a scene around them. Joan Tewkesbury had considerable latitude with her screenplay, although one stipulation was that she write an assassination scene in which the victim would be a "mother figure." Altman was said to have been obsessed with the Watergate endgame—among other current events such as the attempted assassination of South Korean president Park Chung Hee in mid-August.*

Most unusually, *Nashville* featured a nearly autonomous character. The candidacy of the never-seen Hal Phillip Walker was developed by Mississippi novelist Thomas Hal Phillips, who had once managed his brother's campaign

---

* The attack on Park foreshadowed the assassination that climaxes *Nashville*. As the Korean president delivered his Liberation Day address from behind a bulletproof podium at the new National Theater in Seoul, a husky forty-year-old man ran down the center aisle firing a snub-nosed revolver. Seated behind her husband, Mrs. Park was shot in the head; as the screaming, mainly elderly audience, assembled political leaders, and high school choir scrambled for safety, security men gunned down the assailant. A high school girl was mortally wounded in the crossfire. A small boy ran crying to the fallen assassin and tried to kick him until security men pulled him away. Despite the injury to his wife, President Park finished his speech and received a standing ovation. The incident had been televised live. Afterward the Ministry of Home Affairs declared a state of national emergency and the entire government tendered its resignation.

for governor. Given his own budget, Phillips opened a campaign headquarters, ordered buttons and bumper stickers, and sent hired sound trucks through the streets. Altman's only requirements for this simulated politician were that he represent a third party, be someone whom Phillips himself would want to vote for, and was a candidate whom Phillips thought could actually be elected.

Nashville was conceived as an open-ended quasi-documentary, *Jaws* as a tightly plotted thriller; yet, appropriate to *Jaws'* mega-fantasy elements, its transformation into a movie was also somewhat improvisational. Richard Zanuck and David Brown had paid $175,000 for the rights to the novel and a Benchley screenplay. The script then went through three drafts, variously reworked by playwright Howard Sackler, John Milius, and actor-writer Carl Gottlieb. The last version was itself revised continually on location. As Spielberg told one journalist, "We have been making it up as we go along."

Few environments are more self-absorbed than a movie set. Carl Gottlieb's *The Jaws Log* spoofs actor Roy Scheider and camera operator Michael Chapman for their fanatical consumption of each day's *New York Times*, but never bothers to acknowledge the summer's other main drama. Nixon's fall goes similarly unmentioned in a less detailed paperback quickie, *The Making of the Movie Jaws* by Martha's Vineyard resident Edith Blake, although another political scandal is alluded to, for July 18 marked the fifth anniversary of Senator Edward Kennedy's automobile accident on the tiny island of Chappaquiddick, off Martha's Vineyard, and the resultant death of a young campaign worker, Mary Jo Kopechne.

Chappaquiddick was thus something like brother Jack's wartime heroics, as commander of *PT 109*, in reverse—an act of aquatic cowardice that effectively sealed Kennedy's political fate. In the summer of 1969, a year after the assassination of RFK, it seemed inevitable that the last Kennedy brother would fulfill the family destiny and run for president. But after ditching his car in the Atlantic (reportedly the first time in twenty years that anyone had managed to drive off the Dike Bridge) and—without ever providing an adequate explanation either for the circumstances or his subsequent behavior—leaving his passenger to drown, Kennedy consigned himself to political purgatory.

As Vineyard summer resident James Reston would write in his *New York Times* column that season, "Here perhaps more than anywhere else

[Kopechne's death] has remained a live and bitter controversy. On this island—aside from everything else—leaving a body in the water is unforgivable." For Edith Blake,

> It seemed that every news and movie organization was climbing around the satellite island collecting new material on an old subject. . . . Filming crews over the Chappaquiddick dike gave rise to new rumors that Universal was making a movie on the sly about Kennedy at the dike and secretly flying key figures to Hollywood.

(In fact, Bruce—the nickname the crew gave the mechanical shark—was filmed gliding through the same channel where Kopechne drowned and Kennedy supposedly swam to safety.)

Chappaquiddick was consistently in the news during the *Jaws* shoot. In mid-May, as part of its inquiry into the possible impeachment of President Nixon, the House Judiciary Committee requested and received legal papers filed for the inquest into Kopechne's death (preparing for 1972, the White House had dispatched a private investigator to Martha's Vineyard the same day that Kopechne's corpse was pulled from the wreckage of Kennedy's car, and subsequently tapped her roommates' telephones) while the *New York Times* reported that the dead woman's parents had recently visited the Dike Bridge—for the second time—and had lunch with the local sheriff. Two months later, the *Times* noted that the Kopechnes received a $150,000 settlement from the Kennedy family while the *New York Times Magazine* ran a lengthy article—subsequently described by another *Times* columnist as "a major political event"—devoted to the still unexplained circumstances of her death, a subject rehashed by *Time*, the *Boston Globe*, and *60 Minutes.*

For the first half of 1974, Ted Kennedy out-polled all other Democratic possibilities—even though he was considered to be unelectable. Perhaps this yearning for another Kennedy was more Watergate fallout. The trauma of Nixon's resignation was uncomfortably reminiscent of an earlier president's "abandonment'" of his people. But then, as Reston later analyzed it:

> When Nixon finally walked the plank, he took Kennedy over the side with him. Americans of all political persuasions are tired, sad, and ashamed of the frustrations and moral squalor of the age, and worried about the effects of all this on their children. To choose between Watergate and Chappaquiddick

in a savage personal campaign during the 200th anniversary of the Declaration in '76 seemed too much, even to many of the most enthusiastic supporters of President Kennedy and his brother Robert.

Kennedy had removed himself from the race by the time that *Jaws* wrapped, as much over budget as it was over schedule, costing twice the $4 million originally planned.

Like *Earthquake* and *The Towering Inferno*, both of which opened in December 1974, *Nashville* and *Jaws* were positioned—and received—as Events. In a move designed to outflank every other critic in America (not to mention the Paramount executives who had not yet seen his footage), Altman screened a rough cut for Pauline Kael. Four months before the film's eventual release, she published a preemptive rave in the *New Yorker* declaring *Nashville* "an orgy for movie lovers." Thus launched by Kael's influential and notorious review, *Nashville* would enjoy considerable critical success.

Nashville opens with an advertisement for itself. But what was this ironic self-promotion or the ensuing critique of packaging compared to the power of *Jaws*' pre-sold high concept? With *Jaws*, the culture industry began to contemplate itself. The week before the movie began shooting on Martha's Vineyard, the *New York Times Magazine* published a detailed analysis of the novel to illustrate "the making of a bestseller."

On the one hand, Peter Benchley, thirty-four when *Jaws* was published, seemed born to write a best-seller. The son of novelist Nathaniel Benchley and the grandson of humorist Robert Benchley, a graduate of Phillips Exeter and Harvard, he acquired a literary agent at the age of twenty-one. On the other, he had learned to articulate the Voice. After working briefly at the *Washington Post* and *Newsweek*, Benchley served LBJ as a speechwriter during the last beleaguered years of his reign. "I wrote proclamations like 'On Your Knees, America' for the National Day of Prayer," he recalled. In composing *Jaws*, he would be instructed by his editor at Doubleday, Tom Congdon, "to think of the whole country as a child that climbs up on its daddy's knee and says, 'Tell me a story.'"

The *Times* tracked *Jaws*' development from the initial one-page description Benchley submitted to Congdon in June 1971, through the completion of the manuscript eighteen months later, the selection of a title, the choice of cover art, and the development of a sales pitch, to the wild auction for the paperback rights, a full nine months before the hardcover would appear. (One losing editor maintained that she "never would have bid half a million dollars if it hadn't been called *Jaws*."). As the film rights had also been sold before the novel's February 1974 publication, the entire period of *Jaws*' bestsellerdom—much of which coincided with the making of the movie—could be considered a giant publicity trailer for a work in progress.

In a new and particularly self-aware way, the movie's extraordinary box-office appeal further fed that appeal. The audience consciously participated in transforming a hit movie into something larger, a new form of feedback and a new model for the movies. "I have seen the future and it is *Jaws*," is how Kenneth Turan opened his review in *The Progressive*.

Two kinds of filmmaking passed each other that month. *Nashville* was intellectual and exclusive, *Jaws* visceral and populist; *Nashville* looked back to the 1960s, *Jaws* ahead to the 1980s. Altman was a grizzled hippie whose "favorite things," according to his wife, were "smoking dope and having good parties." Spielberg had been an abstinent member of the counterculture. "In my entire life I've probably smoked three joints," he told *Rolling Stone* in 1978. Spielberg's drug experiences were largely vicarious. "I would sit in a room and watch TV while people climbed the walls."

Old enough to be the twenty-eight-year-old wunderkind's father, Altman had fought his way out of television to become the ultimate studio maverick; Spielberg grew up with television and was a precocious industry insider. (Julia Phillips, the Hollywood hipster who would co-produce Spielberg's next project, *Close Encounters of the Third Kind*, considered it her duty to introduce him to a more youthful crowd: "Steven was hanging out with men who were too old for him. Who bet and drank and watched football games on Sunday. Who ran studios and agencies.")

Altman was more direct in stating his intentions, setting his narrative in the Bicentennial Year of 1976 and calling *Nashville* his "metaphor" for America, but *Jaws*, too, was perceived as essentially American: in praising Altman, Kael evoked Fred Astaire and "the great American art of making the impossible look easy." *Time*, meanwhile, termed *Jaws* a "rather old-fashioned, very American way of making a movie."

No doubt that *Nashville* and *Jaws* appeared at a moment when Americans were looking for some way to feel good about themselves. The season's other national success story had seemed similarly old-fashioned and impossibly easy. On May 12, with the new Communist states of Cambodia and Vietnam at war, the Cambodians detained the American container ship *Mayaguez* as it passed through the Gulf of Thailand. Coping with his first international challenge, President Gerald Ford convened the National Security Council, which was informed by Secretary of State Henry Kissinger that there was a greater issue than the capture of a single American merchant ship: in order to reestablish the nation's credibility, at home as well as abroad, it was necessary for the U.S. to exercise its military might.

After a twenty-four-hour ultimatum, American bombers strafed the boat used to transport the men of the *Mayaguez* to Cambodia's mainland and then sunk seven boats harbored around the island of Koh Tang. The next morning, Koh Tang was stormed by U.S. Marines but, once the Americans were pinned down, Ford and Kissinger countermanded Congress's twenty-two-month-old ban on bombing Indochina (along with the War Powers Act) by ordering air strikes on the port of Sihanoukville. After the crew's release, Cambodia was punished with further bombing of industrial installations.

The forty-man crew of the *Mayaguez* was saved at a cost of forty-one American casualties with another forty-nine wounded—and if some were appalled to see the U.S. react so soon and massively against so puny an adversary, the victory nevertheless intoxicated the American media. *Time*'s eight-page cover story provided a detailed day-by-day account of the victory ("THURSDAY. As Betty Ford was gently shaking her husband awake at 6:30 a.m., an hour later than usual, the *Mayaguez*'s crew was stoking the freighter's boilers.") that had "significantly changed the image of U.S. power in the world" as well as that of President Ford, who "had been hoping for weeks to find a dramatic way to demonstrate to the world that Communist victory in Indochina had not turned the U.S. into a paper tiger."*

The *Mayaguez* operation was as star-spangled as *Nashville*, as popular as *Jaws*, as extravagantly praised as both. "I'm very proud to be an American today," Vice President Nelson Rockefeller declared, while his old adversary Senator Barry Goldwater exulted that "it shows we've still got balls in this

---

* While only an estimated thirteen to twenty-five Cambodians were killed on Koh Tang, an unknown number were killed on Swift Boats or during the bombing of the Cambodian mainland.

country," and Senators Frank Church and Jacob Javits, two sponsors of the War Powers Act, echoed their support for what *Newsweek* praised as "a daring show of nerve and steel."

Explaining that "the show of force had many of the gung-ho elements of a John Wayne movie," *Time* did not neglect to describe the home front. Hugh Sidey's sidebar evoked a JFK-era thriller with a happy ending: the crisis, he explained, "was the old-fashioned variety," understandable and enjoyable for Cold War veterans: "a lovely bit of rascality—brief, definable, rightly punishable and done on the high seas, where U.S. men and machines still reign."*

Sidey was among the selected journalists summoned to the White House lawn, where a formal dinner for the Dutch prime minister was underway. "The White House in its spring splendor looked like a Hollywood set. With somber visages and firm jaws, the actors hurried through the mellow night in their sleek black limousines." Carl Albert, the diminutive speaker of the house, seemed three inches taller. Those senators to whom the president had revealed the "scenario" were besieged by reporters. Informed spokesmen hinted that "it was going to be an American kind of show." Henry Kissinger had returned.

> On the big crisis night . . . back in his Washington office, [Kissinger] paced, ordering, listening, waiting. He flashed the V sign out the window once, and then, humor fully restored in the exhilaration of action, he made a lunging movement toward the window as he began to peel off his coat—Henry K into Super K. Deep laughter from the on-lookers, buoyed up by the old-style American confidence, echoed up Pennsylvania Avenue.

---

* The *Mayaguez* crew, several of whom subsequently sued the American government to redress the permanent injuries suffered during their rescue, seemed to think they were in another movie—captured by aboriginal Indians or possibly Martians. "They were a raggedy bunch and they didn't know how to use things," is how fifty-two-year-old Messman William F. Bellinger characterized the Cambodians in *Time*.

> One guy just squatted on the wash basin. So we showed them how to use the toilet. The shower was the big hit. Once we showed them how to use it, they had a ball. One guy held the gun, and the rest piled in under the shower. Sometimes they were afraid of things they did not understand. They wouldn't let us touch the typewriter. I guess they thought we could send messages out on it. I don't think anybody got sick on their food even though it wasn't what you would go into a restaurant and order. They served us first and ate the leftovers.

The Spirit of '56, Twenty Years Later

Nashville was played out in a city of lost souls, of unstable idols and vora-cious fans, and the meretricious hustlers who prey on both—what some saw as a grotesque satire of Hollywood and Altman called a vision of "instant stars, instant music and instant politicians."

A musical disaster film, *Nashville* unfolded against a backbeat of clichés and platitudes, and underscored by the search for a new national anthem. Throughout, self-righteous arias of idiotic boosterism alternate with sche-matic hymns to survival ("I've lived through two depressions and seven dust-bowl droughts"). Joan Tewkesbury's stream-of-consciousness introduc-tion to *Nashville*'s published script positions the movie as the culmination of postwar American history.

"Perhaps the best thing about World War II was going to Sonja Henie movies," Tewkesbury begins a breathless catalogue of Alger Hiss, Richard Nixon, and the Cold War Red Scare. "Somewhere between President Eisen-hower and my boyfriend's navy-blue letterman sweater, the Rosenbergs were executed," and then it's the John Birch Society, JFK ("against everyone else, he was Technicolor"), RFK, Timothy Leary, Angela Davis, Abbie Hoffman, Spiro Agnew, Kent State, George Wallace, Watergate, and finally Robert Altman, who "rounded out the *Rashomon* of the United States."

In the American commercial cinema, *Nashville* was the culmination of the Robert Frank aesthetic—the appreciation of the American vernacular landscape that had nostalgically informed *Bonnie and Clyde* and, intermit-tently, *Easy Rider* (1969), was here programmatic. The once-exotic icons of national identity—the flag, the TV, political hoopla, chewing gum, Dixie; diners and honky-tonks, jukeboxes and motorcycles, preachers and drifters, waitresses and drum majorettes, cowboys and movie stars—appeared as tawdry, discombobulated, secondhand, the open highway now carnival midway.*

---

* Published in *Harper's*, Chilton Williamson Jr.'s furious response to *Nashville*'s visual rhetoric recalls the original response to Frank's 1959 collection of photographs, *The Americans*:

> The images of America captured in *Nashville* are in themselves sufficiently deflat-ing: the twirling, whitewashed muskets of absurdly spangled schoolgirls; the erector-set skyline of the booming provincial American cosmopolis; the flat,

Bracketed by two spectacular crack-ups, *Nashville* opens with a monumental traffic jam extending from downtown to the airport where the plane-carrying country music queen Barbara Jean (Ronee Blakley) is about to land. It winds up at a Replacement Party rally on the steps of the imitation Parthenon in Nashville's Centennial Park, where the warm-up act sings of Watergate and impending food shortages, setting the stage for Barbara Jean's onstage breakdown and her subsequent assassination by the frozen-faced loner who has been orbiting the action all movie.

In the chaos that follows, Barbara Jean's spot is immediately filled by the runaway wife Albuquerque (Barbara Harris), who effectively provides the new American anthem:

> It don't worry me, it don't worry me.
> You might say that I ain't free
> But it don't worry me!

The crowd eagerly joins in. A star is born.

Describing *Nashville* as a "cascade of minutely detailed vulgarity, greed, deceit, cruelty, barely contained hysteria, and the frantic lack of root and grace into which American life has been driven by its own heedless vitality," the *New York Times* political commenter Tom Wicker suggested that the movie was not fundamentally "apocalyptic," quoting Altman on the last scene: "In the face of this disaster, they're going to go on." Or, as Tewkesbury had concluded in her introduction: "Whatever you think about the film is right, even if you think the film is wrong."

In fact, *Nashville* inspired a remarkable critical unanimity—not to mention an extraordinary amount of attention from political pundits and high-profile literati. Reporting in the *Village Voice* on the glamorous advance screenings held a month prior to the movie's release, Arthur Bell noted that

---

stupid walls of modern apartments; the crumbling, greased legs of poor fried chickens; the white plastic belt and white shoes of a sweating, meat-faced lawyer. But it is the people amidst these dreary phenomena that Altman's cameras, with their gleeful eyes, lust to portray. They delight in recording the scabby cross section of the American citizenry indulging itself in nearly every kind of social, cultural, political, and personal malpractice known and feared by right-thinking progressive man: apathy, complacency, slobbish consumerism, the exploitation of women, hypocrisy, the application of greed, leechlike, to the slender swan neck of Art.

"most critics and celebs who have seen *Nashville* this past week are feigning shellshock. Kurt Vonnegut claims it's the best film he's seen in his life. Roz Drexler told us in the elevator she was an emotional wreck. And Mrs. E. L. Doctorow cried so hard she lost her contact lens." (That winter at the annual New York Film Critics Circle Awards, where *Nashville* won best picture and Altman won best director, Doctorow made one presentation and Vonnegut the other. At that time, Altman's announced future projects included an adaptation of Vonnegut's *Breakfast of Champions* and Doctorow's *Ragtime*.)

Robert Mazzocco's thoughtful demurral in the *New York Review of Books* was a rare exception to the general excitement among liberals. Mazzocco accused Altman of presenting "the crack-up of Middle America" as an in-joke and called *Nashville* "an artificial high—a symptom of the disease and not a diagnosis of it," linking the movie to President Ford's post-*Mayaguez* surge in popularity. Greil Marcus was another dissident, bracketing *Ragtime* and *Nashville* as the prime vehicles of what he termed a Failure-of-America fad. Marcus was struck by the enthusiasm with which these two essentially downbeat works were hailed as great fun and sure hits, and how both were instantly cited as "metaphors" for the nation—attributing this phenomenon to a reigning "spirit of passivity."

The consensus was such that even the *National Review* critic thought *Nashville* might "perhaps [be] the most encompassing and revealing film ever made about what it is that defines this nation, this people, this age . . . at least as American as apple pie." Perhaps in response, *Harper's* published *National Review* contributor Chilton Williamson Jr.'s anti-*Nashville* jeremiad. But not even Williamson argued that *Nashville* was essentially false. To him, it was the response that seemed hypocritical; liberals were laughing at the grotesque spectacle they pretended to decry.

If anything, *Nashville* inspired Williamson to call for a right-wing critique of American vulgarity (the "dangers of mass culture and mass living"), hoping that "conservative critics would be able to condemn the more repulsive aspects of American culture without feeling that they are betraying their fundamental stance by sharing certain articles of condemnation with people on the Left." In fact, the significance of the actual Nashville had already been appreciated by more pragmatic conservatives.

Not four months before Altman began filming, Nixon himself had attended the Grand Old Opry in its new $15 million home, located in the midst of the 369-acre Opryland theme park. The first U.S. president to attend an Opry performance, Nixon received a standing ovation after he took the stage, sat down at the piano, and played "Happy Birthday" to his wife. According to the *New York Times*, Nixon then "pulled a yellow yo-yo from his pocket and presented it to Roy Acuff, known as the 'King of Country Music' whose act has used a whirring yo-yo." Noting that country tunes talk about family, religion, and patriotism, Mr. Nixon said, "Country music is America," and swung into "God Bless America" at the piano, raising his voice loudly to lead the singing. "That's what it takes to be a real President," Mr. Acuff said as the Nixons left.*

The movie *Nashville* would scarcely be so warmly received by Opry partisans. Indeed, Altman and Tewkesbury could easily have scripted its gala Nashville premiere—held, after *Nashville* had already opened in thirty-five other American markets, on August 8 (the first anniversary of the Nixon resignation) in the 100 Oaks Shopping Center, where shoppers dodged a country band, square dancers, and baton-twirlers while television crews and journalists jostled fans to get to the stretch limousines bearing the Nashville elite. *The Nashville Banner*, which had previously run a front-page story on the movie's New York press screening, gave the event major play ("'Nashville' Premiere Churns Sour Reaction" was the second headline after the lead story, "Grim Natural Gas Shortages Forecast"), reporting that most of the country music personalities in attendance thought the movie "stunk."

Nashville was lit up by themes as boomingly obvious and brilliantly insubstantial as firework display on the Fourth of July. The rockets whiz skyward, the payloads explode, showering the spectator with flamboyant signs of

---

* Some thought that country music might be appropriated by the liberal left. While *Nashville* was in post-production, producer Jerry Weintraub acquired the rights to *Mr. Smith Goes to Washington*, planning a musical vehicle for his client the neo-country-singer John Denver. ("The issues in the Capra film were, in one sense, ecological," he explained, "so updating the story is logical and also consistent with the way John feels.") During the 1980 campaign, President Jimmy Carter held a town hall meeting at the Opry, but his reception could hardly be compared to President Ronald Reagan's triumphant appearance during the 1984 campaign. In 1988, candidate George Bush campaigned with country singer Loretta Lynn and appeared at the Country Music Awards. Not until 1992 would the Democrats campaign at the Opry—presidential candidate Bill Clinton identified with Elvis Presley, while his running mate Al Gore was a senator from Tennessee.

national confusion, depression, exhaustion, and division—as Robert Hatch would write in *The Nation*, "You could hardly hold a Bicentennial celebration without playing into Altman's hands."

The synthesis of show business and politics predicted by Adorno and Horkheimer, deplored by Elia Kazan and Budd Schulberg's *A Face in the Crowd*, subsequently explicated by *The Candidate* (1972), accepted by *Shampoo* (which opened earlier in 1975 and would be one the year's five top-grossing films), parades through *Nashville* as stridently as a brass band auditioning for John Philip Sousa himself. But Hal Phillip Walker's platform was eccentric. In addition to a new national anthem, his proposals included the abolition of lawyers in government, the Electoral College, and farm and oil subsidies.

Addressing his audiences as "fellow taxpayers and stockholders in America," Walker tells them that "a good man with some one-syllable answers could do a lot for this country." On a more mystical note, he attracts college students with such sincere non-sequiturs as the question "Does Christmas smell like oranges to you?" (In recounting this, TV newsman Howard K. Smith—free to invent his own commentary—remarks that for him, Christmas always has.)

Walker, a true pseudo-candidate, is only manifest in the form of his publicity and his advance man, John Triplette (Michael Murphy). Although *Newsweek* found Triplette "the epitome of Nixon's bright young men," Tom Wicker was reminded of those presidential candidates who refused to be "pinned down," like Lyndon Johnson in 1964 and Nixon in 1972. *The National Review*'s David Brudnoy thought Walker an amalgam of Bobby Kennedy and George Wallace ("perhaps Altman and Co. have derived something very shrewd from those startling 1968 returns"). The vast majority of commentators, however, looked at Walker and just saw Wallace.

To that degree, *Nashville* did anticipate the 1976 campaign which, at least at the time of the movie's release, was characterized by a fear of Wallace and troubled—at least before *Mayaguez*—by the possibility of a conservative third-party candidacy. In February 1975, members of the American Conservative Union and Young Americans for Freedom concluded a four-day Washington conference by creating a committee, chaired by Senator Jesse Helms of North Carolina, to explore the viability of launching a third party, preferably behind Ronald Reagan. (The now-former governor, introduced by Senator James Buckley as "the conservative movement's Rembrandt," declared that "Americans [were] hungry to feel once again a sense of mission and greatness," though he declined to announce his candidacy.)

Simultaneously, the Conservative Caucus, newly put together by Howard Phillips and Richard Viguerie, pushed the idea of a third-party candidacy for Reagan and/or Wallace. "I believe both of them are going to be denied their party's nomination," Phillips said in April, suggesting that "they could come together to run for the presidency."

Nashville noted the inevitable growth of spectacular politics (during the 1976 presidential election, the first under a new campaign finance law that acted to further increase spending on television, media consultants were virtual policy advisers), and it correctly predicted that, after Watergate (and Vietnam), the presidential campaign's major theme would be a longing for renewal. Walker's oxymoronic campaign slogan—"New Roots for the Nation"—evokes the first positioning of Gerald Ford, while rival Reagan was cast as the honest outsider come to clean up the mess on the Potomac.

Even *Nashville*'s climactic assassination, which struck many as a tired cliché (although the Senate Select Committee on Intelligence was preparing hearings on the Kennedy assassination), was echoed by the public. There were two attempts made on the life of President Ford during a three-week period following *Nashville*'s run: September 5 in Sacramento, Lynette Alice "Squeaky" Fromme brandished a .45-caliber Army Colt automatic at the president in an attempt to call attention to the plight of her imprisoned guru, Charles Manson; September 22 in San Francisco, Sara Jane Moore fired a shot at Ford from a .38-caliber Smith & Wesson revolver. (In between, Patty Hearst was captured after seventeen months on the lam.)

Two months later, at a Ramada Inn near the Miami airport, Reagan's maiden campaign appearance was plunged into a *Nashville*-like confusion by the presence of a man wielding a toy gun. The assailant was later identified as a twenty-year-old resident of Pompano Beach who had made a call from a public phone booth and threatened the lives of the president, the vice president and Governor Reagan unless Lynette Fromme was freed.

In short, *Nashville* was recognizable and, in February 1976, the same month that Martin Scorsese's *Taxi Driver* opened, political commentator Kevin Phillips wondered whether fiction had now become fact: *Nashville*, Phillips wrote in *TV Guide*, "has drawn a lot of criticism, but in some ways it was prophetic. Dangerously prophetic. Such a candidate can sneak past television news with a smiling blur of sincerity and generality. . . . Toothpaste-smooth former Georgia governor Jimmy Carter can and has."

Hal Phillip Walker's synthetic populism and cheerful negation of complicated realities anticipated the inspirational message of Carter, the smiling, non-ideological, "born again" outsider—handled by Gerald Rafshoon, a former 20th Century Fox publicist who'd worked on *The Longest Day* and *Cleopatra* before relocating to Atlanta. For Carter, even more than for Walker, America was suffering a spiritual depression that might be dispelled by the regular application of single-syllable words like "right" and "wrong." Carter also reminded his audiences of the country's inherent virtue—a natural goodness only momentarily besmirched by corrupt politicians like Nixon and Agnew, repeating the mantra that the nation deserved "a government that is as good and honest and decent and truthful and fair and competent and idealistic and compassionate and as filled with love as are the American people."

Carter's perhaps-naïve insistence on refracting every issue through the prism of personal morality elevated his quest for the Democratic nomination into something resembling a spiritual crusade for instant renewal and the Great Second Chance. As the campaign progressed, the candidate would be increasingly compared to John F. Kennedy. Some even imagined there was a physical resemblance between the two.

The Entertainment Machine

Where *Nashville* exploded genre, *Jaws* imploded it. Spielberg stripped the disaster film, trimmed the flab, and turned it into a pure mechanism.

Gone were the novel's adulterous wife and Mafia connection, impediments to Benchley's original concept which, as he had proposed to his publisher, was "to explore the reactions of a community that is suddenly struck by a peculiar natural disaster [that] loses its natural neutrality and begins to smack of evil." *Nashville* was fragmented, without the presence of a unifying protagonist, but *Jaws* projected a far crueler fragmentation up front on the screen.*

---

* True to his remarkably untroubled reading of his own motivations, Spielberg explained his attraction to the material less as a career move (although he did lobby strenuously for

Nashville had offered a glibly pessimistic view of American life, predicting the rise of a politics as meretricious and authoritarian as Adorno and Hork-heimer's sense of the culture industry. *Jaws* was glibly optimistic in offering itself as a solution. Altman's complex interplay of sound and image—the over-lapping mix of conversation, traffic noise, radios, and sound truck—was the precise inverse of Spielberg's total orchestration, the musical score (so close to the angst-producing theme from the JFK-era TV show *The Twilight Zone*) functioning like a rheostat, everything working together in harmony to achieve the desired effect.

Nashville was about the entertainment machine. *Jaws* was it—the very post-TV multimedia *Gesamtkunstwerk* that Adorno and Horkheimer had predicted, the total integration of "all the elements of the production, from the novel (shaped with an eye to the film) to the last sound effect," with a meta-narrative celebrating "the triumph of invested capital."

> The machine rotates on the same spot. While determining consumption, it excludes the untried as a risk. The moviemakers distrust any manuscript that is not reassuringly backed by a bestseller. Yet for this very reason there is never-ending talk of ideas, novelty, and surprise. . . . Tempo and novelty serve this trend. Nothing remains as of old; everything has to run incessantly, to keep moving.

To keep moving—just like a shark, which, also omnivorous, devours whatever comes its way. (Indeed, *The Jaws Log* opens by comparing produc-ers David Brown and Richard Zanuck to sharks—nice sharks, hyper-alert but not predatory. "Just as the Great White Shark can sense the erratic vibrations of a swimmer in the water, so can Richard and David sense the movement of a literary property in the publishing world.")

Nashville was supple where *Jaws* was rigid, but *Nashville* was superficial while *Jaws* ran deep. Was it while watching *Nashville* or *Jaws* that Kurt Vonnegut was "thunderstruck" by the realization of "how discontinuous with the rest of the world our culture is," its "pure and recent invention, inspired by

---

the assignment) than a counter-phobic reaction: "I wanted to do *Jaws* for hostile reasons. I read it and felt that I had been attacked. It terrified me, and I wanted to strike back." At whom, one wonders.

random opportunities to gain money or power or fame" so that "even the past is faked"?*

Nashville was a party or a concert or, as Kael proposed, an "orgy without excess"—thus an improved version of the Sixties. *Jaws* was predicated on a more ruthless notion of movie as roller coaster. The buildup, certainly, was as long as the wait for a Disneyland ride. The monster remained invisible until eighty minutes into the movie. Then, with each appearance bigger than the last, it repeatedly violates human space, erupting into the frame from below—drawing on every primal conception of the sea as universal womb or collective unconscious, albeit here a repository of blood, monsters, and death. *Jaws*, said Spielberg, was "almost like I'm directing the audience with an electric cattle prod."

The shark—particularly as it was visualized on the movie's celebrated poster—is at once monstrous phallus and *vagina dentata*. It coalesces a whole nexus of submerged feelings and sadistic sexuality. In one scene, a dead shark is referred to as "Deep Throat." The crew had dubbed the mechanical shark "Bruce"—a name then popularly associated with homosexuals—while, as several analysts noted, "fish" was a homosexual slang term for a woman.

And yet *Jaws* was set in a vacationland—which is to say an American utopia—with the welcoming name of Amity. It is the place to which an ex–New York City cop named Brody has brought his family so that they can live somewhere safe.

Jaws was adapted from a monster best-seller, but it had a narrative that might have been configured by computer, combining aspects of Ibsen's *An Enemy of the People* (in which a town doctor discovers that the mineral springs which sustain his community are polluted and is pilloried for his integrity) with the obsessive mano-a-mano leviathan-battle of *Moby-Dick*. At one point, Spielberg wanted to shoot a scene with Quint watching John Huston's movie version but evidently Gregory Peck, embarrassed by his performance as Ahab, nixed it.

---

* Nature too. Traveling through the United States during the summer of 1975, Umberto Eco noted that "the shark in *Jaws* is a hyper-realistic model in plastic, 'real' and controllable like the audio-animatronic robots of Disneyland." Two sequels, several re-releases, innumerable clones, and nineteen years later a *Jaws* ride finally opened at Universal Studios Florida.

Spielberg credited himself with streamlining the narrative: "I took the Mafia out of it, I took, not the sex out, but the affair out." In the novel, Hooper (Richard Dreyfuss) is sleeping with Mrs. Brody—a relationship that would certainly have complicated the eventual alliance between Mr. Brody and Hooper. But although no one goes to bed with anyone in the movie *Jaws*, Spielberg was certainly correct in acknowledging that he had not denuded the story of sex. On the contrary—and not just because Peter Benchley had publicly complained that the alteration of his material was equivalent to a "gang rape."

Jaws opens with one of the most blatantly eroticized murders in the history of cinema—and one that openly encourages the audience to identify with the killer. A young woman detaches herself from a group of youths partying on the beach, a chaste and diminished orgy, and shedding her clothes, runs wantonly toward the ocean. She's followed down the beach by a less-than-sober admirer but draws far more formidable interest once she plunges into the surf, swims out ten yards, and gaily raises a leg to the sky. Now the viewer, too, is submerged in the ocean, peering at the swimmer from underneath in a point of view that not only coincides with the introduction of the shark's musical cue but also is, in fact, the shark's. Back above the waterline, the woman jerks violently up and down, crying, "It hurts, it hurts," as she rhythmically thrashes around. Meanwhile, back on the beach, her drunken suitor has collapsed on the sand and is moaning, "I'm coming, I'm definitely coming."*

Like the Chappaquiddick inquest, *Jaws* opens with the mystery of a young woman's corpse left in the water. Had Bruce's first victim been a man, *Jaws* would scarcely be the same movie. (Indeed, as if to reiterate the sexual nature of the crime, the novel delays a telephone report of the woman's disappearance so that the policeman on duty can finish reading an account of a woman who castrates a would-be rapist with the linoleum knife she'd hidden

---

* In the novel, the girl has just had sex before her fatal swim, so the shark is enjoying a gruesome example of sloppy seconds. In the movie, this foreplay is scarcely necessary. A surrealist-inspired free-associative exercise in "irrational enlargement," administered to a class of cinema students who viewed only this sequence and then were unexpectedly asked to quickly jot down their impressions of what they had seen, yielded stunningly erotic descriptions of the violence, as well as the widespread assumption of the victim's promiscuity.

in her hair.) *Jaws* is a movie in which sex and violence are indistinguishable forms of oral aggression. The Jack-the-Ripper joke made as the police view the woman's remains is only amplified by Hooper's "professional" excitement when he examines them.

In general, *Jaws* has a surplus of innuendo: "I see you got your rubbers with you," Quint teases Brody. Quint's toast "Here's to swimmin' with bow-legged wimmen" is reinforced by his drinking song "Spanish Ladies," in which a sailor bids farewell to the whores on shore. Misogyny is rationalized when Quint and Hooper compare their (women-related) scars.

"Part of a bracing revival of high adventure films and thrillers," according to *Time, Jaws* "promises to hit right in the old collective unconscious and to draw millions irresistibly to the box office." The movie was "mercifully free of padding—cosmic, comic, cultural," it was (like Bruce) a most "efficient entertainment machine."

It was also everywhere at once—like God or a television event. Released simultaneously at 460 theaters on an unprecedented wave of saturation TV advertising, *Jaws* needed only seventy-eight days to surpass *The Godfather's* rentals and become the top-grossing movie of all time—or at least until *Star Wars* arrived in 1977. The co-producer Richard Zanuck accrued more money from his share of *Jaws'* profits than his father, Darryl F. Zanuck, made in his entire career.*

By late July, the novel *Jaws* had sold over seven and a half million paperback units, with Carl Gottlieb's *The Jaws Log* closing in on one million. Americans had purchased two million *Jaws* tumblers, half a million t-shirts, and tens of thousands of posters, beach towels, shark's-tooth pendants, bike bags, blankets, costume jewelry, shark costumes, hosiery, hobby kits, inflatable sharks, iron-on transfers, games, charms, pajamas, bathing suits, water squirters.

The beach itself was an advertisement for *Jaws*—a beneficial side effect of the movie's extended schedule. (Amazingly enough, Universal had hoped to release *Jaws*—like *Earthquake*—in time for Christmas 1974.) Both *Time* and the *New York Times* ran features reporting, respectively, that "formerly bold

---

* So far as distribution went, *Jaws'* unacknowledged precursor was the 1954 radioactive insect-fear film *Them!*, released to two thousand theaters and accompanied by a then extraordinary TV and radio campaign.

swimmers now huddle in groups a few yards offshore," while "waders are peering timorously into the water's edge." An official for the L.A. County department of beaches now had to "force" himself to go into the water. Each day, lifeguards at Long Island's Jones Beach and the Cape Cod National Seashore received hundreds of inquiries about sharks.

In the *New York Times* "Arts and Leisure" section, Stephen Farber maintained that the only difference between *Jaws* and William Castle's *Bug* was hype. An insistent publicity campaign transformed *Jaws* into the entertainment "event" of the year. Was pervasive advertising sufficient to explain this orgy of participation? *Newsweek* noted that "the spell seemed larger than its merchandising hype alone could account for" and speculated that, as "the summer spectacle of the two years just past was the decline and fall of Richard Nixon," Americans needed a respite. "The palpable hunger in this vacation season was for escape and *Jaws* offered it."

Or, as Vonnegut had written of *Nashville*, *Jaws* was not just "a spiritual inventory of America" but also a spiritual salve, a fulfillment of the hope that art could be "wonderfully useful in times of trouble." There were few American fears that were not displaced onto the shark. That summer alone, the *Jaws* poster was parodied to show the Statue of Liberty menaced by the CIA, Portugal by Communism, Uncle Sam by a Soviet Submarine Buildup, the feminist Gloria Steinem by Male Chauvinism (although here, the swimmer had submerged to attack the shark), American citizens by a New Tax Bite, American wages menaced by Inflation, American drivers by the Energy Crisis, American workers by Unemployment, and Gerald Ford by Recession, Ronald Reagan, and a toothless Congress.

By the summer of 1975 there was no more Vietnam War, no further talk of the space race, no new Miami or Las Vegas to construct. At the summit of American accomplishment, there was now only Bruce. "It looked like a Nike missile, but it was one of the [mechanical] sharks," the *Boston Phoenix* had reported from the set, having casually penetrated Spielberg's security system to note Bruce's "inner workings of pumps, gauges, hoses, and clamps," another daring show of nerve and steel. "*Jaws* should never have been made," Spielberg would maintain, and his description of his "impossible effort" was elaborated by Carl Gottlieb in *The Jaws Log*: "Launching *Jaws* was a film production problem analogous to NASA trying to land men on the moon and bring them back."

They Love Us in Hiroshima!

Nashville created such a compelling confusion that even the disgraced ex-president felt free to weigh in. According to Altman, Nixon himself wrote to the director to request a "copy" of *Nashville* for his daughter Julie, maintaining that it was her favorite movie. (How much hatred of politics and desire for normalcy may be intuited here?) *Jaws*, by contrast, was clear-cut.

To the degree that both movies represented politics as a sleazy con game and capitalism as a selfish, rapacious system, both articulated a populist distrust of big business and governmental leadership. But where *Nashville* was fatalistic, suffused with what Robert Mazzocco called an "air of self-congratulatory befuddlement," *Jaws*—which was, after all, an action movie—proposed a solution.

More than a fad or a marketing ploy or psychosexual roller coaster or middle-class *Moby-Dick*, *Jaws*—as much as it was a new business model for Hollywood—was the promise of utopia redux. Amity's mayor is the tawdriest of glad-handers, shamelessly wearing a stars-and-stripes tie like a creature out of *Nashville*. What would Julie Nixon Eisenhower make of him? The actor (Murray Hamilton) has a marked physical resemblance to her father and, no less than Nixon, the character he plays is undone by an attempt to conceal a crime—compelling the town coroner to falsely report that the shark's first victim, Chrissie, died in a boating accident. (Perhaps, Julie would have been sensitive to the unfairness: in real life, on the real Martha's Vineyard, the mayor would be protecting the interests of the all-powerful Kennedys.)

Like the Watergate cover-up, the mayor's (economically motivated) attempt to fool Amity's citizens and tourists serves to divert attention away from the viewer's own implication in the original crime and to channel it into self-righteous anger. This is compounded, in *Jaws*, when the shark's second victim turns out to be an innocent child. The corrupt mayor's decision to open Amity's beaches on the Fourth of July, despite the presence of the Great White lurking offshore, creates the movie's ultimate debacle. A tidal wave of panic hits the beach. It is with the July 4th collapse—the equivalent of *Nashville*'s ending—that *Jaws*' final act begins.

In *The Jaws Log*, Carl Gottlieb would recall a lengthy cocktail party—perhaps even on Independence Day—at which *New York Times* political columnist and Vineyard regular James Reston buttonholed producer Richard

Zanuck, a public Nixon supporter in 1972, and berated him for Hollywood's apparent lack of interest in celebrating the impending Bicentennial. What Reston couldn't know was that *Jaws* would be that celebration.*

Jaws' characters are almost less than television stereotypes. Brody is easily imagined as the protagonist of a TV cop show. It's the 1968 Clint Eastwood vehicle *Coogan's Bluff* in reverse—a former big-city policeman relocated to a picturesque *High Noon* town where, as Brody likes to say, "one man can make a difference." (Of course, were Brody the actual police chief of Martha's Vineyard, he might well have had to orchestrate his own cover-up.)

Charlton Heston—the Universal savior in *Earthquake* and *Airport '75*—had originally wanted the role for himself; as played by the narrow-shouldered Roy Scheider, the character is necessarily diminished. The actor's broken nose seems more an emblem of vulnerability than machismo. Harried and bespectacled, Brody may represent the Law on land, but he's powerless at sea—rendered impotent through his city-kid fear of the water.

In the novel, Brody is on-island working-class and his wife is mainland upper-crust. In the movie, the fisherman Quint is the blue-collar tough-guy, the would-be Dirty Harry of Shark City. Hooper, initially visualized as a scruffy hippie-type, is shown to be both privileged and educated. Throughout there's class tension between Hooper's "wealthy college boy" (Richard Dreyfuss) and Quint's "working-class hero" (Robert Shaw), as each characterizes the other: hippie vs. hardhat. One has no difficulty imagining their respective stands on the Vietnam War. (*Time*'s cover story helpfully notes that Dreyfuss registered with his draft board as a conscientious objector.) But Brody is a new sort of authority figure. (Scheider had played the good cop to Gene Hackman's racist bad cop in *The French Connection*.) Outside the Hooper-Quint conflict and dependent on both, Brody is more sympathetic to Hooper—thanks to Spielberg's thoughtful elimination of the subplot where the oceanographer is sleeping with Brody's wife.

---

* In addition to several sequels, *Jaws* inspired new sorts of disaster films. *Orca* (1977) concerned a vengeful killer whale while the TV movie *Intimate Agony* (ABC, 3/21/83) substituted genital herpes for the shark: a young doctor comes to the beach community of Paradise Island and discovers that a plague of herpes is being covered up to protect the resort's reputation for relaxed sexual promiscuity. It should be noted that AIDS had been named and publicized, and was a matter of public concern for well over a year.

Spielberg also contributed to *Jaws'* underlying mysticism, or at least, understood it. For it is not just business that is predatory and irresponsible. The shark is nature's revenge. Like *Night of the Living Dead*, *Jaws* is rooted in the cheap drive-in science-fiction and beach-party monster movies of the Pax Americana. The true ancestor of the Great White is the Japanese monster Godzilla who emerged from Tokyo harbor, reactivated from eternal slumber by the atomic bomb. *Jaws*, too, is haunted by the idea of nuclear holocaust and a fear of retribution. The movie's release coincided with the thirtieth anniversary of the Hiroshima and Nagasaki bombings, a subject of some media attention that implied no small desire for expiation.

The *New York Times* travel section for February 16, 1975, for example, ran a cheerful account of present-day life in the city where 78,000 were incinerated in a single blast and another 180,000 perished from the effects of radiation:

> We had come [to Hiroshima] with long faces, feelings of guilt, ready to shrivel under accusing eyes.... And now my wife and I found ourselves in a *Wizard of Oz* city, plump with gaiety like a laughing Buddha, prosperous.... There was a poll recently among the schoolchildren. "Of all the countries in the world beyond Japan who are your favorite people?" the children were asked.
>
> The majority wrote, "Americans."

Oh, doubly blessed relief! Out on the sea, Quint tells the true story of the battleship *USS Indianapolis* which, after delivering the atomic bombs that would be dropped on Japan, suffered a suitably cosmic trial. The boat is hit by a torpedo and goes down, forcing its crew to abandon ship in shark-infested seas. Hundreds of seamen are devoured. Shaw's description of this scene, a virtual radio play in this most visual of movies, is a tribute to language and the intensity of Shaw's performance. (This powerful subplot does not appear in the novel. One wonders whether it was the inspired contribution of John Milius, whose enthusiasm for military history is well known.)

Who shall live and who shall die? Which individual or alliance can best preserve Amity from the terror of the Great White Shark? Which of the three is shark bait? The combination of Hooper and Brody—middle-class law-and-order plus youth-culture technocracy—not only suggests self-consciously hip cop shows like *Mod Squad* (ABC, 1968–73) or the later *Miami Vice* (NBC,

1984–90) but also the coalition that would develop behind Jimmy Carter. The sacrifice of Quint, meanwhile, has the additional advantage of canceling the nuclear guilt he articulates and the historical nightmare represented by his service on the *Indianapolis*.*

Susan Sontag wrote that the "imagery of disaster in science fiction is above all the emblem of an inadequate response," but that is scarcely the case with *Jaws*. Brody is born again—literally, baptized in the sea—to be precisely the Adequate Response. He overcomes his fear of the water and single-handedly slays the dragon. (In the novel, Hooper is devoured along with Quint, and the shark mysteriously expires just as its fearsome snout reaches Brody.) Thus, the film's hero—a family man as well as a cop—triumphs over brute nature and mendacious politicians alike, defeating the Great White Shark where ivory-tower oceanographers and working-class fishermen had failed to do so.

Time ended its cover story with the sentiment that "in *Jaws*, the only thing you have to fear is fear itself." This evocation of the Great Depression and Franklin Roosevelt seems hardly inappropriate to a fantasy in which the American middle class survives the onslaught of a monster to regain control of a vacation paradise. *Jaws* presented a national rite of initiation. Revived in theaters, the day following Carter's inauguration, it imagined the end of an old America and the birth of a new one.†

---

* During the 1976 campaign, Carter's toothsome smile would be used as a syntagma for the candidate himself. A mask with nothing but a set of giant red lips and bared teeth was a novelty hit at the Democratic Convention. It is tempting to view this ferocious grin as an inverted version of a shark's ghastly grimace—perhaps even its negation. The souvenir peanuts that were emblazoned only with Carter's smile have an even more suggestive resemblance to Bruce turned upside down.

† Once more, a year to the day before the 1980 election, *Jaws* would rear out of the collective unconscious and into American presidential politics. On Sunday night, November 4, 1979, *Jaws* had its television premiere on ABC, amassing a 57 percent share of the TV audience to earn it the second-highest rating ever achieved by a televised movie, exceeded only by the premiere telecast of *Gone with the Wind* in November 1976.

NBC counter-programmed with the second part of the film *MacArthur*—which proved to be the week's least-watched network program. Only marginally better attended was the third network alternative, *CBS Reports* on another American political personality, Senator Edward M. Kennedy. Kennedy was at the apex of his popularity on the night "Teddy" was broadcast. In two days, he planned to announce that he was challenging Jimmy Carter for the Democratic nomination, and the press was prepared to anoint a winner; polls published that weekend had Kennedy enhancing an already substantial lead over the president—whose advisers denounced the media's perceived bias in Kennedy's favor.

"Teddy" opened as Carter's worst nightmare, with newsreel footage of the two martyred

II

BORN AGAIN IN THE U.S.A., 1976–80

"There were giants in those days"—but not now, it seems. A
nation hungry for heroes who can fire people's imaginations is
finding no successors to Lucky Lindy, Honest Abe and other
legends of the past.

—"The Vanishing American Hero,"
U.S. News & World Report (July 21, 1975)

America was baptized anew in the Bicentennial year 1976—or in a phrase
made suddenly current, the nation was born again.*

Kennedys that re-evoked the national tragedy, positioning Teddy as survivor and heir, the
leading man in a public drama with a final act yet to be played. Then it was followed by a
relaxed conversation between the senator and newsman Roger Mudd outdoors at the
Kennedy family compound in Hyannis Port. Kennedy dealt easily with questions about his
own fear of assassination and his treatment by the press but seemed to freeze when Mudd
asked after the "present state" of the senator's marriage. Kennedy's barely coherent reply
precipitated a public breakdown worthy of *Nashville*'s Barbara Jean. Over the next few ago-
nizing minutes, the befuddled senator fumbled for words while Mudd broached other aspects of Kennedy's private life, including inevitably the incident at Chappaquiddick—a
memory and a cover-up that the presence of *Jaws*, a mere zap of the channel-changer away,
could only reinforce.

Kennedy proved incapable of even articulating his desire to run for president, responding to Mudd's query with a vague succession of meaningless banalities. Carter had
reason to be pleased—although the same night that Kennedy self-destructed and Spielberg
ruled, Iranian militants occupied the American embassy in Tehran and took the staff hostage, thus setting the stage for a teledrama that would play to an audience even larger than
Jaws' estimated eighty million.

* The most celebrated born-again Christian was Richard Nixon's special council and
hatchet man Charles Colson who, sentenced to prison for his part in the Watergate break-
in and cover-up, underwent a jail house conversion and, in 1976, published a best-selling
book, *Born Again*, about his experience. A movie version was released in September 1978.

On one hand, there was the nostalgia-infused Disneyfication of the past, particularly airbrushing the decade recast as the "Fabulous Fifties." On the other hand, there was a desire for a ritual cleansing. "All the animals come out at night—whores, skunk pussies, buggers, queens, fairies, dopers, junkies, sick, venal," the antihero of Martin Scorsese's *Taxi Driver*, released in early 1976, would muse as he cruised for fares in Times Square. "Someday a real rain will come and wash all this scum off the streets."

After going through a long litany of social ills, Howard Beale, the populist TV demagogue in *Network*, the Sidney Lumet–Paddy Chayefsky movie that would open three weeks after the 1976 presidential election, gave viewers their marching orders: "I want all of you to get up out of your chairs. I want you to get up right now and go to the window. Open it, and stick your head out, and yell, 'I'M AS MAD AS HELL, AND I'M NOT GOING TO TAKE THIS ANYMORE!'"

The fugitive Patty Hearst had been arrested in September 1975, but active terrorist cells remained. The Bicentennial year was punctuated by bombs, some planted by the Bay Area's New World Liberation Front, others—mainly in New York and Chicago—by the Puerto Rican nationalists of the Fuerzas Armadas de Liberación Nacional (FALN). The menace had not yet been exorcized. *The Omen*, the big movie during the summer of '76, wound up with the president of the United States unwittingly adopting a five-year-old Anti-Christ.

All politicians were suspect. The crusading post-Watergate Congress served to pry open the crypt. Hearings held by the United States Senate Select Committee to Study Governmental Operations with Respect to Intelligence Activities opened in September 1975 and, chaired by presidential hopeful Frank Church of Idaho, revealed information on a host of hitherto only suspected dirty tricks.*

As if on cue, the self-conscious post-Watergate thriller *Three Days of the Condor* had its premiere eight days into the Church hearings. Robert Red-

---

* Subjects that were uncovered included the surveillance and harassment of domestic radicals put forth by the White House's Huston Plan and the FBI's COINTELPRO, as well as the FBI's attempts to smear Martin Luther King, the CIA's campaign to bring down Chilean president Salvador Allende's socialist government, and Camelot's clandestine war against Fidel Castro, not to mention information about JFK's amours, including his affair with Mafia moll Judith Campbell.

ford played a shaggy CIA operative—not a spy but a creator of alternative scenarios—who discovers a secret CIA within the CIA and, as Vincent Canby noted in his *New York Times* review, "comes close to wreaking more havoc on the CIA in three days than any number of House and Senate investigating committees have done in years."

As the CIA had been turned, the Western approached obsolescence. An overweight Marlon Brando played a lunatic bounty hunter in Arthur Penn's *The Missouri Breaks*. John Wayne made what was to be his swan song in *The Shootist*, essentially playing himself as an aging gunslinger dying of cancer. *The Last Hard Men* would end with the retired sheriff Charlton Heston dead in the dust. Yet, the Bicentennial Year was also notable for Hollywood's interest in American folk heroes, old and new. The investigative reporters Woodward and Bernstein became household names; Robert Altman cast Paul Newman as Buffalo Bill; the white Indian hero of *A Man Called Horse* was called back to America to re-right Kiowa wrongs. Clint Eastwood directed himself, after firing Philip Kaufman, as a post–Civil War redeemer in *The Outlaw Josey Wales*—the first movie in which Eastwood was taken seriously, not only as John Wayne's successor but a director in the tradition of John Ford and Howard Hawks.*

The Old Left remembered itself; history was revised. *The Front* revisited the Blacklist; *The Bingo Long Traveling All-Stars & Motor Kings* celebrated the Negro baseball leagues. Gordon Parks made a film about the folk singer Lead Belly and Hal Ashby adapted Woody Guthrie's memoir *Bound for Glory* with David Carradine as Guthrie. (The role was dangled before Bob Dylan, who turned it down while offering to direct.) Elia Kazan gave Robert De Niro the lead as a crypto Irving Thalberg in *The Last Tycoon*, part of a Bicentennial cycle in which Hollywood recalled, sometimes through a glass darkly, its glory days.†

---

* In his 1999 Eastwood biography, Patrick McGilligan describes Warner Bros.'s strategy for raising Eastwood's artistic profile through expensive press junkets. Promoted as Eastwood's Bicentennial statement, *The Outlaw Josey Wales* was previewed as the centerpiece of a six-day conference, "Western Movies: Myths and Images," sponsored by the Sun Valley Center for the Arts and Humanities, that was attended by two hundred academics and film critics, as well as several legendary directors. The movie's actual premiere, in Santa Fe, was attended by seventy members of the national press flown in for the occasion.

† Others included *The Day of the Locust, Inserts, Hearts of the West,* and *Won Ton: The Dog Who Saved Hollywood* (all 1975), and *Gable and Lombard, Nickelodeon, W.C. Fields and*

Television seemed poised to assume its world-historical role as chronicler of the American past and mirror of the American present. Starting in October 1975, NBC's new comedy show *Saturday Night Live* subjected President Ford to near-continuous ridicule, although it's arguable that the showcasing of radical comedian Richard Pryor ten months before the release of his concert LP *Bicentennial Nigger* was even more groundbreaking. ABC prepared the miniseries *Roots* which, telecast in January 1977, would be the most watched TV program in history, while the Bicentennial Year began with the syndication of Norman Lear's most experimental show, the meta–soap opera *Mary Hartman, Mary Hartman*.

The counterculture dwindled but movie stars with a measure of countercultural credibility remained ascendant: Redford topped the 1975 Quigley exhibitors' poll of box-office stars, as he had in 1974 when he supplanted Eastwood, and would again in 1976. Jack Nicholson, ranked number eight in 1974, rose to number two in 1976 with Dustin Hoffman at three. (After a four-year hiatus, Hoffman had returned to the top ten, although 1976 marked the end of Paul Newman's decadelong run.) It was during 1976 that *The Rocky Horror Picture Show*, a flop when it opened commercially, would become an ecstatic cult film—the ritually repeated viewings, costumed participation, and celebration of pansexuality suggested the continuation of the counterculture by other means.*

Still, so far as Hollywood was concerned, 1975 was the Sixties' last hurrah. *Nashville* received multiple Oscar nominations and Milos Forman's adaptation of Ken Kesey's *One Flew Over the Cuckoo's Nest*, a novel with an antiestablishment polemic exceeded only by *Catch-22*'s, won five Oscars (best picture, actor, actress, director, and adapted screenplay), befitting a movie that, save for *Jaws*, had been the year's biggest hit.

Not just Westerns but the cycles of the early Seventies—blaxploitation and upscale porn, cop and vigilante films, disaster epics and road movies—were

---

Me, and *That's Entertainment, Part II* (all 1976). *Film Comment*'s industry columnist Stuart Byron was struck by the magical thinking behind such nostalgia. None of these movies, he declared, had been a hit or even made money. "What is this collective madness that has gripped Hollywood's pocketbooks? No trend in Glitter City has ever been more irrational, or financially disastrous." These movies were inept avatars. It would remain for Steven Spielberg, George Lucas, and Ronald Reagan to successfully recapture classic movie magic.
* Some four decades later *The Rocky Horror Picture Show* would become the second-highest grossing film released in 1975, second only to *Jaws*.

fading. There were fewer African American and explicitly Jewish protagonists. Soon new figures and tendencies would take their place. In 1977 and
1978, remakes, redneck comedies, working-class inspirationals, space operas,
and slasher flicks would come to the fore. But first, there was the New Hollywood epitome and cosmic bummer that was *Taxi Driver*.

A powerfully summarizing work directed by thirty-three-year-old Martin
Scorsese from a screenplay by twenty-nine-year-old former film critic Paul
Schrader, *Taxi Driver* was an eruption out of the national id. Embodied by
Robert De Niro, the antihero Travis Bickle—a would-be assassin of a would-
be president—almost instantly became a character in the American narrative
alongside Huck Finn and Holden Caulfield.

Steeped in libidinal politics, celebrity worship, sexual exploitation, the fe-
tishization of guns, and racial stereotyping, *Taxi Driver* synthesized film
noir, neorealist, and nouvelle vague stylistics. The Bickle story—an unstable
ex-marine driven mad by New York City's post-orgy sleaze-pits—assimilated
Hollywood's vigilante and Viet-vet cycles. It evoked gritty, downbeat Fun City
policiers like *The French Connection*, while drafting blaxploitation in the
service of a presumed tell-it-like-it-is naturalism. Indeed, predicated on a
frank, unrelenting representation of racism, violence, and misogyny, it was
even more racist, violent, and misogynist than the movie itself allowed. *Taxi
Driver* is nakedly opposed even to itself, as well as the culture that produced
it. For Travis, all movies are essentially pornographic; had he met his cre-
ators, he would, as noted by Marshall Berman in his history of Times Square,
surely consider them purveyors of "scum and filth." It's the slow deliberation
with which this lunatic kicks over his TV and terminates his connection to
social reality that signals his madness—and the filmmakers'.

In production during New York's festering Summer of *Jaws*, in the midst
of a heat wave and a garbage strike, *Taxi Driver* crystallized one of the worst
moments in the city's history. Mass transit faltered, roads cracked, crime rose,
jobs hemorrhaged, businesses fled, and buildings were abandoned. The city
trembled on the brink of fiscal catastrophe—America's pariah, a crime-
ridden, fiscally profligate, graffiti-festooned moral cesspool.

A native New Yorker, Scorsese upped the ante by returning endlessly to
his boyhood movie realm, 42nd Street, now a lurid land of triple X-rated
movies, skeevy massage parlors, cruising pimpmobiles, sidewalks crammed

with hot-pants hookers and the customers who on any given weekday evening, according to NYPD stats, were patronizing porn shops at the rate of eight thousand per hour. The pagan debauchery that the boy Scorsese witnessed in Pax Americana spectacles like *Quo Vadis* was played out in the Manhattan of A.D. 1975. The movie's co-producer Julia Phillips would recall (or imagine) that it was a project fueled by cocaine: "Big pressure, short schedule, and short money, New York in the summer. Night shooting. I have only visited the set once and they are all doing blow. I don't see it. I just know it."

In early September, the *Wall Street Journal* called on New York to declare bankruptcy; Ronald Reagan repeatedly used his radio show to denounce the city's union leaders, news media, and elected officials, as well as its "wild spending, dirty streets, pornography" and "general decline in civility," citing New York as "an example of what can happen to this entire country if we don't re-chart our course," and praying that the federal government would not bail out the city. It was while *Taxi Driver* was in postproduction that President Ford threatened to veto any federal financial assistance to New York and the *Daily News* ran the headline "Ford to City: Drop Dead."

Brilliant and yet repellant, at times even hateful, *Taxi Driver* inspired an understandable ambivalence both toward the movie and the antihero who called himself God's Lonely Man. For the first time, a Hollywood movie provided a pathology and a human face for the Secret Agent of History, the mysterious Lone Gunman seemingly conjured into existence by the great extinguished Star-Pol, John F. Kennedy.

First visualized in *The Manchurian Candidate* (1962), and more benignly in *Dr. No*, this figure was given material form by Lee Harvey Oswald and subsequent political assassins. Post-Watergate fascination with corporate or governmental conspiracies suggested that the Secret Agent of History might be an avatar of the System (as in *The Parallax View*), but *Taxi Driver* was partially inspired by the diaries of George Wallace's failed assassin, Arthur Bremer, and hence interested in the Secret Agent as a social symptom. In her memoir *You'll Never Eat Lunch in This Town Again*, Phillips recalls Scorsese's concern that the would-be Ford assassin Sara Jane Moore might "hurt the picture."

Scorsese and Schrader may have regarded Travis as a menace but, as Stuart Byron observed, many of the movie's patrons saw *Taxi Driver* as "a more sophisticated, kinkier *Death Wish*, the story of a man driven mad by the realities of urban life, and who therefore reacts in an understandably violent way." Seen through Travis's rain-smeared windshield, Manhattan is a movie—call it "Malignopolis." The cab driver lives by night in a world of myth, populated by a host of supporting archetypes: the astonishing Jodie Foster as Iris, a runaway twelve-year-old hooker living the life in the rat's-ass end of the Sixties yet dreaming of a commune in Vermont, and Harvey Keitel as her affably nauseating pimp. Peter Boyle's witless working-class sage speaks for the salt of the earth, while Cybill Shepherd's bratty golden girl plays a suitably petit-bourgeois Daisy Buchanan to Travis's lumpen Gatsby.

Hysterical yet sublime, the twelfth top-grossing movie of 1976, *Taxi Driver* was not just a hit but, like *Psycho* in 1960 or *Bonnie and Clyde* in 1967, an event in American popular culture—perhaps even an intervention. Inspired in part by one failed assassination, it would inadvertently trigger another.*

The 1976 campaign was well underway when *Taxi Driver*, which included a presidential campaign, opened on February 8, 1976.†

Ronald Reagan, the former two-term governor of California, was challenging the sitting Republican president, Gerald Ford. After perennial heir apparent Ted Kennedy made clear his disinclination to seek the office and in the absence of the old warhorse Hubert Humphrey, Senator Henry "Scoop" Jackson of Washington was the designated front-runner in a crowded Democratic field.

Conventional wisdom was upended on January 19 when former Georgia governor James Earl "Jimmy" Carter handily won the Iowa caucuses over Indiana senator Birch Bayh and Arizona congressman Morris Udall, albeit losing to Uncommitted, 37 percent to 28 percent. Carter was indeed the least conventional candidate in the race—despite the fact that *Time* magazine anointed him "the Face of the New South" in early 1971. Unable to succeed himself as governor, Carter had been running more or less openly since serving as Democratic National Committee chairman in 1974. (Other Southern Democrats who were at least considering a run included Florida governor

---

* *Taxi Driver* capped the Hollywood new wave launched by *Bonnie and Clyde* and, like *Bonnie and Clyde*, projected a violent, sexually frustrated scenario that people—or at least some people—wanted to live.

† That the presidential candidate Senator Charles Palantine is played by TV commentator Leonard Harris enhances *Taxi Driver*'s media verisimilitude.

Reubin Askew, Texas senator Lloyd Bentsen, Arkansas senator Dale Bumpers, former North Carolina governor Terry Sanford, and perennial candidate George Wallace.)

Thus, on the eve of the Bicentennial Year, the *New York Times Magazine* introduced a new and intriguing folk hero in a cover story entitled "A Peanut Farmer for President." The fifty-one-year-old Carter's journey had taken him from "farm boy to naval officer/nuclear scientist to peanut farmer/politician."

Patrick Anderson's article described Carter as "a soft-spoken thoughtful, likeable man" who was a "stubborn" anti-segregationist with a "conservative background" tempered by his "liberal instincts." He also seemed to be something of an opportunist. "Carter and his advisors think that next year's election may be decided more on personality—on character—than on issues," Anderson wrote. "They hope that his aura of honesty and sincerity will make the difference in post-Watergate America."

Most intriguingly, Carter positioned himself as a beneficiary of the counterculture, characterized by Anderson (who became Carter's chief speechwriter during the campaign) as "an introspective man who enjoys the songs of Bob Dylan." Let no one say that this one-term Georgia governor was a man who, like Dylan's Mr. Jones, did not know something was happening.*

Two weeks into *Taxi Driver*'s run, Carter beat Udall in New Hampshire in what *New York Times* columnist William Safire called "a triumph of evangelical pseudo-conservatism." Having edged Reagan in Iowa, Ford prevailed by an even closer margin on February 24 in New Hampshire—a contest that Reagan, campaigning strenuously against the legendary "Welfare Queen," might have actually won, and attempted to spin as a victory.

Another campaign began, less than a week later, when Francis Ford Coppola and his family departed for the Philippines. There Coppola would begin shooting if not the Great American Movie he intended, then certainly Hollywood's greatest periodization of the Sixties, and a supreme disaster film: *Apocalypse Now*.

---

* According to Anderson, Carter also enjoyed "the poems of Dylan Thomas and the writings of James Agee, William Faulkner, John McPhee and Reinhold Niebuhr." It is known that on January 21, 1974, sitting in the sixth row, then governor Carter saw Dylan in concert with the Band at the Omni Coliseum in Atlanta. The set list included "Ballad of a Thin Man," "The Times They Are A-Changin'," and "It's Alright, Ma (I'm Only Bleeding)"; the show began and ended with "Most Likely You Go Your Way and I'll Go Mine."

Few movies have ever identified so closely with their own grueling production stories. Not since D. W. Griffith had a director so blatantly attempted the grandiose simulation of a historical event. Now envisioned as a suitably megalomaniacal postscript to the most convulsive episode in American history since the Civil War, *Apocalypse Now* went into production less than a year after the fall of Saigon.

Like the New Frontiersmen who initiated U.S. involvement in Vietnam, Coppola undertook *Apocalypse Now* for what he believed to be a noble cause, namely the creation of his Zoetrope Studios. And, as the American government had, he found himself confounded by nature, beholden to unsavory dictators, leasing planes and other equipment from the Philippine strongman Ferdinand Marcos, and bogged down in an epic quagmire.

Jimmy Carter's *Rocky* Road

On March 6, Scoop Jackson wins the Massachusetts primary with 23 percent of the vote. Morris Udall and George Wallace trail with 18 percent and 17 percent, respectively. Jimmy Carter comes in fourth, at 14 percent, although his campaign notes that he finished first in Boston's black neighborhoods. In any case, Jackson has peaked.

The rest of March belongs to Carter who, described in the *New York Times* as "one of the smartest men to run for President in a long time," is being widely compared—even by *TV Guide*—to Hal Phillip Walker, the mysterious presidential candidate in Robert Altman's *Nashville*. Carter scores victories over and thus neutralizes his Southern rival, Wallace, in Florida, Illinois, and North Carolina. It is there, for the first time, that Carter begins speaking of his evangelical faith.*

North Carolina also gives Ronald Reagan, who had campaigned extensively with James Stewart, his first win, 52 percent to 46 percent. The victory is attributed to a last-minute, recycled TV address in which Reagan called for the "re-establishment of American superiority." Carter squeaks past Udall in Wisconsin on April 6. The next day, Francis Coppola throws himself a

---

* Dylan himself was "born again" midway through Carter's term, as evinced by the 1979 release of his gospel-inflected Christian LP, *Slow Train Coming*.

birthday bash in the jungle. An enormous cake (forty-eight square feet) and gourmet goodies have been flown in from California—an extravagance that anticipates the *Apocalypse Now* barbecue scene. The memory of the war is merging with the reality of the movie. ("There's a rumor that rebels are in the hills about ten miles away," Coppola's wife, Eleanor, notes in her diary, adding that "several hundred South Vietnamese people were recruited from a refugee camp near Manila to play North Vietnamese in the film.")

Opening on April 9, three days after Carter's win in Wisconsin, *All the President's Men* celebrates the downfall of Richard Nixon while crediting his ouster to a pair of dogged, long-haired reporters, Bob Woodward and Carl Bernstein, played by Robert Redford and Dustin Hoffman. Although in many ways a conventional thriller (Vincent Canby calls it "the thinking man's *Jaws*"), the movie is also a counterculture victory: the Sundance Kid and the Graduate take down Nixon. The project was produced by Redford, whose interest dated to early 1974. William Goldman, who'd written the script for *Butch Cassidy and the Sundance Kid*, and who received considerable help from Woodward, had delivered the first draft of his screenplay the very month that Nixon resigned.

All the President's Men was visualized as the Watergate scandal unfolded; its release melds with the publication of *The Final Days*, Woodward and Bernstein's sensational follow-up to their Watergate reporting which, largely unsourced although clearly drawing on material furnished by Henry Kissinger or secondhand by his aides, depicts a drunken, distraught, possibly suicidal Nixon.*

Deep in the jungle another putsch is underway. Coppola secretly leaves the *Apocalypse Now* set on April 16 and flies to Los Angeles to fire his principal actor Harvey Keitel. His reality testing is such that, while there he telegraphs Secretary of Defense Donald Rumsfeld inquiring as to the possibility of renting U.S. military equipment as had been, for example, made available

---

* *The Final Days* was understood as a sort of TV mini-series waiting to happen. In his *New York Times* review, Richard Reeves would call *The Final Days* a "high-grade *Backstairs at the White House*" and a "film of bureaucratic rats on a sinking ship," comparing its style to "the recreated dramatic history being presented these days on television," such as ABC's 1974 docudrama on the Cuban Missile Crisis, *The Missiles of October*, and the more recent NBC telefilm *Truman at Potsdam*." The six-part mini-series *Washington: Behind Closed Doors*, with Jason Robards Jr. as President Richard Monckton, was telecast by ABC in September 1977—anticipating the official TV adaptation by twelve years.

to *The Green Berets*. He also interviews Martin Sheen, Keitel's replacement—
Clint Eastwood having turned Coppola down—in a lounge at the L.A.
airport.

April 27, the Church Committee releases its final report. Two days later,
former vice president, past candidate, and current senator Hubert Humphrey
distances himself from attempts to draft him as a candidate, unwilling or unable to stand in the path of the Carter juggernaut that the *New York Times*
characterizes as an "almost evangelical campaign" and "one of the most spectacular political ascents in recent history."

With *All the President's Men* in theaters and *The Final Days*, hyped as the
fastest-selling book in the history of Simon & Schuster, already in a third
printing, outsider-ness is ascendant: on May 1, Carter wins in Texas, Georgia, and Indiana. So does Reagan, trouncing Ford 66 percent to 33 percent
in Texas, in part because he attracts Wallace voters. (Ford's unfortunate attempt to eat a tamale without shucking the corn husk did not help.) The same
day Robert Duvall arrives in the Philippines to take part in the "Ride of the
Valkyries" scene that will take over seven weeks to shoot.

May 4, Carter wins Georgia, Indiana, and Washington, DC. *Time* and
Newsweek put him on their covers as the presumptive nominee. Reagan beats
Ford in Georgia, Alabama, and, with a dramatic final surge, Indiana. Eleanor
Coppola observes a Philippine Air Force general escorting ladies to the set
to watch the shoot, as though it were a real war being staged for their delecta-
tion. The following week, Carter edges Udall in Connecticut while suffering
his first defeat since Massachusetts, losing a close race to Frank Church in
Nebraska—a state in which Reagan continues his roll, scoring his first victory
in a closed primary. Some now think Reagan is ahead of Ford in delegates.

May 18, Carter narrowly defeats Udall in Michigan but the same day in
Maryland, his spectacular ascent is unexpectedly derailed by an even more
outside outsider, Reagan's successor as California governor the thirty-eight-
year-old Jerry Brown. Nicknamed "Governor Moonbeam," Brown did not
have to quote Bob Dylan; he dated the beautiful folk-rock singer Linda
Ronstadt, cast himself as a Zen Catholic, and was the first national politician to have had personal experience of the counterculture. His entrance
into the race raises the possibility of an all-California election, the Battle of
Berkeley redux!

The next day, the first of two typhoons hit the Philippines and disrupt the *Apocalypse Now* shoot. For the rest of the month, Carter and Reagan absorb a series of split decisions. May 25, Carter wins Arkansas and Kentucky while losing Nevada to Brown and Oregon to Church; Reagan takes Arkansas, Idaho, and Nevada but loses to Ford in Kentucky, Tennessee, and Oregon. The same day, a second typhoon strikes, splitting and isolating Coppola's crew. Three days later, *Taxi Driver* wins the Palme d'Or at Cannes. (The announcement is greeted with boos.)

On June 8, Reagan takes two more western states, Montana and South Dakota, as well as California. Governor Moonbeam wins his home state as well but ends his chances by failing to contest New Jersey and Ohio. Both go to Carter, who reaches out to another constituency, the future fans of Steven Spielberg's *Close Encounters of the Third Kind* (currently shooting on a closed set in Gillette, Wyoming). The June 8 issue of the *National Enquirer* reports his belief in UFOs and a pledge: "If I become president, I'll make every piece of information this country has about UFO sightings available to the public and the scientists."

Ford has won Ohio as well, going into an open Republican convention with a slender majority of delegates. The same day, *Apocalypse Now* shuts down production and Coppola, who has spent the past three days in a Manila hospital, returns to San Francisco. Bicentennial Day passes without incident. Happening in mid-July, around the time George Lucas wraps *Star Wars*, the Democratic Convention turns out to be a love-in that, as if to exorcize Travis Bickle, is held in New York City. Carter accepts the nomination and the wisdom of the counterculture, telling the convention, "We have an America that, in Bob Dylan's phrase, is busy being born—not busy dying." Watching the speech on television, Norman Mailer notes the candidate's happy, good-humored grin: "If the smile was not genuine, then Carter was not only a political genius but an artist of the first Satanic rank."

During the DemCon, *The Outlaw Josey Wales* opens in Los Angeles: by virtue of his charisma, Clint Eastwood's unreconciled, largely unsmiling Confederate soldier unites Native Americans and white settlers, an anachronistic hippie chick among them, in a sort of ad hoc commune dedicated to doing one's own thing and resisting the corrupt federal government. *Josey Wales* is not only Eastwood's Bicentennial Election Year movie—an ambitious synthesis of the classic Fordian Western with the "dirty" late Sixties and even the counterculture Westerns—but his post-Watergate, post-Vietnam statement as well. "All of us died a little in that damn war!" Josey tells the cavalry man who has been pursuing him over the course of Hollywood's first (and only) Carter Western.

As the Republicans gather in Kansas City in mid-August, sometime after the *Apocalypse Now* shoot resumed, a Harris poll gives Carter a 66 percent to 27 percent lead over Ford and a near-identical 68 percent to 26 percent lead over Reagan. (By now both of Carter's prospective adversaries have also claimed to be evangelical Christians.) The party's first open convention since 1940 has Ford and Reagan locked in a virtual tie. Ford arrives with 1,067 committed delegates, 24 more than Reagan but 63 votes shy of the nomination. The battle over the handful of uncommitted delegates is enlivened by procedural stunts, notably Reagan's surprise announcement that his running mate will be Pennsylvania's young Republican senator Richard Schweiker—a member of the Church Committee and a modified long-haired liberal!

The convention's penultimate night features a televised battle of the wives in which Nancy Reagan is upstaged by Betty Ford, who gamely dances the Bump with leering pop star Tony Orlando. In the end, however, Ford prevails—barely winning the nomination on the first ballot by seventeen votes. Meanwhile, *All the President's Men* has gone back into wide release. September 23, some weeks after Marlon Brando and Dennis Hopper arrive in the Philippine jungle, Carter and Ford meet in Philadelphia for the first of three presidential debates (and the first since 1960). The face-off is notable mainly for the twenty-seven-minute loss of sound that left the men frozen behind their podiums. Three days later, the *New York Times* runs Norman Mailer's gaseous profile "The Search for Jimmy Carter."

Mailer's piece begins with an evocation of Carter's hometown as a vision out of the past: "Plains felt peaceful and prosperous. It had the sweet deep green of an old-fashioned town that America has all but lost to the Interstates and the ranch houses, the mobile homes and the condominiums, the neon strips of hotted-up truck stops and the static pall of shopping centers." Rosalynn Carter struck him as "a movie star of a waitress in a good '30s film— the sort who gives you cheer about the human condition."

The writer envisions "a populist future for America."

Mr. and Mrs. Jimmy Carter, willy-nilly, were going to encourage, by the modesty of their social presence itself, the idea in many an American who had not thought it before that the future was a little more unlimited than one might expect. That was a powerful yeast to bring to a battered democracy looking to recover its second spiritual wind.

After a lengthy, intermittently hilarious interview with Carter, Mailer concludes that "it was not every day that you could pull the lever for a man whose favorite song was 'Amazing Grace.'"*

Carter does seem to be in an amazing state of grace, but the race is tightening. During the course of the second debate, Ford makes a remarkable gaffe. As if scripted by *Saturday Night Live*, he declares that Poland was not a Soviet satellite and under his presidency never would be. On November 2, Carter is narrowly elected, with 50 percent of the popular vote to Ford's 48 percent and, as the last Democrat to carry the once-solid South, an electoral margin of fifty-seven votes.

Nineteen days after Jimmy Carter's victory, another redeemer arrived, although his coming had been heralded for several months: stoical, sweet-natured Rocky Balboa, a character invented and played by Sylvester Stallone.

Stallone had hoped to premiere *Rocky* on July 4, 1976. Even so, his timing was nothing short of miraculous. No less than the born-again Christianity that Carter helped popularize or the Bicentennial rebirth hoopla, the passion of Stallone's burnt-out club fighter was predicated on the grace of a second chance. *Rocky* was an auteurist psychodrama. As with *Apocalypse Now*, the movie's story was indistinguishable from its backstory. The advertising tagline "His life was a million-to-one shot" described both the movie's protagonist and its creator. Scripting his own vehicle, Stallone made the movie he wanted to live—and did. A good-natured palooka fought the world heavyweight champion to a standstill; an obscure thirty-year-old actor knocked out Hollywood.

---

* Mailer's piece was less consequential than Tom Wolfe's sprawling "The 'Me' Decade and the Third Great Awakening," published during the Republican Convention in *New York* magazine. Wolfe identifies Carter and Jerry Brown, both "absolutely aglow with mystical religious streaks," as products of the post-Sixties religious revival triggered by America's self-absorbed hippies and assimilated by the nation's affluent middle class. The great synthesizer Ronald Reagan does not figure in his equation.

Opening with the image of Jesus Christ presiding over a boxing ring, *Rocky* resurrected the sports inspirational (a mode that served Ronald Reagan twice, first as a juvenile in the 1940 *Knute Rockne, All American* and twelve years later as star of *The Winning Team*). At the same time, *Rocky* affirmed traditional American values—evoking and endorsing the importance of honesty, perseverance, and hard work, not to mention love, trust, make-believe, happy-endings, and Hollywood hype. Bickle's New York was hell; Rocky's Philadelphia was purgatory.*

By resuscitating the Horatio Alger myth on the mean streets of South Philadelphia and sprinkling pixie dust on Scorsese's urban grit, Stallone confirmed blue-collar white ethnics as heirs to the American Dream. Putting a positive spin on the fatalistic *Godfather* movies, he implicitly celebrated the rise of Italian-American directors and actors—Francis Coppola, Martin Scorsese, Al Pacino, and Robert De Niro, none of whom would ever make or star in a Western.

Archie Bunker notwithstanding, the luckless club fighter and tender-hearted debt collector Rocky Balboa was the first working-class icon to capture the public imagination in the half-dozen years since the eponymous hardhat in *Joe* opened fire on the hippie spawn of the degenerate middle class—the movie that had been the maiden effort of *Rocky*'s director, John Avildsen. While *Joe*, released a few months after the Kent State massacre and widely shown throughout the 1970 electoral season, was one of the most divisive of American movies, *Rocky* proved to be all but universal.†

---

* Stallone's choice of Philadelphia as a setting was significant as Scorsese's decision to shoot *Taxi Driver* in New York. Philadelphia, where Stallone had spent a measure of his adolescence, was not only the city that produced America's Declaration of Independence but also a city riven by racial tension and suffering a prolonged economic slump, ruled by the tough-talking ex-cop Frank Rizzo (like Rocky, if not Stallone, a product of Italian-American South Philadelphia). The morning after his movie's New York premiere, Stallone presented Rizzo with a pair of red boxing gloves. At one point, Stallone imagined that *Rocky*'s inevitable sequel would end with the lovable pug being elected Philadelphia's mayor.

† *Rocky*'s success inspired a flurry of other semi-serious working-class, white-ethnic films, including *Saturday Night Fever* (1977) and *Blue Collar, Blood Brothers, F.I.S.T.* (in which Stallone played a labor leader modeled on the Teamster organizer Jimmy Hoffa), *Paradise Alley* (written by and starring Stallone), and *The Deer Hunter* (all 1978)—not to mention a liberal, female Rocky, *Norma Rae* (1979). Only the latter, for which Sally Fields won her first Oscar, could be considered a truly inspirational film.

According to the legend, published numerous times in late 1976, Stallone felt that his acting career had stalled. His wife was pregnant. The rent was overdue. Then his mother, an amateur astrologist, advised him to seek success as a writer. Three and a half days later, Stallone had the first draft of a screenplay, inspired by the 1975 Muhammed Ali–Chuck Wepner title bout. The studios saw *Rocky* as a possible vehicle for Burt Reynolds, James Caan, Ryan O'Neal, or even Robert Redford, but Stallone, whose major credit was a supporting role in *The Lords of Flatbush* (1974), a post–*American Graffiti* youth film that also featured *Happy Days*' future Fonzie, Henry Winkler, held out for the starring role.

Rocky was positioned as the ultimate sleeper, even though weeks before the movie opened in New York on November 21, Stallone's media presence was so ubiquitous that the *New York Post* would joke that he had "granted more interviews than any American short of [the president-elect's mother] Lillian Carter." Advertised sans title only as an Oscar contender, the movie had a sneak preview at the Baronet, a first-run Manhattan theater on the Upper East Side, on August 8, a week before Republicans began to gather in Kansas City. *New York Times* reporter Guy Flatley saw the ad and paid his way in. "The audience went wild, and so I—on my own—contacted Stallone in Hollywood for the interview," he recalled.

Flatley's piece appeared in the same edition that reported the "generally genteel" first Ford-Carter debate. Around the time Ford blundered in early October, *Village Voice* writer Pete Hamill, then out in Los Angeles, got wind of *Rocky* and had the movie's co-producer set up a special screening. Almost immediately after, Hamill found himself scooped by *New York* magazine and its sister publication *New West*, both of which ran a lengthy profile entitled "*Rocky*: It Could Be a Contender" in their October 18th issues. Upping the ante, Hamill channeled Hemingway in a cover story, "Rocky KOs Movie Biz," which appeared in the *Voice* the morning after Carter's victory: "The word is everywhere: Stallone is a star. A new star. As big as Brando, maybe. And a writer, too. Maybe even a director. The picture will be huge." Leading the premiere by nearly two weeks, *Time* joined the parade, waxing sociological: "Boggled by grim, paranoid plots like *Marathon Man* and savage heroes like the Taxi Driver, audiences may be ready to buy into [Stallone's] gentler, uncomplicated machismo." Rocky was inherently chivalrous and kind, despite his day job as an underworld enforcer.

Although clearly of an age to have served in Vietnam, Rocky's relation to the war is vague, as was Stallone's. Nevertheless, Rocky provided a paradigm for post-Vietnam masculinity. (Stallone himself felt that it was the manliness of Rocky's character that made the film a hit. "I don't think that even women's lib wants all men to become limp-wristed librarians. There doesn't seem to be enough real men to go around.") A column Beth Gillin Pombeiro wrote for the *Philadelphia Inquirer*, published on the day of Rocky's New York opening, made the essential point: "*Rocky* is a film for our times—with a real hero."

And thus, the Bicentennial Year that began in a city of dreadful night, haunted by the insane would-be savior Travis Bickle, demented Secret Agent of History, ended with the beatification of the sweet-natured long-shot Rocky Balboa, hailed by *New York* magazine critic John Simon as "the most likable and unaggressive of punks." Unlike Travis, Rocky was a modest megalomaniac who deserved his success.

The Next *Next Voice You Hear*

Five myth-making movies, each notable in its way, were nominated for the Bicentennial's best picture: *All the President's Men, Bound for Glory, Network, Rocky*, and *Taxi Driver. All the President's Men* was the first movie that Jimmy Carter would screen in the White House, on January 22, two days after his inauguration. But inevitably, on Oscar Night 1977, it was the endearing folk tale *Rocky*, whose grosses were one hundred times its budget, that the Academy canonized.*

The very day Stallone's vehicle opened in New York, the *New York Times* critic Vincent Canby published a Sunday think piece, "Cynical Cinema is Chic," that cited *Network, Three Days of the Condor*, and *The Parallax View* among other movies demonstrating "the extent to which the political events in this country in the sixties, for which Watergate was the grand finale, have shaped hopelessness as a perfectly acceptable, popular attitude"—the very attitude toward which George Lucas objected.

---

* The second movie Carter screened was *One Flew Over the Cuckoo's Nest* (January 28); his third was *Network* (February 5) and his fourth was *Rocky* (February 19). He does not appear to have screened either *Taxi Driver* or *Bound for Glory*, at least not in the White House.

Aggressively innocent and proudly upbeat, Stallone's underdog psychodrama demonstrated that movies were about making audiences feel good about themselves (and America). The fantasy of realizing an impossible dream against all odds was resurrected as a Hollywood staple, even as the *Rocky* theme would become the default musical introduction for American politicians. "*Rocky* is shameless, and that's why—on a certain level—it works," Pauline Kael noted. The movie was a true found illusion. If *Taxi Driver* was Hollywood's last great feel-bad movie, *Rocky*—which mainly redeemed Hollywood but also boxing, showbiz, America, and post-Vietnam masculinity—created the template for the feel-good movies that would endure for the rest of the twentieth century and beyond. The Bicentennial Year saw a dip in box-office figures, but the setback was only momentary: grosses took off over the next few years as a new zeitgeist came to roost. Powered by the astounding, unforeseen success of *Star Wars* in 1977, the period between November 1976 and November 1978 proved to be a watershed for the themes and trends of the next half-dozen years.

Reporting from Manhattan's Cinema II, Frank Rich noted that "the crowds pouring out of a new American film called *Rocky* are behaving in a most unruly manner."

> These moviegoers just can't contain themselves: They leave the theater beaming and boisterous, as if they'd won a door prize rather than parted with the price of a first-run ticket, and they volunteer ecstatic opinions of the film to the people waiting on line for the next show. It's a Hollywood mogul's wet dream come to life. . . . Amazingly enough, this film offers incontestable proof that American audiences have a latent will to believe in the Protestant ethic, the magic of love, and the Easter Bunny.

Rocky was a thing—or, at least a full-fledged symptom. "The Hollywood Movie Hero Has Returned," the *Philadelphia Bulletin* explained. "Audiences grew restless and silent watching Paul Newman or Robert Redford go down to defeat. It was closer to life. It was depressing. Societies need heroes to carry their hopes." Such was Rocky's burden.*

---

* The redemption of this happy-go-lucky palooka was far more satisfying for audiences than the revenge scenario of Ted Kotcheff's comedy *Fun with Dick and Jane*, in which a pampered bourgeois couple (Jane Fonda and George Segal), deprived of their class privileges,

In 1990, Mark Crispin Miller analyzed a new happy ending, founded on the inscription of cheering spectators among other forms of on-screen audience euphoria, observing that, "Feeling warmly watched by everyone now seems a sweeter fantasy than the fictitious heroisms of past cinema." *Rocky* was the exemplar of this fantasy. Although not unanimously favorable, early reviews were near universal in their analysis.

Canby described Stallone's film as "purest Hollywood make-believe of the 1930s." Frank Rich concurred, writing in the *New York Post* that *Rocky* had "an innocence we associate with the uplifting Hollywood films of the Great Depression." (Not the early 1930s surely: *Rocky* is more akin to the optimistic cinema of the New Deal.) The *New York Daily News* critic Kathleen Carroll was even more specific in comparing it to "the movies of Frank Capra," while the *New Yorker*'s Pauline Kael saw *Rocky*, "a threadbare patchwork of old movie bits," as something that might have terminated the Hollywood new wave initiated by *Bonnie and Clyde*. But there was more. *Newsweek* clinched the connection: "Just as Jimmy Carter prevailed by harking back to the old values of love and trust, *Rocky* resembles nothing so much as a throwback—to the 1950s Cinderella hit *Marty* and to the 1930s brand of optimism known as 'Capra-corn.'"

"I knew Carter was going to win two-and-a-half years ago," Stallone told the *Philadelphia Inquirer*, reveling in his new role as prophet. "I saw him on a television show in Los Angeles with a circulation of about 15 people, the Mort Sahl show. Sahl introduced him and people said, 'Who is he?' They thought he was there to sell aluminum siding, or maybe he was waiting for a bus. He said, 'I'm gonna be President,' and I said, 'He's gonna make it.'"*

In the Dream Life, the restoration of the underdog White Champ and the elevation of a long-shot conciliatory Southern Democrat to the White House coincided with the phenomenon that was *Roots*. Telecast by ABC over the course of a week, starting three days after Jimmy Carter's inauguration,

---

turn to social banditry. The film sneaked in New Jersey on September 11, 1976, and was dumped the following February.

* Stallone was apparently referring to the show *Both Sides Now*, which Sahl co-hosted with *Los Angeles Times* reporter George Putnam. Profiled by the *New York Times* (11/28/76), Stallone again expressed his admiration for the president-elect: "Carter never gets rattled. Rocky never gets rattled either," adding that, "a peanut farmer has just become President of the United States. That's the greatest inspiration story of all time."

the miniseries attracted one hundred million viewers—a record that, appropriately, eclipsed that of NBC's November 1976 telecast of *Gone with the Wind*—and stimulated a national conversation on slavery even as it suggested that it was thanks to their belief in the family unit that enslaved Africans had been sustained as a people.

The candidate of faith and family, Carter made a strong appeal to African Americans; *Rocky*, however, profited from a white backlash. "Race is the force of the original film and of the sequels," Joe Flaherty would write on the occasion of *Rocky III* (1982). From the moment that the hero's locker is taken by a black fighter, through his patronizing treatment by a black TV newswoman, to his titanic clash with the black champion Apollo Creed, *Rocky* is a tale of displacement and revenge.

Creed, who taunts the American public by capering about dressed as Uncle Sam, was transparently modeled on Muhammed Ali and, Flaherty declared, "our lust for revenge was denied until Stallone rewrote history." If Ali were simply the world champion he would not be so potent a demon. He was also an embodiment of the Sixties whose sins included a conversion to Islam, a refusal to be inducted into the army, and identification with the Third World. (Rocky, by contrast, is named for and identifies with Rocky Marciano, the last white American heavyweight champion, who won the crown in 1952 and retired undefeated four years later).

Stallone's movie would hardly work if Creed had been a white champion or Rocky an underdog black challenger. It is necessary that Rocky lives in a reverse Bantustan where blacks have appropriated the power and prestige, as well the entitlement to make overt racist comments. Creed, who cooked up the idea of fighting an unknown club fighter on the very day of the Bicentennial and thus for whom Rocky is less a man than a moneymaking gimmick, refers derisively to his opponent as the "Eye-talian Stallion" and makes other disparaging remarks. Meanwhile color-blind Rocky is incredulous and offended when a bartender calls Creed a "jig clown."*

This, of course, is Stallone's most brilliant sleight of hand. For Creed, the American people are a bunch of media-blitzed rubes. The black champ is arrogant, street-smart, and rich, while Rocky is humble, innocent, and poor.

---

* Not until 2015, the next-to-last year of Barack Obama's presidency, were *Rocky*'s racial wrongs acknowledged, if not righted, in writer-director Ryan Coogler's reboot *Creed*.

Structurally, *Rocky* resembles the second half of *The Birth of a Nation*, with blacks having displaced white and whites—or at least the white protagonist— redeemed when Rocky goes the distance. Creed wins a split decision and refuses a rematch (only to demand one in *Rocky II*). Thus, as Flaherty wrote, *Rocky* borders on a "colonial restoration" in which a creature of the 1950s miraculously returns to defeat a demon of the 1960s. (In Hollywood terms, Stallone dethroned Robert Redford as the number one box-office attraction.)

Rocky was neither the first nor the only movie that sought to change America's mood. Mid-1950, a year of acute Cold War crises, MGM released the heaviest and yet the most ethereal movie in Hollywood history: *The Next Voice You Hear* posits a week during which God nightly addresses the American public, over the radio.

The Next Voice You Hear was generally taken for science fiction, but science fiction would seldom again be so affirmative. Indeed, the nine years following Stanley Kubrick's visionary *2001* (1968) was possibly the grimmest period in science-fiction movie history. Where the films of the 1950s were largely metaphors for Communist invasion or nuclear catastrophe, those of the 1970s were sodden bummers set in stagnant or devolved future societies ranging from the grim postapocalyptic worlds of the *Planet of the Apes* cycle (1968–73), *The Omega Man* (1971), and *Damnation Alley* (1977) to the tacky totalitarianism of *A Clockwork Orange* (1972) and the cannibal-istic, overpopulated world of *Soylent Green* (1973).

Technophobia reigned supreme. In *Colossus: The Forbin Project* (1970), a computer tried to become God; in *Logan's Run* (1976), a computer *was* God. *The Stepford Wives* (1975) replaced women with compliant robots; *Demon Seed* (1977) saw Julie Christie raped and impregnated by a sex-crazed computer. The most cherished leisure activities of American life came under attack: *Westworld* (1973) and its sequel *Futureworld* (1976) carried the robot-crammed Disneyland theme park to its logical conclusion. *Rollerball* (1975) and *Death Race 2000* (1975) extrapolated sports-mania into a bloody, dystopian future. For the first half of the '70s, science-fiction movies were depressed sociological extrapolations, issue-oriented and earth-absorbed.

Such grim worlds would return in the mid-1980s as arenas for the likes of Cro-Magnon movie stars like Arnold Schwarzenegger. But four months into Jimmy Carter's presidency, everything changed: *Star Wars!*

Variety was too awestruck to consider the bottom line:

> Like a breath of fresh air, *Star Wars* sweeps away the cynicism that has in
> recent years obscured the concepts of valor, dedication and honor. Make
> no mistake—this is by no means a "children's film." . . . This is the kind of
> film in which an audience, first entertained, can later walk out feeling good
> all over.

George Lucas caught the movie studios, the toy stores, and the media by surprise. As late as Christmas 1977, a month after *Star Wars* topped *Jaws* (and
even as Steven Spielberg's *Close Encounters* was poised to open), theater
owners fought to keep the movie on their screens. *Rocky* was a Movie-Event,
but *Star Wars* was even bigger—not since Chaplinitis swept America in 1915
had cinema inspired so heady a craze.

Perhaps the decline of mere movies can be dated to that spring. A year
after *The Rocky Horror Picture Show* began building its fanatical midnight
following, *Star Wars* established a cult on an unprecedented scale. Francis
Ford Coppola wasn't entirely kidding when, according to Lucas, he suggested
his onetime protégé turn *Star Wars* into a religion: "With religion, you *really*
have power." (Years later Lucas would describe *Star Wars* as a sort of drive-
in McChristianity, "taking all the issues that religion represents and trying
to distill them down into a more modern and easily accessible construct.")

Star Wars would not have inspired the first sci-fi church. (L. Ron Hub-
bard, the science-fiction writer who founded Scientology, was already in business). Nor was *Star Wars* the first movie to bring divine revelation to the
screen (although it did render Cecil B. DeMille's *Ten Commandments* obsolete). But unlike any previous religion, *Star Wars* used late-twentieth century
technology to bypass church, state, and parental authority in mass-marketing
its vision. Lucas cashed the check that Walt Disney wrote. *Star Wars* was a
faith founded on the imagined community of Disney's Magic Kingdom and
the cash-cow collectability of grade school icon Davy Crockett, center of the
1955 kiddie-craze.

Lucas made *American Graffiti* for sixteen-year-olds; *Star Wars* was created for a younger audience. The filmmaker was addressing those ten-year-
olds who—in his opinion—had been deprived of their mass cultural
birthright. Lucas remembered that, when he was growing up during the Cold

War Pax America, Westerns had been the great repository of mythic narrative and moral value: Cowboys and Indians, Good Guys vs. Bad Guys, every night and Saturday morning on TV and every week at the movies, taught American kids right from wrong. The genre failed to survive the tumult of the Vietnam era—as did many thousands of little Western devotees—and so Lucas took it upon himself "to make a film for young people that would move forward the values and the logical thinking that our society has passed down for generations."

Star Wars was not just a seamless blend of Walt Disney and Leni Riefenstahl, *The Searchers* and *2001*, *The Wizard of Oz* and World War II. Lucas had not only studied Akira Kurosawa but also the mystical anthropologist Carlos Castaneda and even Joseph Campbell's 1949 pop-Jungian treatise on myth, *The Hero with a Thousand Faces*. Moreover, *Star Wars* had politics—albeit confusing ones. The movie's protagonists are in rebellion against an evil interplanetary Empire; their leader is a princess who is also a senator of the overthrown republic (as well as a viceroy's daughter), and they are supported by a spiritual elite, the Jedi masters, protectors of the ancient republic.

The novelist and onetime Hollywood agent Clancy Sigal noted in *The Spectator* that Lucas synthesized "the most imaginatively compelling aspects of the Vietnam-era culture: the technical achievements of scientific hardware (from NASA space probes to helicopter gunships used in search-and-destroy operations) and the ascendency of mushy mysticism." *Star Wars* was an anti-technological technological wonder—an ultra-authoritarian presentation with an antiauthoritarian message. Citing the TV show *Star Trek* as *Star Wars*' precursor, Sigal called the movie "a substitute classroom-church for millions of American kids." As a movie about teenage heroism in an adult universe, *Star Wars* created a pop-cultural divide comparable to the chasm that had split the nation with the arrival of Elvis Presley twenty-one years before.*

Established faiths were already on the case. Lucas's creation was celebrated by *Christian Century* and *The Lutheran*. In *The Force of Star Wars*, an original

---

* In a convenient bit of Jungian synchronicity, the King died of an overdose the very summer of *Star Wars*' release—never to be introduced on planet Vegas by a blast from the cornball migraine-maker that was John Williams's instantly disco-ized theme.

Bible Voice paperback published while the movie was still in first release, a born-again former Disney publicist with the Dickensian name Frank Allnutt compared the plucky crew of the *Millennium Falcon* to the early-Christian true believers. Allnutt expressed his belief that *Star Wars* presaged another imminent "invasion from outer space"—namely the triumphant return of Jesus Christ to Earth.

Steven Spielberg understood *Star Wars* as a religious vision, telling *Newsweek* that "it turns me on to think that when we die we don't go to heaven but to space, to Alpha Centauri, and there we're given a laser blaster and an air-cushion car." Indeed, *Close Encounters of the Third Kind* was nearly as epochal. The *New Republic* characterized Spielberg's follow-up to *Jaws* as less a film than "an event in the history of faith." The Christian fundamentalist publication *Today's Student* asserted that "nothing has ever approached the rapture and enchantment of [*Close Encounter's*] closing scenes. . . . The grand scale that they're working on suggests a magnitude that only approaches God."

Even more than America's new president, *Star Wars* and *Close Encounters* channeled the new religious cults that sprouted like mushrooms from the decomposing counterculture: The Unification Church and the Divine Light Mission, Transcendental Meditation and Primal Scream, Jesus Freaks, Hare Krishna devotes, and practitioners of aggressive self-help therapies like est, Arica, and Synanon. Evoking the notion of "(close) encounter therapy," in the Catholic journal *Commonweal*, Colin Westerbeck Jr. called Spielberg's movie "a touching film, literally" that was "made out of, and for, our touchy-feely culture—the culture of group therapy and group grope."*

Star Wars and *Close Encounters* reflected the countercultural ethos of the 1960s and the spiritual values of Tom Wolfe's "Me Generation" even as they suggested an immersion in childhood enthusiasms—the animated cartoons, comic books, and simpleminded science fiction of Cold War *kinderkultur*. *Close Encounters* in particular demonstrated a visceral understanding of childhood, evoking both the pleasure of making a mess and the dream of an enchanted toy shop. Taken together, *Stars Wars* and *Close*

---

* Julia Phillips, who co-produced *Close Encounters*, imagined that the movie would be pure counterculture: "Anyone who has ever dropped acid and looked up at the sky for a while or smoked a joint and watched the Watergate hearings on TV is waiting for this movie" is the pitch she fancied herself delivering to Columbia boss David Begelman.

Encounters were not only reassuring but regressive: through their genre and sense of wonder, they served to construct the spectator as a child.

As *Star Wars* brought glitzy high-tech and an aggressive innocence to the widely televised space opera serials of the 1930s and 1940s and elevated kindred TV kiddie shows like *Tom Corbett, Space Cadet* and *Rocky Jones, Space Ranger* to Wagnerian heights, so *Close Encounters* infused the alien invasion films of the 1950s with the passion of Beethoven's "Ode to Joy." Resurrecting the Cold War space invader–UFO genre, *Close Encounters* followed the *Rocky* road back to the Fifties—but with a difference. Back then, humanity was menaced by everything from bloodsucking carrots and giant ants to mysterious pods and bellicose Martians. Now, the Implacable Alien Others were positively saintly.

Star Wars and *Close Encounters* were proudly retro and profoundly nostalgic, referring not to social issues but to old movies. Both movies were essentially solipsistic, set in imaginary worlds or a sanitized America. Both were spectacular, a reassertion of cinematic power to create the suspension of disbelief. "Movies for me are a heightened reality," Spielberg told *Rolling Stone*. "Making reality fun to live with, as opposed to something you run from and protect yourself from."

Had God spoken? Were the movies born again?

The *Close Encounters* shoot opened in the midst of the 1976 campaign. Steven Spielberg secured the use of a demilitarized air force base outside Mobile, Alabama, that at 100,000 square feet was perhaps six times the size of the largest soundstage.

Everything was top secret. "If one phrase is operative here, it is secrecy," the *Washington Post* reported. "Security guards ring the Brookley Field hangar area, checking all entrants for Polaroid ID badges. The unit publicist keeps complaining that his job is to keep people away. Some members of the crew and most of the extras have not even seen a script."

While rigorously controlling his own publicity, Spielberg himself was convinced that the government was "sitting on an incredible compilation of information." They feel the public isn't ready for it, he told the *Post*.

Just think what would happen if the President could come on television and say "This administration is pleased to make the most important announcement in history . . ." In many ways, this movie is a cosmic Watergate. Hopefully people will experience something very much like a real UFO experience, and begin to understand some of the social and political ramifications of the subject.

Close Encounters also articulated the post-Watergate mistrust of government. *Newsweek*'s November 21, 1977, cover story "UFO's Are Coming!" asked if fifteen million Americans could be wrong. "That is the number—an amazing 11% of the adult population—who say they have seen a UFO." (Included in that number is no less a personage than the president.) *Time* reported that shooting was abruptly halted one night, so that the cast and crew could observe what Spielberg believed to be a UFO (it turned out to be an Echo communications satellite). Restricting information was part of a strategy to build interest. Originally promoted as "science fact" (rather than science fiction), *Close Encounters* cost nearly $20 million to produce. Columbia, which had banked its future on its success, embarked on what was promoted as the most ambitious advertising campaign in the studio's history with a two-page introductory ad that ran in twenty-seven newspapers, introducing the sell line: "We Are Not Alone."

Stars Wars may have provided the framework for a religion, but *Close Encounters*—which like *The Next Voice You Hear* spoke to the Silence of God—was a story of faith. The adult protagonist, Roy Neary (Richard Dreyfuss), is a Midwestern telephone lineman—and thus, save for the fact he has a wife and children, an incarnation of the lovelorn protagonist of Glenn Campbell's hit song "Wichita Lineman," a country-western crossover hit in late 1968. Roy is redeemed and ultimately beatified by his belief in UFOs. Unlike the aliens in *The Day the Earth Stood Still*, or even God in *The Next Voice You Hear*, the aliens of *Close Encounters* send personalized messages rather than issue a collective transmission.

Roy's faith in the aliens inspires him to drop out, grow a beard, and rebel against an official culture of lies. His female counterpart Jill (Melissa Dillon) is already something of a hippie, eschewing a bra and wearing cut-off jeans, a solitary artist alone with her young son, Barry, on an isolated farm. ("She is living as if she were in a commune, yet doing so chastely and in essential America," Westerbeck noted in *Commonweal*.) Along with Roy, Jill sets out to follow the aliens, after they apparently abduct her child. Virtually sexless, *Close Encounters* confounds generic expectations by not developing a romantic relationship between Roy and Jill; even more bizarrely, it ends not with the creation of a new family but a maternal merge. Just as Barry is reunited with his mother, Roy is led into the "mother ship" by frail, little figures that resemble fetuses. Roy hasn't been reborn—the process of birth has been reversed; he's been taken back into his techno-mother's womb.

Father Andrew M. Greeley published a piece in the *New York Times* extolling *Close Encounter*'s sense of religious wonder, while in *New York* magazine, Molly Haskell demanded, "Who is Spielberg to define religion for us?" Multiple commentators observed that the movie's initial audiences remained seated through the credits as if waiting for the story to continue. I remember standing on line to see *Close Encounters* in early 1978, startled and a bit derisive to see patrons exiting in tears.*

Close Encounters was religious in ways that *Star Wars* was not. For one thing, Spielberg believed in received truth; for another he did not advocate escapism. On the contrary. Whether intuiting the thesis of Richard Dyer's "Entertainment and Utopia," namely that motion pictures were essentially compensatory, or drawing on his own experience, Spielberg understood that movies had the mandate to assuage real-life dissatisfaction with utopian solutions.

That Roy longs to escape adult responsibility raises a legitimate fear of losing his job, his home, his family, and his sanity. Yet the more Roy surrenders to extraterrestrial influence, the more infantile he becomes. Given the dirt he deposits all over the house, one might see him as regressing to the pre-toilet training period. "In his savage retreat—'a heightened reality' divested of the encumbrances of wife and family—his desecration of the home, the monument of dirt, he projects a schizophrenic parody of a child without the civilizing and restraining influence of his parents," Haskell wrote. (He's making reality fun to live with.)

Later we see other adults acting like kids, as when, having acknowledge the probability of extraterrestrial life, the scientists gleefully rolling a globe of the earth. "Only those who are willing to follow instinct can begin to grasp

---

* *Close Encounters* grossed $116 million to finish number three for 1977, edged out by the good old boy Burt Reynolds vehicle, *Smokey and the Bandit*, a trucker action-comedy which, speaking to another segment of the Carter coalition, took in $127 million.

the extraterrestrial's unique, nonverbal language," Frank Rich explained in *Time*. Science itself is downgraded, as when the appearance of the aliens prompts one scientist to exult, "It's the first day of school, fellas," or when another suggests that, as might have been theorized by the Swiss author Erich von Däniken, Einstein was an alien.

In *Close Encounters*, the workaday suburban world is rendered wondrous, and government manipulation is replaced by transparency. Spielberg's aesthetic forbears are the arch-manipulator Alfred Hitchcock and the master of childhood innocence Walt Disney. If *Jaws* is Spielberg's Hitchcock film, *Close Encounters* is his Disney film. In *Jaws*, the crisis must be met. In *Close Encounters*, it's an illusion that only need be dispelled. There are two crises. The first comes when the aliens disable the power grid, the second when the government simulates disaster, with a bogus nerve-gas spill. With its helicopters and jungle fatigues, the fake disaster has obvious intimations of Vietnam and even, as the army loads masses of people into boxcars, Nazi deportation. Nevertheless, it is inconsequential.

Like *The Next Voice*, *Close Encounters* proposed the Department of Amusement as a cosmic panacea—acknowledging the existence of an actual problem and proposing itself as the solution. The movie celebrates itself. The climactic light show is a drama of communication in which nothing (and everything) is communicated. Incredibly, Spielberg had toyed with the idea of ending the movie with the *Disneyland* theme song "When You Wish Upon a Star."*

"In the course of reinventing itself, Hollywood finds trends, follows them, copies them and drops them," Wayne Warga began a *Los Angeles Times* article published soon after Jimmy Carter's inauguration. "One might— just might—predict science fiction as the next course to be followed. There is

---

* Although the idea was discarded after a Texas preview audience responded negatively, Spielberg has credited "When You Wish Upon a Star" with inspiring *Close Encounters*: "I made this movie because of the Disney song," he told *Rolling Stone*, citing "the feeling the song gave me when I was a kid listening to it." Introduced in Walt Disney's *Pinocchio*, a movie *Close Encounters* references several times, "When You Wish Upon a Star" was deployed as the theme to the *Disneyland* TV show—the embodiment of *kinderkultur* zeitgeist when Spielberg was a child. *Close Encounter*'s final shots suggest the show's emblematic image of a Disney-dust-enhanced version of Cinderella's castle.

a project called *Star Wars* on the way, a feature version of *Star Trek* in development and two films before the camera: *Close Encounters of the Third Kind* and *Capricorn One*."

Capricorn One—written and directed by former TV newsman Peter Hyams—might be *Close Encounter*'s stunted, evil twin, not least because Warga quoted a *Close Encounter* publicist asserting that the film was "science fact." Indeed, *Capricorn One* had already benefited from pre-production publicity when Warga's article ran. An earlier *Los Angeles Times* piece headlined "The Space Shot as a Sham" noted the topicality of a movie premised on the notion that the National Aeronautics and Space Administration might use TV technology to fake a landing on Mars. According to the article, Gallup determined that 28 percent of those polled believed the space program to have been a fake. (One wonders how many of these also believed in UFOs.)

Working at Boston's CBS affiliate, Hyams had been impressed by the realistic simulations NASA provided for telecast, to show the progress of the spaceship as it headed for the moon. Soon after, he was struck by the duplicity of the Nixon administration and began working on a script. Hollywood was uninterested but Hyams's friend Paul Lazarus, the producer of *Westworld*, managed to sell the idea to the British impresario Sir Lew Grade, who bankrolled the movie and brought Warner Bros. in on a distribution deal.

Capricorn One even got NASA cooperation, including use of a prototype landing module. Evidently the agency believed that there was no such thing as bad publicity; *Capricorn One* takes it for granted that America is disillusioned and in decline and posits the space program as an apparent antidote. In one early scene, the film's snarky reporter (Elliott Gould) complains to a colleague (Karen Black, like Gould, a signifier of the counterculture and graduate of *Nashville*) that everything in contemporary America was plastic or bogus, while NASA embodied national prestige. "We know how bad we can be," the agency's head (Hal Holbrook) tells the four astronauts about to go on a mission to Mars. "You can show us how good. You are the basic truth in us, you are the reality."*

---

* One of the four astronauts is played by football superstar O. J. Simpson, characterized by Wayne Warga as "one of the few authentic American heroes in recent years."

Of course, the real reality is that Mars is a top-secret TV studio and, in order to protect his agency from defunding, Holbrook is orchestrating a fraudulent show. (An opportunistic liberal senator in *Wild in the Streets* and the informant Deep Throat in *All the President's Men*, Holbrook was a convincing representative of the deep state.) Eulogizing the astronauts who were supposed to have died in a rocket malfunction during reentry, he maintains that "at a time when cynicism was a national epidemic, they gave us something to believe in."

Not only is the government, as manifested by NASA, capable of murdering its own citizens, it has the power to propagate fiction and alter reality, as when NASA minions alter the apartment belonging to one of Gould's sources to suggest that the man never existed. As in paranoid Watergate-era films like *The Parallax View* and *Three Days of the Condor*, there is nothing the state won't do. In addition to dramatizing a widely believed rumor, *Capricorn One* may have been the first movie to employ the sinister black helicopters that, beginning in the 1970s, became a conspiracy theorist trope.

Virtually the last of the old-style dystopian sci-fi films, despite its joyful *Rocky*-like ending, and no less a response to Watergate than *Close Encounters*, *Capricorn One* suffered its own mildly conspiratorial fate. The movie began filming in January 1977 and wrapped by spring. Still, it did not open in the U.S. until the summer of 1978 a year after *Star Wars*. The original fall 1977 release date was pushed back to February 1978 when, according to Hyams, Warner Bros., having soured on the project, planned to dump it in a few Southern theaters. Then the studio's prospective summer blockbuster *Superman* was delayed and Warners rescheduled *Capricorn One* in its slot.

In late May 1978, the *New York Times* reported the studio's unprecedented insistence that "critics see the film, not in the snug cocoon of a special showing but at one of the public previews, arguing that the participation of the audience is an essential part of the event as a whole." Audiences did respond and although soon overwhelmed by blockbusters like *Grease* and *National Lampoon's Animal House*, *Capricorn One* proved reasonably profitable and even the most successful independently financed film of the year. Writing in the *Los Angeles Times*, Charles Champlin singled it out as "virtually the only original American movie" in a summer distinguished by sequels (*Jaws 2*, and *Damien: Omen II*), remakes (*Heaven Can Wait*), and adaptations (*Grease*).

No less than *Star Wars*, albeit on a far smaller scale, *Capricorn One* became a cult film. "It's got to be something other than the intrinsic merit or lack of merit of the movie," Hyams later recalled. "It can't just be that the movie's so brilliant, because it isn't. I think it strikes something a little primal in people."*

Not quite the opposite of *The Next Voice You Hear*, Hyams's movie suggested that while the government lies, the media tells the truth. What *Capricorn One* failed to anticipate was the degree to which, over the next decade, the media would collude with the government and the government would manage the media.

Disc-O-pocalypse Now

Star Wars and *Close Encounters of the Third Kind* were upbeat, feel-good, and coercive—spectacular assertions of cinematic power to create the suspension of disbelief. They were not only reassuring but regressive. Their sense of wonder served to reconstruct the spectator as a child.

If *Star Wars* mixed militarist bombast with teenage rebellion, *Close Encounters* tempered its cheerful theology with a post-Watergate mistrust of government. Super-strength versions of the *Rocky Horror* cult, both movies sought to extend and massify the moribund counterculture, in part through the dialectic of science-fiction and airbrushed nostalgia, the French-dubbed *le mode retro*. So too the third great hit of Jimmy Carter's first year in office: *Saturday Night Fever.*

Star Wars and *Close Encounters* were excitingly extraterrestrial. Opening in December 1977, a month after *Close Encounters*, which it would

---

* Writing in *The Observer*, the British critic Philip French joked that the movie "looks as if it had been scripted by the editorial board of *Krokodil* [the sanctioned Soviet humor magazine] at the height of the Cold War." According to an article published decades later in the *Boston Globe*, "*Capricorn One* found a huge audience in the pre-glasnost Soviet Union, where the government owned every movie theater."

   The film ran for years and years, often on one screen, once a day, all across the country. Why? Not because it was popular; Russian audiences weren't stupid. But because the Soviet regime hoped, in vain, that its populace would assume that America's greatest propaganda coup, the 1969 *Apollo* moon landing, had been faked by some Hollywood trickery.

replace atop *Variety*'s chart of top-grossing movies (where it remained through mid-February), *Saturday Night Fever* was aggressively down to earth—set and largely shot in the working-class, mainly Italian neighborhood of Bay Ridge, Brooklyn. Still, using an actual Bay Ridge disco, it evoked a depressed vision of ecstatic youth culture in a cramped version of outer space: the 2001 Odyssey nightclub.

Star Wars and *Close Encounters* were dependent on special effects. The magic of *Saturday Night Fever* derived mainly from the synergy between twenty-three-year-old John Travolta—who for three seasons had played Vinnie Barbarino, the resident high school greaser on the Brooklyn-set sitcom *Welcome Back, Kotter* (ABC, 1975–79)—and the Bee Gees, a passé pop group converted to disco. The electrifying credit sequence has Travolta sashay through busy Bay Ridge, pausing to scarf a double slice of pizza, as he bops to the infectious anthem "Staying Alive."

Established as a star even before the movie begins, Travolta's teenaged Tony Manero—a hardware store clerk living at home with a devoutly Catholic mother and an unemployed hard-hat father—is prophetically located as a creature of pop culture, his bedroom plastered with posters of Bruce Lee, Farrah Fawcett, Sylvester Stallone (as Rocky), and Al Pacino (as Serpico). A workweek drone and weekend king, Tony reigns supreme in a resplendent white suit, strutting his stuff at the local disco. "Pop rapture" and "futureless squalor" were phrases Pauline Kael coined in her *New Yorker* review, suggestively titled "Nirvana."

Saturday Night Fever had its origins in the British music writer Nik Cohn's *New York* magazine cover story "Tribal Rites of the New Saturday Night," published in the late spring of 1976. Something of an ethnomusicologist, Cohn had begun hanging out in Brooklyn discos that winter, around the time *Taxi Driver* was in release, taking notes on what he considered to be a new youth culture developed by the working-class white ethnics who came of age after the Orgy in the depressed post-Sixties.

"They are not so chic, these kids," Cohn wrote. "They know nothing of flower power or meditation, pansexuality, or mind expansion."

> No waterbeds or Moroccan cushions, no hand-thrown pottery, for them. No hep jargon either, and no Pepsi revolutions. In many cases, they genuinely can't remember who Bob Dylan was, let alone Ken Kesey or Timothy Leary.

Haight Ashbury, Woodstock, Altamont—all of them draw a blank. Instead, this generation's real roots lie further back, in the fifties, the golden age of Saturday nights.*

Still, a few remnants of the counterculture are visible. Named for the trippiest movie of 1968, the 2001 Odyssey features a light show—strobes, moving beams, and a translucent checkerboard dance floor illuminated from below with a cycle of what Kael, channeling hippie bard Allen Ginsberg, called "burning neon-rainbow colors." Every night at the 2001 Odyssey was the climax of *Close Encounters* and *Saturday Night Fever* secured an initial R-rating by dramatizing the closer physical encounters in the parking lot outside as well as the action portrayed on the floor.

Australian music and movie producer Robert Stigwood, responsible for the filmed rock operas *Jesus Christ Superstar* (1973) and *Tommy* (1975) and manager of the Bee Gees, bought the rights to Cohn's story and began assembling a package to reunite Norman Wexler and John Avildsen, the writer and director of *Joe*. Avildsen, who had since directed *Rocky*, would be replaced by John Badham, reportedly for refusing to work with what Andrew Sarris called Wexler's "relatively sordid script."

Saturday Night Fever opened at seven hundred theaters. The movie cost $3 million to make and as much to promote—a campaign immeasurably helped by the mid-November release of the Bee Gees–dominated two-disc soundtrack album. *Variety* was contemptuous, calling it "a fast playoff item" aimed at the "undiscriminating youth market," "nothing more than an updated '70s version of the Sam Katzman rock music cheapies of the '50s," a "more shrill, more vulgar, more trifling, more superficial and more pretentious exploitation film."[†]

---

* Cohn would later reveal that his story was fraudulent. Although he had "put in hard time in Brooklyn," his characters were inspired by mods he had known in London in the 1960s. Still, his observation was driven home when, even as *Saturday Night Fever* enjoyed its seventh week as America's number one box-office hit, Bob Dylan's near five-hour psychodrama *Renaldo and Clara* had its premiere and was universally derided as bloated, passé self-indulgence. It should also be noted that *Saturday Night Fever* coincides with the heyday of punk—a youth subculture programmatically opposed to hippies and the Sixties.

† *Saturday Night Fever* merged into the Fifties revival with Stigwood's subsequent musical *Grease*, the number-one grossing movie of 1978. That same year the Brooklyn-born insult comedian Andrew Dice Clay began incorporating a parody of Travolta's Tony Manero in his act.

Time's new film critic Frank Rich was more precise in detailing what he called the movie's "merchandising assault on the youth market." Not only was *Saturday Night Fever* the first disco feature, it starred TV's hottest juvenile, and was tied to an album that would dominate the national soundtrack, topping the charts from January into July. The Bee Gees' catchy ballad "How Deep Is Your Love" was already heading toward number one. (Three more cuts would follow.) Other reviewers noted the movie's recycling of elements of *Mean Streets*, *American Graffiti*, and *Rocky*.

The least ambivalent, most prescient, comment was Kael's. Five years before MTV, she appreciated *Saturday Night Fever* as a musical: The "sustained disco beat keeps the audience in an empathetic rhythm with the characters." While cognizant of the movie's sources, she saw new subject matter—"how the financially pinched seventies generation that grew up on TV attempts to find its own forms of beauty and release." Less sympathetic observers saw the continuation of the Orgy of the Sixties by other means.

Citing the conservative sociologist Peter Ludwig Berger's notion that "the U.S., by all relevant indices, is well on its way to evolving as a totally pagan society," William F. Buckley wrote in the *New York Post* that *Saturday Night Fever* was "as fascinating as a ritual dance by an aboriginal society, full of feathers, drum beats, blood, and organized lust."*

As the youth culture experienced itself in diminished form, ancient regimes in deepest Eurasia—along what Jimmy Carter's national security adviser Zbigniew Brzezinski called the Arc of Crisis—were crumbling.

November 15, 1977, a day before *Close Encounters* opened, Shah Rezi Pahlavi's state visit to Washington, DC, occasioned violent demonstrations outside the White House. Many in Iran imagined the protests were stage-managed by President Carter to humiliate his guest. Carter paid a return visit to the Shah on New Year's Eve. *Towering Inferno* had just opened in

---

* Rock 'n' roll anarchy continued to be packaged that spring. March brought a nostalgic tribute to Alan Freed, *American Hot Wax*. April evoked Beatlemania with *I Wanna Hold Your Hand*; in May it was Motown's disco musical *Thank God It's Friday* and the '50s-era *Buddy Holly Story*. Stigwood's echt-retro *Grease* opened in June and topped the *Variety* chart for fifteen weeks that summer and fall—supplanted once by *National Lampoon's Animal House*—more than making up for the failure of another Stigwood production, *Sgt. Pepper's Lonely Hearts Club Band*. The only notable science-fiction films were a pair of dystopian stragglers, Brian De Palma's telekinetic thriller *The Fury* and *Capricorn One*.

Tehran, with *Earthquake* and *Jaws* soon to follow. The president praised Iran as "an island of stability." A week later an estimated twenty thousand Iranians took to the streets of the holy city of Qom chanting "Death to the Shah."

UFOs were seen in the skies over Tehran. Some claimed extraterrestrials had invaded a house in the central city. The next month, riots swept the northwestern city of Tabriz. Banks, movie theaters, and appliance stores were trashed. Women in Western dress were chased off the streets and sometimes assaulted. In April, even as the beleaguered Shah met with American military leaders to consider the benefit of a U.S.-sponsored coup, a real coup led by the pro-Soviet People's Democratic Party ousted Afghanistan's self-proclaimed president Mohammed Daoud Khan.

As if on cue, with the Iranian crisis that would result in America's worst foreign policy defeat since the fall of Saigon gathering momentum, the War in Vietnam was newly hallucinated. *Apocalypse Now* remained mired in postproduction but Hollywood released a cluster of films that would establish the basic themes of the Vietnam cycle: there was the returning vet melodrama, *Coming Home,* starring liberal icon Jane Fonda, and the grunt ensemble film, *The Boys in Company C,* both of which opened in February 1978. *Good Guys Wear Black,* a macho back-stabbing fantasy starring the martial artist turned low-budget action hero Chuck Norris and directed by Ted Post, was released in June along with Post's more respectable combat film, *Go Tell the Spartans.* (Apparently loath to associate himself with Vietnam, Clint Eastwood had turned down the lead, which eventually went to Burt Lancaster.)*

Karel Reisz's druggy *Who'll Stop the Rain* (also known as *Dog Soldiers*), adapted from Robert Stone's National Book Award–winner *Dog Soldiers,* opened in early August, several months after competing in Cannes. Here, Vietnam appeared as a crime scene and source of contagion. A disillusioned journalist (Michael Moriarty) is caught up in a scheme to smuggle heroin from Saigon to Berkeley, pressuring his merchant marine buddy Ray (Nick Nolte) to act as his mule. The whole thing is a setup. When crooked cops attempt to hijack the dope, the marine and the journalist's uncomprehending

---

* An absurdist view of the Vietnam War was available throughout the decade in the form of the hit service comedy sitcom *M*A*S*H* (CBS, 1972–83), ostensibly set in Korea but, like the 1970 Robert Altman film on which it was based, recognizably Vietnam.

wife (Tuesday Weld) flee Berkeley for Los Angeles and then the New Mexico hills.

In some ways anticipating *Apocalypse Now*, *Who'll Stop the Rain* conflated the battlefield with the counterculture under the sign of film noir. The movie oozes paranoia and features a climactic, psychedelic light show worthy of the 2001 Odyssey. Ray is not just a real soldier but a hipster who reads Nietzsche and casts the *I Ching*, a characterization for which Nolte received near-universal praise. Forgetting about *Rocky*, Clint Eastwood, and the impending release of *Superman*, *New York* magazine's new critic David Denby saw Nolte's character as a welcome panacea: "In the last five or six years, the macho movie hero—the man of action—has been ridiculed so frequently that we are in danger of forgetting how important physical heroism remains in a pictorial medium like the movies."

Who'll Stop the Rain was still in theaters when Iranians staged the biggest anti-Shah demonstration in Iranian history—a record topped three days later. In Hollywood, however, as the film historian Peter Biskind wrote, "The buzz on the street was all about *The Deer Hunter*"—hyped even while in production as "A Vietnam Movie That Does Not Knock America" (unlike, presumably, *Apocalypse Now*).

The thirty-six-year-old writer-director Michael Cimino, who had both written for and directed Clint Eastwood, succeeded in scooping Francis Ford Coppola, even as he aped Coppola's muscular *Godfather* style. *The Deer Hunter* opens with a lengthy set piece combining a Russian Orthodox wedding celebration with a military send-off as the movie's three male protagonists—all steel workers and at least one, named Michael after the director (Robert De Niro), a future Green Beret—prepare to leave for Vietnam. Indeed, Cimino went even further than Coppola—imagining a western Pennsylvania town as though it were nestled in the Swiss Alps, interpolating footage shot in the Cascade mountains and using a mystical chorus to underscore the misty peaks, as well as the ritual deer-hunting sequence that gives the movie its title. Then, Cimino cuts from the spectacle of elevated male brotherhood to the cesspool of Asian depravity, as demonic Vietcong destroy innocent civilians.

The heroes are captured but, thanks to Michael's superhuman fortitude, manage to escape and Michael eventually returns to the Nam to rescue a lost comrade. The My Lai massacre is reversed. As pointed out by H. Bruce

Franklin, it is the VC, rather than American GIs, who toss grenades into shelters, strafing the escaping women and children with automatic rifle fire; captured Americans, rather than Vietnamese, who tumble from helicopters. "The central structuring metaphor of the film is the Russian roulette the sadistic Asian Communists force their prisoners to play," Franklin writes.

> POW after POW is shown with a revolver at his right temple, framed to match with precision the sequence seen by tens of millions of Americans in which the chief of the Saigon secret police placed a revolver to the right temple of an National Liberation Front prisoner and killed him with a single shot; even the blood spurting out of the temple is exactly replicated.

The Americans were the war's real victims.

Cimino would insist that *The Deer Hunter* was essentially apolitical and that so far as his characters were concerned, the war could have been any war, "simply a means of testing their courage and will power." The movie is grandiose in its affirmation, topping even the ending of *Close Encounters* with the surviving principals breaking into an utterly sincere chorus of "God Bless America."

Would God bless Iran? The Ayatollah Khomeini was now leading the revolution from Iraq, and when driven out, continued from France. In late October, the revolution spread to the oil industry; a few weeks later, Iranian junior officers were reportedly refusing to follow orders. On December 8, one day after Jimmy Carter declared that it was "up to the people of Iran to decide" their fate, *The Deer Hunter* opened to near-unanimous raves and was voted the year's best movie by the New York Film Critic's Circle. Writing with a soupçon of ambivalence in the *New York Times*, Vincent Canby called it "a big, awkward, crazily ambitious, sometimes breathtaking motion picture that comes as close to being a popular epic as any movie about this country since *The Godfather*."

Pauline Kael's brilliant analysis acknowledged the movie's virtuoso mise-en-scène while parsing its pulp ideology, conflating the romance of boys in the wilderness with xenophobic yellow peril (or red Indian) terror. The movie was grandiloquent but simpleminded, "Coppola without brains or sensibility," with "no more moral intelligence than the Eastwood action pictures." But while placing the movie in the tradition of James Fenimore Cooper, Kael ignored the systematic inversion of Vietnam War iconography and the introduction of the POW as American martyr—a perspective that would soon come roiling out of the Dream Life.*

On December 10, even as massive street demonstrations brought Iran to a halt, America unwrapped a long-anticipated Christmas present to itself. *Superman: The Movie* had its world premiere at the Kennedy Center in Washington, DC, at a screening attended by the president and his eleven-year-old daughter Amy.

Superman was advertised simply with the pentagonal S-logo cast in platinum and set against a streaky luminous sky above the words "You'll Believe a Man Can Fly." Keep the faith! A World War II fantasy figure, staple of early 1950s kiddie TV, and comic book titan, eclipsed as a Pop Art icon by brother Batman, Superman was born again in a $55 million production that, its initial budget tripled by the cost of special effects, was then the most expensive movie ever made. Few failed to note the parallels between Hollywood's alien superhero and the babe whose birth is celebrated on Christmas Day.

Conceived in 1974, *Superman* was not the spawn of *Star Wars* but a parallel production that, at one time or another was rumored to star Robert Redford, Paul Newman, Steve McQueen, Clint Eastwood, Al Pacino, Dustin Hoffman, Sylvester Stallone, Arnold Schwarzenegger, and Muhammad Ali. Marlon Brando received a guaranteed $2.7 million for twelve shooting days as Superman's father, Jor-El, thus solidifying *The Godfather* connection established by novelist Mario Puzo, well publicized and handsomely paid for a script that would later be extensively rewritten by David Newman and his wife, Leslie, and then revised yet again by Joseph Mankiewicz's son Tom.

Old Hollywood had come to save itself, although George Lucas had been approached to direct, along with Steven Spielberg and a half-dozen others including Roman Polanski, Francis Coppola, William Friedkin, and Sam Peckinpah, before Richard Donner was hired on the basis of *The Omen,* a cross between *The Exorcist* and *Jaws* that was the number-five grossing film of 1976. Principal photography on *Superman* and its sequel *Superman II*

---

* Kathleen Belew's *Bring the War Home: The White Power Movement and Paramilitary America* argues that previously disparate far right-wing and white supremacist movements, including neo-Nazis and the Ku Klux Klan, made common cause both in the recruitment of disgruntled Vietnam veterans and a belief that the war had been lost by traitorous elements in the U.S. government.

began two months before *Star Wars* opened and, with location shooting in New York during the blackout summer of 1977, continued for over a year and a half into October 1978, during which time Donner was replaced by Richard Lester, credited with *Superman II.*

The most remarkable thing about *Superman* was its production history, an elaborate pyramid scheme, replete with bounced checks and deferred payments, masterminded by the swashbuckling international producer Alexander Salkind on the advice of his twenty-five-year-old son Ilya (who like many involved in the project would wind up suing the old man). Nearly as remarkable was the delight with which this jerry-built contraption was received. *Superman* reigned supreme at the box office for ten weeks, from mid-December to mid-February 1979 (upended once by the Clint Eastwood orangutan comedy *Every Which Way but Loose*); it would gross over $130 million in North America to be the second-highest grossing movie of 1979.*

Superman's antipode as an extraterrestrial invasion film that season was another long-germinating project. Producer Robert Solo got the idea to remake Don Siegel's 1956 *Invasion of the Body Snatchers* in 1975, then spent two years securing the rights. The movie's eventual director, Philip Kaufman, had been working on Paramount's movie version of the 1960s TV show *Star Trek* when, with flawless timing, the studio shut down the project on the eve of *Star Wars'* epochal premiere in May 1977. Kaufman signed onto *Invasion* that summer, bringing Leonard Nimoy, *Star Trek*'s beloved co-star, with him.

Siegel's *Invasion of the Body Snatchers* was so intrinsically a movie of the 1950s that Kaufman felt compelled to link his own version to the epic revival that began around the time of Richard Nixon's reelection (and would continue, unabated, through the middle of Ronald Reagan's second term). "We were all asleep in a lot of ways in the Fifties, living conforming, other-directed types of lives. Maybe we woke up a little in the Sixties, but now we've gone back to sleep again," he told one interviewer, referring to the self-involvement and political disorientation that followed the counterculture's crack-up.

Rather than *The Lonely Crowd*, David Riesman, Nathan Glazer, and Reuel Denney's 1950 analysis of the American character and conformism that

---

* As DC comics were then owned by Warner Bros., *Superman* exceeded even *Jaws* as an example of corporate synergy. The movie's soundtrack was released by Warner Bros. records, its novelizations were published by Warner Bros. books and Warner subsidiary Atari developed a Superman arcade game.

introduced the terms "inner-" and "outer-directed," the pop-sociological con-text for this second *Invasion of the Body Snatchers* was Christopher Lasch's *The Culture of Narcissism*, published just as the movie was released. And, un-like the original, Kaufman's mannerist, alternately self-conscious and rhap-sodic remake—shot by Michael Chapman, the cinematographer on *Taxi Driver*—made little argument in favor of podification. Rather it parodied the pod condition which, in the movie's funniest joke, was spread by flowers and mimics the effect of watching TV.

Kaufman's remake transposed the action from a small town to San Francisco, still the capital of American non-conformism (even if Siegel, to whom Kaufman gave a cameo, visualized the city as Dirty Harry's playground). Populated by a gaggle of smart-mouthed free spirits, former flower children turned welfare state functionaries, and smooth, hustling guru-therapists for-ever asking each other about their "feelings," Kaufman's *Invasion* reeks of local color and urban alienation. Indeed, thanks to two sensational post-counterculture tragedies preceding the film's release, the movie's setting im-bued it with additional resonance.

Less than a month before *Invasion of the Body Snatchers* had its premiere, a deranged former member of the San Francisco Board of Supervisors assas-sinated both the city's mayor and its most public gay activist, Harvey Milk, while members of the progressive, multiracial People's Temple, formerly of San Francisco, committed mass suicide in the Guyana jungle at the behest of their leader, the Reverend Jim Jones. Each atrocity suggested in its way that the wages of lifestyle might be death—not to mention, as Andrew Sarris cyni-cally put it, "a press agent's dream come true." Sarris was struck by an "even weirder subtext" while watching the film's protagonist (Donald Sutherland) pulverize a pod-fetus. "A group of pod people arrive on the scene and begin a throaty subhuman lament. In the ensuing noise, I began to perceive an eerie echo of the Right-to-Lifers, the most powerful pressure group in the country as far as the spreading of fear and the stifling of dissent are concerned."

Pauline Kael was also struck by this effect but made a more apt compari-son. For her, the pod people's wail suggested "an inhuman variant of the rhythmic trilling-screaming sounds of the women in *The Battle of Algiers*." Less concerned with the threat of political subversion and the comfort of the lonely crowd than with the curse of creeping psychobabble and the need to protect the environment, Kaufman's *Invasion of the Body Snatchers* was at once a defense of non-conformism and bitter parody of the counterculture, the cri de coeur of the aging hippie—"an unending wail of confusion and despair," per Sarris—a denunciation of the pod that failed.

The Shah flees Iran on January 16, 1979, as George Lucas, Steven Spielberg and screenwriter Lawrence Kasdan meet to plan their first joint venture, *Raiders of the Lost Ark*. Euphoric demonstrations demand an Islamic Republic, pleading for Khomeini to return. On February 1, he arrives after fourteen years in exile.

The year is off to a jittery start. A few weeks later there is a new war in Vietnam. China has invaded! March 16, the same day that Chinese forces withdraw, *The China Syndrome* opens, dramatizing an instance of nuclear power plant malfeasance uncovered by a TV reporter (Jane Fonda). Twelve days later, a real mechanical failure in a reactor at the Three Mile Island plant in Pennsylvania leads to a meltdown and partial evacuation of the surrounding area. Meanwhile, the Islamic Republic has cut oil production and, for the first time since 1973, there will be gas lines in America.

April 9, Oscar Night 1978: inside the Dorothy Chandler Pavilion the assembled stars sway to disco music, bedazzled by strobes and mirrors as Donna Summer sings "Last Dance." Outside, the building is surrounded by demonstrators from two groups, the Hell No, We Won't Go Away Committee and the Vietnam Veterans Against the War, protesting *The Deer Hunter*, which will win five academy awards, including the Oscar for best picture presented by no less than the gaunt and ailing John Wayne. *Coming Home* is awarded three Oscars and a clever publicist attempts, but fails, to contrive a backstage confrontation between Jane Fonda and Michael Cimino.*

Five days later, Coppola, who had handed his "paisan" Cimino the Oscar for best director, celebrates his fortieth birthday. Guests, who include George Lucas, Robert De Niro (who lost best actor to Jon Voigt), and Dennis

---

* *The Deer Hunter* had already roiled the 1979 Berlin International Film Festival. The Soviet delegation, along with those of other socialist states, charged the movie with maligning the Vietnamese people in violation of the festival's mission to foster "mutual understanding" between nations. There were staged walkouts by the Cubans and East Germans; two members of the jury resigned. After *The Deer Hunter* won its Oscars, the movie was attacked in *Izvestia*, which called it "objectively an attempt at arousing compassion for the invaders and at slandering the heroic people of Vietnam."

Hopper, shout "We will rule Hollywood!" as cheerleaders chanted that "Francis has the power." (Two days later, the shoot for Cimino's ambitious mega-Western, *Heaven's Gate*, opens in Glacier National Park, Montana.)

After the better part of a decade, *Apocalypse Now* was almost ready. Inspired by Joseph Conrad's novella *The Heart of Darkness*, the project had its origin in a 16mm project John Milius and George Lucas had originally hoped to film in Vietnam while war was being waged. Ambivalence was part of the package. The pro-war Milius saw the movie as a celebration of "surfing and bombs," while the anti-war Lucas thought it might be a new *Dr. Strangelove*.

A few years later, still envisioning a 16mm film shot with real soldiers, Lucas imagined *Apocalypse Now* as his follow-up to *American Graffiti*. But Coppola, who produced *American Graffiti* and inherited the rights to *Apocalypse Now*, offered Lucas a deal so penurious that he turned it down. Then, in 1974, with Lucas already involved with *Star Wars*, Coppola became suddenly enthusiastic, deeming it a perfect Bicentennial film. Lucas asked Coppola to wait for him to finish *Star Wars*. Coppola declined and, after failing to recruit Milius to make the film, decided to direct it himself.*

Having made the greatest popular movie of the era, *The Godfather*, Coppola sought to remake the Vietnam War, or so it came to seem. The idea that a madly extravagant movie and an out-of-control imperial war might be kindred forms of endeavor was scarcely lost on him. The filmmaker would assert that *Apocalypse Now* was not about Vietnam, it *was* Vietnam—up to its confused, anticlimactic ending, not to mention its destructive effect on his subsequent career. At the same time, Coppola put himself and his consciousness at the center of the narrative. *Apocalypse Now* was something new—the manifestation of a personal struggle to make a movie, an auteur psychodrama.

Like LBJ, Coppola was tough on his subordinates. He fired Harvey Keitel and drove Keitel's successor, Martin Sheen, to a heart attack. And like Nixon, Coppola had no idea how to end his extravaganza. In a sodden paroxysm of irrationality, he hired Marlon Brando to be his white whale and prayed that once the actor arrived on location, something resembling a climax would

---

* Coppola had actually made an inadvertent contribution to the war, having written the screenplay for the 1970 movie *Patton*—a film portraying the World War II field commander as a megalomaniacal war lover and hero that President Nixon screened at least twice, the second time occurring the night before he invaded Cambodia.

occur. Would Brando be a redeemer like Jimmy Carter or Rocky Balboa? Sheen's character, who spends most of the movie pursuing Brando's, speaks for his director: "I really didn't know what I'd do when I found him."

Apocalypse Now had a sneak preview in the L.A. neighborhood of Westwood on May 11 and was shown in Cannes as a work in progress. (Coppola brought two endings—a 70mm antiwar ending in which the Martin Sheen character drops his machete and renounces brutality amid a cleansing rain, and a 35mm pro-war ending in which he calls in the final airstrike.) "We had too much money, too much equipment and, little by little, we went insane," Coppola bragged.

The reaction was mixed and yet it was clear that Coppola had succeeded in conjuring up the High Sixties purple haze, evoking the feel of the first rock 'n' roll war and the magnitude of American hubris, along with the savage joy of watching so many millions of dollars consumed on the altar of the film's ambition. *Apocalypse Now* shared the Palme d'Or with Volker Schlöndorff's adaptation of *The Tin Drum* and opened in the U.S. on August 15. It soared, crashed, and burned.

The movie's first two-thirds were a succession of spectacular set pieces beginning with the moment, only minutes into the movie, when, synchronized to the sound of the Doors vamping, the jungle tree line explodes just as Jim Morrison intones, "This is the end." Visualizing the Futurist notion of aerial warfare as a total artwork, Coppola managed to evoke the American experience of Vietnam as both a thrilling high and a terrifying bummer: The grunt who can't leave the chopper ("I'm not going, I'm not going"), the wounded guys screaming for Mama, the gyrating Playboy bunnies who descend from the sky, the surfer who drops acid to stumble through a chaotic equivalent of the Khe Sanh siege, the orange flares against the green and gold foliage that give the film what, writing in the *New Republic*, Stanley Kauffmann dismissed as its "jungle discotheque look."

Nothing in *The Deer Hunter* tops the fascist excitement of the "Ride of the Valkyries" air cavalry attack—or its historical resonance. Employing the Wagner composition that D. W. Griffith used for the climax of *The Birth of Nation* to score a godlike view of a Vietnamese village destroyed in flames, the Space Age equivalent of white America's nineteenth-century Indian massacres. Reveling in cinematic power, the movie devolves into the temptation to be a white god. Everything fails in the Brando scenes—first imagination, then language. The actor gets one good line: "You're an errand boy sent by grocery clerks to collect a bill." Much of the rest of his dialogue sounds like lyrics from a bad Doors song ("I watched a snail crawling along the edge of a straight razor") or worse.

Nothing can redeem the movie's final forty minutes. That may not be an ultimate horror, but it is a real one. Perhaps the only public utterance more anticlimactic was Carter's so-called malaise speech—a televised sermon that, after a period of deliberation on the need for energy conservation, the president had delivered a month earlier. The president paid homage to America's vaunted "family values" but deigned to criticize American materialism: "In a nation that was proud of hard work, strong families, close-knit communities, and our faith in God, too many of us now tend to worship self-indulgence and consumption. Human identity is no longer defined by what one does but by what one owns."*

Reasonable as he was, Carter failed to appreciate his countrymen's capacity for self-pity. He screened *Rocky II* at the White House three days after his speech—would that it had been three days before!—as his approval ratings fell to a record low. With its nightmarish rocket-ship factory and born-again monstrosity, the summer's other big movie, *Alien* (also projected at the White House), was closer to the public perception of life in Carter's America.†

Spielberg Strikes Out and *The Empire Strikes Back*

Sometime during the Bicentennial year, John Milius (who then had a production deal at MGM) hired his two protégés, the recent USC graduates Robert Zemeckis and Bob Gale, to write a dark comedy inspired by the suggestive episode of mass hysteria and war-fueled delusion known as "The Great Los Angeles Air Raid of 1942."

Ten weeks after the Japanese bombed Pearl Harbor, an enemy submarine surfaced off the California coast, twelve miles north of Santa Barbara, to fire

---

* Carter's unfairly maligned and programmatically misremembered speech was given in the midst of a series of briefings and conferences involving scientists and government officials on the danger of fossil fuel and the inevitability of global warming.

† The season also brought *More American Graffiti*, a perfunctory sequel that, although directed and written by Bill L. Norton (who made his debut in 1972 with the druggie Righteous Outlaw film *Cisco Pike*), might be considered Lucas's Vietnam film, set between 1964 and 1967 and including several battlefield scenes.

thirteen shells at an oil refinery. Damage was minimal, but panic was wide-spread, particularly in Los Angeles where, the following night, antiaircraft guns unloaded 1,440 rounds of ammunition in a forty-five-minute attack on a fleet of nonexistent Japanese planes.

The war came home and the show was spectacular. Searchlights raked the sky; shrapnel showered the blacked-out city. There were five casualties (three in car accidents and two due to heart failure) and, although the secretary of the navy quickly called a press conference to declare the incident a false alarm due to "war nerves," the story was extensively covered by the Los Angeles press and made national news.*

The initial script, which Milius revised and, with brazen political incor-rectness, titled "The Night the Japs Attacked," would be rechristened *1941* once Spielberg became involved. At the same time, the movie, originally bud-geted at a relatively modest $10 million, morphed into what Spielberg's biog-rapher Joseph McBride characterized as "an elephantine postmodernist farce." The action was pushed back to December 1941 and also now included a version of the June 1943 zoot suit riots. Fighter planes crashed into Holly-wood Boulevard (reconstructed on a studio back lot), a house dropped off a cliff, and a Ferris wheel rolled into the Pacific.

The production involved two studios, Columbia and Universal, and prom-ised everything for everybody. In his interviews, Spielberg evoked Mack Sen-nett, Laurel and Hardy, and the Three Stooges, and hired animator Chuck Jones as a consultant. As befits a disaster film, the director had attempted to recruit old Hollywood icons like John Wayne and Charlton Heston; they de-murred, Wayne angrily, deeming the project unpatriotic. Spielberg did how-ever manage to land Robert Stack, as well as Toshiro Mifune as the sympathetic Japanese submarine captain. At the same time, he had his eye on the youth market and, taking his cues from the hit farce *Animal House*, hired two *Satur-day Night Live* stars, Dan Aykroyd and the notorious coke-fiend John Belushi.

Filming began in October 1978, with Jimmy Carter calling for restraint regarding inflation. Requiring an even longer shoot than *Jaws*, it wrapped seven months later, a few days before *Apocalypse Now* screened at Cannes—

---

* The scenario was an extension of Orson Welles's radio dramatization *War of the Worlds* (in fact, in later years, some would reinterpret the event as a covered-up flying saucer at-tack). It also served to facilitate, only days later, the forcible relocation of Japanese Ameri-cans to concentration camps.

although special effects work would continue for another month. Even during the shooting, Spielberg had begun to panic. "I'm scared," he told *Time* the following spring. "We're taking history and bending it like a pretzel. I would use the words 'stupidly outrageous' to describe this movie. It's really a celebration of paranoia."

It was also a celebration of directorial power. Contempt for Hollywood and its audience felt implicit. Beginning with a riff on *Jaws* (using the same actress devoured in that movie's opening scene), Spielberg declared himself the new King of Comedy. The most maudlin scene in Disney's *Dumbo* held up to ridicule even as its racist representation of jive-talking crows is resurrected; Santa Claus desecrated; the Grand Canyon used for a prop.

Spielberg had his eye on the competition as well, throwing in some *Star Wars* aerial pyrotechnics and a USO dance spectacular beggaring the set piece in *Saturday Night Fever*. It may have been coincidental that *1941* featured a mad commanding officer (played by Warren Oates) comparable to Robert Duvall's colonel in *Apocalypse Now*, but Spielberg's comedy of destruction rivaled Coppola's war epic for firepower—as well as disdain for the armed forces.

Had the thirty-two-year-old director finally vented the anti-Vietnam outrage he might have absorbed as a suburban teenager and at Cal State Long Beach? Was Spielberg satirizing the fears dramatized in *Jaws*, turning the invasion anxiety of *Close Encounters* inside out? Ridiculing Coppola's hubris and mocking the pretensions of *Apocalypse Now* with a movie he jokingly referred to as "Apocalypse Then"?

Attempting to edit his footage, Spielberg had begun using phrases like "utter horror" and "total conceptual disaster" when, just before *Apocalypse Now* opened in New York, the *Village Voice* reported that, based on Milius's assertion that *1941* would come in "slightly under" the $30.5 million spent by Coppola, Spielberg was working on "the most expensive movie ever made on American soil."

October 19, 1979: A poor preview in Dallas in mid-October sent *1941* back to the editing room. The ending was reshot, and the movie's premiere delayed from mid-November to mid-December. By then, the world had significantly altered.

The 1980 presidential campaign was underway. Ronald Reagan made clear the obvious—that he'd again be seeking the Republican nomination—while

Senator Ted Kennedy and Governor Jerry Brown were set to announce chal-
lenges to the first Democratic president since Lyndon Johnson (who'd
been challenged by Kennedy's brother Robert in 1968). The most unforeseen
and transformative development, however, happened thousands of miles
away from Hollywood or Washington when, on November 4, Iranian militants occupied the American embassy in Tehran and took fifty-two Americans hostage.

"I'll spend the rest of my life disowning this picture," Steven Spielberg told
a *New York Times* writer, who thought he was kidding. "From the first day,
I kept saying to myself, 'This is not a Spielberg movie. What am I doing
here?'" (This, even though, no less than *Jaws* or *Close Encounters*, *1941* is an
invasion story with episodes of mass hysteria.)

Spielberg imagined that, watching *1941*, "kids will see similarities with
the hysterics caused by Iran's takeover of the United State Embassy in Tehran.
Except that the film, in a way, is anti-Ayatollah. Our character, played by
John Belushi, would be over there the next day to liberate the hostages personally. Compared to what Belushi does in *1941*, his role in *Animal House*
makes him look like the dean of students at Harvard." (Among other things,
what Belushi does is crash his plane into Hollywood Boulevard, searching
for a secret Japanese airfield "somewhere in the clover fields around Pomona.")

Spielberg was waging a battle in his mind. A *Rolling Stone* profile, published in January, found him a fount of near-hysterical babble: "Making a
movie, any movie, is like fighting a hand-to-hand war," he insisted, "*Every*
filmmaker is a commanding officer. . . . It's a war. The only real winners are
the public. The only real losers, often, are the filmmakers. It's an unnatural
act to make a movie." Rather than his earlier evocations of Ben Turpin, Spielberg now cited the quintessential end of the world black comedy *Dr. Strangelove*, although the only apocalypse *1941* represented was a nightmare death
wish for his own career.*

---

* *Dr. Strangelove* has a particular significance for Spielberg (as for George Lucas, who cited
the Kubrick film as influencing his concept of *Apocalypse Now*). Spielberg told Chris
Hodenfield that he was standing in line for the movie in San Jose when his sister came
running with a letter from the Selective Service: "I opened up the letter and it said, 'Report
for your physical.' It was very apropos at the time, when you're about to spend an hour and
thirty-three minutes with *Dr. Strangelove*." Spielberg has recounted other versions of this
story, including one that puts the event on the movie's opening weekend. Joseph McBride
politely terms the anecdote implausible, pointing out that *Strangelove's* first weekend in

In the Dream Life, Spielberg's "1941" was really "1965"—the year the film-maker graduated from high school and first came to Los Angeles. He was living with his father in a Brentwood apartment when the Watts riots erupted, allowing Spielberg to experience the destruction of Los Angeles firsthand, or at least on live television.

The reviews were brutal. *New West* critic Stephen Farber called *1941* "the most appalling piece of juvenilia yet foisted on the public." Writing in the *Los Angeles Herald Examiner*, Michael Sragow joked that it was "a movie that will live in infamy" and accused it of waging "war against all humanity." *Los Angeles Times* critic Charles Champlin wrote that *1941* "offers a nihilism based not on a rejecting rage but on an arrogant indifference to values." *New York Times* critic Vincent Canby was more restrained, calling the movie "profligate," "dumbfounding" and "ineptly timed." Few noted how impressively Spielberg had crafted his assault.

Overpowered on its first weekend by the long-awaited *Star Trek* movie, *1941* is remembered as a debacle, although it more than made its money back, mainly overseas. Then, on Christmas Eve, ten days after the Spielberg's movie opened, the Soviets premiered their own Vietnam death-wish scenario, sending troops into Afghanistan.

A miscalculation that would reverberate for a decade or more, the Soviet invasion of Afghanistan further helped the incumbent. Still, 1980 seemed destined to be a Republican year—perhaps the first since 1952 when the party could win the presidency and both houses of Congress.

The post-Nixon GOP had no shortage of prospects. All held Jimmy Carter responsible for America's decline and vowed to make the nation great again by enhancing the armed forces while otherwise reducing Washington's power, thus ending regulation and unleashing free enterprise.

Ronald Reagan's long-held positions were now his party's conventional wisdom, although it was Senator Howard Baker of Tennessee, a moderate and

---

San Jose was March 20–22, 1964: "Not only was Spielberg still seventeen at the time, but that was also the last weekend he spent in Phoenix." What's significant is that Spielberg associates the movie with the Vietnam War as well his own anxiety regarding authority. According to Robert Zemeckis, an earlier version of his *1941* screenplay did have something of a *Strangelove* ending, with the bombardier on the *Enola Gay* dropping the atomic bomb on Hiroshima, still angry at having lost the USO jitterbug contest.

rare Republican hero of the Watergate hearings who, as the candidate with the greatest similarity to Carter, was the potential rival that Carter (and Reagan's advisers) most feared.

Reagan made his Southern strategy evident by opening his campaign in Philadelphia, Mississippi, not far from the dam where the bodies of three slain civil rights workers were found, and delivering a nostalgic speech on "states' rights." Baker, meanwhile, was quickly outmaneuvered by George H. W. Bush, a one-term congressman appointed by Nixon multiple times (as CIA chief, UN ambassador, ambassador to China, chairman of the Republican National Committee) who trounced him in an early straw poll. Taking a lesson from Carter's playbook, Bush then concentrated on the Iowa caucuses, where he beat Reagan by 6 percent, setting himself up to go into New Hampshire as the early front-runner.

Reagan, now concerned, changed campaign managers and agreed to debate Bush one on one, thus setting up the primary campaign's crucial performance. A New Hampshire daily, the *Nashua Telegraph*, had agreed to sponsor the debate but was forced to withdraw when the Federal Election Commission ruled its participation an illegal campaign contribution. Consequently, the Reagan campaign picked up the tab and, unbeknownst to Bush, invited the four other candidates—Baker; two Illinois congressmen, John Anderson and Philip Crane; and Kansas senator Bob Dole. Panicked by their unexpected appearance, the moderator, a Bush supporter, threatened to cut off the sound but was confounded by Reagan who, channeling Spencer Tracy, a political candidate in the 1948 Frank Capra film *State of the Union*, paraphrased a line Tracy forcefully delivered in a similar situation: "I am paying for this microphone."

Initially trailing in the polls, Reagan went on to defeat Bush, and while Bush did win the Massachusetts primary, he had been mortally wounded. In fact, the real winner in Massachusetts and Vermont was Anderson who, by finishing second to Bush in both, assumed Baker's mantle as a moderate, commonsense Republican.

Ronald Reagan and Jimmy Carter have established themselves as solid front-runners by early March, but George Bush and Ted Kennedy and John Anderson and even Jerry Brown press on.

Reagan clobbers Richard Nixon's favorite Republican, the former Democrat, Texas governor, and LBJ protégée John Connally, in South Carolina, and then gives an effectively "presidential" performance, playing de facto master of ceremonies at an acrimonious four-candidate debate in Chicago. Watching this, former president Ford realizes that it is too late. Reagan will soon be stressing his historical inevitability with the slogan "The Time Is Now."

Carter has also won in Illinois, handing Kennedy his biggest setback so far, but his campaign—like Kennedy's—has turned terminally negative. Their main talking points are that each is not the other. As the race shifts to the Northeast, Kennedy recruits Carroll O'Connor, the beloved hard-hat racist Archie Bunker of *All in the Family*, as his spokesman. Speaking in (and yet against his persona), O'Conner calls Carter "the most Republican president since Herbert Hoover" and urges viewers to support "my friend Ted Kennedy."

Archie's pal scores upset victories in New York and Connecticut but, the next month, Carter beats Kennedy and Brown in Wisconsin where, hoping to elevate the California governor, Francis Ford Coppola orchestrates a sort of televised domestic *Apocalypse Now* with dazzling strobe lights and swooping helicopter shots. Carter has his own helicopter extravaganza in the works. As underdogs Kennedy and Bush both rally to win in Pennsylvania, the president prepares to launch a daring hostage rescue: Operation Eagle Claw.

This complicated mission requires the creation of two temporary bases in the Iranian desert in preparation for a lightning assault on Tehran. The helicopters encountered problematic weather conditions and when one blows up—leaving eight American soldiers dead—the mission is aborted. Carter has released his *1941*. The lone military operation of his term in office is a humiliating debacle.

For the first time, Carter trails Reagan in the polls. "For Reagan, the Stump Is a Stage," read the headline of Clyde Haberman's article in the *New York Post*. The candidate warms up his audience with well-timed jokes and anecdotes before embarking on a half-hour "nonstop tirade against busing, abortion, gun control, consumer protection laws, revenue-sharing, welfare, marijuana, most federal spending, Administration economic programs, and current U.S. foreign and defense policies."

Haberman compares Reagan's barrage of jaunty one-liners to Bob Hope. Meanwhile, Carter has consoled himself with a Clint Eastwood weekend, previewing Eastwood's upcoming comedy *Bronco Billy* on May 9 and revisiting his mid-'60s Spaghetti Western *A Fistful of Dollars* on May 10. In this, Carter may be prescient. For, somewhat belatedly, a trio of post-Western cowboy protagonists have surfaced late in the primary season.

Released a few days after Kennedy's New York victory, *Tom Horn* stars Steve McQueen in his penultimate movie role as an anachronistic frontier scout, a hero left behind in the changing west. In her *New York Times* review, Janet Maslin characterizes him as "part of a dying breed"—prophetic in that McQueen himself will die four days after the presidential election. As oxymoronic as its title, *Urban Cowboy*—which has its premiere on June 6—imagines the disco-king ethnic John Travolta as a contemporary oil refinery hand two-stepping and line-dancing in a fantastically capacious Houston honky-tonk. Opening five days later, *Bronco Billy* is the most resonant.

Eastwood plays the none-too-bright proprietor and star of an itinerant Wild West show (and former New Jersey shoe salesman) who triumphs over adversity in a diminished, cowboy American landscape by virtue of his optimistic belief in his own legend and the nation's. "This is an emphatically American fable, which is perhaps why it ends with a chorus of 'Stars and Stripes Forever,'" Maslin writes, although *Bronco Billy* like much else has already been subsumed by *The Empire Strikes Back*.

When *The Empire Strikes Back* was previewed in Los Angeles, two weeks after the disastrous Operation Eagle Claw, *Variety*'s reviewer was struck by the movie's aerial bellicosity: "The juggernaut attack on infantry in the trenches with fighter planes counterattacking overhead is straight out of every war movie ever made."

Despite a grade-school level romance between wise-guy Han Solo (Harrison Ford) and Princess Leia (Carrie Fisher, seemingly suffering from indigestion) and the introduction of the adorable wrinkly puppet Yoda, the movie was the celebration of an intergalactic Strategic Air Command, filled with jet pyrotechnics, aerial bombing, spectacular combat, and exotic military hardware, as in the anthropomorphic dinosaur tanks.

As befits the central episode in a trilogy, *The Empire Strikes Back* begins and ends in medias res with the rebel Alliance to Restore the Republic still stymied against Darth Vader and his Imperial forces. Thus, the conservative critic Richard Grenier would find the movie defeatist, writing in *Commen-*

tary that *The Empire Strikes Back* is "the first space fantasy heralding the demise of Western civilization."*

Or is it the demise of the Kennedy dynasty? Sunday, May 17, *The Empire Strikes Back* had its world premiere in Washington as a crypto-Kennedy event. The movie was screened at the Kennedy Center as a benefit for a Kennedy family charity, the Special Olympics program under the chairmanship of Robert Kennedy's widow, Ethel. Ted Kennedy did not attend; other family members who did attend included Eunice Kennedy Shriver and her daughter Maria Shriver, accompanied by her fiancé, Arnold Schwarzenegger. The star of the Carter contingent was the presidential daughter, Amy.

Bush beat Reagan one last time in Michigan on May 20 but lost in Oregon (as did Carter), ensuring Reagan's nomination. The next day, *The Empire Strikes Back* opened at number one. Expectations were high. According to *People*, "the lines and stampedes to see the sequel exceeded even those of the original." Audiences cheered the triumphalist theme and the reappearance of *Star Wars*' favorites, hiding from the dread Imperial star fleet on the icy planet of Hoth.

For the next five weeks, *The Empire Strikes Back* ruled the box office. Carter waited until May 26 to screen the movie at the White House, reportedly per *People*, because Amy had "cajoled her parents into letting her see the movie a second time within a week." *The Empire* was upended by another aerial adventure, the comic disaster film *Airplane!*, over the July 4th weekend, then rebounded another week later as the nation's top box-office attraction during the week of the Republican convention, held in Detroit between July 14 and 17.†

The nomination was a far-gone conclusion; the generally upbeat conclave was characterized largely by Moral Majority self-congratulation and a

---

* For Grenier, *The Empire Strikes Back* showed Lucas to be a pretentious countercultural simpleton whose "heavy emphasis on the 'Oriental' wisdom of Yoda leads me to doubt very much that the victory will be shown as one for 'our side.'"

† The year's top-grossing release *The Empire Strikes Back* overshadowed Stanley Kubrick's ambitious, unconventional horror film *The Shining*, which opening wide over the Memorial Day weekend and was positioned by Warner Bros. as a Movie-Event. The movie nevertheless finished number fourteen for 1980, a year marked by popular comedies including *9 to 5* (#2), the Richard Pryor vehicle *Stir Crazy* (#3), *Airplane!* (#4), Clint Eastwood's *Any Which Way You Can* (#5), and Goldie Hawn's *Private Benjamin* (#6).

measure of suspense regarding Reagan's running mate. An attempt was made to lure Gerald Ford onto the ticket before Reagan invited his last adversary, George H. W. Bush. "Never before in our history have Americans been called upon to face three grave threats to our very existence, any one of which could destroy us," Reagan told the convention. "We face a disintegrating economy, a weakened defense and an energy policy based on the sharing of scarcity." The Democrats were responsible for "this unprecedented calamity."

In the Democratic race, Carter had clearly prevailed, although Kennedy refused to surrender—even managing to win five of the last eight primaries, including California, where he deployed his nastiest attack ads yet. Still, as in 1976, Carter went the distance and staggered victorious to the Democratic convention, held between August 11 and 14, again in New York City. His favorability ratings, which had for the past year gone up and down like a yo-yo, were once more diminished.

III

BAD TRIPS, 1981–82

As the 1980 presidential campaign heated up, during the same week that *The Empire Strikes Back* reclaimed its number one box-office status from *Smokey and the Bandit II*, the *Village Voice* published my unabashedly snarky take-down, here retitled "My Reagan."*

He may have the beady eyes, leathery hide, and social conscience of a stegosaurus, but as an American politician, Ronald Reagan is right on time—and not just because he pioneered the use of pancake on the stump.

Reagan made a successful career out of establishing the "likeability" of his two-dimensional image. He spent three decades practicing a form of hoodoo—the Dr. Strange–like projection of his ectoplasmic form— over radio, in the movies, and on TV. The package may be shopworn, but the historian must stand in awe of its prophetic vision. In the sine

---

* J. Hoberman, "That Reagan Boy: The Education of an All-American" (*Village Voice*, September 10–16, 1980). A shorter version of this article, titled "Ronald Reagan: The Star Who Fell to Earth," was published in the June 11–17, 1976, issue of the *Berkeley Barb*. "That Reagan Boy," which was further informed by Mitch Tuchman's article "Ladies and Gentlemen, the Next President of the United States . . ." in the July/August 1980 issue of *Film Comment*, was originally written for *High Times*, a journal in which I learned, having written pieces on Frank Sinatra's Rat Pack and Walt Disney, I was free to be as scurrilous as I liked. To my amazement, the editor turned the piece down as too obvious. I was even more surprised when the *Voice*, where I was then the third-string film critic, enthusiastically accepted it virtually as written. (It appears here as published, slightly shortened, with footnotes and bracketed interpolations.) My research, which I long ago lost or discarded, was all done at the Library of the Performing Arts in New York.

qua non of American tele-politics, Reagan is the best-trained candidate who ever lived.

The story of Ronald Reagan is the story of his image—how he developed it, refined it, layered it, solved its problems. The key to his behavior as president is not to be found in his eight years as a governor of California. That was, after all, just another role. Reagan presented himself to the American public in successive phases: Good Joe, Patriot, Cowboy, and Corporate Logo. The sum of these is Reagan the politician.*

Very often a performer "finds himself" by using cues from audience responses and making himself into what people want.

—ORRIN E. KLAPP, *Symbolic Leaders* (1964)

Well, an actor has to please people and so does a senator.

—SHIRLEY TEMPLE BLACK, campaigning for former costar George Murphy (1964)

Reagan has always made the most out of what he had. Breaking into show business as a radio announcer, his forte was fabricating Chicago Cubs games out of telegraphed dispatches while a sound-effects man backed him up with the crack of the bat and the roar of the crowd. After five years he followed the Cubs to spring training and landed a Hollywood contract. The studio that signed him was Warner Bros., the major that specialized in "ordinary" (even proletariat) stars like Cagney and Bogie and Joan Blondell. Despite the fact that it was the most pro-Roosevelt studio in Hollywood, Warners was run like an assembly line. Movie stardom was less a condition than a job. Reagan turned out to be a good worker.

In his first three years as a Warners factory hand, he appeared in over twenty pictures. He played news hounds, radio announcers, and Tugboat Annie's son. He was part of gossip columnist Louella Parson's entourage in *Hollywood Hotel* (1937) and the next year shared billing with a horse in *Sergeant Murphy*. The year after that, in *Hell's Kitchen* and *Angels*

---

* It was not then generally known that during the 1940s Reagan had also been an FBI informant.

Wash Their Faces, he was a straight man for the Bowery Boys. They chewed up the scenery; he courted "Oomph Girl" Ann Sheridan and crusaded for slum clearance and reform of the reform schools. In 1939, Reagan was rewarded with his own kiddie series, the four *Secret Service of the Air* flicks, in which he got to rush around like a sexless Errol Flynn protecting top-secret "inertia projectors" from nefarious enemy agents. His attitude was impeccable. "Believe what you are doing is important," he would advise the youth of America in a ghostwritten movie magazine article, "even if it is only grubbing for worms in the backyard."

The ambitious starlet bought the Hollywood myth in toto, marrying co-Warners contractee Jane Wyman in a burst of studio-manufactured publicity. Brokered by Louella Parsons, their match was consecrated at the Wee Kirk o' the Heather chapel of the fashionable Forest Lawn cemetery. It was a storybook union—eight solid years of *Photoplay* fodder. Ronnie and Janie played it the company way. They invited press photographers and fan-mag scribes to document each new acquisition (home, first baby, second baby). Off camera and on, Reagan played the Good Joe. "I'm no Flynn or Boyer," he told the world. "Mr. Norm is my alias." Once pressed to name his hobbies, he replied, "I like to swim, hike, and sleep."

In 1940, the twenty-nine-year-old but still fresh-faced Reagan landed a plum part in *Knute Rockne, All American.* As the Christ-like Gipper, he played a Notre Dame football star who died two weeks after his last game. It was a film to make Richard Nixon weep. (Nixon even incorporated the movie's tagline, "Let's win this one for the Gipper," in his 1968 RepCon acceptance speech. For "Gipper" he substituted "Ike," then conveniently on his deathbed.) Perhaps seeking to probe Ronnie's potential as a tragic ingénue, Warners cast him as the young George Custer in the big-budget *Santa Fe Trail* in 1940; he elicited further sympathy in *Kings Row,* playing a small-town Lothario whose legs are gratuitously amputated.*

---

* The role was Reagan's favorite and he used his plaintive post-operative cry "Where's the rest of me?" as the title for his 1965 autobiography. Garry Wills analyzes the film in *Reagan's America* to show, among other things, the degree to which Reagan reimagined his big scene, which actually belongs to his co-star Ann Sheridan.

The success of the latter led the studio to consider pairing him with Sheridan in *Casablanca*, but when Ingrid Bergman became available they shunted the couple over to *Juke Girl* instead. This saga of a "nickel-hungry broad" was just a bargain basement *Grapes of Wrath* in 1942, but it became a Telegraph Avenue cult film twenty-five years later for casting California's governor in the unlikely role of a militant migrant fruit-picker.*

Although an undistinguished piece of work, *Juke Girl* does communicate a strong sense of solidarity and concern for the underdog. Reagan played "a migrant worker from the Kansas cornfields," as the *New York Times* reviewer described him, who undertakes "a one-man crusade against the local big shot packer, who is a crook." Reagan would subsequently characterize his activities against Hollywood Communists in similar terms.†

Juke Girl epitomizes the flaming liberal past Reagan was wont to evoke with the relish of a dried-out alkie describing his last binge. Playing Cesar Chavez left him with a paucity of sympathy for a real Chavez—hell, if he could marry the eponymous heroine of *Million Dollar Baby* (1941), didn't that show America worked? As governor, Reagan sided with the big growers and corporate plantations against the farmworkers. But then, the two Bowery Boys films notwithstanding, a sense of fair play for the underdog was never to be Ronnie's strong suit. He jettisoned Warners' New Deal ideology, although he did retain the studio's

---

* This was pure fantasy on my part. Having attended movies at Berkeley's Telegraph Repertory Theater during the nightly antiwar, anti-Reagan riots on Telegraph Avenue in the summer of 1968, I imagined that *Juke Girl* would have been a potent attraction. Tom Luddy, who then programmed the Telegraph Rep, has no memory of showing *Juke Girl*. However, Mike Thomas, who programmed the Times Theatre in San Francisco and the Minor Theater in Arcata, did show *Juke Girl* and recalls it surfacing at Market Street grind houses; the movie was telecast by KSBW, Channel 8 in Oakland, twice during the spring of 1969, and may well have been screened on the UC Berkeley campus.

† Inspired by "Land of the Jook," a *Saturday Evening Post* exposé of the conditions under which Florida's mainly black migrant farmworkers lived, *Juke Girl* has only a token African American presence and no acknowledgement of racism—it was nevertheless criticized by the Hearst press for inspiring "class warfare," as well as by the Office of War Information for portraying Americans as exploitative imperialists and generally creating a bad impression.

flare for wisecracking dialogue: "It's too bad we can't have an epidemic of botulism," he quipped in 1974, during the Symbionese Liberation Army's chaotic free food distribution program.

On the eve of Pearl Harbor, Reagan was a rising star—a useful but not yet valuable commodity. The disruption of the war consigned him permanently to Hollywood's second rank. Reagan spent most of it stationed on a Culver City sound stage but he managed to make almost as much publicity out of this military service as he had with his marriage: "Mr. Average Guy on the bright side is now in the Army with your brother Joe" (*Photoplay*, 1943). Even so, Mr. Average Guy remained defensive about his contribution to the war effort and would later complain that "some people can't respect a uniform unless it's on a dead soldier." (Could he have meant a dead gipper?) Reagan's major military assignment was an appearance in the lavish propaganda musical *This Is the Army*.*

Conspiracy buffs should note that Screen Actors Guild activist George Murphy, the man who would test the political waters for Reagan twenty years later, co-starred as his doughboy dad.

Politics is just like show business. You need a big opening. Then you coast for a while. Then you need a big finish.

—RONALD REAGAN, 1966

After the war, Ronnie was ready to resume his career playing what *Silver Screen* called "the typical young American," but nobody was sure that was what they wanted to see. As an actor he had always been a bit limited. His stock-in-trade was a bashful, boyish innocence. His best emotion was "dismay"—a state of mind he would telegraph by raising one eyebrow and compressing his lips. Wondering how to repackage

---

* The movie is a version of *Stand Up and Cheer!* Reagan plays a corporal who is mobilized into the Department of Amusement, charged with organizing a morale-boosting armed forces variety extravaganza. As noted by Michael Rogin, "The movie ends with a command performance of Reagan's show before the president of the United States." Reagan's own performance was singled out for praise by David Platt in the *Daily Worker*, who wrote that he provided "the heart interest in the best Hollywood tradition."

their overage juvenile, Warners put his development on hold. In 1947, to celebrate his return to civilian life, they cast him as the veterinarian hero of *Stallion Road*, an innocuous yawner that the star described as his "favorite picture of all time."

It is a measure of Reagan's good-natured lack of focus that he was designated to play opposite eighteen-year-old Shirley Temple in her first "adult" film, *That Hagen Girl*. Ronnie was cast as a heroic veteran (decorated for his contribution to "the successful launching of atomic warfare") with Shirley as a winsome orphan girl, rumored to be his illegitimate daughter. The issue is resolved when they elope together to Chicago. One of Reagan's most ludicrous films, *That Hagen Girl* has apparently been suppressed. (The authors of *The Fifty Worst Films of All Time* reported that when attempting to obtain a print from its erstwhile distributors, they encountered a wall of "embarrassment" and "frightened silence.")

At the time of its release, *New York Times* reviewer Bosley Crowther considered *That Hagen Girl* so perverse as to be "downright un-American." That same year, Reagan flew to Washington with Gary Cooper, Robert Taylor, George Murphy, and Robert Montgomery (later to be Ike's TV coach). Solemnly, they had told the House Un-American Activities Committee how they had carefully scanned all prospective scripts for "communistic" propaganda, while monitoring Hollywood in general for any "subversive" activities.

As his postwar career faltered, Reagan increasingly immersed himself in the muddy waters of movieland politics. "It was no secret in Hollywood that Reagan had political ambitions," *Time*'s L.A. correspondent Joseph Lewis recalled. "But the cosmopolitans of the movie industry never considered him more than an overgrown Boy Scout constantly crusading for something or other." He was really kind of a bore—forever quoting from the *Reader's Digest*, holding forth at cocktail parties on the horror of the graduated income tax, or earnestly speculating how the proper deployment of mounted cavalry would've hastened the end of World War II. Smitten by Ayn Rand, he publicly offered to dye his hair red to get the lead role in *The Fountainhead*.

As president of the Screen Actors Guild (SAG), Reagan had reason to take himself seriously. During one strike (which he opposed) he began packing a gun—just like in the movies. His actual role in the Hollywood witch hunts was marginal, but by 1965, when he published his autobiography (remarkably titled *Where's the Rest of Me?*) he retroactively cast himself as the anti-Communist messiah. Fancifully, he boasted that when "testifying under oath on the Communist maneuvers to take over Hollywood, Sterling Hayden was asked what tripped him up. His reply: 'We ran into a one-man battalion named Ronald Reagan.'"*

As the Red Scare gained momentum, Reagan's Warners contract expired and left him a free agent. Then Janie left him too. "I'm wearing of being dreary, of being the good, the sweet, the dull, colorless charm boy . . . I'd make a good louse and I hope they're not out of style before I get a chance to find out," he complained to *Silver Screen* in 1950, the same year that *Modern Screen* ranked him among "Hollywood's 10 Loneliest Stars." It was a while before Reagan would get to play the louse of his dreams, but he did manage to shed his juvenile image and pull together a string of films wherein he embodied low-keyed, affable authority figures.†

The most notorious of these is the 1951 Universal production *Bedtime for Bonzo*, a movie ostensibly inspired by the success of *Francis the Talking Mule*. Without quite knowing how it happened, Reagan found himself cast as a pointy-headed college prof attempting to prove the primacy of environment over heredity by raising a chimpanzee as his own child. Publicity stills posed him standing on his head alongside the grinning simian and welcoming the creature into his bed.

Speaking about the film from the vantage point of fifteen years later, Reagan put up a game front: "Like all really good comedy, this one was based on a solid, believable foundation." (The film continued to dog him. While visiting New York in April 1979, he again defended its comic "credibility.") One can only imagine the extent of his paranoia, however, when after *Bonzo's* release, its scenarist Val Burton was named as

---

* Hayden was actually referring to the 1945 Conference of Studio Unions strike and picketing of Warner Bros., calling Reagan "a one-man battalion against this thing."
† The 1951 Warner Bros. melodrama *Storm Warning*, in which Reagan plays a crusading district attorney attempting to reign in the local Ku Klux Klan (an obvious stand-in for the Communist Party), is by far the most notable.

a Communist and banned from the movie industry. Under President Reagan, SAG had already capitulated to the Blacklist, but it was clear that Ronnie would have to toughen up his own image as well.*

He instantly went into training. In 1951, when Paramount cast him in a low-budget Western called *The Last Outpost,* he waxed ecstatic: "I've been itching to sling a six-gun ever since I put on greasepaint. . . . Now at long last I've made the grade and I'd like to keep on making horse operas as long as they'll let me." His next two, even chintzier films gave him an education in foreign policy he's remembered to this day. *Hong Kong* (1952) sent him to a studio-built Orient to save schoolmarm Rhonda Fleming from the lascivious Chinese Reds. Then it was off to the *Tropic Zone* (1953), where he again teamed with Rhonda to protect a Central American banana republic from an "outlaw" takeover. By the time Reagan had introduced compulsory loyalty oaths and non-Communist affidavits into SAG and turned up as an ersatz Wyatt Earp in *Law and Order* (also 1953), he was approached to run for the Senate [to fill the seat left vacant by the new vice-president Richard Nixon]. But such a move would've been premature. "I'm a ham—always was and always will be," he stoutly told reporters.†

---

* This is a bit of fanciful supposition on my part. Reagan maintained a good-humored attitude regarding his most infamous movie, which he screened for a group of friends at Camp David on June 22, 1984, writing in his diary that, "No one had ever seen it. With Nancy gone I had guests—the Laxalts & the Deavers plus a friend, Leslie Leach of Amanda's. We had a birthday cake for Amanda—her 14th. Everyone enjoyed the picture."

† Michael Rogin points out that "Reagan left Warners so he could choose his own roles."

> He wanted to make Westerns, and his first post-Warner Brothers film was *The Last Outpost* (1951). While fighting Communists offscreen, he fought Indians in front of the camera. Just as the Communist threat, Truman supporters hoped, would unite Democrats and Republicans, so the Apache danger in *The Last Outpost* makes allies out of Union and Confederate soldiers. In *Cattle Queen of Montana* (1954), Reagan saves Barbara Stanwyck from Indians; the local reds are being manipulated by a white outlaw. Reagan plays a gunslinging sheriff in *Law and Order* (1953) who brings peace to a western town.

> Rogin also notes *Tropic Zone,* "a Western set in Central America," and *Hong Kong,* "an adventure movie with an anti-Communist backdrop." Clothes make the man. To some extent, Reagan's Western duds were—and

Building his persona as a third-string John Wayne, Reagan took roles in films you practically had to pay people to sit through. In MGM's cheap and lugubrious *Prisoner of War* (1954), he played a counterspy pretending to be brainwashed so that he could investigate a North Korean POW camp. The film was made with government assistance, although the Department of Defense ultimately withdrew support, reportedly because they wanted a harder line. Reagan's role—deprogramming hapless traitors—paralleled his activities as member of the Motion Picture Industry Council committee for the "rehabilitation" of repentant movieland commies. *Prisoner of War*'s fade-out saw him teaching his men an instructional mantra: "Here's a little thought that will get you on the go / Your old Uncle Sam is a better man than their old Uncle Joe."

With this kind of routine, anyone could see that Reagan's screen days were numbered. He must have known it himself. It was around this time [actually March 4, 1952] that he married his second wife, Nancy Davis; he couldn't have done better if he'd called central casting. Perhaps he did. Davis was a post-debutante with an MGM contract whose specialty was playing demure, dutiful, usually pregnant, wives. [Indeed, she was then pregnant: daughter Patti was born on October 21, 1952.] Her greatest role had been in *The Next Voice You Hear*, a deliriously turgid exercise in political apocalypse wherein the Voice of God commandeers the airwaves for six successive nights to endorse the American way of life.

Who has written his speeches? Who—or what board of ghost-writing strategists—has fashioned the phrases, molded the thoughts, designed the delivery, authored the image, staged the presentation, put the political show on the road to win the larger number of votes? Who is the actor reading the script?

> —ad taken out in *Life* by John Wayne to coincide with
> JFK's nomination in 1960

---

would be—more important than his affect. "Mr. Reagan plays an ex-G.I. drifter in his own solid citizen style, laboriously drawling every tattered slang utterance in the books," *New York Times* reviewer Howard Thompson wrote of *Hong Kong*. Neither of these were ever shown at Camp David.

Together with Nancy, Reagan built a second career out of the ruins of his first. The shift was a bit rocky. Surviving from guest spot to guest spot on the tube, he hit bottom in 1954. That was the year he had to take a two-week gig at the Last Frontier lounge in Las Vegas fronting for a comedy dance team with a shtick that reflexively parodied his appearance as a high-class no-talent emcee.*

But if things looked dark, there was an electric light bulb at the end of the tunnel. Casting around for a respectable name (rather than a flashy talent), General Electric signed Reagan to host their new TV show. For eight years he served as a corporate trademark, the Speedy Alka-Seltzer of the all-electric kitchen. He was, in fact, a glorified front man whose stint as a GE flack coincided with a period of rampant electrical industry price-fixing. Meanwhile, Reagan achieved the bland ubiquity of a television personality. *TV Guide* tagged him "the ambassador of the convenience of things mechanical." His work was not only confined to the tube. As GE super-salesman he toured the country speaking at factory outings and pitching what's-good-for-General-Electric-is-good-for-the-U.S.A. to Rotarians and Knights of Columbus. The emotional core of Reagan's speech was always his evocation of his Midwestern boyhood. Its dramatic highpoint was the story of how he beat the Kremlin plot to take over Hollywood.

Then the trademark went out of control (or perhaps found another sponsor) and began to add new material into his act. In 1962, Reagan's persistent criticism of the Tennessee Valley Authority, a major GE customer, prompted the corporation he liked to call "as human as the corner grocer" to cancel his program. The sponsor's official explanation was that *Bonanza* was pulverizing the General Electric Theater in the ratings. In any case, Reagan was prepared. Donning a Barry Goldwater–style Stetson, he signed on for two years as the host of *Death Valley Days*. A nationally televised election-eve speech for Goldwater—the supreme distillation of a decade spieling on the rubber chicken circuit,

---

* Reagan was immeasurably helped by his agent Lew Wasserman whom, as SAG president, he managed to get a sweetheart deal, waiving rules against agents producing television shows. Thanks to Reagan, Wasserman's MCA became an industry powerhouse; thanks to Wasserman, Reagan continued working—mainly on TV—throughout the 1950s and into the 1960s.

complete with inspirational *Mr. Smith Goes to Washington* ending—left him heir apparent to Goldwater's minions and paved the way for his governorship.

Out of the blue, Reagan made one last movie, Don Siegel's *The Killers* (1964). When Manny Farber described the quintessential Siegel opus as "a raunchy, dirty-minded film with a definite feeling of middle-aged, middle-class sordidness," he most likely had *The Killers* in mind.

Made for television shortly after the Kennedy assassination, but released to theaters because it was too violent for the tube, *The Killers* is a key film of the '60s—one of the first to depict the robotic hitman as a space-age American antihero. To the delight of every audience I've ever watched the film with, its cynical arch-criminal, the brains and money behind Lee Marvin's implacable assassin, turns out to be squinty-eyed, orange-conked Ronald Reagan.*

---

* *The Killers* was released during the summer of 1964 (in New York, it opened on a double bill with the 1960 Mamie Van Doren sex farce, *The Private Lives of Adam and Eve*), thus providing an odd trailer for the electrifyingly hardnosed election-eve speech in support of Barry Goldwater that served as Reagan's televised political debut: "We're at war with the most dangerous enemy that has ever faced mankind in his long climb from the swamp to the stars."

I first saw *The Killers* in June 1969 at the Museum of Modern Art's retrospective of postwar Hollywood action films, curated by Lawrence Alloway and originally titled "Violent America" until one of the distributors objected. It was not quite a year since I had spent the summer in Berkeley and it would be difficult to overestimate my loathing of Reagan, whom I saw as the enemy of antiwar students such as myself. Although it was not apparent to me in 1980, my whole sense of the man was informed by his supporting role as a criminal mastermind.

This however was not necessarily how the American people remembered Reagan. In her *Packaging the Presidency*, the political scientist Kathleen Hall Jamieson recounts this anecdote, concerning Carter's media adviser Gerald Rafshoon: After the 1980 election, Rafshoon was told by an unnamed Hollywood producer that the Carter campaign had erred in attempting to portray Reagan as a menace: "'Let me tell you something,' said the producer.

Ronald Reagan is not a good actor. I've known him for years and he's not a good actor. But he played in 59 movies and in all but one he played the same role and that was of a sincere guy. Now, as I say, he is not a great actor but he knows how to play sincere people. And you should have known better. If you play sincere people in 59 roles, it's got to rub off.

Why a man who was already planning his gubernatorial run should have taken this role is a mystery. Nancy claims it was a favor to his agent [Lew Wasserman, who was involved in the production]. Perhaps Reagan needed the money, perhaps he relished the opportunity the script gave him to smack New Frontier sweetheart Angie Dickinson across the mouth. Or perhaps, in a Nixon-like blunder of inadvertent disclosure—he couldn't resist a bit of last-minute practice playing at what he hoped to become.*

I'll probably be the only fellow who will get an Oscar posthumously.

—RONALD REAGAN, 1965[†]

One day in 1966 Ronnie changed out of his working duds, freshened his makeup, and marched onto another set on the *Death Valley Days* lot. It was fixed up like a den from *Father Knows Best* with a phony fireplace, dummy bookcases, and an easy-to-read TelePrompTer. There he told the TV audience that he was a candidate for governor of California. Conventional wisdom held that Reagan's glamorous past would act against him. The reverse, of course, was true. As one campaign strategist explained it, "People say, 'Look at this character, he could be smooching Doris Day and he's worried about the budget.'"

---

* In fact, Reagan was worried about his image and reportedly asked Wasserman not to release *The Killers*. "I have to take full blame for it," Don Siegel told Mitch Tuchman in a 1980 interview. "I talked him into it, and he was really upset about it. . . . We haven't met since, of course." Reagan had never before played a killer, Siegel explained. "I don't think that Ronnie fully appreciated until he saw the film that he was really the most evil person in the picture. I mean I'm sure that he thought that Lee Marvin was really the bad guy." Nevertheless, Siegel had praise for Reagan's political instincts:

> After all he is an actor. . . . He's not going to be frightened when he's having debates with anybody. He feels that he's in better shape than they are, and he is. It's not easy to get up on your own and look out at a sea of faces and mikes sticking up and, God knows how many millions of people are going to be looking at it. It doesn't bother him at all. It absolutely doesn't. It might be a good reason why he's being so successful.

† According to former aide Mark Weinberg, Reagan resented never receiving an honorary Oscar.

"America," observed a denizen of the Saul Bellow novel *Mr. Sammler's Planet*, "is the world's greatest dispenser of science-fiction entertainments." For years we were primed to land men on the moon. When it finally happened, what was really interesting was that the event was telecast "live" (complete with Nixon phone call) into every bar and motel room in the Free World. Intermittently since Elvis Presley, we've been titillated by the vision of a demagogic pop star running for president. When it finally does happen—albeit in the form of a sixty-nine-year-old Hollywood has-been with a cast-iron pompadour—the interesting thing is the media's blasé attitude. But why shouldn't they take Reagan for granted? Isn't the nightly news one more kind of entertainment? And aren't polls just another form of ratings?

What I mean is this: All the hip pols went Hollywood long ago. The persona of Calvin Coolidge—the first modern president and the one whom Reagan most closely resembles—was designed by Bruce Barton, the promotional genius who invented Betty Crocker and wrote a best-selling depiction of Jesus as a go-getter whose success was achieved through a visionary grasp of sound advertising techniques. "The president shouldn't do too much and shouldn't know too much," Coolidge once told his PR man—or was it vice versa? Silent Cal passed the five years of his administration posing for pictures, acting out manufactured pastimes (his real hobby, he once admitted, was "holding public office") and making speeches over the radio. I imagine this is approximately what Ronald Reagan had in mind. [Or so I thought!]

In a totalitarian state, entertainment is an obvious function of politics. But in the American mediacracy, where TV has hopelessly blurred the distinction between art and life, private and public, great and petty, it would seem that the reverse is closer to the truth.*

---

* Mark Crispin Miller coined the useful phrase "National Entertainment State" and edited a special issue of *The Nation*, dated June 3, 1996, devoted to the power of the media. It was followed by two sequels, one on publishing (March 17, 1997) and the other on music (August 25, 1997). It goes without saying that the election of reality TV star Donald Trump to the presidency in 2016 pushed the National Entertainment State—or what I less felicitously called the "mediacracy"—into new territory.

The *Voice's* political writers regarded attention to Reagan's show business career as trivial and degrading; one, who wrote on culture as well as politics, praised my article while disputing its gloomy conclusion regarding the effect of television on politics. It took Garry Wills's "Could He Act?," a chapter from *Reagan's America*, first published in *Newsday* in 1985, and Michael Rogin's essay *"Ronald Reagan*, the Movie," given as a paper at the 1985 meeting of the American Political Science Association before it was published in *Radical History Review* in 1987, to render respectable any analysis of Reagan's Hollywood career.

"It's been a boast of mine, during some years of writing from Washington, that I have never lampooned the old boy as a Wild West ham, an All-American kid, a granite-jawed GI, or any other of the stock repertoire," Hitchens wrote in the *London Review of Books* (10/3/85) by way of acknowledging Rogin's thesis. "Now I wish that I had paid more attention to the obvious."

The Time Is Now

Labor Day 1980: polls putting Jimmy Carter and Ronald Reagan in a dead heat suggest voter dissatisfaction with their choices—despite the numerous alternatives available during the primary season and the presence of an independent third candidate, former Republican congressman John Anderson of Illinois.*

Ted Kennedy is gone but his image lingers, employed by the Reagan campaign to attack Carter in states that Kennedy won where Republicans hope to inherit his white working-class voters. Carter is regarded as incompetent; Reagan as ill-equipped; Anderson, who appears to draw equally from Democrats and Republicans, seems unlikely to win more than 10 percent of the vote.

---

* In the Dream Life, each candidate has retained his core supporters. Country-western singers Johnny Cash, Tom T. Hall, Loretta Lynn, Willie Nelson, Dolly Parton, Hank Snow, and Tammy Wynette back Carter. The president's biggest celebrity is Muhammad Ali. Reagan's camp has enlisted a few country-westerners (Merle Haggard, Marty Robbins) and aging swingers (Dean Martin, Frank Sinatra) but is strongest on his Old Hollywood cohort (James Cagney, Irene Dunne, Ginger Rogers, James Stewart, Gloria Swanson, Loretta Young). Paul Newman has endorsed Anderson while Warren Beatty, along with fellow Kennedy supporters Angie Dickinson, Goldie Hawn, and Martin Sheen, has decided to sit out the election.

An ABC-Harris poll released in mid-September, shortly before Reagan and Anderson have a debate that Carter refuses to attend, asks whether Reagan is too apt to make ill-considered statements that demand an explanation or apology (blaming trees for air pollution, supporting creationism). A remarkable 82 percent agree that Reagan is gaffe-prone, but Carter overplays his hand, denouncing his opponent as an inherently divisive, racist warmonger. In an October 6 speech, the president warns that, should Reagan be elected, "Americans might be separated. Black from White, Jew from Christian, North from South, rural from urban."

Up until then, Carter had been seen as decent (if hapless). Now, his "meanness" becomes an issue. Reagan, who had gently reproved the president as "reaching a point of hysteria that's hard to understand," appears to be moving ahead and away from his more extreme positions. In mid-October, Carter promises TV interviewer Barbara Walters to restrict himself to criticizing his opponent's stated views. However, the Reagan campaign does not let up: the candidate's wife Nancy is drafted to rebut Carter's presumed unkindness.

Meanwhile, Carter's campaign has hinted that there are hints that the Iranians, now engaged in a war with Iraq, might be inclined to make a deal to release their American hostages. Carter inches back up in the polls and Reagan, still resisting a challenge to debate the president without Anderson's presence, abruptly changes his mind.*

October 28, the two men face off in Cleveland before a television viewership estimated at eighty million, the largest ever for a presidential debate. Carter is superbly prepared, calm, rational, and highly disciplined in sticking to his talking points. But amiable Reagan, who has a lifetime of experience in enlisting an audience's sympathy as well as access to purloined copies of Carter's briefing books, is even better prepared. He deflects the president's mastery of the facts and deflates his insistence on them with a simple, spontaneous complaint: "There you go again!" Carter's complex arguments appear ridiculously pedantic. In closing, Reagan brilliantly personalizes the election, asking viewers to ask themselves, "Are you better off than you were four years ago?"

---

* Carter's administration did negotiate the release of the hostages, although the Iranians stuck a thumb in his eye by announcing the agreement on the first day of Reagan's presidency, twenty minutes after he had been sworn in.

Election Eve features a bizarre replay of John Ford's classic Cold War cavalry Western, *Fort Apache*—a relic of the 1948 presidential campaign, as much American myth as Hollywood movie. Rival addresses delivered on primetime TV involve the movie's two rival military leaders, the stubborn Custer figure played by Henry Fonda and his more sympathetic successor John Wayne. Fonda (a former Ted Kennedy supporter) introduces Carter's final appeal to the voters, while Reagan's primetime address evokes the memory of the Cowboy Warrior. "Duke Wayne did not believe our country was ready for the dustbin of history. Just before his death he said in his own blunt way, 'Just give the American people a good cause, and there's nothing they can't lick.'"*

Reagan, whose victory is projected by TV network exit polls announced early afternoon on Election Day, exceeds all expectations. The final tally has him beating Carter with 51 percent to 41 percent of the popular vote. (Anderson receives 7 percent.) The electoral count is even more impressive. Reagan's 489 to 49 win is the third-largest in U.S. history, after Franklin Roosevelt's reelection in 1936 and Richard Nixon's in 1972. (Carter carries only six states plus the District of Columbia.) The Republicans win their first Senate majority since 1954, with George McGovern and Frank Church among the losers, and gain thirty-three seats in the House of Representatives.

The last months of the Carter presidency are a season of escalating omens: Carter's avatar, Rocky, merges with the antihero of 1976, Travis Bickle, in Martin Scorsese's *Raging Bull*; Michael Cimino does his rival Francis Ford Coppola one better in wrecking a Hollywood studio with *Heaven's Gate*

---

* I have been unable to track down the source of this quotation, which echoes the last line in Fonda's great vehicle, *The Grapes of Wrath*: "They can't wipe us out; they can't lick us. We'll go on forever, Pa, 'cause we're the people." Perhaps the phrase was Reagan's own. In any case, interoffice correspondence found in the Reagan Library suggests that Wayne's family periodically asked President Reagan to return the favor by allowing them to reprint a presidential endorsement on the covers of various books or in filmed tributes. With regard to the use of Reagan's remarks praising Wayne as "the personification of the American ideal" and "a self-image to Americans that challenged us to live up to what we professed to be," in a BBC documentary, a 1983 memo from White House lawyer (and future Supreme Court chief justice) John G. Roberts expresses concern over "the absence of a consistent policy governing our willingness to permit the President to participate in these private, commercial tributes. . . . Once you do one it becomes impossible to turn down countless others." While serving as president, Reagan screened eight John Wayne movies at Camp David, seven in his second term: *Stagecoach* (August 1982), *Chisum* (April 1985), *Big Jake* (June 1985), *Rio Bravo* (June 1986), *Red River* (November 1986), *Rooster Cogburn* (January 1987), *The Searchers* (May 1988), and *How the West Was Won* (December 1988).

(a movie that carries America's suffix for scandal in its very title); the most political of Sixties pop stars, John Lennon, is assassinated.

Opening on November 14, ten days after Reagan's triumph and four years after Sylvester Stallone's, *Raging Bull* was the anti-*Rocky*—a feel-bad movie starring Robert De Niro as a loathsome real-life protagonist, the former light-heavyweight boxer Jake LaMotta.

The most artistically ambitious Hollywood film since *Apocalypse Now*, as *Heaven's Gate* was the most grandiose, *Raging Bull* might almost be an expiation, having been made with *Rocky*'s profits by the same producers, Robert Chartoff and Irwin Winkler, for the same studio, United Artists. *Rocky*'s hero was a fantasy redeemer, the white '50s heavyweight champ Rocky Marciano born again; LaMotta was a mob-controlled middleweight who briefly held the title, throwing one bout and losing two others to the black fighter Sugar Ray Robinson.

If *Rocky* was about denial, *Raging Bull* was a confessional. Rocky's success celebrated American agency; LaMotta's career embodied American impotence. Both movies embody a particular masculine crisis. In *Rocky*, the motor is race; in *Raging Bull*, it is sexual anxiety. Violent and pathologically macho, LaMotta uses the ring to work out his paranoid personal obsessions. Here, the Other is not black but female. Too arty, critical, and emotionally complex, *Raging Bull* could not enter into the national discourse except insofar as it dealt with celebrity. Much was made of the fifty pounds that De Niro gained for the part, an Oscar-winning exercise in extreme acting that rivaled the unknown neophyte Stallone's writing the Oscar-winning script for his own vehicle.

Thanks to *Rocky*, Stallone became an icon. The movie concluded with a conflation of the actor's stardom and that of the character. Like *Taxi Driver*, *Raging Bull* drew attention to the viewer's spectatorship in the Dream Life, ending with LaMotta as a downscale nightclub entertainer whose act consists of lamely impersonating Marlon Brando in a scene from Elia Kazan's *On the Waterfront*. As the 1954 movie informed *Rocky* as well as offering parallels to LaMotta's life, De Niro's intentionally clumsy Brando imitation might have parodied Stallone's.*

---

* In *On the Waterfront*, some twenty-three years before *Rocky*, Marlon Brando had played another over-the-hill palooka mixed up with gangsters and looking for self-respect. "What

November 19, five days after *Raging Bull*, *Heaven's Gate*, Michael Cimino's long-awaited follow-up to *The Deer Hunter*, opened. The movie was an extreme outlier, being a big-budget, rampantly pictorial, antiestablishment "Gilded Age" Western produced four years after the last cycle of Western spectaculars were released to box-office ignominy during the Bicentennial.

The Western was over, but *Heaven's Gate* was something else—inspired by, if freely reworking, the Johnson County War, an 1890s conflict over Wyoming range rights portrayed by Cimino as a struggle between state-sanctioned ranchers and a polyglot collection of German and Slavic immigrants. *Heaven's Gate* was a movie of near-continuous choreographed tumult in which mise-en-scène trumped script.

Twice as long as its screenplay warranted, *Heaven's Gate* meant to be an epic rivaling the *Godfather* films. Cimino finished his original script in 1971 and, as the last gasp of Hollywood anarcho-leftism, *Heaven's Gate* was a belated successor to *Bonnie and Clyde* and *The Wild Bunch*. The movie's closest character to a Righteous Outlaw was Isabelle Huppert's endearing little frontier madam, beloved both by the immigrants' lackadaisical but eventual defender (Kris Kristofferson) as well as the reluctant enforcer hired to kill them (Christopher Walken). A series of generally overwrought, barely coherent set pieces representing America as a xenophobic plutocracy administered by a killer elite, *Heaven's Gate* rose to the truly horrifying once the combined forces of law, order, and capital begin engaging in Nazi behavior, massacring the helpless immigrants, including the movie's heroine.

The movie had its world premiere at the Cinema 1 in New York to an incredulous audience and devastating reviews. *Heaven's Gate* "fails so completely that you might suspect Mr. Cimino sold his soul to the Devil to obtain the success of *The Deer Hunter*, and the Devil has come around to collect," Vincent Canby wrote in the *New York Times*. Running for only a week before United Artists yanked it, Cimino's muscle-bound colossus would ultimately be blamed for pulling down the studio.

Canby ended his review with the observation that "*Heaven's Gate* is something quite rare in movies these days—an unqualified disaster." Worse was yet to come. On December 8, John Lennon was shot and killed by a

---

separates Stallone from Brando is that everything Stallone does has one purpose: to make you like him," Pauline Kael wrote.

twenty-five-year-old ex-security guard, Mark Chapman, as the ex-Beatle and his wife, Yoko Ono, entered their New York City apartment in the Dakota, the imposing building off Central Park West that thirteen years before had served as the location for the movie *Rosemary's Baby*. As recently as 1977, in Wim Wenders's *The American Friend*, Dennis Hopper riffed on bringing the Beatles back to Hamburg. That could never happen now.

Heaven's Gate closed. Lennon's death shut the door on the Sixties, resoundingly and for good—although a handful of quasi-countercultural movies remained. Two were conspiratorial thrillers. Brian De Palma's *Blow Out*, then in production on location in Philadelphia, starred John Travolta as professional soundman who becomes embroiled in a plot combining aspects of Watergate, Chappaquiddick, and the Kennedy assassination. Ivan Passer's *Cutter and Bone*—a United Artists production once intended as a vehicle for Dustin Hoffman and, already shelved, a casualty of *Heaven's Gate*—was a neo-noir comparable to early 1970s downers like *Chinatown* and *The Long Goodbye*, presciently set in Santa Barbara, not far from Ronald Reagan's Rancho del Cielo.

As the veil over America's secret history parted for De Palma's hapless protagonist, so it did for Passer's. Three counterculture left-behinds—notably John Heard's raspy-voiced Viet-vet, who lost an arm, a leg, an eye and possibly his mind in the Nam—are drawn by chance and paranoia into a sordid murder mystery. Both movies used patriotic displays as ironic backdrops. De Palma's invented Liberty Day Jubilee conceals a brutal political killing while San Barbara's annual Old Spanish Days celebration is a cover-up for fat-cat malfeasance, the late-afternoon golden light contributing an atmosphere of malign ripeness equal to downtown Philadelphia sleaze.

Not the movie America wanted to see, this premature critique of Reaganism was retitled *Cutter's Way* and dumped into release. The third movie, reemerging from the Dream Life a few days after *Cutter's Way* sank, was *Taxi Driver*.

Being There with Ronald Reagan

Ronald Reagan's inauguration raised the curtain on a new era. Anticipated a week by the premiere of ABC's new primetime soap opera *Dynasty* (ABC, 1981–89), the saga of a patriarchal Denver-based oil oligarch and his dysfunctional family, the festivities included eight separate balls, with Elizabeth Taylor and Charlton Heston among the hosts, and a gala concert by the National Symphony Orchestra that opened with a suite from the score for the new president's favorite movie, *Kings Row*.

"In white and black tie, in sequins and sables and clouds of perfume, Republican revelers stepped out tonight to the most lavish series of inaugural balls ever held in the nation's capital," the *New York Times* reported. "It was an evening of shiny black limousines and nostalgic swing bands, of glittery Hollywood celebrities and wealthy Western oil men. The aura of big money was everywhere." And yet, the president declared in his first State of the Union on February 5, the nation was in "the worst economic mess since the Great Depression." And, a bit less than two weeks later, he would present Congress with a utopian budget. The Program for Economic Recovery would cut taxes by $54 billion, increase military spending by $750 billion, reduce assistance to the poor by some $40 billion, and produce a $500 billion surplus by 1984! Who better than a movie star to enact such a program?*

Thus, the thirty-four-year-old former congressman David Stockman, once a youthful New Left zealot and Harvard divinity student, appointed to head the Office of Management and Budget in part because he had played Jimmy Carter in the preparation for the 1980 presidential debates, became the administration's first media celebrity. The Saint-Just of the Reagan revolution, Stockman was prepared to slash welfare, education, energy, housing, and health—as well as defense and even corporate welfare.

Reagan sought to emulate Franklin Roosevelt's First Hundred Days. He promised to boost morale and restore authority. But before that, however, he would have to exorcise a curse: ever since his election, superstitious Americans wondered if their new maximum leader, a man who turned seventy the day after his State of the Union address, would live out his term. For beginning in 1840 with William Henry Harrison and ending with JFK in 1960, every American president elected or reelected in a year ending with a zero had died in office: Abraham Lincoln (1860), James Garfield (1880), William

---

* Given his belief in less government, fewer regulations, and lower taxes, Reagan was a ready convert to so-called "supply side" economics—a theory that held these policies would stimulate entrepreneurs and the accumulation of wealth.

McKinley (1900), Warren G. Harding (1920), Franklin D. Roosevelt (1940). Four of the seven had been assassinated.

Indeed, Reagan was a marked man. As the 1980 presidential campaign heated up, John Hinckley—a twenty-six-year-old college dropout and would-be songwriter, devoted to John Lennon and fixated on *Taxi Driver*, a movie he had seen some fifteen times—was suffering a prolonged nervous breakdown. Shades of *Dynasty*: ever since leaving his family's Colorado home on September 17, Hinckley, who told his parents that he had enrolled in a writing workshop and was given $3,600 for tuition, had been frantically traveling around the country, compulsively returning to New Haven where the object of his obsession, Jodie Foster, had just begun her freshman year at Yale. Hinckley left letters and poems in Foster's mailbox and managed two brief awkward phone calls to her dorm room.

Reprimanded by Foster, Hinckley returned home, then almost immediately took off for Lubbock, Texas. There he purchased two .22 pistols, and headed back east to Washington, DC, a new self-appointed Secret Agent of History gunning for a president. Waging his own insane campaign, Hinckley followed Jimmy Carter to several Ohio rallies, reappeared in New Haven, then went down to New York City, in apparent hopes of meeting a preteen prostitute like the character Foster played in *Taxi Driver*. October 6, Hinckley was in Lincoln, Nebraska, planning, as a secret agent might, to make contact with a leader of the American Nazi Party. The get-together never happened and the would-be assassin zipped off to Nashville for a Carter rally. He intended to fly on to New York, perhaps in pursuit of third-party candidate John Anderson, but his weapons were confiscated at the airport, and he was briefly arrested.

After a quick trip to Dallas to replenish his arsenal, Hinckley returned to DC. Two weeks later his money was gone. Back home with his parents in Colorado, he began therapy but took to the road within a month. Once more in Washington, Hinckley had begun stalking the president-elect when, on the evening of December 8, his idol John Lennon was shot. Tumbling further into the abyss, distraught Hinckley boarded a train to New York to join the vigil outside the Dakota. He then spent several days in New Haven, before returning to his family in Denver in time for Christmas where, horribly depressed, he recorded a New Year's Eve monologue: "John Lennon is dead. The world is over. . . . I still think about Jodie all the time."

January was a blur. Hinckley reappeared in New Haven on February 9, four days after the president's apocalyptic State of the Union, considered invading and opening fire on Jodie Foster's classroom but changed his mind and took a bus to Washington. "He had a fantasy of shooting up Congress," an examining psychiatrist would later explain. Hinckley thought "he might shoot [Senator] Kennedy. He went as far as Kennedy's office. He wasn't there. [Hinckley] took a tour of the White House and saw no metal detector. He thought he might shoot up the White House."

Hinckley also considered shooting himself and came back to New York planning to commit suicide on Yoko Ono's doorstep. But he couldn't do that either and, defeated, returned to Colorado on February 19, informing his credulous parents that he'd lined up a newspaper job.

March 1, Hinckley makes his final pilgrimage to Yale, with a note addressed to "Jodie Foster Superstar." Slipping it under her dorm room door, he retreats to New York and, on March 7 (four days before *Blow Out* wraps in Burbank), yo-yo's back to Colorado where his exasperated father hands him a couple of hundred dollars and tells him to get lost.

It's on March 15, with Hinckley checked into a Denver motel as "J. Travis," that the president unveils his plan for "supply-side" tax cuts and a $1.3 trillion boost in defense expenditures. (The next day, Jerry Lewis drops by the Oval Office—apparently the first of the new president's Hollywood friends to pay a visit.)

For weeks, the psychohistorian Lloyd deMause and his colleagues have been monitoring the news media, noting concern regarding a new wave of lawless criminal behavior. In a highly unusual coincidence, on the last Monday in March, *Time* and *Newsweek* both feature cover stories on the epidemic while, in what deMause takes to be a subliminal death threat, the cover of the *New Republic* represents the Washington mall as the Western cemetery, Boot Hill. DeMause and his colleagues at the Institute for Psychohistory find so many such "hidden messages" that they fear for Reagan's life.*

---

* DeMause cites additional violent newspaper headlines as well as a *U.S. News & World Report* cover on which "Angry Americans" were shown falling in space as an indifferent father-figure towered above them. The cover line "$60 Billion of Federal Waste—Reagan's Next Target" seemed a "subliminal suggestion" to "waste Reagan."

Journalists have begun to suggest that the Reagan honeymoon is over. March 25, Hinckley takes a plane to Los Angeles, stays a day and buys a bus ticket to New Haven, with a stop-off in DC. There, he picks up the *Washington Star* and sees the president's schedule. This, he will later tell a psychiatrist, was his cue. Hinckley has come to believe that he's living in a movie. (Later, when asked why he had so many guns he replies, "Ask Travis.") The next day, Hinckley stakes out the Washington Hilton Hotel where Reagan is giving a luncheon speech addressing 3,500 members of the AFL-CIO. As the president and his party leave the hotel, Hinckley fires six shots—one of which ricochets off the presidential limousine, enters Reagan's left side, bounces off a rib, collapses a lung, and lodges an inch from his heart.

However weak and disoriented, Reagan manages to walk into George Washington Hospital—sinking, once past the cameras, to the floor. He jokes to the doctors that he hopes they are all Republicans and, upon seeing his frightened wife, quotes a line attributed to fighter Jack Dempsey after losing to Gene Tunney: "Honey, I forgot to duck." Paul Schrader hears the news in New Orleans, where he is scouting locations for his remake of the 1942 thriller *Cat People*, and remembers a crazy message from Hinckley he received a few months back. When he returns to his hotel, the FBI—which has already searched Hinckley's possessions and found an unmailed letter to Jodie Foster—is waiting for him.

The president leaves the hospital after a two-week stay on the afternoon of April 11, giving another bravura performance. Walking out arm and arm with his wife, Reagan flashes a broad smile for the cameras although, once back in the White House, nearly passes out from the exertion—and will require several more weeks of recuperation from his physical and emotional pain.

After ten days, Reagan watches his first post-recovery movie in the White House screening room. In addition to Mrs. Reagan, known guests are the president's son Ron Jr. and daughter-in-law Doria; and his friend the producer Charles Z. Wick, best known for the 1961 film *Snow White and the Three Stooges*, soon to be the new head of the United States Information Agency; plus Mrs. Reagan's protégée, the decorator Ted Graber. The movie is *Being There*—directed by Hal Ashby from the novel by Jerzy Kosinski and starring Peter Sellers as the enigmatic naïf Chance.

Recent but not new, screened by Jimmy Carter on January 14, 1980, *Being There* was a curious choice. Did Mrs. Reagan select the movie? Did the president request it?

Albeit taken as a one-joke comedy, *Being There* had been generally well received. Critical attention focused on the simpleton Chance who, having spent his entire life working in a rich man's garden and watching television, becomes one of the most influential figures in America. Without losing his naivete, he effortlessly plays the role of a TV personality and adviser to the president (Jack Warden, previously cast by Ashby as the cuckolded would-be kingmaker in *Shampoo*). As the movie ends, he is even seen as a potential presidential candidate.

Critics wondered if this inoffensive creature was the subject or the object of television or perhaps represented the medium itself. Reviewing for the *Village Voice*, Tom Allen described Chance as "a supreme personification of the channel-switching TV addict who has seen everything and understood nothing." Writing in *Time*, Frank Rich noted that "having been nurtured by the medium, Chance has all the attributes of a perfect TV star; he is bland, non-threatening and always cheery." Indeed, Chance was something of a blank screen. The crafty old plutocrat (Melvyn Douglas) who takes a liking to this amiable dunce (as, in late 1981, former secretary of defense Clark Clifford would describe Reagan), tells him, "You have the gift of being natural. That's a great talent, my boy!"

As early as March 1980, the political columnist Ellen Goodman compared candidate Reagan to the protagonist of *Being There*, "praised because he is perceived as consistent, straightforward, understandable." That summer, the *New York Times* titled an opinion piece on the Republican National Convention "Being There," noting that "the convention was something going on between the television screen and the national audience and the way truly to attend it was to watch." Some fifteen months after Reagan came to power, Garry Wills would identify America itself with Chance: "A character like that of Peter Sellers in *Being There* who just sees television without hearing words, would think the whole job of a modern president is to get on and off helicopters and horses. Ronald Reagan has perfected that routine, and he knows he is playing to a nation of Sellers characters."

No less enigmatic than Chance is the logic—or lack of same—that caused this wildly inappropriate movie to be selected to entertain the president. Was it because *Being There* satirized Washington society and politics? Was it because Reagan's peer Melvyn Douglas—something of a political ally during the long-ago 1940s—won an Oscar for best supporting actor? *Being There* is filled with things that Reagan might well have found disturbing, ranging from the incapacity and death of the Douglas character to the scene in which his younger wife (Shirley MacLaine) propositions Chance and, misunderstanding his statement that he "likes to watch," masturbates to climax on a bearskin rug beside his bed. Nor is this the only instance of embarrassing sexual behavior. There are two scenes in which the president is shown as stressed out and impotent. ("This never happened when you were a senator," his wife complains.)

Reagan had already, even before the attempted assassination, been dubbed the Great Communicator. Yet, trying to fathom his reaction to these scenes is like trying to figure out Chance. Still, the movie made something of an impression. At one point, Chance draws on his horticultural experience to advise the president: "As long as the roots are not severed all is well and all will be well in the garden. In the garden, growth has its seasons. First comes spring and summer, then we have fall and winter, then we have spring and summer again." In February 1983, at the start of Reagan's third year in office, a letter to the business editor of the *New York Times* pointed out a statement by the president that was clearly inspired by Chance: "Economic recovery is like a seedling. For a while, it grows underground and you don't see it above ground. And then it shoots up and seeds are sprouting all over the place."

A week after screening *Being There*, Reagan was there—live on national television, "pale but beaming," according to the *New York Times*—to address a cheering joint session of Congress. His "sense of political theater" was intact, the *Times* reported, "even as his delivery and sometimes wavering voice suggested the physical toll of the chest wound he suffered."

The curse had been exorcised and the national trauma of November 22, 1963, dispelled. The shadowy Secret Agent of History faded away; the Hollywood Freedom Fighter was resurrected. Reagan was the only American president to take a bullet and live. Suddenly, deMause noted, "all violent language in the media simply disappeared, and was replaced by images more appropriate to a new, strong president."

The *New York Post* had already anointed "Iron Man Reagan." After the speech, New York's Republican senator Alfonse D'Amato declared that

Reagan "out-Wayned John Wayne." Democrats had no choice but to endorse his economic program. The president's recovery was the nation's.

Raiders, *Reds*, and the Return of the Hollywood Freedom Fighter

"Got word of Israel bombing of Iraq—nuclear reactor," Ronald Reagan wrote in his diary on June 7, 1981. "I swear I believe Armageddon is near."

Five days later, the first real Reagan movie opened: *Raiders of the Lost Ark*. Conceived by George Lucas and directed for his production company by Steven Spielberg, it presented an American hero, Indiana Jones (Harrison Ford), who bestrode the Third World like a colossus. Yet, he was not exactly a Hollywood Freedom Fighter in the sense that John Wayne in *The Alamo*, or Kirk Douglas in *Spartacus*, or the stars of *The Magnificent Seven* (all released in 1960) undertook missions of liberation. Indy, who would be described by Molly Haskell as "a grave-robbing imperialist mercenary looting Third World cultures and killing the natives," liberated something else.

Not just the twenty-year curse but the curse of *1941* was lifted. "By Raiding Hollywood Lore and His Childhood Fantasies, Steven Spielberg Rediscovers an Ark That's Pure Gold," *People* magazine's headline read. Like the new president, the Lucas-Spielberg collaboration promised to bring back "the good old days," as *Variety* called them, delivering "an exotic atmosphere of lost civilizations [and] Nazi arch-villains" which, while it might be too "exuberantly violent," was "deftly veiled" in a "sense of mystical wonder."

What, *Time*'s reviewer pretended to speculate, "did people do in the summers before George Lucas started making movies?" *Raiders* was more than just a movie (or a movie-movie):

> In a "troubled time" of runaway costs, indifferent craftsmanship, and stiffening competition from new entertainment technologies, *Raiders* is, in fact, an exemplary film, an object lesson in how to blend the art of storytelling with the highest levels of technical know-how, cost-control planning, and commercial acumen. Most of its relatively low, $20 million budget (half of what Michael Cimino was permitted to squander on his out-of-control flop, *Heaven's Gate*) is, as they say in Hollywood, "on the screen."

But were *Raiders* and *Star Wars* really, as *Time* put it, "affectionate and gracious acknowledgments that after almost 100 years movies have built up an honorable set of visual traditions and character conventions"? Or, as the more skeptical Stanley Kauffmann suggested in the *New Republic*, was *Raiders* something more sinister? "The picture is offering you a pact: you agree to be a kid again, in return for which *Raiders* will give you old-time movie thrills expressed in slick modern cinematic terms."

Indeed, the Spielberg-Lucas collaboration introduced two new templates. One was movie as choreographed thrill machine. ("My films are closer to amusement-park rides than to a play or a novel," Lucas would say.) The other, as anticipated by *Chinatown* and exemplified in *Star Wars*, was the movie as hyperreal, streamlined pastiche. Indiana Jones was something else—a positive version of what would in the Sixties have been described as an Ugly American. For some, the movie's key moment came in an Egyptian souk when, menaced by an outsized, sword-twirling Arab adversary, blasé Indy pulls out a revolver and—the punchline to a gag—shoots him point blank.

Like the Reagan administration, *Raiders* had been germinating for a biblical seven years.

Finishing *American Graffiti*, Lucas began to daydream about making an action movie modeled on the Republic serials of the 1940s—a farrago of cheap thrills and impossible cliff-hangers. He imagined his protagonist as a "shady archeologist," whose trademarks were a turned-down fedora hat and a coiled bullwhip.

Lucas's first collaborator was Philip Kaufman, who worked on the concept for several weeks. Kaufman introduced the Ark of the Covenant, mythical repository for the stone shards of the original Ten Commandments, and the idea of Nazi villainy (inspired by Trevor Ravenscroft's just published pseudo-history *Spear of Destiny*, an assertion that Adolf Hitler waged World War II to possess the Lance of Longinus, which supposedly pierced the side of Jesus Christ). Thus, anticipating *Star Wars* and *Close Encounters* (and similarly rooted in countercultural notions), Lucas's glorified B movie took on a religious aspect.

However, the project stalled when Kaufman was engaged to direct Clint Eastwood's Bicentennial Western, *The Outlaw Josie Wales* (from which he was fired), and lay dormant while Lucas created *Star Wars*. The month that *Star Wars* opened, Lucas paid off Kaufman and enlisted Spielberg. *Close Encounters* was still in release when Lucas and Spielberg met with Lawrence Kasdan in early 1978 to hash (and act) out the *Raiders* story over the course of five nine-hour days of exuberant masculine bonding.

Preproduction on *Raiders* coincided with a period of tumult in and around the Middle East, as well as growing ties between American evangelical Christians and Israel's right-wing government. Kasdan was working the script when Communists staged a coup in Afghanistan in April 1978; Lucas was revising it when the Egyptian-Israeli peace treaty was signed, the Shah left Tehran for Egypt, the Islamic Republic was declared, and Pakistani strongman General Muhammad Zia-ul-Haq had former prime minister Zulfiqar Ali Bhutto hanged.

Locations were being scouted in October 1979, a few months after President Carter authorized clandestine aid to the anti-Soviet elements in Afghanistan, even as the Iranian militants took fifty-two American hostages in the U.S. embassy. The script went back to Kasdan when, fearing what some saw as a U.S. plot to reestablish the Ottoman Empire, the Soviet Union intervened in Afghanistan; while Kasdan was working, Carter warned the Soviets not to interfere in the Persian Gulf and called for greater defense spending, his new posture underlined by national security adviser Zbigniew Brzezinski's photo op at the Khyber Pass.

ABC-TV's *Nightline*, a half-hour news program that began as a daily report on the U.S. hostages in Iran, was only a few weeks into its run when Kasdan completed his fifth and final draft, the same month as Carter's failed mission to rescue the U.S. hostages. The shoot opened in La Rochelle, France, during the summer of 1980 (before moving on to Tunisia) and wrapped seventy-three days later, two weeks before Iraq invaded Iran.

It is unlikely that instability around the oil-producing regions of North Africa, the Middle East, the Persian Gulf, and what Brzezinski named the Arc of Crisis had any effect on the men who made *Raiders*—although Spielberg did make the provocative statement in the movie's press notes that "the thing to keep in mind about this film is that it is only a movie. *Raiders* is not a statement of its times."

Spielberg needn't have worried. No geopolitical analogies were drawn by the movie's enthusiastic initial reviewers (although their excitement does seem a portent of that which would, two and a half years later, greet the Conquest of Grenada). On the contrary, *Raiders* was welcomed as exemplary escapist spectacle and a return to a presumed golden age. It "devotes itself exclusively to the glorious days of the B-picture," *New York Times* critic Vincent Canby wrote. "Spielberg has unleashed the floodgates of nostalgia," Ernest Leogrande declared in the *New York Daily News*, while colleague Rex Reed opined that the filmmaker "makes kids of us all."

Bill Hootkins, the heavy-set, Princeton-educated character actor who played a military intelligence officer in *Raiders*, exuberantly characterized the movie as "the Bible with Nazis!" But there was even more than that. Modeled on the radioactive "whatsit" in Robert Aldrich's *Kiss Me Deadly*, the Ark of the Covenant was a stand-in for the Atomic Bomb, and the battle between the echt-American hero and his German adversaries was something like a Saturday afternoon version of the Manhattan Project, albeit one that wound up with the super-weapon melting the bad guy's face before it could be used to end World War II.

Both Lucas and Spielberg identified with Indiana Jones. For Lucas, the rogue archeologist was an ego ideal: "If I could be a dream figure, I'd be Indy." Spielberg's view was no less romantic. For him, Indy was a soldier of fortune: "I was the Indiana Jones behind the camera. I felt I didn't have to shoot for a masterpiece." He also maintained that he and Lucas approached their deal with Paramount as "mercenaries." But the character was even larger than that.

Although it would become a commonplace, *Raiders* appears to have been first linked to Ronald Reagan by Frank P. Tomasulo in a paper presented in July 1982 at the annual Conference of the Society for Cinema Studies: Characterizing the movie as one that "must harken back to a past era of national greatness and achievement in the international arena in order to restore and dynamize a cultural renewal in a nation beset with problems foreign and domestic, political and economic," Tomasulo had little difficulty finding geopolitical analogies. He compared "the warm, smiling and gregarious Sallah," an Egyptian digger, "who is friendly and cooperative to American interests" to Egyptian leader Anwar Sadat (assassinated October 10, 1981, as *Raiders* enjoyed its last week atop the box office). And he noted that Indiana Jones wears the same leather jacket and fedora outfit as Reagan in *Hong Kong* (1952).*

Raiders was the year's number one box-office attraction, nearly doubling the returns generated by the runner-up *Superman II*, and the highest-grossing Paramount release ever. Reagan, who screened the movie at Camp David on July 10, would not fully dramatize the *Raiders* scenario until he invaded Grenada in autumn 1983, but he did adopt the role of Indiana Jones at the height of the movie's success. On August 19, with *Raiders* still at number one and the president still asleep, American F-14 Tomcats shot down two Libyan jets over the Gulf of Sidra. Briefed upon waking, Reagan greeted his aides with a performance, miming the quick-draw of a Western gunslinger or Indiana Jones. A few weeks earlier Reagan had shot down the striking air traffic controllers, whose union, PATCO, had supported him in the election. On August 13, he signed the largest tax cut in American history as well as the Omnibus Budget Reconciliation Act.

Some seven hundred thousand working-poor families were deprived of some or all of their benefits. Hundreds of thousands more lost their food stamps; school lunches and breakfasts were defunded, and a billion dollars in Medicaid grants disappeared. August 1981 was in many respects the highpoint of Reagan's presidency.

The president screened a dozen new movies that fall. The most inappropriate or, alternately, most totally apt, was *The Fan*, a horror film in which a famous actress played by Lauren Bacall is stalked by a crazed admirer, whom—in a switch from its source, Bob Randall's 1977 epistolary novel—she kills. In his diary, Reagan characterized *The Fan* as "a bloody one."

Because the Reagans were spending the weekend in Washington, the

---

* While *Raiders'* frequently listed inspirations include *King Solomon's Mines* (1950), *Journey to the Center of the Earth* (1959), *That Man from Rio* (1964), and "Uncle Scrooge" comic books, it more generally recalled a Hollywood cycle described in *Hollywood Review* by the blacklisted screenwriter Michael Wilson as movies about a "free-booter hero who brazenly interferes in the affairs of another nation—usually a colonial country." In addition to *Hong Kong,* examples included another Reagan vehicle, *Tropic Zone,* as well as *His Majesty O'Keefe, Appointment in Honduras, Plunder of the Sun, Wings of the Hawk,* and *East of Sumatra* (all 1953), along with *Secret of the Incas* (1954), in which Charlton Heston wears the same outfit as Reagan in *Hong Kong* and Ford in *Raiders.* The Lucas-Spielberg movie not only harked back to the glory days of B pictures but a particular stage in the Cold War.

movie was shown at the White House with only the first couple and Ted Graber in attendance. As with *Being There*, this selection begs the question: Who
chose the evening entertainment and why? Heralded by trailers that attempted
to distance it from the death of John Lennon, *The Fan* had opened to poor
reviews in mid-May, less than two months after John Hinckley's attempt on
Reagan's life. Bacall was neither a friend nor a political ally. Did the president not see the analogies between Hinckley and the movie's monster? Or
was it rather that, the novel having been found by the police in Hinckley's
hotel room, his curiosity was piqued?

At Camp David, where Reagan most often watched movies alone with
Nancy, his selections included the Australian war film *Gallipoli*, the World
War II spy thriller *Eye of the Needle*, the space Western *Outland*, and the British sports inspirational *Chariots of Fire*, a movie about the 1924 Olympics
that left a lasting impression, cited by Reagan seven years later at the conclusion of a speech given at the Royal Institute of International Affairs in
London. Over a long Columbus Day weekend, the Reagans watched the crime
drama *True Confessions*; *Paternity*, a Burt Reynolds farce about surrogate
motherhood; and *Continental Divide*, a comedy produced by Spielberg's new
company and written by Lawrence Kasdan, featuring John Belushi in his most
romantic role.

Reynolds was the nation's number-one star and Belushi was popular
among young males, but Reagan did not ignore the last manifestations of
his own Hollywood cohort. Months before the movie's opening, the president secured an early screening of *On Golden Pond*. The number two top-
grossing movie of 1981, *On Golden Pond* was unkindly described by Pauline
Kael as "a doddering valentine" to Hollywood's greatest generation, represented by seventy-six-year-old Henry Fonda and seventy-four-year-old
Katharine Hepburn, as well as to the eternal values of WASP America. (As
noted by Kael, *Time* magazine's cover story extolled the stars' respective
pre-Revolutionary War pedigrees.)

The soon to be seventy-one-year-old president completed his first year in
office as newfangled home video was heading for its first billion-dollar year.
Thanks to the VCR, fans might replay the lives of the stars on tape, perhaps
in perpetuity. In essence, *On Golden Pond* replayed Hollywood's first truly
self-referential movie, *Sunset Boulevard*, for nostalgic pathos rather than
nightmare comedy. The casting of Henry's real daughter, Jane, as the couple's

estranged offspring gave *On Golden Pond* additional documentary status. It also, some thought, provided a parallel for the Reagans' strained relationship with their daughter Patti Davis, a fervent admirer of Jane Fonda whom, according to her mother's biographer Kitty Kelley, Nancy Reagan particularly despised.*

Reagan was also given a preview of *Ragtime* at the White House, with featured actor and early supporter James Cagney in attendance. At Camp David, during the last weekend, the Reagans ran George Cukor's final movie *Rich and Famous*, a remake of the 1943 Warner Bros. film *Old Acquaintance*. The updated version struck the president as pornographic, perhaps because Jacqueline Bisset's various trysts include sex with a stranger in an airplane toilet.

The documentary *From Mao to Mozart: Isaac Stern in China*, treated as a state occasion, screened at the White House three days after the president met with the National Security Council and approved a plan to provide $20 million in covert aid to the Nicaraguan Contras, was "wonderful." But the most impressive movie Reagan saw that season, with unemployment at 8.9 percent and his approval slipping below 50 percent, was Warren Beatty's epic biography of the revolutionary journalist John Reed, *Reds*—not least because the Reagan Revolution was already over.

The December issue of *The Atlantic* featured a long article by *Washington Post* journalist William Greider entitled "The Education of David Stockman," in which Reagan's young firebrand complained that because Congress had failed to cut spending by some tens of billions of dollars he felt it to be necessary to delay or even reduce the president's tax cuts. To this apostasy, Stockman admitted that "supply-side" economics was only "trickle-down" by another name. Having obtained an advance copy, Senator Gary Hart read the entire article into the *Congressional Record*.

Instantly, Stockman went from the administration's poster boy to its pariah. He kept his job but lost his voice—although presumably had the

---

* Mark Weinberg, the former Reagan speechwriter and chronicler of his movie-watching at Camp David's Aspen Lodge, devotes a chapter of his memoir *Movie Nights with the Reagans* to *On Golden Pond*. Although present for its Camp David preview, he was not privy to—or has forgotten—the Reagans' response and so can only speculate on how personal an impact the film had.

last laugh when several years later he completed the generational shift from SDS instigator to Wall Street investment banker.

Warren Beatty had been mulling *Reds*, a three-hour-and-fifteen-minute movie (plus intermission) that he co-wrote, produced, directed, and starred in, even longer than George Lucas contemplated *Raiders of the Lost Ark*. Indeed, it had been on his mind for perhaps as long as Ronald Reagan had been plotting his way to the White House.

The same year Reagan found himself heir to Barry Goldwater's army, Beatty—who once told a reporter that his earliest childhood ambition was to be president of the United States and who turned down the role of John F. Kennedy in the 1963 adaptation of *PT 109*—discovered John Reed, perhaps, some have speculated, as a result of his love affair with the Bolshoi prima ballerina Maya Plisetskaya.

Even as Reagan campaigned to be elected California governor, Beatty was bruiting the possibility of a Reed movie on the set of *Bonnie and Clyde*. During the summer of 1968, a few months after Reagan's first bid for the Republican presidential nomination fizzled, Beatty and his then romantic partner Julie Christie flew to Moscow to explore the possibility of making a Reed biopic in the Soviet Union. Four years later at the Democratic National Convention, in the immediate euphoria that followed the nomination of Beatty's favored candidate, Senator George McGovern, he began writing a script.

In the aftermath of McGovern's defeat, Beatty solicited advice, from screenwriters (Robert Towne, his collaborator on *Shampoo*), politicians (McGovern's campaign manager, senatorial hopeful Gary Hart), and pundits (the liberal columnist Max Lerner). Although most advised him to drop the project, Beatty persevered and, in 1976, after Reagan lost his second bid for the Republican nomination, was working on a script with the radical British playwright Trevor Griffiths.

Beatty was now pushing forty, seven years older than Reed was when he died and another six years older than when Reed makes his first appearance in *Reds*, galloping through the Mexican Revolution. The age difference may account for the actor's perpetual boyish enthusiasm. (A possibly apocryphal story has Beatty explaining to his editor that Warren Beatty is not playing

Jack Reed, Jack Reed is playing Warren Beatty.) The part of Reed's companion Louise Bryant was taken by Beatty's then partner Diane Keaton with a sort of defiant, defensive embarrassment.*

Principal photography on *Reds* began around the time that Reagan launched his second campaign in 1979. The picture wrapped during the spring primaries as Reagan beat back a challenge from George Bush; post-production occurred in Manhattan next door to Studio 54 during the presidential campaign, and continued past Reagan's inauguration and into the first year of his presidency. Preceded by rumors of disastrous previews and wild cost overruns, *Reds* opened on December 4, 1981. The initial box office was good and the notices were even better. *Variety* hailed *Reds* as "a courageous and uncompromising attempt to meld a high-level socio-political drama of ideas with an intense love story." *New York*'s critic David Denby declared *Reds* "the most entertaining large-scale American movie in years" and, at the *New Republic*, Stanley Kauffmann pronounced it "a big achievement." *Reds* "radiates intelligence, sincerity and creativity," Dave Kehr wrote in the *Chicago Reader*, calling it "the most complete, most mature epic I know."

In the *New York Times*, Vincent Canby maintained that "*Reds* dramatizes with great emotional effect—better than any other entertainment film I can think of—a remarkable period in America's intellectual development and self-awareness." But what period was that? Without explicitly saying so, Max Lerner suggested that *Reds* was a film of the Sixties that "works best as a story of love and revolution, of sexuality and ideology, of the heady mixture that hit the sons and daughters of the affluent in the first American erotic-political revolution of the century . . . poised precariously at the convergence point of Eros and power."

The alternative press was less coy. Kehr understood *Reds* as political autobiography. ("What went wrong for John Reed in the teens is also what went wrong for Warren Beatty in the '70s.") Veronica Geng, who reviewed *Reds*

---

* There is evidence that Beatty would have preferred Julie Christie in the role (the movie is dedicated to her), and the star told Jeremy Pikser, his research assistant and an uncredited screenwriter on the film, that he really should have made *Reds* in 1973, when the battles of the 1960s were still fresh, with Jane Fonda, who had turned down the role of Bonnie in *Bonnie and Clyde*.

for the *Soho Weekly News*, was more direct, tartly noting of Beatty's Reed that "radical chic gets him the girl," and adding that "this is certainly what goes on among political people, as anyone who was active in the '60s remembers, but it's a folly, not a point of view on a folly." Skeptical of Beatty's intentions, Geng found the movie personal in other ways: Beatty "was brave to stick to the sex comedy he knows so well, and perverse to stretch his style over this vast scope."

While critics writing for left-wing and even Communist journals were generally thrilled by *Reds* (some perhaps onetime Yippies or former members of SDS who had loved the far more inflammatory *Bonnie and Clyde*), mainstream critics simply chose to normalize the movie as industry product. Writing in the *National Review*, John Simon declined to see Beatty's epic outside of a Hollywood context: "War and revolution are mostly an exotic background to spice up the screwball comedy of battling, wisecracking lovers." Andrew Sarris began his favorable *Village Voice* notice by stating that "*Reds* is more a love story than a revolutionary chronicle, and as it happens, I prefer love stories to revolutionary chronicles."

Writing in *Harper's* magazine, John Podhoretz (then a twenty-year-old undergraduate at the University of Chicago) located *Reds* both in the context of traditional Hollywood as "an amalgam of almost every cliché we have ever witnessed in a movie theater," and the New Hollywood of the 1970s, "with its conventions about 'feelings' and 'emotions' and its socially conscious themes." Reed and Bryant, Podhoretz joked, "spoke to each other as though they were at an Esalen retreat." Beatty's protagonists, Podhoretz thought, were not so much Communists as "progressives," who believe in "sexual liberation, women's liberation, birth control, and, of course, honesty about one's emotions," and, "rather than chronicling the years 1915 to 1920," *Reds* ran "the gamut of the 1970s, from feminism to the Helsinki Watch, from encounter groups to the human-potential movement, and all this" while dramatizing Beatty's "own version of a time very much on certain people's mind these days—the McCarthyite 1950s—by lavishing special attention on the first American Red Hunt in 1919."

Was that how the movie appeared to the prominent Hollywood anti-Communist Ronald Reagan when, one day after *Reds*' theatrical premiere, he hosted a Saturday afternoon screening at the White House for a group that included Beatty and Keaton?*

Reds' first half exudes excited chaos and evokes an alternative America, as the charming, vaguely comic Reed dashes about raising money and knocking off articles for *The Masses*, playing a prolonged game of "I Dare You" with the would-be adventuress Louise Bryant both in Greenwich Village and Provincetown, where Eugene O'Neill (Jack Nicholson) creates a romantic triangle.

Jack and Louise struggle with a proto-hippie ethos and join the antiwar movement. Then he gets serious, experiencing the thrill of making a political speech, and the movie's first part ends with a rousing version of "The Internationale" that could bring the susceptible close to tears. According to Beatty, Reagan spoke to him during the intermission, asking him how he did "all those jobs at the same time," remarking that he didn't understand how anyone could be president without being an actor: "He wasn't joking. He was talking about the performance of it," Beatty remembered. (In fact, this was one of Reagan's stock lines.)

If *Reds'* first half is the mid-1960s, the second half—which begins with congressional hearings and the World War I Red Scare—starts in the early 1950s before fearlessly plunging into the sectarian weeds as rival Communist parties compete for Soviet recognition and Reed makes a pilgrimage to revolutionary Russia. Confounded by Bolshevik fanatics, jailed for a time in Finland, he burnishes his revolutionary credentials by attending the 1920 Congress of the Peoples of the East in Baku, Azerbaijan, where he denounces American oil imperialism. In the final hour, he is reunited with Louise, who has fearlessly made her way to him before he dies.

After the movie, as reported by the *New York Times*, Reagan jokingly told Beatty and Keaton that he had been "hoping for a happy ending." But of course, from Reagan's point of view, this drama of revolutionary failure was a happy ending. Asked why he was showing *Reds*, the president had a ready quip: "I look at it as showing up the Reds."

---

* The White House guest book lists other guests as Mr. and Mrs. Cary Grant; Mr. and Mrs. Douglas Fairbanks Jr.; the actress Audrey Meadows and her husband, California businessman Robert Six; the retired producer Armand S. Deutsch, recently appointed to the Presidential Task Force on the Arts and Humanities, and his wife; Mr. and Mrs. George Bush; Michael Deaver; and, of course, Ted Graber.

For Beatty, the mere existence of the movie demonstrated his capacity to put one over on Hollywood. Still, some like David Denby saw a paradox: "In the past year, as the country has lurched to the right, the three biggest of the big-budget movies, massively supported by banks and conglomerates— *Heaven's Gate*, *Ragtime*, and *Reds*—have all been overtly leftist. Which might be a 'contradiction' of capitalism that neither Marx nor Lenin could have imagined." (Perhaps, although it might not have seemed strange to Herbert Marcuse, who had written of "repressive desublimation" in *One-Dimensional Man*.) Podhoretz addressed this contradiction while contradicting himself. Because "*Reds* is less a pro-communist movie than a Hollywood romance with communism as an almost arbitrary backdrop providing 'color,'" he blandly explained, "no one accuses Beatty of serving up propaganda."

Actually, some did. *Reds* was characterized as "pro-Communist poison" by the financial magazine *Barron's* and, along with Jane Fonda, was denounced in Congress by Representative Larry P. McDonald (a Georgia Democrat who, as chairman of the John Birch Society, was likely the House's most right-wing member). The White House screening was criticized by Howard Phillips, chairman of the Conservative Caucus, and Reed Irvine, chairman of Accuracy in Media, but Reagan was largely immune. Indeed, William Buckley took a notably relaxed view of the movie, reminding his readers that the Russian Revolution had initially attracted idealists like John Reed. Some blamed the deputy chief of staff, Michael Deaver, perceived by his enemies as enthralled by Hollywood glamour, for arranging the screening; others thought that Beatty cleverly used the White House to inoculate himself against red-baiting.

Podhoretz compared *Reds* to several older movies, including Robert Altman's *Buffalo Bill and the Indians*, Martin Ritt's Blacklist comedy *The Front* (1976), and the Jane Fonda vehicle *Julia* (1977), based on a memoir by Lillian Hellman. All, he thought, were indebted to the novel *Ragtime*, "which made it intellectually respectable for popular artists to revise America's past" as "a metaphor for the present." (In other words, the movie industry was engaged in rewriting history in Hollywood terms . . . like the president!)

As an epic psychodrama, allowing a movie star to present himself as a world historical figure, *Reds* was in the rarefied tradition of *Spartacus* and *The Alamo*, two movies released during the same season that John F. Kennedy was elected president. But if Beatty cast himself as the last Hollywood Freedom Fighter, Reagan could lay claim to be the greatest.

Indeed, no critic made a connection to Reagan apart from Podhoretz, who began his essay on the movie by coyly observing that "for whatever reasons, actors are now firmly ingrained as personages in both American low and high cultures." While Beatty made this movie, Reagan made history.

Noisy Ghosts

> You *must* have a varied viewing pattern. You can't see *Taxi Driver* and *Mean Streets* together on a double bill. You must see *Taxi Driver* and . . . *His Girl Friday.*
>
> —MARTIN SCORSESE with regard to John Hinckley's obsession, *The Village Voice* (February 1983)

As he begins his second year in office, Ronald Reagan is looking at the sort of old movies most Americans see on TV: Tay Garnett's 1932 romantic weepie *One Way Passage*, George Cukor's 1949 romantic comedy *Adam's Rib*, and the all-star 1932 version of *Grand Hotel*, the latter two screened while the president is working on a State of the Union address in which he will acknowledge that the American economy is in recession.

Speech delivered, Reagan turns to recent treatments of contemporary history, inviting Romuald Spasowski, the newly defected Polish ambassador, to the White House to see Andrzej Wajda's paean to Solidarity, *Man of Iron*, a movie that the martial-law Polish government unsuccessfully tried to have removed from Oscar consideration. It's followed the next weekend at Camp David by Costa-Gavras's Cannes-winner *Missing* ("a pretty biased slam at Chile and our own government," Reagan notes in his diary) and Terence Young's *Inchon* ("a brutal but gripping picture about the Korean War and for once we're the good guys and the Communists are the villains"). Reagan speculates that the producer was Japanese or Korean—in fact *Inchon*, starring Laurence Olivier as Douglas McArthur, was bankrolled by Reverend Sun Myung Moon's Unification Church, which soon founded the *Washington Times*, a daily newspaper dedicated to advancing the Reagan agenda.

The president also creates his own fanciful scenario when he is asked by a reporter about the history of CIA involvement in Vietnam. According to the *New York Times*, Reagan explains that "North and South Vietnam had been two separate countries."

> He said that at the 1954 Geneva conference, provisions had been made that "these two countries could by a vote of all their people decide together whether they wanted to be one country or not." He continued that Ho Chi Minh, the Vietnamese Communist leader, "refused to participate in such an election." The President went on to say that American military advisers were then sent to South Vietnam to work in civilian clothing and without weapons, until they were attacked with "pipe bombs." Ultimately, Mr. Reagan said, former President John F. Kennedy authorized "sending of a division of Marines."

"Nearly all of these statements are either wrong or open to challenge," the reporter noted.*

In March, Reagan is looking at current movies (and also agreeing to a tax increase). The March 12–14 weekend includes a suggestive, even poetic, pairing, at least in terms of the titles: Alan Parker's *Shoot the Moon* and Guy Hamilton's *Evil Under the Sun*. (The former is a downbeat drama about a dysfunctional marriage, the latter is an Agatha Christie murder mystery set in Majorca.) The next weekend the president and first lady watch another comic murder film, Sidney Lumet's *Deathtrap*, and a German World War II film, Wolfgang Petersen's *Das Boot*. The latter, a tremendous success in West Germany, leaves an impression: "Very good but strange to find yourself rooting for the enemy," the president mused in his diary. The same night, CBS News airs the ninety-minute documentary "Central America in Revolt," split between reports from three hot spots—El Salvador, Nicaragua, and Guatemala.

March 27, two nights before the Oscars are televised and three days before the first anniversary of John Hinckley's thwarted assassination, Nancy

---

* In fact, the French divided Vietnam into three units and reunified the country in 1950. The 1954 Geneva Accords provided for temporary partition and called for national elections in 1956. South Vietnam and the United States did not sign the accords; it was not Ho but the South Vietnamese leader Diem who refused to participate. The first uniformed American military advisers arrived in the mid-1950s; Kennedy authorized "combat support" in late 1961 and eventually dispatched nineteen thousand combat advisers. Lyndon Johnson sent the first ground combat units, a marine brigade, in March 1965.

scores a hit at the White House press corps' annual Gridiron Club dinner. After a reporter in drag sings a parody version of "Second Hand Rose," an old Jewish-dialect song associated with Fanny Brice and more recently Barbra Streisand, here revised to burlesque the first lady's reputation for getting free designer clothes, Mrs. Reagan suddenly appears in a get-up described by Kitty Kelley as "yellow Donald Duck boots, a white feathered boa, strings of pop-it beads, a floppy plumed hat, and a red and yellow Hawaiian skirt held together with safety pins" to sing yet another version.

"The smash of the evening was Nancy," Reagan writes in his diary.

> She had left the head table supposedly for the powder room. Suddenly there she was on stage—even the cast wasn't in on the secret. She was dressed in a hokey costume and sang a parody of "Second Hand Rose"—Second hand clothes. She was carrying a plate which she smashed as a finale. It brought the house down. She got 2 standing ovations. Maybe this will end the sniping.*

The next week, it's back to movie-movies with vintage screwball, Leo McCarey's 1937 *The Awful Truth*—a movie in which the Manhattan (or Hollywood) sophisticates, played by Cary Grant and Irene Dunne—both friends of the Reagans—get considerable comic mileage riffing on the rich cornball rube played by Ralph Bellamy.

As winter turned to spring, unemployment approached 9.5 percent, the highest rate in forty years. Housing foreclosures set a new record. The Census Bureau reported that 14 percent of American families were living in poverty, the greatest total since the late 1960s. Meanwhile, a new hero was rumbling through the land: the eponymous, muscle-bound hero of John Milius's *Conan the Barbarian*.

On the night of February 19, a thousand people were turned away for the sneak preview of Milius's film, starring bodybuilder Arnold Schwarzenegger as the long-haired "Hyborian Age" hired sword, a character invented by pulp writer Robert Howard in the 1930s and, since 1970, a Marvel comic book hero (as well as a childhood favorite of future president Barack Obama).

---

* It did, for a time. A White House staffer told Kitty Kelley that Mrs. Reagan rehearsed "every day for a couple of months" in preparation.

Universal hastily scheduled three screenings the next night in Las Vegas and still could not accommodate the crowds.

There were previews in thirty cities on March 12. Some precipitated total bedlam. In Los Angeles, people reportedly fought to gain admission. In New York, two capacious Broadway houses were mobbed, per Carlos Clarens in *Film Comment*, by "a restless, loud, volatile compound of young adults, mostly male," police forced "to intervene and keep late-comers from crashing the already sold-out houses." Opening on May 14, *Conan* grossed $9.6 million on its first weekend, and reigned as the nation's top box-office attraction for two weeks, coinciding with the height of the war between Britain and Argentina over the Falkland Islands.

The most aggressively personal of recent sword-and-sorcery films, *Conan* was very much a product of the new Hollywood—a spectacle of brute violence rather than snazzy special effects, taking its cues from *Alexander Nevsky*, *Samson and Delilah*, and *Triumph of the Will*. Although inspired by the popularity of the Marvel comic book, the project was propelled by the success of *Star Wars* and, even before that, by the prescience of George Lucas who counseled would-be producer Edward Pressman to recruit Schwarzenegger. By the time Pressman cleared the tangle of rights, professionally bellicose Milius was set to direct, and former Scorsese student Oliver Stone (who would win an Oscar in 1979 for writing *Midnight Express* and independently imagined Schwarzenegger as Conan) was working on a script which, after dropping out of the project and returning, Milius revised.

Schwarzenegger would tell the press that Milius ran the set in mock-military fashion, complete with "Nazi salutes" and drills and "General Milius" inscribed on the back of his director's chair. Nothing if not gung-ho, Milius presented Schwarzenegger—a hunk of Hegel's world spirit made material—as the Übermensch embodiment of paranoid individualism and the Nietzschean will to power. (Nietzsche is invoked at the onset of the film with a quote filtered through Watergate burglar G. Gordon Liddy: "That which does not kill us makes us stronger.") Even more than Lucas, Milius proposed to elevate a twelve-year-old's Saturday matinee epiphany into a world religion although, when Conan prays to his god Crom for victory and, by way of amen, adds "if you do not listen, then the hell with you!," he seems more the apostle of secular super-humanism.

Indeed, like Ayn Rand, who might well have enjoyed the movie, *Conan* is markedly anti-religious. The arch-villain Thulsa Doom (James Earl Jones in a braided Beatle wig) is a cult leader whose temple was said to be the largest free-standing set in Hollywood history and whose hippie followers are ready to commit mass suicide if so commanded. It is also anti-urban, as when Conan first visits the degenerate city of Zamora, and—given its phallocratic adoration of the loincloth-clad muscleman—strategically homophobic, as when Conan violently rebuffs an advance made by Doom's swishy priest.

Reviews were mixed. Many deemed *Conan* a ludicrously violent and pompous cartoon. (The editors of *Mad* magazine evidently regarded it as so outlandish that, rather than their master caricaturist Mort Drucker, they assigned their "maddest" cartoonist Don Martin to illustrate "Conehead the Barbituate.") Milius "treats the material as solemnly as if it were an authentic Norse myth or Icelandic saga," *New York* magazine critic David Denby wrote. Perhaps because of Schwarzenegger, or Milius's Wagnerian pretentions, or both, *Conan* had the best opening in West German history, topping the World War II submarine drama *Das Boot* both in its first week admissions and grosses.

Denby was one of the few critics to address Milius's ideology ("Milius worships force, but he doesn't have the consistency or the visual skills to be a good fascist filmmaker"), although this would soon be commonplace. Some years later, in his book *From Vietnam to Reagan*, Robin Wood would call *Conan* the lone 1980s fantasy film to "dispense with a liberal cloak, parading its Fascism shamelessly in instantly recognizable popular signifiers: it opens with a quotation from Nietzsche, has the spirit of its dead heroine leap to the rescue at the climax as a Wagnerian Valkyrie, and in between unabashedly celebrates the Aryan male physique with a single-mindedness that would have delighted Leni Riefenstahl."

The *Village Voice* critic Carrie Rickey also declared *Conan* "crypto-Fascist" and further joked that, like Reagan, the movie's protagonist was an "invincible patriarch" who could not "utter a comprehensible sentence." Actually, Schwarzenegger was a vocal Reagan supporter as *People* magazine pointed out in a June profile that, although pegged to *Conan*, seemed mainly interested in the bodybuilder's romantic relationship with the TV news personality Maria Shriver, Senator Ted Kennedy's niece.

Conan was the first of the Reagan era's "hard body" protagonists identified by the academic Susan Jeffords in her book of the same title a dozen years later. The Schwarzenegger torso was crucial, and some reviewers associated *Conan* with *Jane Fonda's Workout*, just released and soon to become the year's top-selling VHS tape. Schwarzenegger himself regarded Conan as the new Rocky, telling the *New York Post* that "the picture is a winner because Conan is a winner. . . . He's the kind of person an audience can identify with. He never gives up."

Appropriately, *Conan* was knocked from its perch by *Rocky III* and Conan would be surpassed as a hard body by a new Stallone creation before the year's end. But first, America's reigning action hero cast himself as a two-fisted Cold Warrior as well as a bona fide Hollywood Freedom Fighter.

As the self-directed star of *Firefox*, a movie that his company Malpaso also produced, Clint Eastwood plays a heroic bomber pilot traumatized by his experience in Vietnam, where he was shot down and had been a POW—like John McCain, then poised to run for Congress in Arizona.

Eastwood's Major Mitch Gant is forcibly re-recruited by the air force to go undercover in Russia. Stealing the top-secret Soviet weapon Firefox, a super MiG powered by mental telepathy, is a mission that, as a top pilot fluent in Russian, only he can accomplish. Warner Bros. had pitched the scenario, based on a 1977 techno-thriller by the Welsh writer Craig Thomas, to the Pentagon in early 1980, soon after the Soviet invasion of Afghanistan.

Despite the ridiculous premise, the idea was enthusiastically received not only because it promised to dramatize post-Vietnam redemption but because it presented the opportunity to show an air force flier engaged in a spectacular aerial battle à la *Star Wars*. Indeed, once his company Malpaso took over the project, Eastwood enlisted George Lucas's special effects genius John Dykstra to supervise the climactic dogfight.

Budgeted around $20 million (mainly for effects), *Firefox* was the most expensive Malpaso movie yet. It went into production during Reagan's Libyan summer, and Eastwood had been anxious to secure the president's endorsement as well as the Pentagon's. Back in April, he wrote a personal invitation to the movie's June 11 gala Washington premiere, a $1,000 a ticket benefit for the USO. The event was attended by Secretary of Defense Caspar Weinberger (who pronounced *Firefox* "exciting and good for morale," adding "we won") but Reagan, returning that evening from a nine-day European trip, took a pass.*

Eastwood arranged for a screening at Camp David a week later on June 18, the same day that the movie opened theatrically and the president had a forty-five-minute National Security Council meeting as well as telephone calls with six of his fellow former Warner Bros. contractees (James Cagney, Priscilla Lane, Joan Leslie, Pat O'Brien, Ginger Rogers, and Alexis Smith), plus Eastwood, with whom he spoke before screening the movie. The following evening, after Reagan watched the Neil Simon comedy *I Ought to Be in Pictures*, the men spoke again for eleven minutes.

According to his diary, Reagan was "impressed" with Eastwood's work. Other reviewers were less enthusiastic. *Variety* called *Firefox* "a burn-out," Vincent Canby deemed the film "a Superman movie without a sense of humor," David Denby characterized it as "a neo-conservative espionage drama that might have been commissioned in a wild moment by the armchair Cold Warriors at *Commentary* magazine." (In fact, while acknowledging *Firefox* as "the most resolutely anti-Soviet film to be made in this country in a very long time," *Commentary*'s Richard Grenier found it "wildly implausible and rather awful.")

Denby further noted that "Eastwood lets himself look confused, weak, even stupid, as if to say that Americans are too straightforward for this cloak-and-dagger stuff," something that the filmmaker's most sophisticated exegete, the *Chicago Reader* critic Dave Kehr, saw as an example of near-pathological ambivalence: "Eastwood the director doesn't simply serve Eastwood the actor, but actively undermines him, exaggerating his sense of grandeur with parodic, low-slung camera angles, and puncturing his pretensions with suddenly elevated points of view, in which the camera looks down ironically on the character."

A good deal of *Firefox* is concerned with acting. Eastwood poses as a businessman in Moscow, where he stages a fake mugging and, operating in a

---

* The next night in Camp David, Reagan screened Robert Altman's political satire *Health*, set in a convention of food faddists and originally intended for release during the 1980 campaign, noting in his diary that it was "the world's worst movie." Did he find the competition for president of the organization, replete with dirty tricks, conspiracy theories, absurd TV interviews, and partisans parading around as giant vegetables, to be insulting or merely unfunny? *Health* was followed by Alfred Hitchcock's *Notorious*.

nightmare world of continuous surveillance, keeps switching his identity—on occasion even speaking a few words of phonetic Russian. (Russians, however, mainly use English.)

Although only a middling success—out-grossing *Conan* with just under $50 million to finish as Warners' top box-office release, and number fifteen for 1982—*Firefox* has been credited with inspiring government research into a form of enhanced jet-fighter command controls based on an "ocular attention-sensing interface system," perhaps the subject of the phone call Reagan placed to Eastwood after seeing the film.

The next weekend at Camp David, the Reagans switched genres, choosing to watch the classy hit horror film *Poltergeist*, produced by Steven Spielberg and directed (or co-directed) by Tobe Hooper.

Was this uncharacteristic choice made in preparation for the upcoming White House screening of Spielberg's all but simultaneously released blockbuster *E.T.: The Extraterrestrial*? Or perhaps *Poltergeist* was relevant to a recent White House exorcism. Early that week, John Hinckley was judged to be insane and thus innocent of attempted murder. "Quite an uproar has been created," Reagan serenely observed in his diary.

While noting that he and Nancy watched Secretary of State Al Haig (who had used the attempted assassination as a clumsy means to assert his own control in the White House) read his letter of resignation on TV, the president made no notes on *Poltergeist* in his diary. Still, it did provide a significant form of media feedback, being most likely the first current Hollywood release in which Reagan saw his own image—emblazoned on the cover of the *New York Times* collection of essays *Reagan: The Man, the President*.

That scene, early in the movie, is the quiet before the special effects storm—hostile spirits have not yet taken control of the Freeling household. The father, Steven Freeling, is shown reading or perhaps only perusing the book in bed while his wife Diane tokes on a joint and engages in a giggly riff on the book she's reading about Carl Jung. In another room, the family's two younger kids Robbie and Carol Anne are being spooked, and the 1943 patriotic fantasy *A Guy Named Joe*, a Spielberg favorite, beams out of the haunted TV.

If the telecast of a World War II movie presents the TV as a source of historical memory, Reagan's mediated presence is a nod toward social realism—not unlike the clutter of *Star Wars* memorabilia in Robbie's bed-room. *Poltergeist* is America 1982, haunted by its past. ("I can't think of many other directors who could raise goose bumps by playing 'The Star-Spangled Banner' behind a film's opening credits," Vincent Canby noted ap-provingly in his *New York Times* review.)

Although seen as mirror opposites, *Poltergeist* and *E.T.* both treat what Spielberg called "the lifestyle of suburban America" as essentially apocalyp-tic, TV normality refracted through the Book of Revelation. A photo-realist appreciation for the nuances of tract-house life barely conceals the hysteria that underlies the two movies (not to mention *Close Encounters*). In *Polter-geist*, the suburb (which Spielberg would maintain was based on Scottsdale, Arizona, where he grew up) has been constructed atop a graveyard; in *E.T.*, it is a pit stop for a sentient being from outer space.*

In some ways, *Poltergeist* and *E.T.* are the same movie. Both have their origins in an earlier treatment, known in one version as *Night Skies*, com-missioned by Spielberg and written by John Sayles, and in another as *Night Time*, developed by Spielberg with input from Tobe Hooper. *Night Skies* was a sort of anti–*Close Encounters* in which marauding extraterrestrials, under the command of the very nasty Scar (a reference to the villainous Comanche chief in *The Searchers*), terrorize a rural family—save for one kindly ET, named Buddy by the family's autistic child.

Even as *Night Skies* began pre-production at Columbia in April 1980, Spielberg, then preparing *Raiders of the Lost Ark*, was working on *Night Time*, in which the hostile forces are ghosts who take possession of the Freeling family and then their idyllic suburb, described by Spielberg in his treatment as a large "child-infested community." The four Freeling kids are character-ized as "children of the 80's. They watch more TV than they should, see all the new 'PG' movies at the local six-plex, and do just enough homework to get by in school."

The premise seems to have stimulated Spielberg's imagination. Pos-sessed by forces flowing through the family television set, father Freeling undergoes a personality change that among other things provides an exciting

---

* Spielberg lived in Arizona during the heyday of great Southwestern sci-fi—including *It Came From Outer Space* (1953) and *Them!* (1955) among many others—and atmospheric testing at Yucca Flat.

new dimension to his conjugal relations. Thanks to "ectoplasmic manifestations" that beset their home, the Freelings become "unwitting celebrities" and then community scapegoats as the contagion spreads, via TV, first to the neighboring family (remarkably named the Eisenhowers) and beyond.

The suburb, which was developed by Freeling, is—as in *Poltergeist*—constructed on a graveyard, albeit one that was far grislier. Spielberg described it as the site of "a massive massacre of white settlers, perhaps 150 years ago. . . . Children, babies, pioneer men and their women. Arrow heads, scalping knives—a horrible way to die." The ending was open. Spielberg suggested that one possibility was a mass evacuation: "As we slowly pan through the empty town and its deserted homes, we see ghost fires being lit." The suburb burns, TV sets implode, and "the souls are set to rest in peace." Now let's hear the national anthem.

In early 1981, as soon as he finished *Raiders*, Spielberg explained to Columbia's president Frank Price that he no longer wished to make *Night Skies*, describing a benign version of what would be *E.T.* Price rejected it and Spielberg brought the project to Universal. At the same time, he offered *Night Skies/Night Time*, renamed *Poltergeist*, to MGM. Contractually unable to direct it because he was already working on *E.T.*, Spielberg handed the film to Hooper—while exercising such on-set control as producer as to be the dominant creative force.

Poltergeist was steeped in its own contested history. The movie was haunted by negative pre-release publicity—conflicting accounts of who directed the picture—and an initial R rating. Reviews were mixed. Vincent Canby thought it "marvelously spooky" and David Denby wrote that it was "sensationally effective." West Coast critics were less amused. *Variety* found the movie "annoying" in its lack of development and the *Los Angeles Reader* complained that "the relationship between the family and the spooks that pester them is totally arbitrary." *San Francisco* magazine called *Poltergeist* "a ghost story without catharsis, without conviction."*

Perhaps because Spielberg and Hooper were working at cross-purposes,

---

* Nevertheless, *Poltergeist* was a success, placing third, behind *Star Trek II: The Wrath of Khan* and *Rocky III*, during its opening weekend; it wound up grossing over $76 million, number eight for the year and MGM's biggest hit.

Poltergeist is an exemplary instance of what Robin Wood would call an incoherent text. On the one hand, the movie concerns a childhood fear of separation and an adult fear of loss, most apparent in the vanished Carole Anne's plaintive cries: "Mommy, help me, please!" Birth imagery is apparent as when Carole Anne and her mother emerge together, covered with blood and goo, from the supernatural void.

A current of submerged female sexuality runs through the movie. Not only is Diane "raped" and levitated by the spirits, her sexual history haunts the film in the person of the family's teenage daughter Dana, who is nearly a decade older than her siblings. Dana is not harassed by ghosts but rather, in a scene meant to be comic, by the uncouth workers who, in order to build a swimming pool, are excavating the family's backyard. Diane's age is given as thirty-two, which suggests that she herself was a teenager when she gave birth to the daughter she apparently named for herself.

On the other hand, *Poltergeist* appears to have something to do with American history—or rather, a-history. As the Western faded, so did the flurry of historically minded movies released in time for and in the years following the Bicentennial. Movies would traffic in nostalgia or, as in the case of *Poltergeist*, myth. Thus, the titular ghosts are the result of rapacious capitalism. The suburb is built on a desecrated graveyard (headstones removed but not bodies), and it plans to expand by relocating another cemetery. As the developer's star salesman, Steven is the first to have his household haunted—first by ghosts and then, in the ludicrous finale, by the army of corpses erupting out of the unfinished swimming pool.

Spielberg, of course, had his own interpretation. *Poltergeist*, he told *Time*, would be his "revenge on TV." In what sense? Although television is most closely associated with Carole Anne, the only member of the family to receive actual messages as well as the movie's poster child, the Freelings are inundated with cathode rays. The household has at least three TVs, one of which can be manipulated by the neighbor's remote control—and monitors proliferate once a crew of scientists arrive and place the entire house under video surveillance.

Was the movie meant to be a critique of the medium? Was television our national "noisy ghost"? The repository of collective memory? A force of nature? The omnipresent tube is the first thing one sees. It is also the last when, his family forced to leave their home for a Holiday Inn, Steven evicts the room's television. (A final image, cut from the film, had the displaced set rolling off on its own.) Monday, June 27, President and Mrs. Reagan hosted a White House screening of *E.T.* for guests who included the new Supreme Court justice Sandra Day O'Connor, several astronauts, and Steven Spielberg himself.

The president's post-screening comments would become legendary among UFOlogists for suggesting that Reagan had taken the opportunity to express his own belief that extraterrestrials had visited Earth. "Nancy Reagan was crying towards the end," according to Spielberg. "And the president looked like a ten-year-old kid."

Then, as the filmmaker recalled decades later, Reagan stood up and after thanking him for the film, remarked, "'There are a number of people in this room who know that everything on that screen is absolutely true.' . . . The whole room laughed because he presented it like a joke, but he wasn't smiling as he said it." (The next morning, Reagan was briefed on the U.S. Space Program.)

If *Poltergeist* was the return and reburial of the historical repressed, *E.T.* was something else. The fallen paradise of suburban America was redeemed by an innocent savior from outer space. In both, the Implacable Alien Other was dispelled.

The Whatsit of the Year: *E.T.* or *Blade Runner*?

The summer of 1982 saw the worst recession since the end of World War II. Unemployment hovered around 10 percent. Spring had brought a record number of foreclosed mortgages. Now there were two million homeless, and cars with Michigan plates were pouring into Texas. That summer, Congress would pass and the president would sign the largest tax increase in American history, raising nearly $100 billion in taxes and restoring a third of the reductions Reagan had achieved the previous year.

British prime minister Margaret Thatcher had invaded the Falkland Islands; Israeli prime minister Menachem Begin occupied southern Lebanon; and for the first time in twenty years, the U.S. administration was thinking about the unthinkable, floating scenarios for a winnable nuclear exchange. The *New Yorker*'s "Talk of the Town" waxed grim: "The first thing that people want to know when they turn on the news is [if] World War III has started." Armageddon angst was echoed in the nationwide poison scare kicked off by *Time*'s cover story, "Today's Scarlet Letter: Herpes," which appeared midsummer around the time that the term "AIDS" (acquired immune deficiency syndrome) was first used to describe what was imagined to be a "gay plague," and amplified with the serial Tylenol murders that began in the Chicago area that September.

Cosmic portents were everywhere. All spring, according to the hypervigilant psychohistorian Lloyd deMause, "images of the rebirth group-fantasy [had] multiplied in the media. . . . Discussions of abortion multiplied. . . . A new 'baby boom' was proclaimed." And now, a savior was at hand. For kids and Hollywood alike, 1982 would be the summer of *E.T.: The Extra-Terrestrial*, in which a lonely suburban kid named Elliott discovers and befriends a stranded visitor from outer space—the cutest alien life-form to visit earth, in no sense the Implacable Alien Other.

Reporting from the Cannes Film Festival, where *E.T.* had its world premiere as the festival's closing attraction in May, the *Daily News* critic Rex Reed wrote that Spielberg "showed the Godards and the Antonionis and the Fassbinders who had bored everyone into a state of catatonia for the past two weeks how real movies are made." Real movies, indeed: Was any film ever more protective of its fantasy? When some neighborhood wise guy wonders why the alien doesn't just "beam up" to his ship, Elliott snaps back that, "This is reality, not a movie!"

Some weeks after Cannes, *E.T.* opened at a thousand or so American theaters on June 11, one day before the massive—and, in its unexpected popularity, equally mysterious—Nuclear Freeze rally in New York's Central Park that, with crowds estimated upward of six hundred thousand, some thought the largest demonstration in the city's history. Although its initial weekend gross was weaker than either of the current summer hits, *Star Trek II* or *Rocky III*, *E.T.* did astonishing midweek business and, in unprecedented fashion, went on to top its first week's box office for the next four consecutive weeks. Thanks to *E.T.*, 1982 would become Hollywood's record year to date—only two weeks into 1983, Spielberg's film would surpass *Star Wars* as the highest-grossing movie in American history.

Made for a moderate $10.6 million, *E.T.* returned some $228 million to Universal from the U.S. and Canada alone. Although *E.T.* did not match the sensational 100:1 return of the late-1960s sleepers *Easy Rider* or *Night of the Living Dead*, it left its own mark on Hollywood's forehead. As thousands, perhaps tens of thousands of American children were enrolled in dance school in the wake of Shirley Temple, so every Hollywood movie might now aspire to *E.T.*'s achievement: universal appeal, repeat viewings, ancillary merchandise.

Six weeks into *E.T.*'s run, there were licensing deals with forty-three separate firms—each item Spielberg-approved. The E.T. not only graced T-shirts, trading cards, and lunch boxes but also children's shoes and female undergarments. The alien-hawked bicycles and Speak & Spells. He (for so the E.T. seemed gendered) was not only embodied in stuffed plastic and wind-up metal but gold pendants. The sales of Reese's Pieces, the candy that Elliott uses to lure the space creature out of hiding, tripled. *E.T.* spoke with the authority of brand names: Coke, Raid, Fritos, Coors. (As late as November 1988, Pepsi was happy to spend $25 million on a home-video tie-in.)

Spielberg too was now a brand-name bard who sang the song of American normalcy: "I had wanted to explore what it was like growing up in suburbia because I grew up in suburbia," he explained. (No buried bloody past or revenge on television here.) "Falling asleep in your lounge chair with a glass of lemonade by your pool [is] not as exciting as being mugged near the corner drugstore à la *Taxi Driver*," he allowed. "But I've always found it, in my own way, very engaging."

In *E.T.*, as Pauline Kael pointed out in a generally favorable review, "suburban living, with its comfortable, uniform houses, is seen as a child's paradise—an environment in which children are protected and their imaginations can flourish." European fairy tales typically concern the youngest sibling and sometimes the oldest—Elliott's position in his family helps make *E.T.* an American fantasy. The suburban middle child is emblematic of the suburban middle class. *E.T.* defines the joy of life as childhood, TV, and candy. The toy closet is the peaceable kingdom; the home is the temple of consumption.

There is no work, no social conflict, no racial difference, no sense of the past. The one unavoidable serpent in the garden is disintegration of the nuclear family—the real drama seems to be that Elliott's father has abandoned his wife and gone to Mexico with a girlfriend. Elliott misses him ("Dad would believe me"); of the three kids, he's most bereaved. Structurally, the extraterrestrial is Elliott's missing father, in some respects an ideal Dad—at least he phones home.

In some ways, *E.T.* is a very liberal movie. Just as the spaced-out ex-hippie on the TV sitcom *Taxi* (ABC/NBC, 1978–83) took to wearing an "E.T. Lives" button, so the conservative pundit George F. Will took issue with the most popular movie of all time, belligerently titling his July 19, 1982, *Newsweek* column "Well, I Don't Love You, E.T." The movie, which he saw with his young son, seemed to advance three subversive ideas: "Children are people. Adults are not. Science is sinister." When *E.T.* equates school with the murder of frogs, the movie idealizes feeling over reason. The E.T. itself associates emotion with tolerance, empathy, and acceptance. The kids must protect it from the world of adult males—outsized, half-glimpsed oppressors who aggressively beat the bush and ultimately invade the house as sinister spacemen.

Spielberg, Will suggested, "should be reminded of the charge that got Socrates condemned to drink hemlock: corrupting the youth of Athens." (In this case, Elliott told his annoying older brother to "shut-up, penis breath.") Stricken by a mysterious illness, E.T. is on the verge of death, Will wrote, just as "a horde of scary scientists" invade Elliott's house:

> Throughout the movie, they have been hunting the little critter, electronically eavesdropping on the house and generally acting like Watergate understudies. They pounce upon E.T. with all the whirring, pulsing, blinking paraphernalia of modern medicine. He dies anyway, then is inexplicably resurrected.

Will, who didn't see this as a triumph for religious faith, joked that his criticism of *E.T.* was "illiberal and—even more unforgivable—ethnocentric." But actually, *E.T.* is liberal mainly with its own complacent stereotypes. The movie is a remarkable domestication of the Other. Spielberg called his suburbanization of wonder "a broad-based story about an ugly duckling who didn't belong, someone who wasn't like everybody else . . . a minority story."

Is that little E.T. more advanced or more primitive than us? Certainly, its evolved state poses no threat; it's so simple that our children intuitively understand him. In some ways he's a wise yet modest Third World native, like Yoda in *Star Wars*. In Japan, where the E.T. was dubbed "our little friend from space," the alien became a corporate icon for the national telephone and telegraph company—perhaps a sentimentalized vision of the Japanese businessman abroad. More hysterically, author Shintaro Ishihara's 1989 diatribe *The*

Japan That Can Say No would rail against his countrymen as a brainy but helpless "Nation of E.T.'s."

Like any true star, the E.T. reconciles contradictions. He is a fount of patriarchal wisdom (joining forces, when necessary, with TV) but also a helpless orphan. He's powerful yet vulnerable, androgynous yet coded as male. The E.T. is a godling, at once father and son—a symbiotic relationship suggested in the grotesque death scene with the poor creature and Elliott "in bed" together connected by extravagant sci-fi tubing. Kael observed that "E.T. isn't just Elliott's friend; he's also Elliott's pet." And, of course, it's in Elliott's room that the E.T. takes his place among the toys—the best toy a child ever had.

The end of *E.T.* is a classic example of what Roland Barthes calls "Neither-Norism"—a situation wherein alternatives are dismissed because it is "embarrassing to choose between them." If *E.T.* is a movie meant to reconcile the generations, it can neither endorse dominant norms nor offer another possibility to them. The E.T. neither instructs Elliott to listen to his parents, nor encourages him to rebel. There is neither the acceptance of the adult world nor the promise that, inspired by the E.T., Elliott will be able to remake its terrors.

Toward the end of *E.T.* summer, President Reagan was given a utopian notion by the so-called father of the H-bomb, Edward Teller. "Dr. Teller came in," the president noted in his September 14 diary entry. "He's pushing an exciting idea that nuclear weapons can be used in connection with Lasers to be non-destructive except as used to intercept and destroy enemy missiles far above the earth."

Uncanny toys and mysterious Otherness also figured in *Blade Runner* which, directed by Ridley Scott from the Philip K. Dick novel *Do Androids Dream of Electric Sheep?*, opened two weekends post *E.T.*

E.T. brought together the two master tropes of 1980s Hollywood—the narcissistic fantasy of the stranger in (our) paradise and the joyful recuperation of the authoritarian Fifties—presenting them in such a way as to restore universal faith in smoke and mirrors. A competing fantasy for the Age of Reagan, *Blade Runner* was everything that *E.T.* was not. Where *E.T.* was set in an idyllic all-white suburb, *Blade Runner* invented a horrific multicultural inner city.

Both movies, however, eschewed the Implacable Alien Other of the Fifties. While *E.T.* resurrected Jesus Christ in the form of a lovable alien, *Blade Runner* featured robot "replicants" more soulful in their mortality than the Homo sapiens, like Harrison Ford, who hunted them.

While *E.T.* proved the most universal movie ever made, Scott's $30 million bomb was relegated to the midnight circuit almost immediately. (Indeed, *E.T.* made Reese's Pieces while *Premiere* magazine once humorously listed the corporations that vanished after being plugged in *Blade Runner*: Atari, Bell Telephone, Cuisinart . . .) Reviews were generally negative. "All visuals and no story," David Denby complained in *New York*, calling it the summa of a "hundred naïvely bad experimental films." Denby's verdict ("terribly dull") was mild compared to that of his colleagues. "*Blade Runner* has nothing to give the audience," declared Pauline Kael, while Michael Sragow concluded his *Rolling Stone* pan by declaring *Blade Runner* a movie "best suited for zombies" and, writing in the *Boston Phoenix*, Stephen Schiff condemned *Blade Runner* to a moral gulag as "a film without sense . . . a film without soul, without conscience."

One of *Blade Runner*'s few critical supporters was the conservative *Commentary* critic Richard Grenier who, like George Will, didn't much care for *E.T.* (Of Spielberg's film he wrote that "the trick, if one wants to make a film showing American society as brutal and aggressive, is to concoct a story without the faintest hint of an adversary, revealing a tranquil, peaceful universe in which we, only we, disturb the loving order of nature.") For Grenier, *Blade Runner* was "by far the best and most interesting of this year's big summer movies," at once a technically bravura "nightmare vision of what our society would become if it were overrun by what we call the Third World" and a film about the human condition that ends "with a startling burst of Christian symbolism."

E.T. was the ultimate middlebrow cult film, *Blade Runner* outflanked it at both ends of the spectrum. At once a touchstone for the cable station MTV, which had been launched the previous summer, an avatar of cyberpunk, an F/X head trip, and an object of academic discourse, praised in fan magazines like *Starlog* and parsed in serious journals like *Camera Obscura*, *Blade Runner* spent a decade proselytizing itself on video and in classrooms.

Blade Runner was hated for the very things that give it grandeur. Visual rather than literary, blatantly post-authorial, the movie was a ready-made metaphor, a treasure trove of vulgar postmodernism that seems to have escaped human control and thrived on disjuncture. In an essay on cult films, the semiotician Umberto Eco declares that *Casablanca* is not a movie but the movies—it transcends personal artistry or even human intent; the clichés themselves are "having a conversation." The same reading can be applied to *Blade Runner*—a glittering mishmash of *Frankenstein* and *The Big Sleep*, *Metropolis* and *Love Story*, Josef von Sternberg and George Lucas.*

As splendid as the assemblage of *Blade Runner*'s sources is its look—a fantastic amalgam of locations, back lots (including Warner Bros.'s old New York set), and miniatures. Although this futuristic vision of acid rain and eternal night, where advertising is the landscape and hovercrafts zip past the animated billboards as punks slurp ramen in the Casbah below, owes little to Philip K. Dick, it does anticipate William Gibson ("Night City was like a deranged experiment in social Darwinism, designed by a bored researcher who kept his thumb permanently on the fast-forward button," to quote a passage from his 1984 novel *Neuromancer*), not to mention the hallucinatory inner city of Frederic Jameson's "Hysterical Sublime," in which the decay of urban life produces its own heightened exhilaration.

The inspiration must be Hong Kong, although Scott told one visitor to his set that he was "constantly waving [a reproduction of Edward Hopper's painting *Nighthawks*] under the noses of the production team to illustrate the look and mood I was after." *Blade Runner* has come to seem the quintessential Los Angeles film. The 1988 report *L.A. 2000: A City for the Future* specifically invokes the "*Blade Runner* scenario" as "the fusion of individual cultures into a demotic polyglotism ominous with unresolved hostilities." For the film theorist Peter Wollen, the opening shots seem modeled on a "view across the flatlands from San Pedro, a city in which 'white flight' has left a ramshackle downtown to a throng of Third World immigrants and intellectual

---

* Like Orson Welles's *Touch of Evil*, *Blade Runner* would be a film without a fixed version, ultimately existing in several director's cuts, the 1982 release version with Harrison Ford's hard-boiled voiceover and a tacked-on "happy ending" (which recycled aerial outtakes from *The Shining*), and the cut shown to preview audiences (with disastrous results) that concluded with a melancholy reminder that Ford's replicant love (Sean Young) is fast heading for a preprogrammed obsolescence. The old phony ending was hardly inappropriate. After all, it features a secondhand image used to construct a pseudo-escape—precisely the sort of simulation that *Blade Runner* is all about.

misfits, presided over by a single giant high-security corporate headquarters, while the middle class has fled to 'off-world,' a kind of interplanetary Simi Valley"—indeed, as he was writing in 1991, Wollen likely knew was the very home of the Reagan Library.

The *Blade Runner* dystopia is hardly novel—a sinister corporate oligarchy responsible for making Earth a squalid ecological nightmare, its population pacified by image-induced dreams of consumption. As in *Metropolis*, capital transforms labor into machines. But here, where every desire is reproduced and amplified in an endless chain of simulation, there's a continual dialogue between human and replicant, nature and culture. The human protagonists are all defined by their relation to the replicants. Are the replicants people who are treated as objects or are they objects who have somehow become human? (The snapshots they use to document their simulated memories suggest the universal past of *American Graffiti*.)

As the lacquered replicant of a noir heroine, Sean Young's Rachael is a multiple simulation. (She's the ultimate android in that she has no awareness of being anything other than human—her implanted memories are identical to actual experience.) In the movie's most discomforting scene, the Ford character—who knows what she is—compels her to love him, prompting her response step by step. Does he feel so free to dominate her because she's female or because she's a machine? Is teaching a machine to love you a form of masturbation?

The replicants are products of human vanity—but with a difference. They bear the burden of existential angst and romantic rebellion. Thus, lead replicant Roy Batty (Rutger Hauer) wrests the movie away from its nominal hero, and the slogan of the Tyrell Corporation, which manufactures the replicants, turns out to be true: these artificial creatures are "more human than human." Predicated on the pathos of machines who know they are programmed to shut down, *Blade Runner* suggests that, far from a state of grace, humanity is barely a state of mind—something perhaps that a sympathetic Alien Other is best suited to understand.

Time's year-end issue devoted a special section to Spielberg's movie: "*E.T.* emerged from a sweet communal dream: of fellowship, loyalty, ordinary heroism, unfettered fun. He is every child's secret best friend, every adult's reverie of the innocence that once was, once upon our time. He is also a magical money machine."

Indeed, *Time*'s "Man of the Year" was a machine—not E.T. but the home computer, pondered on the cover by a humanoid George Segal plaster sculpture.

Drawing *First Blood*

Seven years after it ended, the Vietnam War continued to play out where the battle had originally been fought for the hearts and minds of the American viewing public . . . on television. Midway through the summer of 1982, ABC telecast *Vietnam Requiem*, an hourlong documentary—originally titled *VIPs: Vets in Prison*—that profiled five decorated veterans, all of whom were incarcerated for committing violent crimes.

Staring directly into the camera, these still-young men discussed their wartime experiences. Each had suffered the traumatic death of a buddy. "You're eighteen years old and you're wearing somebody's brains around your shirt because they got their head blown off right next to you, and that's not supposed to affect you?" one asked. Some recalled taking revenge on innocent Vietnamese; others turned the violence inward. Reviewing *Vietnam Requiem* in the *New York Times*, John J. O'Connor pointed out that World War II veterans had also been afflicted by what was now called "post-traumatic stress disorder" and noted that, "The great majority of the veterans who saw combat in Vietnam have never been arrested." Was society really responsible? *Vietnam Requiem* raised the specter of collective guilt. The show effected a disturbing displacement: the war itself, not a bungled armed robbery, was the crime.*

But that was old news. The TV cop shows that embodied the mood of Richard Nixon's foreshortened second term—an irate, self-lacerating confusion compounding an enraged sense of loss, a general exhaustion, and an overall longing for order that included the sacrifice of Nixon himself on the altar of public opinion—had long featured psychotic or shell-shocked veterans

---

* *Vietnam Requiem* would subsequently inspire and provide material for the British musician Paul Hardcastle's hit single "19," an early use of sampled and synthesized speech, much of which was drawn from the documentary. Although the single was number one on the British charts for five weeks and received the Ivor Novello award for the best-selling single of 1985, the U.S. reception was negligible.

while, with few exceptions, movies were less interested in battlefield heroics than in the nightmarish situation of returning warriors. The crazy Viet-vet was a cultural cliché, alternately shown as a guilty society's violent redeemer or as its victimized scapegoat or, sometimes, as in the case of Travis Bickle, an ambiguous combination of the two.*

Firefox was in 1,300 theaters and ABC broadcast *Vietnam Requiem* at the very moment that the struggle over a Vietnam memorial on the Washington mall came to a head. Yale student Maya Lin's submerged, V-shaped black marble wall—to be inscribed with the names of the 58,000 American casualties—was selected in May 1981 by a design commission underwritten by the Texas data-processing billionaire and future presidential candidate H. Ross Perot.†

Lin's design was another battle in the postwar war. During a televised Commission of Fine Arts hearing in late 1981, Tom Carhart, a Pentagon civil lawyer and Vietnam veteran, called the proposal a "black gash of shame and sorrow" and complained that "in a city of soaring white monuments, we get a black ditch in the ground." Other critics piled on. The monument was a "degrading ditch," an "open urinal," a "black spot in American history," a "tombstone," a "slap in the face," a "wailing wall for the draft dodgers and New Lefters of the future." The Marine Corps withdrew its support, referring

---

* One of the few positive Viet-vets was the hero of the TV show *Magnum, P.I.* (CBS, 1980–88), a former Navy SEAL played by Tom Selleck, who turned down the world-historical role of Indiana Jones because of a commitment to the show. A world-historical figure in his own right, Thomas Magnum was a Hawaii-based private eye whose sleuthing activities were regularly interrupted by flashbacks to his tour of Vietnam. Praising *Magnum* in the October 19, 1982, issue of the *Village Voice*, TV critic Tom Carson called it "the first action show with a sense of history": Its "schizoid Vietnam (the obscene nightmare doubling as macho proving ground . . .) suggests how illogic can have its own accuracy." The show enjoyed its highest ratings in the 1982–83 and 1983–84 seasons, finishing number three and number six, respectively.

† Perot was the founder of the organization United We Stand. In May 1970, shortly before the invasion of Cambodia, he organized a POW/MIA multimedia extravaganza at Philadelphia's Constitution Hall. As described by H. Bruce Franklin in *M.I.A., or, Mythmaking in America*, the show served to transform "America's vision of the war."

> The actual photographs and TV footage of massacred villagers, napalmed children, Vietnamese prisoners being tortured and murdered, wounded GIs screaming in agony, and body bags being loaded for shipment back home were being replaced by simulated images of American POWs in the savage hands of Asian Communists.

to the memorial as "a tribute to Jane Fonda," an epithet picked up by Tom Wolfe who reported on the controversy, which also served to support his disdain for the art-world "mullahs" with their close-minded devotion to Bauhaus architecture.

The V-shape was variously interpreted as standing for Vietnam, victim, victory, veteran, violate, and valor, while reference to the black marble was so vitriolic that at a late 1982 meeting, General George Price, one of the army's highest-ranking African American officers, felt obligated to ask people to "please stop referring to black as the color of shame."

Visitors to the not-yet-opened memorial were already jumping the gun when another sort of Vietnam monument materialized. The war's restless ghost, its *poltergeist*, had been given human form: John Rambo, the muscle-bound lump of grievance embodied by Sylvester Stallone in *First Blood*, directed by Ted Kotcheff and adapted by Michael Kozoll and the veteran TV producer William Sackheim, with Stallone's input, from the novel by David Morrell.

The surprise hit of late 1982, as well as Stallone's first commercial hit outside of the *Rocky* cycle, *First Blood* opened on October 22, edging *E.T.* from its spot atop *Variety*'s weekly grosses chart. It held its number-one position for the next week as well when, with unemployment over 10 percent and America's trade deficit at a new high, the Republicans lost twenty-six seats in the House of Representatives, while maintaining control of the Senate, and Jane Fonda's husband, the SDS rabble-rouser Tom Hayden, was elected to the California State Assembly. (In vain, the president had urged Americans to "vote your hopes, not your fears.")*

Morrell's novel, published in the late spring of 1972 and quickly optioned by Warner Bros., spent nearly a decade on the studio's shelf, awaiting its moment. "It is not strange that this fine novel should be released at a time when newspapers and magazines are reporting stories of returning veterans

---

* Reagan campaigned against the growing grassroots movement for a nuclear freeze, asserting that it was not led by "sincere and honest people who want peace but by some who want the weakening of America." Citing a *Reader's Digest* report titled "The K.G.B.'s Magical War for Peace" as evidence, the president charged that the movement was instigated and supported by "foreign agents." (The piece itself drew on articles by John Rees, a discredited police informant who, some fifteen years before, had furnished then governor Reagan with reports on Berkeley activists.)

whose wartime expertise has altered the whole concept of civilian violence,"
the *New York Times* review ended. *First Blood* "contains its warning: When
Johnny comes marching home this time, watch out." (What goes around
comes around. The review ran on June 18, 1972, the day after the Watergate
break-in.)

The conflict between hard-assed cop, sheriff Will Teasle (Brian Dennehy),
and crazy Viet-vet, John Rambo (Sylvester Stallone), was overt in *First Blood*,
which made a few changes in Morrell's conception. The location was switched
from rural Kentucky to the Pacific Northwest, transposed from a Southern
border state to America's last frontier. Teasle's Korean War experience was
downplayed, and—most importantly—Rambo survived the carnage he precipitated. (In the novel, Rambo is a Frankenstein monster who kills the entire
posse that chases him up into the hills, returns to burn down Main Street, and
is finally terminated by the very Green Beret officer who trained him.)

Few critics liked the movie or recognized its originality. *Variety* thought
it "really pretty awful." Writing in the *New York Post*, Rex Reed called *First
Blood* "an experience so thoroughly nasty, you might not be able to sit through
it without retching." The figure of the crazed Viet-vet struck Roger Ebert as
a cliché; he further pointed out that the notion of countercultural guerillas
wiping out naive National Guardsmen had already been anticipated in 1980
by Walter Hill's more artful *Southern Comfort*. (David Giler, who wrote
Southern Comfort, contributed uncredited revisions to *First Blood*.)*

First Blood turned the assumptions of the returning vet films inside out.
Dressed in an ambiguous uniform of mixed patriotic and countercultural signifiers, Rambo is first seen visiting a poor black family—that of one of his
former "teammates"—only to discover that his buddy died of "the cancer
brought back from Nam," a result of the chemical defoliant, Agent Orange.
From the beginning, the movie stores up rage. The former Green Beret is
treated like a dirty hippie, told to get a bath, relentlessly persecuted by a
crypto-redneck sheriff.

Teasle might have been the hero of a dozen cop shows, the sort of tough

---

* Not unlike Rambo, the Nietzschean Viet-vet played by Nick Nolte in *Who'll Stop the
Rain* demonstrates a Vietcong guerrilla's capacity to confound the corrupt authority figures assigned to bring him in; the protagonist's inhospitable town is comparable to the one
on which crypto Viet-vet Clint Eastwood wreaked vengeance in the 1973 Western *High
Plains Drifter*.

guy many Americans would want to protect their neighborhood. Spotting Rambo, he's quick to note the stranger's flagrant "crime," namely the juxta-position of his long hippie hair and the American flag on his jacket: "We don't want guys like you in this town." After escorting Rambo to the city limits, he offers some paternal advice. Get a haircut and take a bath, followed by the classic American kiss-off "Have a nice day."

In many respects, *First Blood* is extremely antiauthoritarian. Teasle, in-troduced with a screen-filling close-up of the Stars and Stripes, personifies law and order, but considering how sweet and harmless Rambo has been seen to be, the sheriff is also a grotesque bully. Rambo himself is a very fluid char-acter. Simultaneously or in rapid succession, he can be read as a grunt, a hippie, an Indian, an anti-American guerrilla fighter (which is to say a Viet-cong), and a war hero, what his mentor, Colonel Trautman (Richard Crenna), calls "the last of an elite group." The Canadian-born Kotcheff, a self-identified leftist, maintained that "Rambo's treatment by the redneck sheriff and his deputies was a microcosm of the way America had treated their re-turning veterans."*

This incendiary plea for tolerance was designed to appeal to both hawks and doves. Rambo's violence is totally justifiable—not just at home but, ret-roactively, in Vietnam. As co-producer Andrew Vajna explained: "We tried a new approach. We made the protagonist a hero instead of a psychological killer." Only after the initially sympathetic Rambo has been driven to go King Kong is it revealed that he is not simply an ex–Green Beret but a Congres-sional Medal of Honor winner.

Formerly licensed to kill, Rambo has been persecuted by the society he once protected. *First Blood* brings the war home, complete with firefights, as-sault rifles, and jungle-style guerrilla warfare. Even the media is on hand to offer bogus assurances of public safety. The troops start losing their morale. The national guardsmen won't obey their commanding officer. Trautman contemptuously cites the relative comfort of civilian life, and when Rambo remarks that "there are no friendly civilians," the notion cuts two ways. He's applying the lesson of Vietnam to the home front.

Rambo's humanity is continually being denied. The cops repeatedly

---

* *First Blood*'s third week as the nation's box-office champ coincided with the three-day celebration that marked the official opening of the Vietnam Veterans Memorial.

employ Dirty Harry's term for perpetrators by referring to him as an "animal." (Trautman more kindly terms him a "machine.") The cops are identified with the North Vietnamese as Rambo's enemies. Teasle is Nixonian. He embodies the law and takes his war with Rambo personally: "I wanted to kill that kid. I wanted to kill that kid so bad I could taste it," he tells Trautman.

Thus, *First Blood* articulated Viet-vet resentment while incorporating all manner of free-floating leftist critiques. Rambo's ambiguous mixture of left- and right-wing symbols anticipates the "Born in the U.S.A." Bruce Springsteen of 1984. A killer who is also a kind of reverse neutron bomb—destroying property rather than lives—Rambo manages to combine the humble, long-suffering attitude of the grunt with the expertise of the Green Beret.

Rambo is everything: super-grunt, Green Beret, hippie protester, VC guerrilla, righteous outlaw, Hollywood Freedom Fighter, total violence, the War itself. His taciturn nature facilitates audience projection up until the movie's final minutes. Face to face with Trautman, he explodes into language: "Nothing is over! Nothing! You don't just turn it off!" The war has not been resolved. *First Blood* may have redeemed the war as entertainment but Rambo has utter contempt for American society: "Civilian life is nothing!" At the same time, he disclaims any individual responsibility. "It wasn't my war! You asked me, I didn't ask you! And I did as I was told! And I come back to the world and see those maggots protesting me! Spitting! Calling me baby-killer and all that vile shit! Who are they to protest me?"*

Rambo establishes himself as the war's primary casualty—clinching the point with the story of a buddy blown up by a Vietnamese shoeshine boy. America wins and America loses and Rambo is unreconciled. When this victimized victor is hauled off to prison, it's for our sins. *First Blood* ends with a freeze-frame on Rambo's proud, paranoid look back at the camera—another signifier of hipness, identified with the French new wave, popularized in Hollywood by *Butch Cassidy and the Sundance Kid*.

---

* Jerry Lembcke's 1998 book *The Spitting Image* makes a convincing case that accounts of returning soldiers being spat upon by anti-war protesters are by and large an urban myth that began to gain currency after the war was over (and perhaps after *First Blood*). Although "there were actual acts of hostility toward GIs and veterans," he writes, "the fact that most of the documentable hostility emanated from pro-war groups and individuals is a detail that is often lost."

First Blood surely benefited for being released under the first American president to defend the rightness of the Vietnam War without the inconvenience
of having to wage it. "We're beginning to understand how much we were led
astray at that time," Ronald Reagan declared at the dedication of the monument. "We are just beginning to appreciate that [our troops] were fighting
for a just cause." Trautman is the part that might have been played by
Reagan.

There's nothing to suggest that the president screened *First Blood*. In late
November he was given a preview of Clint Eastwood's *Honkytonk Man* at
Camp David, noting in his diary that the Eastwood character "dies of T.B.
in the end" and that the movie seemed unsuitable for Nancy, whose step-
father had recently passed away. Reagan spent the following weekend at his
Santa Barbara ranch and there met personally with Eastwood, who had flown
down from his Shasta ranch. The filmmaker, Reagan would note in his diary
entry for November 28, arrived "with a man named Gordon Wilson who is
part of a small group trying to get P.O.W.'s out of Laos. Clint has contributed
to this. I'm checking the group out with [national security advisor] Bill
Clark—right now it looks a little questionable."*

Wilson was the "executive officer" of a group led by retired Special Forces
colonel James ("Bo") Gritz, who had taken it upon himself to produce a raid
into Laos to rescue the imagined POWs. Gritz was already the inspiration
for a character on the soon to premiere action-adventure series *The A-Team*
(NBC, 1983–87), best remembered for showcasing Mr. T, a former professional wrestler. William Shatner, captain of the Starship *Enterprise*, most
recently in *Star Trek II: The Wrath of Khan*, had contributed $10,000 in re-
turn for the Gritz caper's movie rights. The scenario, which Gritz dubbed Operation Lazarus, had a generic resemblance to John Ford's Korean War
Western *Rio Grande*. Eastwood, a pal who had given Gritz another $30,000—
or more—was dispatched to brief his other friend, the president.

The idea was that once Gritz and his men crossed the Mekong into Laos
and freed the POWs, he would transmit the news to their base in Thailand,
which would alert Los Angeles and then, via Eastwood, Reagan who would

---

* Whether or not the Reagan administration was funding a clandestine search for POWs,
as was suggested by Gritz's subsequent testimony before a House subcommittee in
March 1983, the president was familiar with such an operation, having himself gone undercover as a POW in *Prisoner of War*.

dispatch American forces to complete the rescue. The script, however, did not go according to plan. To keep with Eastwood's schedule, the Gritz team forded the Mekong before they were fully armed and, upon entering Laos, were ambushed by a rival anti-Communist Laotian group. Retreating to Thailand, Gritz found Wilson's message: "CLINT AND I MET THE PRESIDENT ON THE 27TH. PRESIDENT SAID: QUOTE, IF YOU BRING OUT ONE US POW, I WILL START WORLD WAR III TO GET THE REST OUT, UNQUOTE."

But even if there were no POWs to bring out, a movie was already in the works. In early December, *First Blood* again dethroned *E.T.* as the nation's top-grossing movie and in late January 1983, Paramount handed Kotcheff a POW rescue script, eventually known as *Uncommon Valor*, by neophyte screenwriter Joe Gayton, which would be revised throughout the winter and spring. Meanwhile, at a meeting of the National League of Families of American Prisoners and Missing in Southeast Asia, Reagan promised that the "intelligence assets of the United States [were] fully focused" on their issue and, pressured by growing public awareness, "the government bureaucracy" would now be compelled to give it the "highest national priority."*

Three days later, even as the *New York Times* broke the story of Gritz's raid, the colonel was engaged in a sequel. "We are the gladiators—not the arm-chair critics, bureaucrats, politicians and pot-bellied has-beens," Gritz wrote in a twelve-page handwritten letter brought by courier from Laos. "There may be better than us—but where are they?" Within the year, he would see them on the screen.

---

* According to H. Bruce Franklin, *Uncommon Valor* drew heavily on *Mission M.I.A.*, the best-selling novel by J. C. Pollock, which Franklin characterizes as "a rabidly racist and militarist tract explicitly designed to incite popular demand for mercenary raids to rescue American POWs allegedly still being brutalized by demonic Asian Communists." The writing of *Mission M.I.A.* coincides with the organization of Gritz's Operation Lazarus. The novel was excerpted in the same March 1982 issue of *Penthouse* magazine that published an interview with Gritz, a perennial figure in "white power" and Christian Identity politics; ten years later he would run for president as the candidate of the Populist Party.

IV

"I AIN'T AFRAID OF NO GHOST!," 1983–84

First Blood was a manifestation of the nation's unresolved Vietnam trauma; *E.T.* had intimations of post-Watergate disillusionment. Both were rooted in an earlier political zeitgeist.

Perhaps the Eighties became the Eighties on January 2, 1983, when, chanting (while denying) "I am the One," the era's greatest pop star Michael Jackson released the second cut from *Thriller,* soon to become the top-selling LP of all time—an infectiously urgent song that would be his best-selling solo single, "Billie Jean."

Or perhaps, from another perspective, it was on January 8, when President Reagan lifted the Carter administration's "human rights" ban on military aid to repressive Guatemala, announcing, in effect, that We are (still) the One. Or maybe, later that month when, normalizing the business and sexual shenanigans of a plutocratic oil family, the glitzy primetime soap opera *Dynasty* first entered the television Top Ten: They are the One.*

Intimations of a new era were evident in a February 15 *New York Times* story acknowledging that where the president's aides had once been "visibly alarmed at suggestions that he had given mangled and perhaps misleading accounts of his policies or current events in general," they no longer seemed to be so: Reagan "continues to make debatable assertions of fact, but news accounts do not deal with them as extensively as they once did. In the view

---

* Conceived in the late 1970s, the show—like Ronald Reagan—was a repudiation of Jimmy Carter's perceived holier-than-thou lack of pretention and ostentatious austerity, as well as cultural New Age-ism and political protest. Its co-creator Esther Shapiro said as much when she told the *New York Times* that while she "wore granny dresses in the 1960s, baked bread, marched and made speeches," toward the end of the Carter presidency, she "felt like dressing up again."

of White House officials, the declining news coverage mirrors a decline in interest by the general public."

The article went on to detail a number of recent Reagan misstatements in policy matters ranging from budget cuts to increased spending to the state of social security, ending with a quote from unnamed officials that, far from obfuscating or misleading the public with these half-truths or falsehoods, the president was "simply trying to make a larger point." This capacity to misrepresent the facts without consequence would soon be known as Reagan's magical "Teflon" factor.*

But Teflon suggested something more. "The Carter Administration lives in the world of make-believe," candidate Reagan had declared in accepting the Republican Party nomination. "The rest of us, however, live in the real world." That so-called real world was now his.[†]

As the president began to master the Department of Amusement, February 1983 brought the first Eighties critiques of Eighties culture. David Cronenberg's *Videodrome* and Martin Scorsese's *The King of Comedy*, two downbeat fables that—perhaps pondering the mystery of Ronald Reagan, as

---

* The phrase appears to have been coined by Colorado representative Pat Schroeder who, in remarks delivered to the House of Representatives on August 2, 1983, credited Reagan with a "breakthrough in political technology—he has been perfecting the Teflon-coated presidency. He sees to it that nothing sticks to him. He is responsible for nothing—civil rights, Central America, the Middle East, the economy, the environment. He is just the master of ceremonies at someone else's dinner."

† Writing in *Artforum* in the aftermath of the 1984 election, Greil Marcus noted that, ever since Michael Jackson's 1984 so-called Victory tour, "performer after performer has been brought-forth-to-come-forth as a unitary, momentarily complete symbol of individual fulfillment and public conquest. As Jackson was replaced by Prince, Prince was replaced by Madonna, who has been replaced by Springsteen."

> At a given moment their faces appear on every magazine cover . . . Every single and LP, every tour, sets "records," generates "unprecedented" amounts of money. . . . It's no matter that much of this is pure hype; what counts is the result, and the result is a sort of consumer-fan panic, a *Konsumterror* (the phrase was Ulrike Meinhof's) that suspends one's very identity in the fear of missing out on what's happening, or what is said to be happening.

Marcus's unavoidable conclusion: "Just as, in the pop milieu, there is at any given time only one real star, in the United States, today there is only one real person: Ronald Reagan." (Even in 1984, no one could imagine that there might someday be an American president, Donald Trump, who was, in effect, individually addressed by an entire cable network, Fox News.

well as the impending arrival of George Orwell's dread 1984—dramatized the nature of celebrity in the context of mass-mediated reality.

Although released by major studios, neither movie was precisely a Hollywood job. Scorsese, however well-versed in Hollywood history, was a stalwart New Yorker; Cronenberg, a philosophically inclined avant-garde artist who took gross-out genre films as his medium, was a confirmed Canadian. Still, their films made Hollywood's traditional anti-TV argument linking the medium to demagoguery, mind control, and madness, as well as taking for granted the ideas advanced by the Canadian media theorist Marshall McLuhan—that television was a technology for altering consciousness. What distinguished *The King of Comedy* and *Videodrome* from earlier movies like *Network* or *A Face in the Crowd* or the independent quasi-documentary *Medium Cool* was the assumption that TV had prevailed.

"In postmodern culture, it's not TV as a mirror of society, but just the reverse: it's society as a mirror of television," Arthur Kroker, another Canadian McLuhanist, put it in *The Postmodern Scene*. He might have been describing *Videodrome*. The *Toronto Star* film critic Geoff Pevere wrote that Cronenberg's movie satirized "the apparent ease and acquiescence with which the masses, as represented by the dominant media, embraced the surge in communications technology that occurred in the mid '70s"—a surge that not only involved "developments in video, cable and satellite technology" but the universal cinematic blockbuster exemplified by *Star Wars*.

Successors to audience-driven Movie-Events like *Bonnie and Clyde*, *2001*, and *Taxi Driver*, blockbusters were the entertainment exemplars of a TV-driven Totality—or Global Village—that, having coalesced in the Sixties, was instrumental in codifying popular memory, consolidating public opinion, and creating a national identity based on shared material fantasy. For a brief moment, sometimes identified as "1968," it seemed as though that Global Village might abolish the distinction between Media makers and Media consumers. While a similar impulse animated the first stages of punk rock in the late 1970s, the gap had grown wider than ever. Such was *The King of Comedy*'s concern and *Videodrome*'s subject. Their protagonists strive to master or even become the Media; both men are deranged, albeit in different ways.

Max Renn (James Woods), the manager of a small, exploitation-minded television station, amusingly named Civic TV, is captivated by the rogue TV transmission called "Videodrome" that appears to deliver instances of actual torture and death. The malign spectacle appeals to his sadism as well as his commercial instincts, with the result that the transmission colonizes his mind and body. An avant-pop filmmaker with a Salvador Dalí–like taste for visual shock, Cronenberg gives Renn's hallucinations a gross physicality. Organs explode out of the TV set as he himself is transformed into a flesh-and-blood VCR.

The King of Comedy put a more recognizably human face on the Media. A thirty-four-year-old messenger still living at home, Rupert Pupkin (Robert De Niro) is a borderline psychotic driven to become a celebrity—crossing over from passive Media consumer to elite Media subject. Pupkin has no discernable talent other than a ferocious, unrelenting need for recognition. Although he has never performed for an audience, he has studied obsessively to be a talk show guest, planning to start his career on a TV program watched each night by half of America.

In part, the Pupkin pathology hyperbolizes the ambivalent relationship Americans have with the aristocracy of winners who, as presented on TV or paraded through the pages of *People* magazine, live their lives as performers in a public drama. Where do these celebrities come from? Are stars invented and imposed upon or are they chosen by the public? "Modern man deeply craves friendship, confidence, close personal relationships," Jacques Ellul notes in *Propaganda*.

> But he is plunged into a world of competition, hostility, and anonymity. He needs to meet someone whom he can trust completely, for whom he can feel pure friendship and to whom he can mean something in return. That is hard to find in his daily life, but apparently confidence in a leader, a hero, a movie star, or a TV personality is much more satisfying. . . . The hero becomes model and father, power and mythical realization of all that the individual cannot be.

The King of Comedy might have been written to dramatize Ellul's thoughts on the social use-value of celebrity. In *The King of Comedy* as on TV, famous people appear onscreen playing themselves—their presence a form of naturalism, like the brand-name products in a Spielberg movie. The most important is Jerry Lewis, as television talk-show host Jerry Langford.

Radiating celebrity, Lewis (the first star to hobnob with Reagan in the White House) carries his whole showbiz history into this film. Playing the first serious role of his career—which turns out to be his brusque and exasperated self—the star is an objet trouvé. The scenes where Pupkin and his date (De Niro's then wife, Diahnne Abbott) invade Langford's Long Island weekend house, or the one in which Pupkin's confederate, the high-strung and unpredictable Masha (Sandra Bernhard), holds Langford captive come close to documentary fiction.*

Langford unavoidably evokes Ronald Reagan, nearly killed by an assassin who imagined himself as Travis Bickle, but so does Rupert Pupkin—a mediocre comic who is brilliantly delusional. Nearly every scene in *The King of Comedy* starts as a potential fantasy; the movie ends with his fantasy realized. *Videodrome* is cooler, yet more bizarre. Here the Media is an impersonal—almost evolutionary—force. Humorously pushing McLuhanist ideas to their limit, Cronenberg suggests that television changed everything, even our brain functions and hence our understanding of the world: "Television is reality—and reality is less than television," says the movie's resident savant Professor Brian O'Blivion.

Videodrome proposes that it doesn't matter what you watch on TV, it's that you watch it. (Or, as in Orwell's *1984*, that it watches you.) O'Blivion is an oracle who communicates only through the tube and believes in television as therapy: "Watching TV will help patch them back into the world's mixing board." As a radical McLuhanist, Cronenberg has no problem recognizing the Media as the extension of man. *Videodrome* is most outrageous in suggesting that humans are merely the sex organs for the machine. Civic TV advertises itself as "the one you take to bed with you." Pop star Debbie Harry, a celebrity playing a celebrity, is aroused by the violent Videodrome signal; Renn is physically transformed by it.

---

* Lewis was genuinely angry during this sequence, and he wasn't alone. *The King of Comedy* made people uncomfortable. Pauline Kael concluded a highly unfavorable review by calling the movie "a training film for pests, and worse." As a journalist then writing a profile of Scorsese, I attended a number of early screenings, among them opening night at the 1983 Cannes Film Festival and a showing organized for the editors of the *New York Times Magazine*. The postmortem that followed was particularly irate. The movie was irresponsible—might it not inspire some kook to kidnap Johnny Carson? The starstruck crowd at Cannes, however, was nonplussed. Expecting to see a movie in which the most stylish and violent of American filmmakers directed the funniest man in the Gallic world, they got what amounted to a critique of their fandom—a comedy predicated on pain, need, and embarrassment.

Where *Videodrome* is a malignant hallucination, *The King of Comedy* aspires to a form of naturalism. (The words "king" and "comedy" evoke the rituals and public theater of ancient civilizations, suggesting a connection between patriarchal authority and entertainment—or the rules that govern the social spectacles.) Devoured by the Videodrome and literally remade by the Media, Renn is a victim who stands in for those that the leftist Pevere called the "masses." Pupkin, however, is a winner who imposes his personal fantasy on social reality to supplant his model, Jerry Langford, as the King of Comedy.*

Entertainment, as Richard Dyer explains it, "presents what utopia would feel like rather than how it would be organized." Yet, two years into the Reagan era, America was not feeling so hot.

"The stench of failure hangs over Ronald Reagan's White House," the *Washington Post* declared on January 16, 1983. Unemployment was nearly 11 percent; public opinion polls put Reagan's midterm numbers ten points below Jimmy Carter's.

The president was the ultimate Star-Pol and the greatest of the Sixties Survivors: unlike JFK, he died and had been resurrected. He was the keeper of the faith, the personification of America's newfangled old-time religion. More than anyone in Hollywood ever had, he understood that stardom was the

---

* Another related allegory appeared that summer. Woody Allen's pseudo-documentary *Zelig* used all manner of motion-picture clichés to portray a fictional celebrity famous for his chameleon-like capacity to blend in, a talent that inspires songs, dances, merchandise, and even a Hollywood biopic. Writing in the *New Yorker*, Pauline Kael called *Zelig* "a fantasy about being famous for being nobody" but, as embodied by Allen, Zelig is a blank icon who personifies a desire to be mass man as well as mass culture, delivering everything to everyone: "I just wanna be liked." Is he the creation of the Media, or its audience—or both? Allen dissolves this tension in a conventional romance. Still, the movie is blatantly intertextual, filled with signifiers of the 1920s and 1930s (the creation of the Hollywood studio system, the ubiquity of radio, the rise of Hitler), as well as invented crazes; *Zelig* seamlessly blends archaic and new material into home movies or archival footage, as Orson Welles did in *Citizen Kane*'s fake newsreel. Allen further parodies *Reds* in his use of witnesses (including Susan Sontag, Irving Howe, and Bruno Bettelheim) to support the factual basis of his imaginary story.

Each in its way, *Zelig*, *Videodrome*, and *The King of Comedy* encouraged viewers to look critically at the Media and its creatures. But, so far as mass culture was concerned, this distance from the ultimate media hero, Ronald Reagan (who screened *The King of Comedy* and *Zelig*, but not *Videodrome*, at Camp David), would soon disappear.

ultimate form of public service: the Department of Amusement. The Western was moribund, yet Ronnie le Cowboy, as the French dubbed him during the 1980 election, lived.

Like a good star and an adroit politician, Reagan reconciled contradictions. But, his survival of an assassination attempt notwithstanding, he had yet to fulfill his mandate to conjure the socially cohesive illusion of an intimate, imperial America, untouched and untouchable. For that, he would need to become the greatest of Hollywood Freedom Fighters.

Videodrome and *The King of Comedy* appeared at the climax of what Lloyd deMause called the "Great Reagan Poison Alert." The Media was filled with "images of disintegration, disease, and poisoned blood." Headlines pleaded for war: "We couldn't take all those free-floating poisoning fears indefinitely without having *someone* to blame them on," deMause maintained. "Reagan could no longer mistake the urgency of our demand. He would have to find us an enemy and prepare for war so we could shift the poison abroad."

Or put another way, the president would have to become the Media. It was time for Ronald Reagan to occupy the Videodrome and crown himself the King of Comedy. A war scenario, code-named Big Pine, was already in production. American forces were in Honduras, conducting joint training exercises and building up sanctuaries that Nicaraguan counterrevolutionaries, or Contras, now grown into a guerrilla army of 7,500, could use to attack the Sandinista regime. Perhaps a victory in Central America would expunge defeat in the Nam.

"Star Wars," *WarGames,* and Yuppies

"Took time off to run slides & sound tape on Shroud of Turin," Ronald Reagan wrote in his diary entry for February 26, 1983. "I'm convinced it is the burial cloth of Jesus and it certainly gives credence to the bodily ascension."

On March 8, after meeting with high school students at Disney World, Reagan delivered a speech before the National Association of Evangelicals in Orlando mainly devoted to social policy and designed to head off any clerical support for the burgeoning Nuclear Freeze movement. He cautioned against, without actually citing, the Antichrist who cloaked his intentions in "soothing tones of brotherhood and peace," and characterized the Soviet Union in terms Luke Skywalker might use—as an "Evil Empire."*

There was also El Salvador, the subject of Joan Didion's newly published book. Didion, who had visited the country in mid-1982, describes the nation as a place where "the dead and pieces of the dead" are ubiquitous and "taken for granted," and calls it the setting for "a horror movie." Two days later, Reagan warned the National Association of Manufacturers of the danger posed by the insurgents in El Salvador and the revolutionary junta governing the island of Grenada, the smallest nation in the Western Hemisphere. The president's audience assumed that he'd be addressing the issue of taxes. "I suppose I fooled them somewhat by talking on El Salvador & why it was necessary that we help," he noted in his diary.

Then, speaking from the Oval Office on March 23, Reagan blindsided both his secretaries of state and defense with a televised speech announcing a space-based antimissile shield that he called the Strategic Defense Initiative. Congressional Democrats immediately labeled the proposal a "*Star Wars* scenario."[†]

Lloyd deMause would call this telecast "Reagan's masterpiece."

It would be cited in the media hundreds of times in the coming months as the turning point of his foreign policy. The speech had two aims. It had to show that the Evil Empire was very close and was growing more dangerous

---

* In the course of the speech, Reagan also recounted a favorite anecdote:

A number of years ago, I heard a young father, a very prominent young man in the entertainment world [most likely the singer Pat Boone], addressing a tremendous gathering in California. It was during the time of the Cold War, and communism and our own way of life were very much on people's minds. And he was speaking to that subject. And suddenly, though, I heard him saying, "I love my little girls more than anything." And I said to myself, "Oh, no, don't. You can't—don't say that." But I had underestimated him. He went on: "I would rather see my little girls die now, still believing in God, than have them grow up under communism and one day die no longer believing in God."

Noting this story in *Reagan's America*, deMause remarks that "holy wars often begin with a child sacrifice, symbol of the coming sacrifice of the group's vitality."

† Reagan objected to this tag, but also reveled in it. In a speech given in March 1985, he would explain that SDI may have "been labeled Star Wars but it isn't about war, it's about peace. It isn't about retaliation, it's about prevention. It isn't about fear, it's about hope, and in that struggle, if you will pardon my stealing a film line, the force is with us."

by the minute, and it had to make us feel that if we got into war once again we would be safe from nuclear retribution.

The eventual projected cost of the space-based laser battle stations, as well as the ground lasers, was well over $100 billion. The setup was fragile—a nuclear explosion in space could knock out the infrared sensors and radar—as well as self-defeating. Some said that even sand could derange the system, let alone a flotilla of dummy missiles. Moreover, the laser stations themselves would be a target for a preemptive strike.

While it was unclear whether Reagan's SDI would protect Europe, it was likely that it would produce an escalation in the arms race with the Soviets or prompt them to re-aim their warheads at large cities and other soft targets. In any case and even if it were possible, the shield offered scant protection against submarine-launched cruise missiles. No matter, the president proposed "a vision of the future which offers hope" and, by rendering nuclear weapons "obsolete," would change the course of human history. The Democrats' nickname might have been lifted from Lucas, but the tone of bland reassurance, the mystification of technology, and the downgrading of science were pure Spielberg.*

Reagan was sufficiently confident by the weekend to make a surprise appearance at an exclusive journalists' gathering, the annual Gridiron Club dinner. The caboose of a conga line, and wearing an outsized black and silver sombrero, with a scarlet and gold serape over his white tie and tails, the president broke away to sing a self-satirizing version of the 1948 Peggy Lee hit "Mañana (Is Soon Enough For Me)." "My 1st time ever singing a song on stage," Reagan noted in his diary. It is unclear whether he employed the broad Mexican accent with which Lee and others delivered the song.

If the president was thinking about the upcoming election, so were his fans.

A Utah lawyer named Timothy B. Anderson had come up with a new Rocky scenario in which the fighter took on a Soviet Übermensch and had

---

* Michael Rogin and Garry Wills have seen an antecedent to the Strategic Defense Initiative in the 1940 movie *Murder in the Air*, wherein Reagan's character Brass Bancroft prevents a spy from stealing a death ray known as the Inertia Projector that can bring down distant enemy airplanes; National Security Adviser Robert McFarlane told Reagan's biographer Lou Cannon he was "convinced that Reagan's interest in antimissile defense was the product of his interest in Armageddon."

persuaded the White House deputy chief of staff Michael Deaver to broker a meeting with Sylvester Stallone. "I assume that you realize the possible positive impact that my version of *Rocky IV* could have upon the national electorate should it be released in mid-summer, 1984," Anderson wrote Deaver. "For my story to be placed before as many as 60 to 80 million Americans in the four months prior to the election, it will very possibly ignite a groundswell of both support and understanding for the President."

In April 1983, Reagan acknowledged American support for the Nicaraguan Contras. After an initial turndown, the House of Representatives approved the administration's request to fund the first-strike MX missile. "President Reagan looked wonderful the morning after the MX vote," Mary McGrory wrote in the *Washington Post*. "His eyes were bright, his cheeks rosy." Deficits continued to mount but . . . the light saber was his!

McGrory's story ran May 25, the same day that the Senate passed the MX bill and *Return of the Jedi* was released to complete the *Star Wars* trilogy. *Return of the Jedi* was notable mainly for its successfully resolved hostage drama (Han Solo rescued from the giant slug Jabba the Hut) and prolonged denouement ("The joyous mood at the end of *Jedi* is about a split-second away from getting slightly ridiculous," Gary Arnold noted in the *Washington Post*). "Star Wars" was about to become a reality.

New York Times critic Vincent Canby made no attempt to conceal his boredom—the movie "doesn't really end the trilogy as much as it brings it to a dead stop [and] is by far the dimmest adventure of the lot"—but *Return of the Jedi*, which the Reagans screened at Camp David on June 2, was the nation's number one box-office attraction for six weeks through July 14, its reign disrupted only by the one-week ascendency of the new James Bond film *Octopussy* which, given a sneak preview at Camp David in late May, opened June 10.*

The movie that most fascinated Reagan, however, was *WarGames*, which

---

* *Octopussy* was "the first new Cold War Bond flick," I wrote in the *Village Voice*. "The real threat to Bondland is neither [the Afghan warlord] Kamal nor the eponymous international smugglerette [Maud Adams] but one General Orlov [Steven Berkoff, a specialist in such roles] who has been surreptitiously pillaging the Hermitage—that is, selling off the precious heritage of the czars—in order to finance his mad scheme for Russian world conquest." Orlov "plots to detonate an atomic bomb at a West German military base, thus creating a NATO 'accident' that will stampede timorous Western Europe into unilateral disarmament."

opened on June 3 after having its world premiere at the Cannes Film Festival in a slot that was identified with the Hollywood sensation of 1982, *E.T.* The premise suggested a Spielbergian remake of *Dr. Strangelove*: a high school computer whiz (twenty-year-old Matthew Broderick) hacks into the North American Defense Command, mistaking one of its programs, Global Thermonuclear War, for a sophisticated computer game. The fate of the world is in his hands, along with his accomplice (twenty-one-year-old Ally Sheedy).

The film had begun shooting the previous summer. Replacing Martin Brest twelve days into the shoot, John Badham was charged with making a more light-hearted movie. He succeeded (although the studio evidently tested a version ending in nuclear holocaust). *Variety* deemed *WarGames* "a terrifically exciting story charged by an irresistible idea for today's young audience." *New York* critic David Denby, who also found the movie "irresistibly entertaining," noted that "the cameras zip around the large war-room set, circling the big black computer and racing down corridors with the same fluidity displayed in Badham's first triumph, *Saturday Night Fever*."

Unenthusiastic but resigned, and impervious to the movie's underlying anxiety, Andrew Sarris called *WarGames* "the latest entry in the summer kiddie blockbuster series," and predicted that "it will probably sweep up whatever loose currency there remains in the nation's cookie jars and piggy banks after the inexhaustible appetites of the Jedi-worshippers have been appeased," while "cashing in on what is left of the videogame craze." An embedded portrait of President Reagan was, he reported, "good for a derisive laugh."

Reagan himself saw *WarGames*, which was conceived in the late 1970s and co-written by Lawrence Lasker, the son of the actress Jane Greer, a Reagan family friend, over its first weekend at Camp David. The following Wednesday, he met with a bipartisan group of congressional leaders, including several Democrats who had supported the MX, and, departing from his prepared cue cards, inquired if any of them had seen the movie. "As the president started to describe the movie, one congressman said, 'his face lit up,'" Lou Cannon reported in the *Washington Post*. "Reagan became so engrossed in relating the plot that one congressman even said to him: 'Don't tell the ending.'"

The president was in "very good humor," another participant told Cannon. "He said, 'I don't understand these computers very well, but this young man obviously did. He had tied into NORAD!'" At one point, Reagan twitted

Army General John W. Vessey Jr., the chairman of the Joint Chiefs of Staff, who was also present, with the observation that the movie "portrayed the general as this slovenly, mean unthinking guy."

The government was divided over the question of *WarGames*. In mid-August, *People* magazine reported that it was "a blast at the box office, but a bomb at the Pentagon." One member of the NORAD high command, Air Force Major General Thomas C. Brandt, went on record to denounce the movie as "unfair and grossly inaccurate," maintaining that, "it's a disservice to the public to mix fact and fiction." On the other hand, the movie was praised by the former secretary of state and retired four-star general Alexander Haig, now serving on the MGM/UA board of directors and as a paid consultant to the studio, which distributed *WarGames*: "I'm confident that saboteurs or other enemy agents could penetrate segments of the system in an even more competent way than depicted by the teenagers in *WarGames*."*

For a moment, *WarGames* seemed to eclipse "Star Wars," at least in terms of the media speculation on the probability of its scenario. Meanwhile, the president's ratings were beginning to rise and so were expectations of a new crusade that might redeem the ignominy of Vietnam.

On the eve of a not-so-secret and far larger sequel to Big Pine, *Time* magazine called Reagan "a laid-back god." His favorability rating climbed back to 47 percent. As the president sent five thousand troops and nineteen ships staffed with 16,500 troops to Central America ("the idea is to intimidate," a Pentagon official told *Time*), polls showed that 54 percent of Americans thought Reagan was preparing for a war.†

Powered by record federal borrowing and a 14 percent expansion in the

---

* On October 14, 1983, the *New York Post* reported, "FBI 'WarGames' Raid Nets 10 Whiz Kids." The teenage hackers were arrested in Detroit and Irvine, California. *WarGames* was not only a popular hit, the fifth top-grossing movie of 1983, but became something of a Silicon Valley cult. Hosting a twenty-fifth anniversary screening in May 2008, Google co-founder Sergey Brin told an enthusiastic audience that *WarGames* "was a key movie of a generation, especially for those of us who got into computing."
† This, evidently, was not enough for America's white supremacists and neo-Nazis who, after the Aryan Nations World Congress, called for a revolution against the state, which they referred to as the "Zionist Occupational Government." This was a more extreme formulation of Reagan's inaugural address assertion that "in this present crisis, government is not the solution to our problem; government is the problem."

money supply, the economy was beginning to recover. The gross national product had grown by 8 percent, and corporate profits by 20 percent. A bull market was running on Wall Street. "The euphoria just keeps building and building," one stock broker told *Inquiry* magazine, comparing the scene to "a wild New Year's party." Making money was fashionable! Jane Fonda was making workout tapes. Reinvented as "young urban professionals," or "yuppies," even counterculture radicals were in business as professional Sixties Survivors. Jerry Rubin, a founder of the Youth International Party and member of the Chicago Seven who had turned Wall Street broker in 1980, was organizing networking parties for young professionals and entrepreneurs, culminating in a college tour with his old comrade Abbie Hoffman under the rubric, "Yippie vs. Yuppie."

Two hit comedies that summer seemed to herald the Reagan turn. *Risky Business*, written and directed by Paul Brickman, and *Trading Places*, directed by John Landis from a script by Timothy Harris and Herschel Weingrod, the team that would later be behind the Arnold Schwarzenegger comedies *Twins* (1988) and *Kindergarten Cop* (1990), were outspoken in their celebration of capitalism and the profit motive. Each featured an ascendant performer, Tom Cruise and Eddie Murphy, both post-counterculture youth stars if not prototypical yuppies. In both, the respective leading female characters—played by Rebecca De Mornay and Jamie Lee Curtis—were business-minded young prostitutes.

Risky Business was positioned as a raunchy youth comedy but, with its surplus of style—including a score by the avant-pop, techno-rock ensemble Tangerine Dream—was something odder, a parodic Spielberg idyll that was also premonition of High Eighties movies like *Blue Velvet* and *Something Wild*. The *New York Times* critic Janet Maslin described it as "part satire, part would-be suburban poetry and part shameless showing off."

Enterprising high school student Joel Goodson (Cruise) hires an even more enterprising hooker, Lana (De Mornay), whose last name would logically be "Badgirl." Noting that Joel has his family house to himself, Lana helps turn it into an impromptu brothel. The movie is a paean to yuppie self-actualization. Joel manages to lose his virginity and secure admission into Princeton over the course of the same long weekend. Still, the most famous scene has Joel celebrating his parents' absence by blasting the living room stereo playing air guitar, making like a rock star and cavorting about in his underwear. Fairytales can come true. Lana is not just the greatest high school girlfriend a boy could imagine, but the spirit of free enterprise—"what a capitalist!" Joel exults—a foretaste of Madonna's "Material Girl" some eighteen months before the song and music video materialized. Praising Joel's initiative, the college interviewer gives the would-be MBA credit: "Princeton can use a guy like Joel."

Of course! Joel "surmounts his sex and career anxieties by turning himself into a pimp," David Denby wrote in *New York*, adding "this is presented, without irony or a hint of criticism." But if the movie lacks irony, it may be because its neophyte producer David Geffen imposed a new ending. Originally, the boy doesn't get the girl and doesn't go to Princeton. The imperatives of the marketplace effectively blunted the movie's critical edge, tilted it toward sociological propaganda, and made Brickman a prostitute in spite of himself. (Significantly, perhaps, he only once more directed a Hollywood film, the 1990 *Men Don't Leave.*)

If *WarGames* was a high school *Dr. Strangelove*, Joel and Lana were a post-hippie Bonnie and Clyde, no longer Righteous but Self-righteous Outlaws. The same could be said of *Trading Places'* two male stars, Dan Aykroyd and Eddie Murphy, both graduates of *Saturday Night Live* and thus certified TV hipsters. As class conscious as any Hollywood movie since the 1930s, *Trading Places* united a flagrant yuppie and a lumpen hustler against the super-rich and their flunkies.

The Duke brothers, a pair of fabulously wealthy commodity traders (Reagan contemporaries Ralph Bellamy and Don Ameche), play God to settle a philosophical debate regarding the primacy of environment or heredity. Having made a bet, they contrive to have their pampered prize trader Louis Winthorpe III (Aykroyd) unwittingly switch his life with that of the impoverished black street hustler Billy Ray Valentine (Murphy). Winthorpe and Valentine, who turns conservative the instant he has property to protect, join forces to teach the Dukes a lesson, driving them into bankruptcy on the floor of the World Trade Center ("the last bastion of pure capitalism left on earth," according to Winthorpe). They are aided immeasurably by a good-natured whore (Curtis), who sees Winthorpe as an investment opportunity.

Shot on location in Philadelphia, home of the Liberty Bell, *Trading Places* completes an unofficial trilogy begun with optimistic *Rocky* (whose statue appears amid a montage of local patriotic monuments) and continued with pessimistic *Blow Out*, which *Trading Places* obliterates with a genial nod to the power of the marketplace. The *Wall Street Journal* approved of the new comedy: the film "does for commodity traders what [*It's a Wonderful Life*] did for bankers: It makes them heroes for a change." (That is, the ones who aren't villains.) *Newsweek*, which called *Trading Places* a "Reaganomics comedy," fell into the spirit, hailing Murphy as "the movie's hottest—and funniest—commodity."

Some saw the movie as social satire. *Time*'s critic Richard Schickel called *Trading Places* "one of the most emotionally satisfying and morally gratifying comedies of recent times," and David Denby wrote that "the jokes on the rich, and on people who fall down dead before the rich, are good to hear at a time when the accumulation of wealth has been blessed by the current administration as the only virtuous human activity." Returning to *Trading Places* in his review of *Risky Business*, Denby recognized a hidden agenda. "Landis and his screenwriters must have decided that in Ronald Reagan's America no one really wants to identify with the poor."

> At the last minute, they turn the heroes into big winners, leaving them on a Caribbean beach with luxurious ladies in tow. Since the movie, up to this point, insists that money corrupts, we might expect success to corrupt the heroes too. But *Trading Places* isn't the kind of movie that resolves its conflicting fantasies: it just ends.

Other critics had already spotted the contradiction. "This extravagant-looking film is itself too obviously enamored of wealth and prosperity to rail at the establishment with any real conviction," Janet Maslin wrote in the *New York Times*. "Everyone in the film aspires to the prosperity that is also so cleverly mocked here."

Describing without recognizing the Reagan magic, Andrew Sarris wrote that "in this overall context of Reaganish me-ness and meanness run amok, *Trading Places* seems almost like a beacon of humanism, simply because the entire cast somehow projects an aura of amiability and camaraderie."*

---

* The Reagans screened *Trading Places* at Camp David on June 17. The movie is notable for including a small portrait of the president (along with one of Richard Nixon) on the Duke brothers' shared desk, as well as for the presence of future Minnesota senator Al Franken as a baggage handler.

More direct than either *Risky Business* or *Trading Places* in its repudiation of the Sixties ethos was *The Big Chill*, which opened in September, and more than any movie since *American Graffiti*, defined the Boomerography.

An intended lament for the death of Hippie, the movie instead celebrated the birth of Yuppie—not a tale of failure but success. Written and directed by Lawrence Kasdan, *The Big Chill* concerns a group of college friends (University of Michigan, class of '70, like himself) who come together a dozen years after graduation to mourn the suicide of their erstwhile comrade Alex, a brilliant ne'er-do-well whose death represents the end of the Sixties or youthful idealism or simply youth itself. He was, as somebody says at the funeral that opens the movie, "too good for this world."*

Over the course of a long weekend, the seven voluble friends (Tom Berenger, Glenn Close, Jeff Goldblum, William Hurt, Kevin Kline, Mary Kay Place, and JoBeth Williams), along with Alex's younger girlfriend (Meg Tilly), bemoan their respective accommodations to adult life, wonder if their unspecified "commitment" was only "fashion," pair off (or not), wistfully smoke weed, and—far more lamely than Tom Cruise in *Risky Business*—prance around the kitchen of Close and Kline's sumptuous suburban South Carolina house to the Temptations singing "Ain't Too Proud to Beg."†

Big chill or warm bath? Originally meant to evoke a cold shiver of mortality, the movie's title came to signify a nostalgic reunion for a generational game of Trivial Pursuit, inadvertently suggesting the new meaning of "chill," namely "hang out." Dave Kehr, who reviewed *The Big Chill* in *Chicago* magazine, called it "a machine movie that manufacturers complacency." The term "machine" was apt. Like Kasdan's previous film, the 1981 neo-noir *Body Heat*, *The Big Chill* was something of a pastiche, giving the premise of John Say-

---

* A legendary flashback epilogue—cut during previews—showed the Chillsters as the Love Children they were in 1970, complete with a long-haired Kevin Costner as Alex. (He'd get to wear his fringes and beads again seven years later in *Dances with Wolves*.)

† The soundtrack of what was not yet known as "classic rock" is an even more Pavlovian substitute for feeling than Lucas's selection of "golden oldies." The trade press found the success of *The Big Chill* soundtrack LP a bigger surprise than the movie's considerable popularity. (It was the year's thirteenth top-grossing film and Columbia's biggest hit.) Conceived in the shadow of Ronald Reagan, the movie anticipated the ascension of Bill Clinton. In 1996, a *New York Times* article on Clinton's fiftieth birthday party began by noting that the president "led his generation into its sixth decade last night with the ultimate in boomer birthday bashes: a Radio City fund-raising extravaganza of self-celebration and reflection drenched with more Top-40 nostalgia than *The Big Chill*."

les's 1979 independent feature *The Return of the Secaucus Seven* a sitcom slickness while borrowing the war-wounded character played by Hurt from Ernest Hemingway's "Lost Generation" novel *The Sun Also Rises*.

Reporting from the Toronto Film Festival in the *New York Post*, Rex Reed quoted an anonymous Canadian critic who joked that the movie's characters were "all the same person—they all sound like they'll go back to Hollywood and write *Return of the Jedi*."*

The Day After the Conquest of Grenada

A sadder and more confused nostalgia film had been released earlier that summer. Not the Big Chill but the Big Heat. Sidney Lumet's *Daniel*, adapted by E. L. Doctorow from his 1971 novel, was a historical fiction inspired by the Cold War left's great cause célèbre, revisiting the execution of convicted atomic spies Julius and Ethel Rosenberg from the perspective of the couple's young children.

Although the movie evoked the same nuclear anxiety underscoring *WarGames*, it was crammed with historical signifiers that many viewers would find unintelligible. Worse, it evoked the wrong Fifties. (The movie had been Lumet's dream project for over a decade, repeatedly suggested to and rejected by Hollywood studios. Its time, if it ever had one, would have been the revisionist mid-1970s.)

Unsurprisingly, given *Daniel*'s basis in a historical controversy, reviewers responded along generational or political lines. Janet Maslin was able to separate the movie from the actual case, calling it "a work of noble and unusual ambitions," while older critics like Pauline Kael and Andrew Sarris were contemptuous of what they saw as Lumet's sentimental special pleading. Kael even took a dig at Paul Robeson, whose recordings are used throughout, revealing the less than atomic "secret" that he was "a very monotonous singer."

Lumet wore his heart on his sleeve: no Hollywood movie has ever more fully dramatized what the author Vivian Gornick termed "the romance of

---

* That *The Big Chill* opened both the Toronto and New York Film Festivals is worth noting in view of the competition between festivals; as a member of the NYFF selection committee that year, I can attest to how eager the festival was to have it. The Reagans screened the movie a month into its run on October 29.

American Communism," nor employed more untranslated Yiddish. "I'm getting paranoid," the director told the *Boston Globe*. "I've never had such bad reviews for any picture I've ever done. Virtually every major corporate publication has come out against it." Perhaps the greatest bummer of Reagan's first term, *Daniel* encourages the viewer to imagine what it would be like to be a child whose parents were accused of a monstrous crime and put to death in the electric chair.

A thought experiment that possibly one had to appreciate Paul Robeson as entertainment to get, *Daniel* was a disaster that even an ending showing the troubled title character participating in the Central Park Nuclear Freeze demonstration of May 1982 could not mitigate.

Less noticed than the mounting American pressure on Nicaragua or the president's fulminations regarding the Evil Empire were the large-scale maneuvers held that spring by the U.S. Pacific Fleet, complete with navy war planes overflying Soviet military installations in the Far East and violating Soviet airspace. Paranoia was such that the new Soviet leader, Yuri Andropov, issued a "shoot to kill" order for border intrusions.

U.S. intelligence agencies had determined that the Soviets planned to test a new missile over the Kamchatka peninsula on September 1. That very night a South Korean passenger liner, KAL 007, unaccountably strayed into Soviet airspace and, after being tracked for hundreds of miles, was shot down over the Sea of Japan. Air Force Intelligence concluded that the attack was a confused blunder. Four days later, Ronald Reagan—who had been vacationing at his Santa Barbara ranch—appeared on television, charging the Soviets with a "crime against humanity." Soon after, Andropov, who had told visiting former ambassador Averell Harriman he feared the U.S. might be planning a preemptive strike, accused Reagan of having deployed KAL 007 as a deliberate provocation.

Intentional or not, Reagan did cast American marines—stationed for over a year in Beirut as part of a multinational peacekeeping force—into the Lebanese civil war. Ordering the bombardment of Druze positions, the president used his weekly radio address to link the U.S. presence in Lebanon to the global struggle against Communism. Scarcely two weeks later, on October 23, a truck crashed through the gates of the American compound in Beirut, detonating some twelve thousand pounds of explosives and killing 241 marines.

Two days after that, on the other side of the globe, the administration un-leased Operation Urgent Fury against the Caribbean island of Grenada—the smallest nation in the Western Hemisphere.*

Waves of A-7 Corsair fighters materialized out of the bright tropical sky. Seven thousand troops in eleven warships converged. Grenada is but twenty-one miles in length and twelve miles at its broadest point although, as the travel writer Patrick Leigh Fermor pointed out, it seems much larger, "owing to the mountainous ridge running along its spine, and the deep valleys that radiate from it on either side." So it would loom in the Dream Life . . . at least for a few years. The Conquest of Grenada was a triumph for the image—a successful Bay of Pigs, a zipless Nam.

Not since the capture of the *Mayaguez* eight years before had America stood so tall. Reagan had found an unlosable war. Justified in part because tiny Grenada, helped by Cuba, was constructing an alarmingly large airport, the invasion was described by one American diplomat as "the most thor-oughly planned crisis" in which he had ever participated. U.S. forces were ten times larger than the Grenadian army, which had neither air power nor artillery weapons. "We blew them away," exulted the operation's command-ing officer. Over eight thousand medals were given out to commemorate what the *Washington Post* hailed as "the most popular invasion since *E.T.*"

Much was made of the American medical students—aspiring yuppies!—rescued from the native population from no apparent danger. Reflexively, young people turned to Reagan. "In Grenada he showed he will stand up to the Soviets," a twenty-one-year-old senior at Pitzer College told *Time* maga-zine. "We don't have a wishy-washy human rights foreign policy. We say what we're going to do and do it."

As 1984 approached, new Cold War narratives consolidated.

Two days after Operation Urgent Fury, Reagan made a nationally tele-vised speech conflating Grenada, Beirut, and KAL 007 into a single plot

---

* Grenada's socialist prime minister, Maurice Bishop, was overthrown by a leftist coup on October 12 and, as Secretary of State George Shultz counseled Reagan to prepare for mili-tary intervention, murdered a week later. Plans were advanced after the Organization of Eastern Caribbean States called for U.S. military aid, on October 22, the same day that a bearded gunman named Charles Harris stalked the president as he relaxed on an Augusta, Georgia, golf course.

orchestrated by Moscow. *Washington Post* journalist Bob Woodward was invited to watch the speech with CIA director William Casey at his home. Before the speech Casey, who managed Reagan's 1980 campaign, told Woodward that he considered the shooting down of KAL 007 to have been the result of a "foul up" on the part of Soviet military intelligence. But as Reagan spoke, Casey appeared to Woodward to be mesmerized, praising the president's address as "perhaps the best speech he has ever given."

The Soviets had reason to feel jittery. In late September, their satellite defense system erroneously reported five incoming American ballistic missiles. (War was averted when duty officer Stanislav Petrov decided, correctly, that the launch reports were most likely a false alarm.) Between November 2 and 11, NATO forces began an elaborate military exercise code-named Able Archer 83 that—more sober and less entertaining than *WarGames*—involved some forty thousand American, British, Canadian, Dutch, and West German soldiers.

The grand finale of a series of exercises that, beginning in August, simulated a European land war, the Able Archer scenario dramatized the segue from conventional to chemical and nuclear weapons, positing successive Warsaw Pact invasions of Yugoslavia, Finland, and Norway. These were followed by Soviet air attacks on West Germany and Great Britain, which triggered NATO's deployment of tactical nuclear weapons to destroy designated East European cities. The exercise ended November 11 with the all-out use of nuclear weapons. Fearing that the game was real, the Soviets placed their nuclear forces on high alert and sent an unprecedented number of spy planes over the Baltic and Barents Seas.

Coincidentally, another dramatization of another nuclear exchange would be projected into America's living rooms. Announced on October 6, ABC's made-for-TV movie, *The Day After*, a graphic depiction of a full-scale nuclear attack on the American heartland, was scheduled for broadcast on November 20, two days before the twentieth anniversary of the Kennedy assassination. It was, according to the president of ABC Motion Pictures, Brandon Stoddard, "the most important movie we or anyone else ever made." ABC News's Moscow bureau chief previewed the film for Soviet officials, who must have wondered about its connection to Able Archer.

VHS tapes of the movie had been circulating among antinuclear weapons activists and pro-Freeze politicians since early fall. "It is going to be the most powerful television program in history," Massachusetts representative Edward J. Markey predicted. California senator and presidential hopeful Alan Cranston planned a fund-raising blitz tied to the movie.

Editorial writers for the *National Review* and *Human Events* attacked *The Day After* sight unseen; Moral Majority leader Jerry Falwell denounced it as "a preemptive strike" on the president's policies. Having read the *National Review*'s concern that the movie would "generate an ignorant public hysteria," Reagan called his U.S. Information Agency director Charles Z. Wick and was given a tape, which he ran on the Camp David VCR on October 10. The movie struck him as effective propaganda and dubious entertainment, not to mention a questionable undertaking in the annals of show business. "It is powerfully done—all $7 mil worth," he noted in his diary. "It's very effective & left me greatly depressed. So far they haven't sold any of the 25 spot ads scheduled & I can see why."

Reagan was sufficiently impressed; his administration perceived *The Day After* as a threat. In early November, the White House put out talking points on the film—the subject of a senior staff meeting on November 18. While op-ed pieces were prepared for publication following the telecast, it was stressed that the administration should not attack the network or the film itself: "We agree with the premise that nuclear war is horrible; the key question for debate is how to prevent it. Guidance regarding a particular news report is that the president has seen the film, but did not suggest that changes should be made." (In fact, Reagan noted in his diary that, "We know it's 'anti-nuke' propaganda but we're going to take it over & say it shows why we must keep on doing what we're doing.")

The same day that the *Chicago Tribune* reported "Clamor Grows for Replay of Grenada in Nicaragua," an audience estimated at one hundred million gathered to watch *The Day After*, exceeded only by that for *Roots* and the final episode of *M*A*S*H*, with some clustered around TVs in churches and college lecture halls. Some deemed the movie a bomb—literally. Fifty minutes of exposition—in which a confrontation over Berlin leads to a barrage of escalating news bulletins, increasing mass hysteria, and finally ICBMs blasting out of silos beneath the Kansas cornfields—are followed by a four-minute Armageddon. *New York Times* critic John Corry, a self-identified "conservative in a media culture dominated by liberals," wrote:

There is a white light in the sky . . . then a blinding yellow light. There is the mushroom cloud, full of flame, followed by fire storms and wind. Buildings explode and implode. A popular forest bends. People, vaporized, turn into images on an X-ray film. A moment or two later, Jason Robards, who survives, says it looked "like the sun exploded."

Dramatically speaking, that's about it.

The next hour was devoted to the "relentless depiction of radiation poisoning," Corry complained. "The drama is carried along by latex, gelatin and wigs. The makeup man is the star." *The Exorcist*, he thought, was more frightening.

Although *Night of the Living Dead* would have provided a more apt comparison, Corry's focus on the production design is understandable given the movie's relentless downward spiral into utter hopelessness—ending with a baby born of an unwilling mother into a shattered, toxic world and two decaying near-corpses dramatizing the indomitable human spirit with a feeble fraternal embrace.

The next night ABC replayed the Cuban Missile crisis after a fashion, initiating a four-part "war game" miniseries, starring former senator and vice-presidential candidate Edward Muskie as the president as he reacts "live" to an imaginary crisis with two former defense secretaries, James Schlesinger and Clark Clifford, playing members of his cabinet. War fever had scarcely abated. Two days after *The Day After*, the West German Bundestag approved the deployment of Pershing II and cruise missiles.

Concrete barriers were placed around the White House; ground-to-air missiles were reportedly installed; Senator Patrick Moynihan was predicting war; and, as the year ended, Dirty Harry reappeared.

Born in late 1971, San Francisco police detective Harry Callahan was Clint Eastwood's most enduring character—the personification of political reaction, the antidote to the permissive Sixties and Lyndon Johnson's Great Society.

Harry embodied Richard Nixon's promise to restore Law and Order. He anticipated Ronald Reagan's notion that the system was the problem, not the solution—even as he took it upon himself to clean up the mess in Reagan's

California. His enemies were the black militants, hippie crazies, loose women, and bleeding-heart liberals the governor had railed against. At once a hero cop and what the Panthers called a "pig," Harry—like Reagan—was a walking contradiction, the authoritarian who hates authority. In opposition to the Righteous Outlaws of the Black Panthers and the New Left, he was the Legal Vigilante.

Returning once more under Nixon in *Magnum Force* (1973) and then under Gerald Ford in *The Enforcer* (1976), Harry went into remission during the Carter administration when Eastwood variously played an alcoholic cop, a hardened convict, a rodeo cowboy, and twice opposite a chimpanzee. Then, with Eastwood directing himself, Dirty Harry reemerged during the post "Star Wars" surge in Reagan's approval ratings. Filmed in late spring and early summer of 1983, *Sudden Impact* would gross an impressive $67 million. It was the number-seven box-office hit of 1983 and the most successful Dirty Harry film ever, the one that introduced his taunt to a malefactor poised to attack: "Go ahead, make my day."*

The movie's first half is a straightforward procedural dramatizing the protagonist's ritual battle with an effete liberal officialdom that regards him as a Neanderthal or worse. Some critics, like David Denby, saw Harry as the embodiment of a "lumpen despair" regarding "the modern bureaucratic state" and even capitalism. *Sudden Impact* was "a grim parable about a country in which the criminal justice system has failed." But at the same time, this perpetually glowering cop was the toughest, nastiest guy in the universe—immune to self-pity, busily intimidating everyone with whom he comes in contact.

The most significant break with the formula was Harry's delegation of his vigilante responsibilities to a female serial-killer, Jennifer (played by Eastwood's consort Sondra Locke). Following Reagan's lead in appointing Sandra Day O'Connor to the Supreme Court, Eastwood gave right-wing law

---

* Dirty Harry uses the phrase twice in the movie; Reagan quoted him in March 1985 while addressing the American Business Conference. Citing the current tax bill before Congress he assured his audience, "I have my veto pen drawn and ready for any tax increase that Congress might even think of sending up. And I have only one thing to say to the tax increasers. Go ahead—make my day." Harry returned once more, to diminishing returns, in *The Dead Pool*, released during the summer of 1988 and the least remunerative of the cycle.

and order a feminist makeover. Harry not only saves Jennifer's life but covers up her crimes. Together, they form a two-person death squad, ridding San Francisco of miscellaneous scum.

Sudden Impact was not Hollywood's lone Christmas gift. The same day that brought Harry introduced a lively antipode: *Scarface*, a remake of the classic 1932 gangster film, conceived by producer Martin Bregman as a vehicle for Al Pacino. Sidney Lumet, originally hired to direct the movie, came up with idea of transposing the criminal rise-and-fall story to Miami and making the antihero a Cuban refugee who arrives in Florida as part of the 1980 Mariel boatlift and, through ruthless force of personality, becomes a kingpin of the booming cocaine racket. The update was impressively trendy, and Lumet evidently had other ideas as well. Some years later, Bregman would recall that "Sidney's take on the material was totally political, incorrect and unfair to the president. He felt there was something sinister happening"—namely that the Reagan administration was playing a role in international drug trafficking.*

Lumet was replaced as director by Brian De Palma, looking for a hit after the failure of his ultra-conspiratorial *Blow Out*. The result was a smashing synthesis of two 1970s mega hits, *The Godfather: Part II* and *Saturday Night Fever*. Pacino's Tony Montana wore the most iconic white suit since John Travolta's dance king, climbing a mountain of corpses to a synth disco backbeat. Controversial before it opened, *Scarface* was attacked by representatives of Miami's Cuban community and branded with a scarlet X—too violent, too profane (by one estimate a record-breaking 226 uses of the word "fuck" and its variants), and so coked-up that it was taken by some to be a satire of the New Hollywood.

De Palma managed to throw off the X by excising a scene in which Tony's partner has his arm removed with a chain saw, but his fans were not mollified. While critics previously sympathetic to De Palma, including Pauline Kael and David Denby, were put off, skeptics like Vincent Canby and Richard Corliss were impressed, seeing the movie as a provocative evisceration of American greed and self-indulgence—"a serious, often hilarious

---

* Lumet's scenario was also impressively prescient. Although the role of Panamanian strongman Manuel Noriega in simultaneously smuggling drugs and supplying arms to the Contras dates back at least to 1983, it would not draw public attention until 1985.

peek under the rock where nightmares strut in $800 suits," Corliss wrote in *Time*. Still, most reviews were dismissive. Joking that it should be "marketed as camp for the coke crowd," Andrew Sarris called *Scarface* "more a disaster than an outrage."*

The stylized TV crime series *Miami Vice* was already in the pipeline, but the pop monster de jour in the winter of 1983–84 was Michael Jackson, and the most innovative movie of the season was the fifteen-minute music video "Thriller," directed by John Landis. Evoking the Fifties revival, it raised and diffused issues of race and sexuality. Michael and his date (former *Playboy* centerfold Ola Ray) run out of gas on lover's lane. "What are we going to do now?" she asks him, the portrait of innocence in a poodle skirt and bobby socks. Michael, whose red jacket evokes the one worn by James Dean in *Rebel Without a Cause*, proposes that they go steady, albeit he warns, "I'm not like other guys." In fact, he's even more so—the full moon transforms him into a beast.

The idea was Jackson's. He wanted to play a monster and recruited Landis on the strength of his 1981 movie *An American Werewolf in London*. The video is highly self-reflexive and proved highly profitable. (The VHS tape *Making Michael Jackson's Thriller* sold nine million copies, topping *Jane Fonda's Workout* as a best-selling VHS release.) Following an off-screen assault, the couple is seen in a movie theater watching the previous scene. Ola gets frightened and splits; Michael follows, singing and dancing to entertain her, oscillating between normal and zombie. Even the corpses are cavorting—at times in formation with Michael as leader. It's *Night of the Living Dead* as entertainment.

Free to be himself, Michael tells the truth as the narrator (Vincent Price) warns viewers that creatures (like Michael?) may "terrorize your neighborhood." "Thriller" presents its star as a sacred monster—conjuring the dead,

---

* Actually, *Scarface* was less financial disaster than box-office disappointment. Grossing $45.6 million to finish number sixteen for the year, just behind *Jaws 3-D*, the movie was a decade ahead of its time. Thanks to cable TV and VCRs, it had become a cult object by the mid-1990s. Marking the transition from gangster to gangsta, sampled in rap recordings and evoked by music videos, *Scarface* was a talisman for hip-hop moguls like Snoop Dogg, Puff Daddy, and the Notorious B.I.G. By 2003, when it finally appeared in DVD, selling two million units in its first week, *Scarface* was arguably the most heavily merchandised and fetishized relic of the 1980s, an ambivalent critique of Reagan-era greed embraced as a manifesto three decades later.

beyond gender conventions and racial stereotypes. In 1983, MTV was almost exclusively white—Jackson integrated the world of music videos. But the movie *Uncommon Valor,* a sleeper hit that finished number twenty-two for the year, was even more utopian.

Like *Sudden Impact, Uncommon Valor* was rooted in the rhetoric of the Nixon administration which, as early as 1969, had decided to make a major issue over American POWs and MIAs.

First Blood had suggested that Rambo and, by extension, all the grunts who fought in Vietnam had been sold out on the home front only to be "spat upon" when they returned. This line was consolidated with *Uncommon Valor,* in which a retired U.S. Marine officer (Gene Hackman) trains guerrillas to spring his son and other MIAs held captive in a Laotian prison camp.

With its emphasis on patriarchal authority, mutilated genealogy, and male rites of passage, *Uncommon Valor* took the lead in visualizing Indochina as the site of America's symbolic castration. Unlike *Apocalypse Now* or even *The Deer Hunter,* it offered itself as a clear-cut exorcism of the shame and dishonor of American defeat. Some critics, notably Pauline Kael, scored *Uncommon Valor*'s underlying racism. But if Kael cited the "exultant, patriotic music" that burst forth during the climactic massacres of the film's "little yellow peril targets," most praised it as a solid, old-fashioned action flick.

When it came to the subtext, audiences were definitely more alert: the *New York Times* quoted one patron leaving the theater who might have been celebrating the Conquest of Grenada: "We get to win the Vietnam War!"*

The Right Stuff at the Wrong Time

No American president since the Christian Soldier, Dwight D. Eisenhower, had enjoyed two full terms; Ronald Reagan's reelection was far from assured.

---

* Co-produced by John Milius, the movie had some New Hollywood elements. However, salted with references to *The Searchers, Uncommon Valor* basically appropriated the premise of *The Losers* (1970), in which a group of bikers returned to Nam on their motorcycles to rescue a captured presidential adviser from a Chinese prison camp. (Anticipating the self-pity endemic to '80s Nam films, the surviving gang members have to hear themselves denounced as "trash" for their troubles.)

Polls during the summer of 1983 had the president losing to both of his likely Democratic opponents, former vice president Walter Mondale and Ohio senator John Glenn, the first American to orbit the earth.

Other candidates included the senators Alan Cranston of California, Gary Hart of Colorado, and Ernest Hollings of South Carolina; former Florida governor Reubin Askew; and 1972 nominee George McGovern. Cranston was strongly identified with nuclear-freeze advocates and had in fact beaten Mondale in Wisconsin's straw poll; Hart, who had managed McGovern's 1972 campaign, sought to position himself as a new-generation candidate and the one most committed to women's issues. There was also the specter of JFK haunting the 1984 election, as it had in 1976 and 1980.

In the absence of Ted Kennedy, who declared his non-candidacy in late 1982, the forty-six-year-old Hart was the most Kennedyesque contender. Throughout 1983, however, Reagan's team regarded Glenn as their most potent adversary. The former astronaut was a bona fide hero and de facto knight of JFK's Round Table, exuding patriotic glamour even as he embodied Midwestern family values. Such was the dialectic regarding Glenn that many Democratic leaders also regarded the candidate, who in some polls led Mondale 39 percent to 33 percent, as a potential Reagan. This was not altogether a complimentary comparison. New York's governor Mario Cuomo, a presumed Mondale supporter, criticized Reagan as a "celluloid hero" while suggesting that Glenn was a "celluloid candidate." For his part, Glenn understood Reagan's appeal. ("I want to have that kind of vision," he told his staff. "I don't see why America can't be like those Styrofoam fingers at the football game— We're Number One! We're Number One! We're Number One!") Correspondingly, Reagan's handlers proved diligent students of Glenn's campaign.

When, at an October 6 candidates' forum at New York's Town Hall, one of the three designated questioners, suggested that Glenn's orbital flight might have been a stunt, the senator took the opportunity to compare himself favorably to Reagan. "I wasn't doing *Hellcats of the Navy* on a movie lot when I went through 149 missions," he pointed out. "And when I was on top of that booster down there getting ready to go, it wasn't *Star Trek* or *Star Wars*, I can guarantee you that. It was representing the future of this country." (This reply, the historians of political advertising Edwin Diamond and Stephen Bates thought, was the highpoint of Glenn's campaign.)

Twenty years before, Glenn had been the subject of a half-hour documentary made under the "personal supervision" of Jack L. Warner on behalf of five federal agencies (the National Aeronautics and Space Administration; the Department of Health, Education and Welfare; the Department of Justice; the Department of the Navy; and the Marine Corps). Opening with a brief statement by President Kennedy (and released four months ahead of Warner Bros.'s JFK feature, *PT 109*), *The John Glenn Story* was, per *Variety*, "sure to stir the patriotic fervor of every red-blooded American." Even more enthusiastic, the *Hollywood Reporter* gushed that "if it were necessary to create an ideal man" who could "sum up and project in one person the American dream at its shiniest, the creation could not have been bettered than in the real-life man, Lieut. Col. John Glenn." The astronaut glowed with "decency, intelligence, humility and courage."

Not surprisingly, the Glenn campaign placed great hopes in *The Right Stuff*, Philip Kaufman's adaptation of Tom Wolfe's 1979 best-selling New Journalistic account of America's space program, from the breaking of the sound barrier in 1947 through Gordon Cooper's twenty-two earth orbits in 1963. Months before the movie would open it was seen as Glenn's *PT 109*, described by one Republican consultant quoted in the *Philadelphia Inquirer* as "a great piece of advertising [Glenn] couldn't buy for 10 million bucks." Another plus, the consultant added, was Glenn's "murky image on the issues."*

"As the 193-minute movie had its initial private screenings this week, it was clear that no Presidential candidacy has ever had a send-off quite like that afforded Mr. Glenn," Howell Raines wrote in the *New York Times* in late September, noting that "the priggish self-righteousness attributed to Senator Glenn in the Wolfe book is toned down in the movie."

In fact, Glenn's character was idealized and rendered more sympathetic

---

* Glenn also had something of a reputation as a national klutz. Attorney General Robert F. Kennedy had encouraged Glenn to challenge incumbent Democratic senator Stephen M. Young in the 1964 primary election. Glenn resigned from NASA, then suffered a bathroom fall that caused him to withdraw from the race. In 1970, Glenn again ran in the Democratic primary for Ohio senator, only to be narrowly defeated by Howard Metzenbaum, who subsequently lost to the Republican, William Saxbe. In 1974, Glenn got on track—rejecting the Ohio Democratic party's demand that he run for lieutenant governor and instead challenging Metzenbaum, appointed to the Senate after Saxbe resigned to become attorney general. Glenn won the primary and, defeating the Republican mayor of Cleveland in the general election, began a Senate career that continued until 1999.

while *The Right Stuff* was in production—if not after it wrapped in October 1982. Glenn himself had read the screenplay in late 1982, telling *New York* magazine that its irreverent tone struck him as "Laurel and Hardy Go to Space." Interviewed soon after by the *Boston Globe*, Glenn called the script "frivolous," although he denied any involvement with the movie.

The filmmakers would subsequently claim that neither Glenn nor his staff had sought changes in the script (and in any case the senator was mainly concerned with the depiction of his wife Annie's severe stutter), but the *Globe* reported that, according to Hollywood sources, Glenn contacted military and space administration officials requesting that the filmmakers be banned from government installations. "I'm not going to try to influence anyone," Glenn told the *Globe*, although he would later acknowledge having called NASA's head "once or twice."

"The politics caught up with the movie, not the movie with the politics," co-producer Irwin Winkler explained. The director Philip Kaufman maintained that he had taken for granted that Ted Kennedy would be the Democratic nominee in 1984 and it was only after December 1, 1982, when Kennedy declared his non-candidacy, that Kaufman realized *The Right Stuff* might have political implications. It was then, Raines reported in October, that Kaufman's thinking changed: "I decided we should start making copies of the scenes that we had just for protection." (How many exclamation points would Wolfe have accorded such self-important paranoia?) Raines continued:

> Mr. Kaufman said he called his film editors together and told them, "You never know, now that our film might have some political significance—thinking back to Watergate—what might happen."
>
> According to the director, memories of break-ins and tape erasures made him determined to see that the original negatives were locked away and that all of the editors' work prints were duplicated.
>
> Mr. Kaufman said that later a 9,000-foot work print that "included all of the Glenn flight" was lost or taken from his workplace in San Francisco.

But the Dream Life would not be denied, and like some monster-movie protoplasm, *The Right Stuff*, which Warner Bros. planned to heavily merchandize and extensively promote, inexorably merged with Glenn's presidential bid. *The Right Stuff* paraphrased Glenn's campaign slogan "Believe in the

Future Again" with the tagline "How the Future Began," while Glenn's TV spots ended by plugging the movie: "The right stuff? You better believe it."

Out on newsstands well before the Town Hall forum, *Newsweek*'s October 3, 1983, issue featured major coverage of the Glenn campaign. The cover line read "Can a Movie Help Make a President?" while, rather than the expected portrait of the senator and his wife, the cover image featured the actor who played Glenn in *The Right Stuff*, the near-lookalike Ed Harris in costume and close-up. Inside, the "battle of image and style" that Glenn waged against Mondale was characterized as a "thematic campaign—long on patriotic imagery but still short on specifics—[that] conjures up happy memories of another era when small-town virtues prevailed, Americans sat tall in the saddle and the Russians regularly received their comeuppance."

Glenn's main image-makers were a former cinema verité documentarian, David Sawyer, and the adman Scott Miller, famous in the industry for his Coca-Cola spots; Glenn, the image-makers explained, was the human equivalent to a can of Coke, a familiar, feel-good "hero symbol." The candidate's TV commercials emphasized patriotism while promoting his iconic status: one spot placed Mr. and Mrs. Glenn before an American flag, Glenn declaring, "We believe in America, and the red, white and blue values that make America great."

Newsweek described the filming of a campaign rally, replete with parade and rally where a country-western trio played "The Marines' Hymn," calling the footage "the right stuff for countless political spots to come," with Glenn "performing as the candidate of the future, the candidate of flight, space, high technology and a strong national defense." At the same time, "in a more subtle way, the camera also caught Glenn as the candidate who harks back to better times, back to an era when test pilots and space flight meant simple pride in America." Glenn hit all the marks—Fifties, Camelot, and the Space Age. As depicted in *The Right Stuff*, Glenn was "Luke Skywalker materializing from the celluloid future to enter Campaign '84."

The first national TV ad for Glenn was scheduled for the night before the movie's Washington, DC, world premiere. Afterward, Reagan was advised to associate himself with John F. Kennedy and the space race. His 1984 State of the Union address would paraphrase Kennedy in calling space the "next frontier" and include a vow to establish a permanently manned space station "within a decade."

The Right Stuff had its world premiere at the JFK Center in Washington on Sunday, October 16, and opened at 229 theaters the following Friday, along with two other political movies—*The Dead Zone*, an assassination story directed by David Cronenberg from the 1979 thriller by Stephen King, and Roger Spottiswoode's foreign-correspondent drama *Under Fire*, both a good deal darker than *The Right Stuff*.*

At three hours, *The Right Stuff* was twenty minutes longer than *Nashville*, and no movie in the near-decade since that film's opening was more rapturously received as a portrait of America. The reviews were enthusiastic. *Newsweek* critic David Ansen called *The Right Stuff* "an irreverent epic" that was "about nothing less than our brash, tenacious, straining-at-the-bit soul. It recaptures, with all its rough edges exposed, a vibrant chunk of our heritage, and shows the grace hidden beneath the flimflam." Writing in *Time*, Richard Schickel praised the movie for reviving a "great figure of American myth," namely "the job- and goal-oriented man, more strongly bonded to his companions in silent striving than he is to his wife and children."

The movie's inspirational patriotic score recalled the music Ronald Reagan had in his voice, yet Schickel's description suggests Reaganism without Reagan—although Harris's portrayal of Glenn, characterized by Raines as "an heroic square with a self-depreciating sense of humor about his squareness," sincerely thanking God for America, had a Reaganesque quality. "Upon seeing the film, it is hard to believe that Glenn once harbored reservations about it," the *Boston Globe* observed. But *The Right Stuff*—which opened four days before and was quickly upstaged by the Conquest of Grenada—did not burnish Glenn's image so much as submerge his once-upon-a-time celebrity in a vision of the Eisenhower and Kennedy eras as a period of sanctimonious hokum.

Nashville was a hit; *The Right Stuff* bombed. Its tepid $1.6 million put it seventh on *Variety*'s list of weekend grosses, behind even *The Dead Zone* and

---

* In the former, Christopher Walken—a New England schoolteacher cursed with prophetic powers after a traffic accident—wrestles with the necessity to kill Martin Sheen's demonic demagogue, a New England politician with an incongruous Southern accent, before he becomes president and triggers a nuclear war. As Ronald Reagan survived an assassin's bullet in 1981, the scenario was less compelling than it might have been. *Under Fire*, which dealt with the final days of the Somoza dictatorship in Nicaragua, was more topical (and also featured Ed Harris as a cheerfully sociopathic CIA agent).

Under Fire. (The big winner was *Never Say Never Again*, with Sean Connery returning as James Bond.) The narrative changed as producers blamed Glenn's candidacy for the movie's failure. "We made a mistake in following the lead of the press," co-producer Robert Chartoff declared. "The press picked the movie up as a political polemic. We thought that any kind of publicity space was good space. Now we think certain segments of the public aren't going to the movie because they think it's a *responsibility*—not a fun movie."*

But while Chartoff held Glenn responsible, others cited the movie's length or the retro quality of the space travel. For his part, Kaufman blamed the marketers. One day after Operation Urgent Fury, he wrote a memo to Bob Dingilian, the Ladd Company's vice president in charge of publicity, criticizing the ad campaign as "too restrained" and "too dignified." Suggesting that *The Right Stuff* "needs a 'dynamic' pose of some sort" in order to reach a younger audience, Kaufman cited a number of reviews, underlining key words. In the *San Francisco Chronicle*, Judy Stone described the movie as "the whole 3-ring rip roaring American circus—hoopla, hypocrisy, and heroism." In the *Los Angeles Times*, Sheila Benson called *The Right Stuff* a "brash, beautiful, deeply American film . . . with a generous, high-spirited look at the bravery and lunacy that was that era," and featuring "the nicest sexuality the screen has had in years," while the *Los Angeles Examiner* critic Peter Rainer called the movie "alternately goony, elegiac, lyrical and cartoonish, it's a genuine piece of new style Americana."

Kaufman's movie was not the only disappointment. The early November polls had Mondale and Reagan running neck and neck but, as post-Grenada euphoria mixed with neo–Cold War anxiety and with the threat of *The Day After* successfully neutralized, Reagan pulled ahead, 51 percent to 44 percent. Glenn polled marginally better against Reagan but, by December, among Democrats the former astronaut was trailing the former vice president, 43 percent to 29 percent.

---

* Although *The Right Stuff* was nominated for eight Oscars, it had by March only grossed $20 million. "I was a hero before the picture opened. People said it was the best publicity job in the history of the business," Bob Dingilian told *New York Times* reporter Aljean Harmetz, who ended her piece with the observation that "perhaps no matter what was done to promote it, *The Right Stuff* would have remained a good movie on a subject that interested too few people." The same might have been said of the Glenn campaign, which would end a week after the story ran on March 7, 1984.

Perhaps Glenn's problems were identical with the movie. Audiences found both to be self-important, corny, and, as Nancy Reagan said of candidate Glenn, "boring." Still, Glenn's "thematic" advertising campaign supplied much usable material for the president's. As 1983 ended, *Time* chose Reagan, whose approval ratings would soon be unprecedentedly high for an incumbent president seeking reelection, and Soviet leader Yuri Andropov as "Men of the Year," positioned back to back on the cover.

One week into the fearfully anticipated 1984, the first mines were laid by the CIA in Nicaraguan harbors. On January 24, Reagan was pleased to note that his numbers were rising in the polls.

Democrats meanwhile are making problems for themselves. Walter Mondale wins nearly half the votes in the Iowa caucuses, but the national conversation is preoccupied with civil rights leader and presidential candidate Jesse Jackson's reported use of the term "Hymietown" to characterize New York.

"I can only say I wish the election was tomorrow," Reagan writes in his diary on February 23. Five days later, Gary Hart wins the New Hampshire primary with 37 percent of the vote. Mondale finishes second with 28 percent and Glenn runs a poor third at 12 percent. "I like Gary Hart," Johnny Carson tells his *Tonight Show* audience after the results are announced. "I like his slogan—'Vote for me. I have Kennedy hair.'" (The next morning, Senator Cranston, who had applied orange dye to his eyebrows and fringe of hair in an attempt to appear more youthful, drops out.)

Media attention now focuses on Hart. TV anchors wonder who he is, what he believes, and why he changed his name (from Hartpence). At a March 11 debate in Atlanta, Mondale paraphrases a fast food TV commercial, telling Hart that "when I hear your ideas, I'm reminded of that ad, 'Where's the beef?'" Mondale presents himself as a traditional Democrat working-class hero and Hart as some sort of elitist twerp—someone that Mondale aides are telling the press is a "yuppie."*

---

* A *New York Times* piece headlined "Hart Taps a Generation of Young Professionals" outlined Hart's appeal:

> Since "realism" is one of the favorite words in the "yuppie" lexicon, they respond favorably to Mr. Hart's suggestion that Democrats can no longer simply take labor's side against management, but must be concerned with long-term economic

On March 13, Hart wins primaries in Florida, Massachusetts, and Rhode Island. Glenn withdraws and Hart is free to run as Kennedy redux except that the media decides he is a poseur. "Why do you imitate John Kennedy so much?" NBC newsman Roger Mudd wants to know and when Hart demurs, Mudd offers proof. "All the motions with the necktie, and the chopping of the air, and the hand in the pocket—all those people, people all over the country say, all he's doing is imitating John Kennedy." Soon after, Mudd poses another question: "Why do you think, Senator, so many politicians are phony today?" In conclusion, Mudd asks Hart to do his Teddy Kennedy imitation and when Hart refuses, eggs him on, saying "I've heard it's hilarious."

With Glenn out of the race, Mondale has no problem winning important primaries in Michigan and Illinois; still, even as Mondale amasses delegates, a late March Gallup poll puts Hart ahead of Reagan, 52 percent to 43 percent. In recognition that Mondale's casting his remaining opponent as the yuppie candidate has definite use-value, Jimmy Carter's media consultant Pat Caddell advises Hart to define himself in generational terms. "You're out there by yourself," he warns.

> You open yourself to much greater scrutiny than if this becomes a movement generationally that you happen to be the head of. This movie is not called "The Lone Ranger." This movie should be called "The Return of the Magnificent Seven." And you get to be Yul Brynner. It is a generation coming back to get involved again.

The Magnificent Seven (1960) was a Kennedy Western. Envisioning U.S. intervention in the most self-evident and flattering manner imaginable, it introduced a new sort of Hollywood Freedom Fighter, one as easily understandable as . . . Ronald Reagan. In April, the *New York Times* reports, "The Pentagon is now in a position to assume a combat role in Central America should President Reagan give the order."

In early May, the runners of the Olympic torch relay departed New York City

---

growth. And they do not automatically believe government has the answer to all problems.

Their sense of realism extends to the November elections, and one reason "yuppies" tend to favor Mr. Hart is they believe he will appeal to a broad spectrum of voters, particularly moderates and independents.

for Los Angeles; at the end of the month, the first flurry of Reagan spots appeared. "Spring '84 in America," which features a white farmhouse, the Grand Canyon, some happy old folks, a group of kids playing basketball, a bustling factory, and a space capsule, might have been made for John Glenn. "For the first time in a long time," the narrator maintains, "hope for the future is coming back."

It was then that *Indiana Jones and the Temple of Doom* opened, and the *Village Voice* movie critic assigned to review (me) lost it. The following diatribe began on the *Voice* cover before jumping to the film section, and is reprinted here in abbreviated form.

George Lucas and Steven Spielberg are the most successful filmmakers who ever lived, with six of the top grossing movies in American history. Millionaires many times over, they can do whatever they want. Lucas even insists that what he would like to make are experimental, non-narrative films. But who's kidding whom? What these guys want, apparently, is *Indiana Jones and the Temple of Doom*.

There's a poetry to pulp and everyone knows that many artists are engaged in working through the junk of their childhood. Few, however, seem as blithely uncritical as Lucas and Spielberg. When Kate Capshaw, who has the thankless task of playing *Indiana Jones*'s bimbo-in-residence, asks Harrison Ford why they're about to go off after the sacred Sankara stone of Pankot palace, there's a cut to close-up that turns his patronizing reply into a virtual manifesto. The reason, since you asked, is "fortune and glory." The fortune will belong to Messrs. Spielberg and Lucas. But the glory, on the other hand, is something grosses can't buy.

Strictly speaking a "prequel," this latest pastiche of the Saturday afternoon serials and adventure TV shows George Lucas loved as a kid picks up more or less where *Raiders* left off. Ford meets Capshaw during an intricately choreographed brawl in a Shanghai cabaret, and they dive out the window together, plunging through six canopies to land in a car driven by a ten-year-old street urchin (Ke Huy Quan), named Short Round in tribute to Sam Fuller's *The Steel Helmet*. Beating their pursuers to the airport, this surrogate family takes off in a plane, only to watch the crew bail out (and the fuel meter read empty), leaving them just a

life raft with which to jump into space, go tobogganing down the Hima-
layas, sail over a cliff, tumble into a river, and ride the rapids to India.

Like *Raiders*, *Indiana Jones* is filmmaking at its most smugly
mechanistic—the celluloid equivalent of a day in Disneyland, a point
Spielberg brings home late in the movie with a reflexive action sequence
that simulates an old-fashioned roller coaster ride. But *This Is Cinerama*
spends most of its time in the Spook-a-Rama, activating one jack-in-the-
box after another. I won't belabor the Freudian implications of the secret
passage Ford discovers in Capshaw's boudoir (particularly in a film as
breezily male supremacist as this one); suffice to say it leads to a cham-
ber of horrors inhabited by more roaches than the Furry Freak Brothers'
crash pad and thence to the Temple of Doom, a flaming red-on-red set
that suggests Maxwell's Plum as redecorated by Julian Schnabel. . . .

[*Indiana Jones*] is inordinately racist and sexist, even by Hollywood
standards. There's a kind of willful ignorance here, as though the magnitude of their success exempts Lucas and Spielberg from any moral consid-
erations. Like white boys just want to have fun! As the film's only woman,
Capshaw is compelled to play a bitchy gold digger (her desire for fortune
implies no glory) who takes her ritual lumps toppling backward off ele-
phants, being terrorized by jungle animals (while the boys argue over
cards) or yo-yoing up and down above the Sacred Lava Pit while wrapped
in the embrace of the hero's equally fetishized whip.*

Remaking the 40-year-old pulp serials they adore—without, apparently, pondering what it is that fascinates them so—these new Kings of
the Earth have no qualms about reproducing 40-year-old assumptions
as well. The film's only humanized nonwhite is necessarily 10 years old.
Indeed, when not pathetically downtrodden, the denizens of the third-
world theme park where Indiana seeks his fortune and glory are all
duplicitous evil scum whose favored cuisine is a suitably yucky repast of raw
snakes, giant beetles, and chilled monkey brains. For all its insistence on
innocent pleasures and the primacy of entertainment, *Indiana Jones* is a
joyless film—mean-spirited, preening, and lacking in grace.

---

* Spielberg and Capshaw were married in 1991.

Forget John Glenn. Later that summer, *Newsweek* would compare Ronald Reagan to Indiana Jones and conjure the Conquest of Grenada: "Rather than pretending to present the American people with the complexities of international relations, Reagan presented the invasion in movie terms. He scorned dialectic for drama, discarded fact in favor of fantasy. . . . His talent for selling illusions to the Indiana Jones generation is the greatest gift a modern president can have."

A demonstration of American superiority, *Indiana Jones* was itself number one when President Reagan flew to France to participate in celebrations marking the fortieth anniversary of the Allied invasion of Europe.

June 5, Reagan spoke at Pointe du Hoc, the spot where U.S. Rangers landed on D-Day. Unlike the other Normandy beaches, evidence of war was preserved—a cratered landscape cut by corroded barb wire. On this dramatic site, the president addressed an audience of veterans, hailing them as "the champions who helped free a continent."

That afternoon, Reagan gave another address, along with French and British dignitaries, at the site of D-Day's worst carnage, Omaha Beach. Reagan's biographer Lou Cannon regards these speeches as his strongest overseas performances, in part because they allowed him to relive his own experience of World War II, wearing a uniform and making propaganda films in Hollywood: Reagan "seemed to be returning to Normandy because he had already been there in his mind."

The D-Day footage would play a significant part in Reagan's campaign film, *A New Beginning*, used for a scene in which he not only appeared but narrated—at once a humble participant and the omniscient voice of history, the remembered past, recalling both the war, which he knew only from the movies, and, more importantly, his role in its commemoration.

We begin bombing in five minutes . . . who you gonna call?

On June 8, two days after Ronald Reagan's D-Day performance, two summer-defining movies materialized—Ivan Reitman's *Ghostbusters* and Joe Dante's *Gremlins*—both special effects–driven comedies readable as occult fantasies of foreign invasion, D-Day in reverse. After the Democrats held their national convention but before the Republicans held theirs, a film dramatizing a more straightforward attack opened: John Milius's *Red Dawn*.

In addition to dramatizing instances of alien aggression, *Ghostbusters* and *Gremlins* offered the spectacle of disaster. *Ghostbusters* brought together two trends—the technology of wonder associated with *Close Encounters* and *E.T.*, and the cynical, post-countercultural attitude of *Saturday Night Live*. *Gremlins* was even more dialectical. A movie about, if not for, children of all ages, predicated on the venerable and quintessentially Spielbergian fantasy of toys come to life, it was understood equally as the triumph of Spielbergism and its antithesis.

This double apprehension was instantaneous. As David Chute put it, with a nod to *Forbidden Planet* in a *Film Comment* cover story, *Gremlins*' eponymous creatures were the "monsters from E.T.'s id." Sugar laced with strychnine, Dante's movie reveled in the horror that lurks beneath the surface of the cute. Rand Peltzer (Hoyt Axton), the feckless inventor-salesman dad, follows his nose into a Chinatown novelty store to discover the original cute and cuddly, big-eyed Mogwai, soon to be known as Gizmo, and unwittingly opens the gates of Troy.

Rand's motto, "I make the illogical logical," should be flipped. Is there a rational reason, even in the storybook world that *Gremlins* creates, why Gizmo—a furry, pet-able pet far more lovable than the reptilian E.T., presented to Rand as a Christmas present for his too-old-for-toys son Billy (Zach Galligan)—should, if carelessly sprinkled with ordinary water, erupt in icky pustules that hatch altogether less adorable versions of the Mogwai, and that these fur-balls, if allowed to feed after midnight, turn into hilariously mean, scarifying black-leather creatures from the pit of hell?

Gremlin's climactic Walpurgisnacht takes place, for maximum carnage, on the holiest night of the Christian calendar and on the innocuous Warner Bros. "small town" set that, among many other things, was occupied by Soviet troops in the 1962 public service film *Red Nightmare*. Part flashback to Frank Capra's *It's a Wonderful Life*, part preview of Ronald Reagan's campaign film *A New Beginning*, *Gremlins*' highpoint is a desecration of Main Street by a monstrously uncouth alien army.

The xenophobic notion of the infernal critters as foreigners is occasionally articulated throughout the movie, but the gremlins' gleeful destruction is against interpretation and beyond good and evil. They begin their reign of terror by hanging the Peltzer family dog, then, after doing battle with Mom (Frances Lee McCain), go on to torment the town's meanest resident with yuletide carols and then take over a local bar—where the younger Peltzer's chaste girlfriend (Phoebe Cates) is inexplicably employed—trashing, flashing, and otherwise staging the nastiest puppet show in Hollywood history before adjourning to Kingston Falls' local bijou, to first destroy the projection booth and then treat themselves to a special screening of *Snow White*.

This bravura bit of double animation allows Dante to hold up a less-than-flattering mirror to his audience, identified by reviewer Scott Rosenberg in the *Boston Phoenix* as "American youth sotted and crazed from a steady diet of exhausting Spielberg and Lucas flicks." It is as though Dante created an ambience of cozy, all-American wholesomeness purely for the fun of staging an adolescent or—appropriate to the post–*E.T.* world—infantile desecration. *Gremlins*' key image is one of its loathsome monsters blowing its snout on the living room drapes.

Even during the movie's blatantly innocent first third, Dante uses an exploding juice squeezer to stage an excremental attack on Mom's spotless kitchen; later, Mom herself is compelled to employ assorted kitchen appliances as instruments of (extremely messy) pest-control. As *New York Times* reviewer Vincent Canby realized, Dante's movie was ("unfortunately") at its funniest when being "most nasty."*

"Who is this picture for?" Dante mused in his interview with David Chute. "Is it for kids, or is it for grownups, or is it for grownups who wish they were

---

* Preoccupied with *Indiana Jones and the Temple of Doom*, much of which was shot on location in Sri Lanka. Dante's executive producer, Spielberg, was something of an absentee landlord—albeit one that *Gremlins* evokes throughout. The local movie theater is showing *Watch the Skies* and *A Boy's Life* (the original titles for *Close Encounters* and *E.T.*), a billboard advertises a radio personality with a distinct resemblance to Indiana Jones, a toy shop features an E.T. figure. Gizmo harmonizes with Billy on something very close to the *Close Encounters* communication song. Dante told Spielberg biographer Joseph McBride that his patron was a bemused good sport. "He got the joke right away. . . . But I don't think he was prepared for how wacky *Gremlins* was. I remember sitting with him in a Warner Bros. screening room, and I saw him in the row behind me hitting his head [again and again] while he was watching the movie." According to Dante, Spielberg's "major change"—and consequently *Gremlins*' major concession to Spielbergism—was keeping Gizmo alive throughout the movie long after logic dictates his demise. The decision would reap millions in adorable Mogwai dolls and *Gremlins* ancillary rights even as it contributed to the movie's schizoid self-awareness as a prank.

kids?" Screenwriter Chris Columbus's protagonists were initially young teen-agers but, according to Dante, "Steven saw that as 'way too close to *E.T.*'" and instructed Columbus to raise their age levels, thus adding a discordantly backward quality to their portrayals.

Gremlins' mise-en-scène is characterized by Spielberg's then current form of brand-name naturalism, with logos for Burger King, Coors, Snickers, and Mobil gas all prominently on display. Thanks to Gizmo, however, the movie was also a magnificent advertisement for itself. As reported by *Variety, Gremlins* spawned the greatest promotional blitz in Warner Bros. history—a mix of radio spots, mall banners, and store signage designed to produce a hundred million "shopper impressions." The audience was primed. Janet Maslin attended an early preview and told *Times* readers that on first glimpse of Gizmo, spectators "emitted what sounded like the 'Aaah!' heard round the world."

If *Gremlins* is conspicuously absent from Andrew Britton's brilliant es-say of analysis "Blissing Out: The Politics of Reaganite Entertainment" (all the more impressive for having been written in the heat of the moment), a text devoting considerable space to *Red Dawn, Ghostbusters,* and *Indiana Jones in the Temple of Doom,* as well as *E.T.* and even *Poltergeist,* it may be because Dante's movie was so shocking an anomaly.

Gremlins alone succeeded in using what Britton called "the ritualized re-petitiveness of Reaganite entertainment . . . with its delirious, self-celebrating self-reference [and] interminable solipsism" to critique Reaganite entertain-ment, along with its travesty of Spielbergian childhood innocence. It's sug-gestive that after Billy successfully blows up the movie theater and destroys the gremlin horde, the gremlin leader remains, hidden in a toy store behind an E.T. doll. *Gremlins* was a mass of contradictions. Indeed, as was often observed, the movie was as schizoid as its Mogwai mascot.*

---

* This built-in travesty may be why *Mad* magazine's parody "Grimlins," written by Stan Hart and illustrated by Mort Drucker, doesn't quite work. And yet, "Grimlins" does point to *Gremlins'* critique of American self-delusion: "This is Stinkton Falls . . . a typically American small town!" Bilgy Setzer explains. "Our drinking water is polluted with car-cinogens! Our streets are paved with radioactive materials! Our classrooms are lined with asbestos! And we've got a toxic waste dump that's emptying into our basements! Man, if that doesn't make us typically American . . . I don't know WHAT does!!" *Mad's* suggestion that *Gremlins* is *E.T.* with "an extra-added wrinkle" or characterization of Gizmo as "a midget YODA . . in drag!" are not without merit, but the notion of Kingston Falls as a

Yet, thanks to Spielberg's intervention, *Gremlins* also succeeded as a Spielberg blockbuster, allowing the audience to participate in Dante's critique by negating it with the purchase of millions of dollars of worthless paraphernalia. *Gremlins* surpassed the studio's two previous box-office champions, *Superman: The Movie* and *The Exorcist*; it needed only forty-two days to gross $100 million and finished number three for the year.

Ghostbusters was an even bigger hit and the one that, albeit haunted by the phantom of 1968, most fully embodied the 1984 zeitgeist.

Gremlins inspired critical misgivings; *Ghostbusters* none. Although rapturously received as a comedy classic, the movie is often plodding, overly dependent on special effects, and frequently infantile in its fixation on mucous textures. The script was written by Dan Aykroyd and Harold Ramis, and they didn't give themselves much to do as actors—eclipsed on screen by the arch-nerd Rick Moranis. Bill Murray, unflappably self-interested and sleazy, is the only strong lead—although Sigourney Weaver is more than game in a severely limited role as the movie's only significant female character.

Aesthetically weak but ideologically potent, *Ghostbusters* portrayed and spoke to the same generation as *The Big Chill*, albeit with a giddy cynicism and engaging absence of angst. Not unlike the Party in Orwell's *1984*, *Ghostbusters* sees through everything—even itself. Making significant use of the old New Left battleground, Columbia University, the movie mocked academic research, countercultural idealism, and governmental regulation to celebrate, even as it parodied, an entrepreneurial free market and skillful merchandising.

Far more than *Gremlins*, *Ghostbusters* merged with its own advertising, exhibiting what the culture critic Fred Pfeil characterized as "a kind of horror and disgust towards those trapped in and defined by the endlessly proliferating codes, clichés, and slogans of everyday life"—the people who for one reason or another won't "get" the movie. (In utopian terms, the movie marries manipulation and its opposite, transparency, the awareness of manipulation.) Thus, the Ghostbusters' TV spots are presented as particularly brilliant in flattering prospective customers, telling viewers: "We're ready to believe you!"

Potemkin village is the key insight. Hart and Drucker's most pointed joke is found on the side of the microwave oven used to incinerate a gremlin: "At G.E. Reagan Was Our Most Important Product."

That the Ghostbusters might be con artists is preempted by the film's villainous Environmental Protection Agency agent, who accuses them of creating apparitions so that they may exorcise them with tricks. Reagan's opposition to governmental regulations in general and his disdain for the EPA were intrinsic to his program. Significantly, the EPA agent, whom Murray refers to as "pencil dick," is not an iconographic square. He has a beard and groomed, longish hair; he seems to belong to the same generational cohort as the Ghostbusters. Unlike them, however, he is a strident idealist, a clueless do-gooder—his presence allows the Murray character to critique his own presumed hippie-peacenik past.*

Doubling as publicity for the movie, the *Ghostbusters* theme song was number one on the *Billboard* Hot 100 for three weeks. "I've been in this business for years, and I've never experienced [this] kind of phenomenon," a Columbia vice president told the *New York Post*. "I'm receiving hundreds of calls from people wanting *Ghostbusters* T-shirts and other items. People want anything with the *Ghostbusters* logo on it." There were some one hundred items in all. When Macy's Herald Square sold out of *Ghostbusters* T-shirts, a desperate fan broke the window and stole the display. Airlines promised "pricebusters," mortgage services were "ratebusters." The media was filled with references to budgetbusters, cropbusters, nukebusters, and litterbusters. CBS News blithely dubbed their DemCon commentators "Conventionbusters."†

---

* Democrats attempted to rally these forces during the campaign, as when their candidate Walter Mondale adopted the sappy Crosby, Stills & Nash song "Teach Your Children," making an appeal that only made them seem lamer than Reagan.

† The *New York Post* called *Ghostbusters* "the first movie in which the logo has become as famous as its stars," noting that "Columbia's strategy for building anticipation for the film relied heavily upon the power of suggestion."

> Newspaper ads were small, and appeared anywhere but in the movie pages. The logo and its accompanying copy line turned up in the business pages, in the fashion pages, in the sports section. Television advertising worked similarly. Columbia purchased 15-second spots during the short news spots separating prime time network programs. Again, all that was shown was the logo and its one line, without as much as an indication that the commercial was for a motion picture.

The campaign was wildly successful. *Ghostbusters* triumphantly illustrates the condition of American motion pictures in the Age of Reagan and beyond as glumly described by Todd Gitlin: "The sum total of the publicity takes up more cultural space than the movie itself."

The logo was ubiquitous on political cartoons. The *New York Times* reported that supporters of both Reagan and Mondale "picked up on the theme and have used it at college rallies, substituting caricatures of the candidates for the perplexed spirit that appears in the 'no ghost' sign. Youth groups for both parties report that T-shirts and bumper stickers are selling well, and both sides have originated choreographed skits performed to the Ghostbuster theme song."

In *Close Encounters*, Spielberg used the occult belief in extraterrestrial beings as a means to dispel certain rational contemporary fears—the instability of the nuclear family or mental illness. No less than Spielberg or Ronald Reagan (fascinated by prophesies of Armageddon) or Nancy Reagan (who employed a personal astrologer), *Ghostbusters* takes the supernatural as a given. What *Ghostbusters* satirizes is not belief in the occult but merely the special-effects movies that appeal to it. In referencing male urination, the ultimate Ghostbuster weapon was a mildly scatological parody of the light sabers that produced such childish awe in *Star Wars*. As skeptical as he is, the Murray character believes in karma; he and his partners were fated to go into business. Having developed a form of spook removal, tacitly compared to Reagan's Star Wars, as "the indispensable defense science of the next decade," the self-proclaimed Ghostbusters—Murray and his buddies Aykroyd, Ramis, and Ernie Hudson—gloat that "the franchise rights alone will make us rich beyond our wildest dreams."

Like Reagan in his pre-election mode, these commercial exorcists invoke "a disaster of biblical proportions." But this Judgment Day (in which the dead rise from their graves in the manner of the ultimate Sixties' horror vision, *Night of the Living Dead*) is prevented through the power of denial. Murray's character, identified by Sigourney Weaver's as less a scientist than a game-show host, refuses to admit the supposed gravity of what is happening—and *it doesn't happen*. However business-school perfect, the movie is remarkably cynical in its view of capitalism and the marketplace, happily ending with a blitz of ancillary merchandising—Ghostbuster T-shirts hawked at the very site of the Ghostbusters' triumph.

By representing Judgment Day as entertainment, *Ghostbusters*, rather than *Red Dawn* or *Rocky IV*, was the antidote to *The Day After*. The dreadful future that George Orwell in *1984* imagined as the "boot stamping on a human face—forever" vanished. Prophetically, if prematurely, *Ghostbusters* celebrated the end of the Cold War. Its slogan—"I ain't afraid of no ghost"—includes the very specter that, 136 years before, Marx and Engels saw haunting Europe.*

Both *Ghostbusters* and *Gremlins* were of a piece with the season's delirium.

Ronald Reagan's early summer polls were higher than ever, comfortably ahead of both Gary Hart and the eventual Democratic nominee, Walter Mondale. On June 23, the president screened *Bedtime for Bonzo* for some guests at Camp David (Nancy was away) and followed it up with *Star Trek III* (noting "it wasn't too good"). Three weeks later, at a convention distinguished by orations from Jesse Jackson and Mario Cuomo, Mondale chose as his running mate, New York congresswoman Geraldine Ferraro, the first woman on the ticket of a major party. Mondale made history but, however prematurely, history was over. With the Russians boycotting the Los Angeles Olympics, America effectively ruled the world.

Strategically opened in the hammock between the Olympics and the Republican convention, John Milius's *Red Dawn* was the quintessential cine-celebration of Cold War II—and indeed, a sort of remake. Even as Steven Spielberg's *E.T.* was a cannier, cuddlier version of *It Came from Outer Space*, so *Red Dawn* seemed a monumental upgrade of the hysterical, 1952 Korean War cheapie *Invasion USA*.

An introductory text spells out a backstory worthy of Able Archer 83:

SOVIET UNION SUFFERS WORST WHEAT HARVEST IN 55 YEARS.
LABOR AND FOOD RIOTS IN POLAND. SOVIET TROOPS INVADE.
CUBA AND NICARAGUA TROOP STRENGTH GOALS OF 500,000. EL
SALVADOR AND HONDURAS FALL. GREEN PARTY GAINS CONTROL
OF WEST GERMAN PARLIAMENT. DEMANDS WITHDRAWAL OF
NUCLEAR WEAPONS FROM EUROPEAN SOIL. MEXICO PLUNGED
INTO REVOLUTION. NATO DISSOLVES. UNITED STATES STANDS
ALONE.

Alone and vulnerable as an innocent babe, this America is visualized as a

---

* Reitman's personal history—he was born in Slovakia to Jewish Holocaust survivors who emigrated to Canada from Communist Czechoslovakia in 1950—may account for the movie's political subtext.

grittier version of Spielberg's *E.T.* suburbia and given additional verisimilitude with references to Chevy, Coke, Coors, Gulf, and Ralston Purina. Invaded by the combined forces of Russia, Cuba, and Nicaragua (if not Grenada), the nation is defended to the death by a cadre of teenaged guerrillas who call themselves "the Wolverines," named after their high school football team by their self-appointed leader, quarterback Jed Eckert (Patrick Swayze).

The notion of a Nicaraguan invasion, as depicted in *Red Dawn*, had been planted by the president in April 1983 when he warned a joint session of Congress that "El Salvador is nearer to Texas than Texas is to Massachusetts" and "Nicaragua is just as close to Miami, San Antonio, San Diego, and Tucson as those cities are to Washington." Still, the movie has a half-intended camp quality that belies its macho posturing; its real audience wasn't only Reagan's America but the aging hippies and limousine liberals of the film industry. Who else but a UCLA-educated nuclear-freezenik was likely to notice that *Red Dawn* opens in the clouds like *Triumph of the Will*, or that, after the Russian takeover, Sergei Eisenstein's nationalist epic *Alexander Nevsky* is playing at the local bijou (for free).*

Avenging the fatherland is literalized when the Russians execute Jed's own dad (Harry Dean Stanton) as he defiantly sings "God Bless America." Somewhat more exotic is the identification of these American insurgents with various Third World liberation struggles. *Red Dawn* also expresses Milius's professed admiration for Yugoslavia anti-Nazi partisans and his covert fondness for Fidel Castro. ("I'm a Castro fighting in the hills against those fraudulent, narrow-minded, bigoted and destructive people," the director once said of New York's film critics.) Milius loved the idea of guerrilla warfare right down to its fashion accessories. By the end of the movie, Swayze's heroic quarterback is even wearing a homemade burnoose. While the Russian occupiers compare Colorado to Afghanistan, the Cubans are notably less at ease in their imperial role, not to mention depressed by the frigid *yanqui* winter. By the end, the film's main Cuban (Ron "Superfly" O'Neal) is so taken with the

---

* One of *Red Dawn*'s most iconic images—used in publicity stills but cut from the film just prior to its August 10 opening, presumably because of the previous month's mass murder at a McDonald's in San Ysidro, California—has a fearsome Red Army quartet hoisting their Kalashnikovs beside a Golden Arch.

gutsy Wolverines that he actually lets them escape unharmed, offering a "*Vaya con dios*" blessing.

In essence, *Red Dawn* is more xenophobic than anti-Communist. Rather than imagining a military failure caused by insufficient defense spending, the movie invents a new form of sneak attack. In this grim extrapolation of the survivalist worldview, the Soviets are starving for want of American grain. The initial invasion force came disguised as commercial airliners—an armada of Aeroflot planes stacked up over New York's JFK International Airport. This followed by a few "selective nuclear strikes." The coup de grace, however, has been years and years of illegal infiltration from Mexico—a nativist fear that would only grow more potent in the decades following the movie's release.

Red Dawn was shooting in New Mexico during the time that *The Day After* was telecast. The Pentagon had refused to assist MGM, but the project was not without quasi-official sanction, having been vetted by Reagan's former secretary of defense and current MGM/United Artist board member, Alexander Haig.

According to *Variety* editor Peter Bart, then an MGM/UA senior vice president for production, the studio's chief executive officer Frank Yablans enlisted Haig as a consultant: "Yablans declared in no uncertain terms that he wanted to make the ultimate jingoistic movie and that Al Haig would take him there." Consequently, Haig took Milius under his wing, bringing him to the Hudson Institute, the conservative think tank founded by Herman Kahn, to develop a plausible scenario.

Bart, who had acquired Kevin Reynolds's screenplay "Ten Soldiers," says that *Red Dawn*'s original concept resembled *Lord of the Flies* in focusing on the situation of children who cope with the absence of parents by brutalizing one another. Milius, however, imagined the *Red Dawn* scenario as a Third World liberation struggle in reverse; Haig hypothesized that, with the collapse of NATO, a left-wing Mexican regime would participate in the Soviet invasion, effectively splitting the U.S. in half. It's not clear if Haig also introduced the idea of a survivable—which is to say, winnable—nuclear war, but even the gun-toting Milius, who took part of his payment for rewriting Reynolds's script and directing the picture as what Bart called "an exotic new weapon of his choosing," was taken aback by Haig's alterations. "Wandering into my office one day," according to Bart, Milius "confided his concern that he was being railroaded into what he described as 'a flag-waving, jingoistic movie.'"*

Haig, who hailed *Red Dawn* as "one of the most realistic and provocative films" he had ever seen, with an important lesson regarding "the maintenance of American strength," organized an invitational preview in Washington for select Pentagon and CIA officials and their dates. Noting that the evening marked ten years since Richard Nixon resigned, Haig (once Nixon's chief of staff) joked that the screening was "a traditional event here—we do it every Watergate anniversary." The reaction was diplomatic. "A party for a movie like [*Red Dawn*] is the kind of party that just demands some delicacy," the *Washington Post* reported. "When the audience walked out at the end of the first screening two hours later, some weren't quite sure how to handle the transition from guerrilla war to teeny-tiny ham sandwiches and meat-balls on toothpicks."

Red Dawn had already had its all-media preview at the Samuel Goldwyn Theater in Beverly Hills on August 3. The response there was mixed, with *Variety* reporting "laughter" and "hooting" among the assembled journalists. Such derision was not in evidence when the movie opened a week later. "Newly patriotic crowds cheer rabble-rousing film," reported the *Los Angeles Herald Examiner*. A thirty-six-year-old man, leaving the Sherman Oaks Cinema with his jubilant buddies, told the *Herald Examiner* reporter that "people were shouting 'Wolverines!' but nobody was laughing." Some patrons related audience excitement to the Olympics, others to the campaign. "If Mondale gets elected, that is what's going to happen," one nineteen-year-old UCLA political science major maintained.

Displacing *Ghostbusters*, *Red Dawn* was the number-one movie the week it opened on 1,800-plus screens. Chicago journalist Roger Simon attended a weekday matinee "at a theater that usually caters to kids who carry large radios and talk to the screen" and instead found the theater "filled largely with young men in suits and ties who looked as if they were playing hooky from the commodities exchange."

A piece that would be published some months later in *Policy Review*, house organ of the conservative Heritage Foundation, pointed out that the

---

* Although *Red Dawn* was among the movies screened at the March 1987 U.S.-Soviet "Entertainment Summit," Milius was not invited or perhaps chose not to attend.

Wolverines were neither idealists nor patriots. *Red Dawn* "holds not a single mention of freedom or democracy. . . . In fact, the audience is never given any reason to believe these young Americans know what such principles mean, or even that they exist." The writer, Susan Vigilante, identified the movie's key scene in which, as the Wolverines prepare to execute one of their members for treason, another asks, "What's the difference between them and us?," and the quarterback screams, "We live here!"

"The simplicity of the Wolverines' claim may be one of the prime reasons for *Red Dawn*'s popularity," Vigilante suggested, linking it to Reagan's invasion of Grenada. Most Americans, especially young ones, "not only supported President Reagan's decision, they cheered him. He had made things simple—and right—and that always feels good."

One day after *Red Dawn* opened, Reagan delivered his infamous sound check: "My fellow Americans. I'm pleased to tell you today that I've signed legislation that will outlaw the Soviet Union forever. We begin bombing in five minutes."

In the summer of 1984, the New Totality first glimpsed in the 1960s came to full fruition. Movies merged with life as life merged with TV in a common media spectacle. Pundits had ceased invoking George Orwell at the moment when the campaign was at its most "*1984*."*

The Republican convention was an extension of the Los Angeles Olympics (or *1984*'s "Two-Minutes Hate"), filled with fanatical patriotic fervor. "At the slightest provocation, cadres of young Republicans would flood the aisles, pumping their arms in the air and shouting 'U.S.A.! U.S.A.!'" Jack W. Germond and Jules Witcover reported.

Reagan developed a little ritual with the crowds. He would tell them he was going to give them a little test. Then he would proceed to ask them what

---

* Israeli academic Bernard Avishai observes that Orwell especially feared television, noting the dissident Emmanuel Goldstein's assertion in *1984* that "with the development of television, private life came to an end." Telescreens cannot be turned off. They are not only a technology of surveillance but also one designed to debase personal space. "Who can read Orwell's account of [these] violent and pornographic telecasts without thinking about American crime shows, the soaps, the Big Events and the commercials that interrupt them?" Avishai asked. "The print media have not been immune to television's standards, of course. In *Time* and *Newsweek*, writers take for granted a democracy of shifting perceptions. Their relentless polls imply that simultaneous opinion is our only hard fact."

country had cut inflation, interest rates, and unemployment. He was not going to give them the answer, he would say, but he would tell them it was known by three initials. The audience, and particularly the young people in the crowd, invariably would start the chant.

As the president made a joke of the Soviet Union by pretending to announce its demise, the *Ghostbusters* theme went to number one on the Billboard Hot 100. The song, which repeatedly posed the question "Who ya gonna call?" and answered with a resounding "Ghostbusters!," was still at number one when Senator Paul Laxalt nominated the president to run for a second term on the final night of the Republican convention. "Let me ask the American people," he said. "Whom would you rather have sit down at the bargaining table and negotiate a responsible arms-reduction agreement with the Soviet Union? A tough confident leader like Ronald Reagan, eyeball to eyeball with the steely-eyed Soviet masters, or Walter Mondale?" Ghostbusters! (Reagan may not have blinked then but, as his radio gaffe regarding bombing Russia suggests, he did occasionally wink.)

On August 30, a week after Reagan's renomination and one week after *Variety* reported Pittsburgh pickets attacking *Red Dawn* as "Reagan propaganda," the chairman of the South Carolina Federation of College Republicans wrote to the president:

> I had the recent pleasure of seeing the new movie entitled *Red Dawn* at a local theatre. After talking with a few friends, we decided it is a movie you should see. Entirely on my own, and without suggestion from anyone able to benefit from your seeing the film, I encourage you to see it.

"If you are indeed able to view it," he optimistically added, "I would appreciate the opportunity of viewing it and discussing it with you." Reagan's reply is unknown but less than a week later, on September 7, the president took his correspondent's advice and screened *Red Dawn* at Camp David. (Reagan's official schedule suggests that he may have watched the movie with his chief of staff James Baker, Baker's assistant Margaret Tutwiler, and his naval aide Commander William G. Sutton, all of whom were at Camp David that weekend.) Meanwhile in Los Angeles, MGM/UA was picketed by the Santa Monica Alliance for Survival and the Los Angeles Peace Coalition.

Although the National Coalition on Television Violence declared *Red Dawn*—the first film to be rated PG-13—to be the most violent movie ever

made, with an average of 134 acts of mayhem committed per hour (exceeding *Gremlins* and *Indiana Jones in the Temple of Doom*), the movie grossed
$38 million ($1.5 million less than *Conan the Barbarian*) to finish number
twenty for 1984, behind the Tom Hanks comedy *Bachelor Party* and ahead
of the sleeper hit *The Terminator*. Soviet protests, Cuban complaints, and West
German freeze-nik demonstrations only added to the movie's glory. *Red
Dawn* was promoted with a picture spread in *Soldier of Fortune* magazine.
Milius was honored by the Gun Owners of America.*

Released less than a decade after America's Indo-Chinese adventure
came to its inglorious conclusion, while claiming as collateral damage the
Cold War's most durable genre, the original *Red Dawn* was—like *First
Blood*—a crypto-Western, made from an imagined or unintentional Native
American perspective. At the same time, the Milius-Haig scenario encouraged its American audience to wallow in triumphalist self-pity. The movie
was pure projection: we didn't attack Vietnam, they attacked us. Moreover,
subliminally rhyming "Wolverine" with "Mujahedeen," *Red Dawn* taunted
the Soviets with their current Afghan quagmire.

The summer of 1984 brought Reagan: the Movie. "Of all the phenomena of
Mr. Reagan on the stump, none are so fascinating as his ability to generate
emotional effects from the distinct areas of fact and fiction," the *New York
Times* reported.

> In addressing the American Legion convention in Salt Lake City, the Presi-
> dent created a patriotic surge in the hall by alternating between such refer-
> ence points as the joyous homecoming of the Iranian hostages ("that

---

* Even lefties were impressed. Writing in *The Nation*, Andrew Kopkind called *Red Dawn*
"the most convincing story about popular resistance to imperial oppression since the in-
imitable *Battle of Algiers*." Still, it was the right that made *Red Dawn* into a cult film; indeed, *Red Dawn* would rival *The Turner Diaries* as an inspiration for advocates of white
power and apocalyptic survivalists. In late 1995, the *New York Times'* front-page analysis
of "[Timothy] McVeigh's mind" coyly led with the Oklahoma City bomber's obsession
with *Red Dawn*: "He rented movies, playing one about a Colorado football team over and
over." Red Dawn ranked number fifteen on the *National Review*'s list of the twenty-five
"Best Conservative Films" of the last twenty-five years (published in 2009): It "has survived
countless more acclaimed films because Father Time has always been our most reliable
film critic. The essence of timelessness is more than beauty. It's also truth, and the truth
that America is a place and an idea worth fighting and dying for will not be denied."

unforgettable moment") and the commercialism of television military fiction ("Maybe you've seen the television show 'Call to Glory' that celebrates Air Force officers serving in the 'twilight struggle' of the cold war?").

A few days later, the *Times* covered Reagan's endorsement by the country singer Roy Acuff:

> The event in the packed Opry theater was one of the more spectacular efforts from the Reagan campaign engineers, ending in a storm of confetti and a mass rendition of "God Bless the U.S.A.," the red-white-and-blue song used on Reagan television commercials. Mr. Reagan, who sang along with his partisans . . . said the Opry was no place for his opponents.
> "They'll just sing the blues," he said as the crowd laughed and applauded.

It was *Nashville* remade as *Close Encounters*, with an acknowledgment of the crowd's whiteness, and a hint of *Rocky*, a movie that hapless Mondale had taken to evoking to remind people of his underdog status.

Videodrome had suggested the radical McLuhanist position that television no longer mirrored reality—now, reality was the mirror of television. Thus, the thirty-minute campaign film given the redundant title *A New Beginning* and sometimes referred to as "Morning in America" would be the template for Reagan's actual rallies.

First shown at the Republican convention as a prelude to Reagan's nomination, *A New Beginning* was reedited to include convention footage and used to announce the Reagan campaign with an unprecedented buy on all three networks in mid-September. The main author was the adman Phil Dusenberry, inventor of the Pepsi Generation. The mode is Reaganist pastoral. Intentionally or not, the bucolic opening montage is reminiscent of that which set the table for annihilation in *The Day After*. America's essential goodness is found in ordinary people, small towns, and farms, as well as cowboys— the president who has a statue of one in the Oval Office is committed to "giving the government back to the people."

Reagan's apparent mandate, according to the campaign film, is the restoration of a lost innocence, a noble past, a primeval America. There are no cities. Nationalist anthems ring out. "America the Beautiful" underscores the president's acceptance speech. One Reagan supporter comments, "I even hear songs on the radio and TV saying I'm proud to be an American," which serves to cue Lee Greenwood singing those very words in his Grammy-winning composition "God Bless the U.S.A."

A New Beginning is a paean to self-interested populism (asking, "Are you better off now then you were four years ago?") and self-congratulatory patriotism. One of the few civilian black men in the film makes a virtue of patience, explaining "we're gonna be better off in the long run." Like the Party members in *1984*, no one has a thought in their head that is not a slogan. The Korean War and particularly World War II stand in for history. There are no direct references to the Soviet Union, Central America, the Middle East or—although South Korea appears as a pacified, U.S.-adoring New Frontier—Vietnam. All have been exorcised, gone down the Ministry of Truth "memory hole."

The movie casts Reagan as a second FDR as people declare, "He gave me a job!" or "He put me to work!" Repeated shots of a wedding correlate to a concern with home construction and ownership. President and Mrs. Reagan are identified as exemplary parents without reference to their actual children. Skillful editing sets them at the center of an imagined community, participating in one Close Encounter after another. Thanks to the failed assassination attempt, Reagan is able to suggest God is sitting on his shoulder. (Even the president was impressed. "Boy, is that a powerful documentary—is that really me?" he was said to have asked Dusenberry.)

God might seem the ultimate character reference, but the president gets a better one. "I think he's just doggone honest," exclaims a young business woman in a foulard tie.

> It's remarkable. He's been on television—what have I heard, about 26 times, talking to us about what he's doing? Now he's not doing that for any other reason than to make it real clear. And if anybody has any question about where he's headed, it's their fault. Maybe they don't have a television.*

Television is the ultimate authority and final arbiter. To not own a set is to be un-American. During the 1984 campaign, according to Germond and Witcover, "the single most important objective for a candidate was scoring well on the evening news shows on a particular night. Campaign managers closed

---

* In fact, although Reagan was frequently on TV he had given relatively few televised press conferences.

their office doors at 6:30 or 7:00 every night to watch what 'really' had happened that day."

Candidate Reagan had appeared tired and confused during the first debate with Walter Mondale, so much so that the managers of his televisual campaign were prepared to denounce TV as superficial and essentially meaningless. An in-house memo declared that "debates can be and frequently are misleading and deceptive: Winning a debate often depends more upon an effective 'cheap shot' than anything else." There was even a built-in rejoinder to this obvious Orwellian doublethink: "The media will notice that for the first time we are minimizing the importance of words and television; but they will just have to understand, along with the voters, that Ronald Reagan takes the presidency and his incumbency seriously."

No need, no worries. Early in the second debate, with regard to JFK's stamina during the Cuban Missile Crisis, Reagan was asked about his vigor. The president was prepared with a quip. After assuring America of his strength and determination, he added with a twinkle and consummate timing that he would not be making an issue of age. "I am not going to exploit, for political purposes, my opponent's youth and inexperience." With these words, Reagan clinched his reelection. The live audience laughed and applauded. Caught on camera with a sheepish grin, Mondale was helpless.

Stars & Hype Forever

Ronald Reagan spent Saturday, November 3, campaigning in Iowa. His last stop of the day was a pilgrimage to John Wayne's birthplace. On Tuesday, Reagan was reelected with nearly 60 percent of the popular vote. He carried forty-nine states, losing only his opponent's home state of Minnesota—and that by 3,761 votes. It was the greatest landslide in American history, exceeding even Nixon's 1972 reelection and FDR's in 1936.

The January 29, 1985, issue of the *Village Voice* marked the president's second inauguration by putting Andy Warhol's image of Reagan as a model in a Van Heusen Century shirts ad on the cover, under the headline "Stars & Hype Forever," and running five articles on the Reagan era. The same title graced my piece, reprinted here with minor excisions:

How will Americans remember the Reagan years?" *Newsweek* wondered last February. "Will they recall the worst recession in 40 years with unemployment at 10.8 percent . . . ? Will they believe that the hardship and suffering—the tent cities and bedraggled cars with Michigan license plates pouring into Texas—were worth the victory over inflation? Will they remember the more than 280 American fighting men killed from Syria to Honduras, or the jubilant medical students from Grenada kissing the ground at the airport?"

As late as last summer, *Time* was being even tougher: "By usual standards of presidential performance, Reagan might be judged a failure. He regularly loses track of facts, or gets them wrong, and he follows his ideology wherever it leads. Several of his subordinates have shown egregious lapses in judgment. Many others are mediocre. His budget is so preposterously out of balance, and generally his programs have tended to hurt the poor." And yet, and yet, and yet—"with most citizens, he seems to have established an uncanny rapport beyond political agreement or disagreement."

Superb as they are at rationalizing all world history from the imagined point of view of these United States in any given week, *Time* and its competitor are incapable of pondering the obvious question. Does this "uncanny rapport" mean that Ronald Reagan gave us what we wanted? Beyond political agreement or disagreement—if not good and evil?

On the surface, Reagan's reelection was the triumph of the irrational. As he had in California, the president sought a second term as a crusading outsider (Congress, the bureaucracy, and—thanks to Walter Mondale—Jimmy Carter were the government, not him). But his flamboyant negation of logic went even deeper. The most racially, economically polarizing president of the postwar era (polls revealed that even his supporters believed his policies favored the rich), Reagan regularly invoked the names of popular Democrats, taking credit for the military buildup, anti-entitlement, and tight money policies that began in the last years of the Carter administration and reveling in an economy that had only just returned to the 1979 level. *I made it through the wilderness . . .*

If Reagan had run in 1980 on a platform to balance the budget and subsequently inflated the federal debt to a cool $3.5 trillion, it was equally true that, the Conquest of Grenada aside, his administration could not boast of a single foreign policy success. But while the restraint that enabled the hostages to return from Tehran alive was proof of Carter's ineffectuality, the bungled posturing that resulted in the death of 280 marines in Beirut was taken as a no-fault act of God, forgotten as quickly as Reagan's sacred promise to never abandon Lebanon. When arms talks shut down amid the war hysteria of late '83, Reagan's poll ratings as a peacemaker shot up.

However distanced from his government or its actions, Reagan was scarcely outside the irrational desires to which it appealed. Au contraire. The president, as one biographer noted, "believes that he gained fame through forces beyond his control." John Hinckley's unsuccessful assassination attempt was only one more proof of Reagan's magical good fortune. *Newsweek* reported that the president's aides had seen his feeling of vocation take on almost a spiritual hue after March 1981—"*As if,* one of them thought, *he felt touched by destiny.*" And despite his professed faith in the future—"'Greatness lies ahead of us,' he said, and in a storm of hurrahs and a blizzard of laser-lit metal confetti, he offered himself as its instrument"—the president has pondered, along with various cabinet members and close advisers, whether ours wasn't the generation that will see the Day of Judgment. *I ain't afraid of no ghost!*

The polls showed that the president's popularity transcended widespread disapproval of his policies, but then irrationality isn't simply a side effect of Reagan's rule, it's part of the program: the vision of the future as Smalltown U.S.A. circa 1925, the Toyotas—"Buy American!"—emblazoned with Nuclear Freeze *and* Reagan-Bush stickers, the pro-ERA, pro-choice college coeds who were gung ho for Reagan because he was "upbeat" like Dad. A politician who had won his first two elections running against the kids at Berkeley demonstrated an unholy appeal for a new generation of collegians, disciplined by the recession of 1981–82, grateful for Reagan's promise of unlimited growth, and frantically studying "communications," the better to understand the Great Communicator himself.

Reagan's every promise concealed a threat. Who was this Great

Communicator if not some babbling version of our national unconscious? "I have signed legislation outlawing the Soviet Union. The
bombing begins in five minutes!" In its most virulent form, the mass
Reaganism of 1984—a true pop phenomenon like Beatlemania—was a
combination of yearning and denial, puritanism and greed, all tied up in
one jumbo family-sized package of all-natural space-age old-fashioned
new-and-improved jingoistic hoopla.

The 1984 Olympics were a metaphor for the new world order. The
Evil Empire and its allies had simply vanished, leaving the U.S. to run
roughshod over Belgium and the Philippines, racking up one gold
medal after another. Deliriously, the nation celebrated its newfound as-
cendancy and Reagan, whose denial of reality dovetailed so exactly with
the zeitgeist, reaped the benefit—"a patriotism," said *Newsweek*, "un-
matched in peacetime American politics since the age of Teddy Roosevelt." *Somehow I made it through . . .*

"Not since Dwight Eisenhower has the U.S. public felt such fondness
for its leader," crowed *Time*, while *Newsweek* hailed Ronald Reagan as
"the most popular president since Roosevelt. . . . He *plays* the role better
than anyone since John F. Kennedy." At the height of the campaign,
NBC News put together a report on the amazing, media-manufactured
Ronald Reagan Show the president had taken on the road. But even the
correspondent Tom Brokaw had to admit that this exposé was most
likely one more promotion. The public, Brokaw told the *New York
Times*, would probably "be impressed by it, rather than horrified. Why
shouldn't they be? He's good at it." *Didn't know how lost I was until I
found you . . .*

Is Ronald Reagan the greatest American who ever lived, or is he only
the most American? Only a few recalcitrant minorities seemed able to
resist the spectacle of a seventy-three-year-old ex-actor waxing nostalgic for God, neighborliness, the nuclear family, strong leadership, the
work ethic, and the small-town community. Especially since—as everyone knew—he himself seldom attended church, rarely gave to charity,
was divorced by his first wife, communicated badly with his children (and
indeed everyone else if there was no script), failed to control his own
staff, kept bankers' hours, hung out with a passel of corrupt billion-
aires, and had fled his small town (scarcely a Norman Rockwell paradise

but a place where his father had been the local drunk) for the flesh-pots of California at the earliest opportunity.

Not simply the McLuhan paradigm of old wine in a glitzy new bottle—a be-rouged creature of the consumer culture endorsing the old-time puritan religion the way he once promoted Chesterfields or General Electric ("Progress is our most important product")—our Ronald was a walking, talking, preaching, leaching contradiction. What do you call a Social Darwinist who rejects the theory of evolution? A president who smashes the New Deal in the name of Franklin Roosevelt?

Jimmy Carter had promised the American people he would never lie to them. His mistake? There's a sucker born every minute. The American people, Ronald Reagan knew, aren't interested in the truth when a lie can be so much more beautiful.

Intense imaginary relationships with media figures have become a prevalent, statistically normal feature of contemporary American social organization.

—JOHN L. CAUGHEY, *Imaginary Social Worlds*

"He probably spends two or three hours a day on real work," one aide confided to a news magazine. "All he wants to do is tell stories about his movie days."

—ROBERT DALLECK, *Ronald Reagan: The Politics of Symbolism*

Does Reagan know he's lying? We could spend our lives puzzling that one out. "Even when his rhetoric turns maudlin and manipulative, he seems sincere, for the president believes the patriotic pieties simply and intensely," *Time* observed. "He gives himself goose bumps."

Reagan is his own best audience. He's Reaganism's first convert. The president is so deep inside his own head, so immersed in his own world-view, so gifted at projecting his psychic dramas on the public sphere, that he literally cannot see when his actual policies (e.g. deficit spending), let alone reality, diverge from his ideological beliefs. In 1980, Reagan was a movie star who threatened to become president: today, he can only be analyzed as a man who became a movie star in order to be president.

"Reagan is a mystery to a lot of us," the former United Auto Workers president Douglas Fraser told *Time* last August, "but he is very, very effective with the American worker." Fraser, it would appear, is not exactly up with the American people—or even his own. In the very same issue, a UAW regional director explained Reagan's appeal quite succinctly: "He looks good and he's an actor. He's the kind of guy you could strike up a conversation with if he lived in the neighborhood."

Ronald Reagan has been dramatizing his normality before audiences all his adult life. It's his specialty. "Mr. Norm is my alias," he told a Hollywood fan magazine back in the 1940s. The president has never exuded the rampant ego or mad ambition that drove other stars or politicians—but that scarcely means he avoided self-dramatization.

Reagan's persona, "Mr. Norm," is literally his second nature. Now, of course, we are inundated with the language of fan magazines: "At Camp David," *Time* recently reported in its Nancy Reagan cover story, "the two former movie stars cozy up on a sofa in the dark, holding hands and sharing a bowl of popcorn as they watch good, wholesome films." (*I ain't afraid of no ghost.*)

Amiable Ron sees the world in reassuring black and white (or Technicolor red, white, and blue). He steers clear of ambiguities, anything complex: "I never suggested where the weapons should be or what kind. I'm not a scientist," he said when questioned about his Star Wars program. His confusion of countries in South America, his blatant ignorance of arms control (which handily keeps him from implication when talks collapse), his proud lack of cultural sophistication endears him to the public. Far from threatening, the gaps in the president's knowledge are positively . . . normal.

One could write books on how the development of the star system before World War I not only changed the role of motion pictures but led to a new consciousness of personality as a thing, a flood of popular biographies, even the new profession of Celebrity. One could discuss how Ronald Reagan is the end result of politics in California—which, with its early suburban population, weak party organizations, and ready-made pool of media professionals (the first public relations firm was established there in 1933), anticipated the national mediacracy we enjoy today. One could further speculate on the importance of John F.

Kennedy—a president whose father once ran a movie studio and who was even the subject of a biopic while still in office—and how his telegenic image and thousand-day reign altered forever America's sense of its chief executive. But the bottom line is, Ronald Reagan knows that showbiz rules.

Perhaps the campaign's most incisive analysis of the president's appeal was delivered by one Dan Luch, a twenty-eight-year-old engineer, described by the *New York Times* (which published his remarks on September 17, 1984) as "one of the young urban professionals that the Democrats courted in the primaries with the promises of new ideas." Reagan, Luch explained with a dreamlike free association, is "a man who, when he says something, sticks to his guns. It's a John Wayne type of thing, you know, the Cavalry. . . . I have to say Mondale's just not as forceful. At work the guys stick to Reagan primarily because they see the race as women versus men, with Reagan standing for the values of the men." (And as if to underscore the point, two days later the *Times* noted that while "Mr. Reagan and Mr. Bush posed in cowboy hats with a pair of cheerleaders waving to a Texas audience, Mr. Mondale appeared in the *Mondale Family Cookbook* wearing an apron.")*

Trustworthy yet telegenic, Mr. Norm and John Wayne, the good neighbor with the gun, and most, most definitely not a woman. Reagan was "America as it imagined itself—the bearer of traditional Main Street values of family and neighborhood, of thrift, industry, and charity," (*Newsweek*). Like any modern politician, Reagan's image is pure feedback. He showed the visage that every other directed person in America might present had they the benefit of scientific polls, demographic statistics, and an endless knowledge of old movie clichés. Even his post-assassination ripostes were quotations: "Honey, I forgot to duck," he told Nancy just as Jack Dempsey had quipped to his wife after losing to Gene Tunney in 1926. Faced with death, he thought of the epitaph on W. C. Field's tombstone: "All in all, I'd rather be in Philadelphia."

Perhaps because he himself is so utterly a product of American mass culture, mass culture proved unusually responsive to Ronald Reagan.

---

* Given the misogyny of the 2016 election, one can only speculate how many votes Geraldine Ferraro cost the 1984 Democratic ticket.

The 1984 campaign was dominated by movie imagery. "Star Wars" and the "Evil Empire" remained buzz words while Vice President Bush mocked the Democratic convention as the "Temple of Doom" and Reagan appropriated the slogan that made his erstwhile employer Warner Bros. famous. "You ain't seen nothing yet," he affably threatened the screaming crowds that turned out to see him—the slogan in its proudly illiterate use of the double negative, echoing the punch line of the summer's number-one song, "I ain't afraid of no ghost!" Yes, as everyone was lining up for the same film, both Democrats and Republicans realized on some level that the party that controlled *Ghostbusters* would win the election—and the Democrats had about as much chance of that as Walter Mondale had of wearing his apron to Wyoming and serving the cowboys quiche.

An Officer and a Gentleman (with its militarism, old-fashioned values, and near-petulant demand that something "lift us up where we belong"), *E.T.* (with its promise of rebirth and celebration of innocence), *Indiana Jones and the Temple of Doom* (with its shameless woggery and utter bimbosity), *Red Dawn* (with its bellicose fear of a Nicaraguan invasion and chipper denial of nuclear war), *Beverly Hills Cop* (the title tells all) are all key Reaganoid texts. But only *Ghostbusters*—the highest-grossing movie ever made by anyone other than George Lucas and Steven Spielberg—mirrored Reaganism in full flower.*

Hailed by the *Wall Street Journal* for its glorification of the free enterprise system, Ghostbusters was indeed business-school perfect—celebrating a Silicon Valley–like high-tech venture devoted to the creation and exploitation of a false need. In further Reaganite touches, the Environmental Protection Agency furnished a villain, academia was mocked, Sigourney Weaver's sexuality got exorcised, and even the Star Wars defense plan was extolled.†

---

* *Ghostbusters* ranks tenth on the *National Review's* list of the twenty-five "Best Conservative Movies."
† True yuppie heroes, the Ghostbusters are even involved in gentrification, fixing up an old firehouse in Manhattan's soon-to-be fashionable TriBeCa neighborhood. The firehouse interiors, however, were shot in a station on L.A.'s Skid Row. As described in *Film Comment*,

Back in 1973–74, media analysts tripped all over themselves reading the fall of Richard Nixon into the runaway success of *The Exorcist* (even though, for years, the children of America had been possessed by the devils of drugs, sex, and rock 'n' roll). A decade later, as yippies gave way to yuppies, *Ghostbusters* replayed *The Exorcist* for laughs.

The rhetoric of consensus was built on the rejection of limits; it inspired its adherents to reshape reality in accordance with prophecy and vision; it thrived on the perils of Gog and Magog; but it may not be able to survive the reduction of "America" to the level of common sense.

—SACVAN BERCOVITCH, *The Rites of Assent*

I made it through the wilderness—somehow I made it through. Didn't know how lost I was until I found you.

—MADONNA, "Like a Virgin"

The disasters of the past twenty-five years—the Bay of Pigs, the Kennedy assassinations, Vietnam, Watergate, the CIA revelations, our humiliation at the hands of OPEC sheiks and Iranian mullahs, the black and sexual revolutions, the end of economic growth, the burden of history, the blah blah blahs—blistered the paint and dulled the chrome on the American dream.

And yet, between April 1978 and April 1979 when, according to *Time*, the number of Americans who felt that their country was "in deep and serious trouble" jumped from 41 percent to a record 64 percent, the most terrifying things facing us were the knowledge of our limitations and an awareness of the horrors we were capable of inflicting.*

Jimmy Carter's mature willingness to reduce "America" to the level

---

Derelicts passed brown paper bags around. One slept on the sidewalk, using a dog as a pillow. Some stumbled by, feet far apart to keep their balance. The irony of making a $30 million comedy here was not lost on the cast and crew. "This is very strange," said Joe Medjuck, the associate producer. No one left the set except in pairs.

* I think that I greatly underestimated the panic induced by inflation. On the other hand, 1979 was the peak year for employment in the American steel and automobile industries, to be followed by a precipitous drop.

of common sense, his complicity in this secularization of the American myth, was among his most grievous errors. Ronald Reagan's blithe denial of the self-evident—that America could not be omnipotent in a complex world, that our system did have certain built-in inequities, that we were hogging (if not squandering) an undue share of the earth's resources—is the bedrock of his appeal and reason his followers could so easily forgive his lesser irrationalities.

Reagan restored the illusion of consensus. (He had the balls to put the blacks and women in their place—namely, the Democratic Party.) The Reaganist vision of "America" is founded on religious certainty, which is to say supernaturalism—something the president made quite clear with his chilling assertions that the U.S. was God's country and folksy reassurances of an afterlife. (*I ain't afraid of no ghost.*)*

Ronald Reagan's political achievement, in an era when more than one-third of all Americans claimed to have been "born again," was to package his reactionary program as a rebirth and not a return. He was the savior who would redeem the misery of the last two decades as Jimmy Carter and Gerald Ford had promised but proved incapable of doing. By exaggerating the nation's weakness and projecting all of its hostile and aggressive tendencies onto a monolithic Soviet Union (the root of all evil in the world today—despite the evidence that Iran, for one, was not a Soviet client state), the new president prepared America for, as psychohistorian Lloyd deMause put it in *Reagan's America*, a rebirth through sacrifice.

Reagan pandered to a latent bellicosity waiting to be released. To be truly reborn, America would have to "kick ass" (as George Bush said, reasserting his manhood after the humiliation of debating Geraldine Ferraro). Where ineffectual Carter chose to scold America for its indulgence, Reagan would show us how to punish the weak to make ourselves feel strong.

Inflation was already subsiding when Reagan moved into the White House, yet the nation, he warned us, was in "greater danger today than we were the day after Pearl Harbor." It was a sensational opening—anything short of all-out thermonuclear war could then be sold as an

---

* This was particularly astonishing in view of Carter's genuine religiosity.

improvement. What was really out of control, deMause surmises, was our own murderous rage. When Reagan took power in January 1981, the media was filled with eagerly anticipatory images of the new president wielding an ax. The only question was, would he be a strong enough vessel "to contain our poison"?

If America's problems could be said to have begun on November 22, 1963, with the assassination of John F. Kennedy, Ronald Reagan's miraculous survival made him a kind of JFK redux. Now, having proved himself strong enough to contain the nation's violence, Reagan was mandated to wield it. Immediately, the president set about attacking the weakest strata of American society (schoolchildren, the elderly, the unemployed) while orchestrating the largest peacetime military buildup in American history.

When the social fabric is straining at the seams, when capitalism reneges on its promise of universal abundance, when humiliation is in the air, military nationalism is the time-tested recipe for the new unity. Even before double-digit inflation set in during the summer of '79, Jimmy Carter was the least popular reigning president in American history. Yet his approval rating doubled as soon as the Iranians took our embassy personnel hostage. Only when Carter refused to go to war to save the hostages did his popularity decline. Reagan's recession set in during late 1981, and the president's approval rating began to slide.

War fever began with the excitement over the Falklands and Israel's invasion of Lebanon in 1982, then flared in earnest in early 1983—our Year of Living Dangerously. In this context, Reagan's March '83 "Evil Empire" and "Star Wars" speeches were masterpieces of applied irrationality. As one conjured up the menace of an implacable deadly foe, poised to strike, the other raised the promise of risk-free nuclear war should we, understandably, choose to smash the aggressor first.

The president spent the summer of 1983 trying to lure the Sandinistas into a war. According to a *Time* poll, the percentage of Americans who felt that the state of the nation was good took a dramatic rise—proof positive of Reagan's successful image-making. When, in September, Flight KAL 007 violated Soviet airspace under circumstances that have never been satisfactorily explained, war fever reached an almost hysterical crescendo, reminiscent of the anti-Khomeini madness of 1980.

Unlike Carter, however, Reagan proved willing to give the American people a taste of what they craved. Shortly after the Korean airline incident, the administration began baiting the Syrians in Lebanon—a tactic that boomeranged when the terrorist attack on American marines couldn't be pinned on Damascus. A few days later, the marines landed in Grenada and Americans went berserk. At last, Reagan had provided a war. The remarkable thing about Grenada, cited again and again during the 1984 campaign as Reagan's supreme triumph, was its disproportionate effect upon the American public. As tawdry as the spectacle of the greatest power of earth subduing the tiniest nation in the Western hemisphere may have been, it actually sufficed to get America "standing tall."

Considering how infinitely more costly wars against the Sandinistas or Syrians—not to mention a confrontation with the Evil Empire itself—would have been, one actually has to be grateful for Grenada. If all it takes is shooting down two Libyan jets a year to keep Reagan from nuking Moscow—then, by all means, fire away.

Perhaps Hannah Arendt was expressing the conventional wisdom when, shortly after the fall of Saigon, she wrote that the Vietnam War "was exclusively guided by the needs of a superpower to create for itself an *image* which would *convince* the world that it was indeed 'the mightiest power on earth.'" With Reagan, the chickens come home to roost once more: Reaganism, it would appear, is exclusively guided by the needs of a superpower to create images which will convince *itself* that it is the mightiest power on earth.

"Politics is just like show business," the president mused back in 1966. "You need a big opening. Then you coast for a while. Then you need a big finish." Threaten Pearl Harbor and end with Grenada. By early 1984, Reagan enjoyed a 56 percent approval rating, even though nearly two-thirds of the American people had yet to feel the vaunted recovery. By the time of the election, *Time*'s count of America-is-all-rightniks was over 70 percent.

It's more than appropriate that, in the weeks preceding Reagan's second inauguration, the nation's number-one hit record would be Madonna's "Like a Virgin." The song, whose bizarre religious overtones are paralleled by its singer's nom de pop, is at once prurient and puritanical. The ideal video for "Like a Virgin" would present Madonna dressed as the Statue of Liberty leading a motley chorus of yuppies and steelworkers, fundamentalists and bankers, all wearing smile buttons and brandishing big sticks, addressing her words toward a giant telescreen image of the president.

Yeah, Ronald Reagan made us feel "shiny and new" all right—the better to fuck us again.*

---

* This piece got a violently mixed reaction at the *Voice*, with some of the political writers particularly incensed. On the other hand, the *New York Times* senior film critic Vincent Canby, a man whom I only knew to say hello to at screenings, went out of his way to congratulate me.

V

FORWARD INTO THE PAST, 1985–86

The weeks before and after Reagan won a nearly unprecedented reelection, another superman emerged from the Dream Life. Dropping naked from The Future into present-day Los Angeles, Arnold Schwarzenegger materialized as the most implacable killer robot in the history of movies: *The Terminator*!

Los Angeles Times film critic Charles Champlin made an immediate connection between the president and the movie, written and directed by thirty-year-old James Cameron. Two days after Reagan's victory, the front page of the *Times'* entertainment section was wholly devoted to election stories. "The Medium Itself Emerges with All the Spoils" revealed that an independent TV station had won the local ratings battle by counterprogramming the British miniseries *A Woman of Substance*. "Coverage Blankets Election" quoted *New York Times* political columnist Tom Wicker's declaration that television was "the new political reality." "Election Post-mortem on Light-Night Call-ins" reported on the talk-radio response. "Stars Turn Out for Reagan Victory" was accompanied by a photograph of comedians Bob Hope and Phyllis Diller sharing a laugh.

Champlin's piece (REWARDS OF REASSURANCE: BIG VOTES, LARGEST GROSSES) began, "It is oddly relevant, in the hours after the presidential election, to consider that the largest-grossing film in the United States last week was *The Terminator*."*

---

* A Hemdale production released by Orion, *The Terminator* was a true sleeper, "advance screened only at the last second," according to *Variety*'s reviewer, who saw the movie a mere two days before it opened, recognizing it as "a blazing, cinematic comic book, full of virtuoso moviemaking." *The Terminator* was the nation's number one box-office attraction for two weeks. On November 9, the *New York Times* called it "the surprise hit of the moment" with "such good word of mouth that its business is even improving."

Although set in 1984, the movie's premise, Champlin noted, was posited on events in a postnuclear holocaust world some forty-odd years hence. The Future is intermittently visualized as a dreadful wasteland with intelligent tanks crushing human skulls, but The Present is hardly Reagan's New Morning. Much of *The Terminator* takes place in nocturnal downtown Los Angeles, a veritable free-fire zone that, with its near-constant car chases and massive construction sites, might have been designed by the machine-based performance artists of the Survival Research Laboratories.

A murderous cyborg (Schwarzenegger) is sent back from 2029, programmed to terminate the Los Angeles waitress (Linda Hamilton) who gave (or would give) birth to the leader of the human resistance to robot rule. At the same time that Schwarzenegger's hyper-macho humanoid machine attempts to perform what is described as a "retroactive abortion," a member of the human resistance (Michael Biehn) is dispatched to The Present to protect humanity's savior from her would-be assassin—and impregnate her as well. In other words, an apparently omniscient savior sends his unknowing father back in time to ensure that he will indeed be born.

The Terminator was a canny synthesis of several key early Reagan-era films—not just the 1983 hit *WarGames* and the increasingly appreciated *Blade Runner*, both pitting humans against robots, but also *First Blood*, which introduced the human war machine, John Rambo. All three movies were variations on the Frankenstein myth. Like *WarGames*, *The Terminator* expressed an overt fear of nuclear war (started, in a bleak extrapolation of the Strategic Defense Initiative, by computers).

And like *Blade Runner*, *The Terminator* pondered the merger of men and machines. Even more than Stallone's impending *First Blood* sequel (based on a treatment by James Cameron), *The Terminator* might have been made to fulfill the Italian Futurist dictum that "War is beautiful because it initiates the dreamt-of metallization of the human body." Indeed, as the first action film to employ the zap-pow rock-video aesthetic pioneered by the musical *Flashdance* (the number-three grossing movie of 1983), *The Terminator* is beautiful—as well as exciting to watch.

Nevertheless, this flashy, violent version of the annunciation with its Möbius strip genealogy, suggesting both Christian dogma and Freudian psychoanalytic theory, was difficult to parse. Champlin struggled to pinpoint the film's appeal, comparing it to the original *Invasion of the Body Snatchers*, a movie that both thrilled and confused its audience in 1956. "If in its time *Body Snatchers* was a metaphor for the paranoia of the McCarthy days," Champlin wrote, something that only became apparent in retrospect, "*The Terminator* rides atop a troika of pre-apocalyptic jitters, deep and even subconscious fears of computers getting too smart and taking over, and a thin but resolute hope that the individual (in this case, significantly, a woman) can dig heels in and fight back."

Champlin thought that, in a manner similar to Reagan, *The Terminator* conjured up a dystopian vision that it might then dispel and that the movie's clearly defined conflict between good and evil and underlying hopeful message explained its popularity. But neither *The Terminator*'s morality, nor its optimism, appeared unalloyed. What was totally unambiguous was Arnold Schwarzenegger's star-making performance. The movie's awesome villain was its most compelling protagonist. As played (and gendered) by Schwarzenegger, originally offered the part of the movie's nominal hero, the machine was the Übermensch. Schwarzenegger's exaggerated "perfect" form exemplified those sci-fi cyborgs whose bionic techno-bodies rendered the human obsolete. Appearing as he did as a machine among machines, his impassive acting and lugubrious delivery were positive elements.

The most single-minded action film in the near decade since *Jaws*, *The Terminator* was an entertainment mechanism that allowed audiences to identify with, even while fearing, its killer robot, a creature that might be humanity's future self. Not restricted solely to the pleasures of destruction, the movie invited viewers to share machine consciousness, providing numerous point-of-view shots from the perspective of the Terminator's computerized video-terminal brain. Machines are ubiquitous, not just vehicles for action but sources of humor, as when the Terminator drives a car over a toy truck and crushes it or a telephone answering-device is programed to tell callers that "machines need love too."

The Terminator is a self-sufficient machine—at one point it plucks out and repairs its damaged eye. But there is a Luddite quality to its activities as well. The cyborg is "born" in 1984 alongside one trash compactor and dies in another. The movie's key scene may be the one in which the Terminator invades the Tech Noir discotheque, a suitably robotic environment, which it proceeds to destroy, wreaking vengeance on technology, authority, and women.

Although he would not achieve full apotheosis until the early 1990s, Schwarzenegger was a world-historical character. His appeal was universal. Like the disaster films, he returned cinema to its fairground origins, embodying the notion of the movie star as an expensive expanse of well-lit torso. His freakish, seemingly indestructible body was, as *Time* magazine would observe, "its own stunning special effect." He was the blockbuster given human—or at least, humanoid—form.

A bodybuilder born in Austria, Schwarzenegger was also an actor "whose Teutonic intonation rivals Henry Kissinger's," Nancy Collins noted in the introduction to her January 17, 1985, *Rolling Stone* interview. Schwarzenegger was both a foreigner and an American success story—a self-made man and a citizen since 1983, the greatest of the extraterrestrial-immigrant-supernatural strangers in paradise who wandered through the Hollywood movies of the 1980s, validating America's suburbs and shopping malls.*

Soon to marry Maria Shriver, Schwarzenegger was a self-identified Republican who, interviewed by *Rolling Stone*, included Reagan, along with John Wayne and Clint Eastwood, in his list of his actor heroes. "He's done the impossible—he's never gotten beaten in any election," Schwarzenegger asserted (unaware of Reagan's numerous primary losses). But Schwarzenegger had also done the impossible. While generations of would-be movie stars had been compelled to anglicize their names, Schwarzenegger proudly sported the least pronounceable, most problematic moniker to ever emblazon an American movie marquee.

The president never screened a Schwarzenegger film while occupying the

---

* Beginning with *E.T.*, the representation of America through alien eyes defines a whole cycle of mid-1980s films, including independent films *Liquid Sky* (1982) and *Stranger Than Paradise* (1984), the science-fiction romance *Star Man* (1984), and the studio comedies *Splash* (1984), *Moscow on the Hudson* (1984), and *Coming to America* (1988), suggesting that America's wondrous New Morning could only be confirmed from the uncritical born-again perspective of a mermaid, a Russian immigrant, or an African prince.

Schwarzenegger's films would gross a billion dollars worldwide during the 1980s. In a story knocked off *Time*'s cover late in December 1990 by a piece wondering whether Kuwait was worth the price of war, Richard Corliss called him "the most potent symbol of worldwide dominance of the U.S. entertainment industry." Schwarzenegger was a strategic asset, listed eighth—the highest-ranked actor—in *Entertainment Weekly*'s 1991 "101 Most Influential Power People in Entertainment." He achieved his apotheosis as a star in the mid-1990s and as a political figure, following Reagan's path when he was twice elected governor of California.

White House. Still, as the first Austrian-born superstar since Hedy Lamarr (if not Adolf Hitler) and a credit to the American Dream, Schwarzenegger deserves at least a footnote in the first great PR disaster of Reagan's second term. Anxious to lay World War II to rest and salute America's West German ally, particularly after its chancellor, Helmut Kohl, agreed to have Pershing nuclear missiles on German soil, Reagan accepted Kohl's invitation to mark the fortieth anniversary of V-E Day by visiting the German military cemetery at Bitburg and there lay a wreath.

Kohl felt left out of the 1984 D-Day commemoration extravaganza and, reportedly with tears in his eyes, told Reagan. Reagan had already experienced a measure of sympathy for America's former adversaries—at least at the movies, where his feelings were most susceptible. After screening the Oscar-nominated West German wartime submarine drama, *Das Boot*, in March 1982, he had characterized it in his diary as "very good but strange to find yourself rooting for the enemy." The following March, Arnold Schwarzenegger—the son of an Austrian policeman who had been a member of the Nazi party—was invited, along with his mother, to a White House state dinner for Argentine president Raúl Alfonsín.

Although the president assumes Americans as well as Germans lie buried at Bitburg, it soon becomes clear that the cemetery holds only Germans and, even more inconveniently, that the dead include forty-seven members of the Nazi Waffen-SS, storm troopers condemned for war crimes by the Nuremberg tribunal.

The story breaks over the April 13–14 weekend. Press furor is intense, particularly as the president had decided against visiting the concentration camp at Dachau. Some at the White House think that such a concentration camp visit would contradict the "theme of reconciliation." Others feel Reagan is temperamentally unsuited to visit such a place: "You know, he is a cheerful politician," a White House spokesman told the *New York Times*. "He does not like to grovel in a grisly scene like Dachau."

April 18, as fifty-three senators go on record opposing the Bitburg visit, the president makes things worse by maintaining that most of those buried at Bitburg were draftees and thus victims of the Nazi regime "just as surely as the victims in the concentration camps." PR Disaster! The *New York Times'* page-one headline reads: "Reagan Likens Nazi War Dead to Concentration

Camp Victims." The president is accused of coddling Nazis, insulting the memory of American war dead, and forgetting the Holocaust.*

Strongly supported by his new communications director Patrick Buchanan, Reagan professes not to understand the objections. "What is wrong with saying 'let's never be enemies again?'" he had written in his April 14th entry. "Would Helmut be wrong if he visited Arlington Cemetery on one of his U.S. visits?" The crisis is further complicated on April 20 when Reagan (who refers to the incident as his "'Dreyfus' case") presents a Congressional Gold Medal to the author Elie Wiesel, chairman of the U.S. Holocaust Memorial Council. Wiesel uses his remarks to implore the stony-faced president not to visit Bitburg. The incident is widely reported and the next day, Kohl telephones Reagan, warning that any cancellation of the Bitburg visit would be an insult to the German people. All of this is front-page news.

The president's advisers are divided, but a compromise is devised. It is determined that Reagan will now tour the concentration camp Bergen-Belsen with Wiesel before going on to Bitburg alone. The uproar fades, only to be revived three years later with the revelation that Reagan's German schedule has been micromanaged by Nancy on the advice of her astrologer Joan Quigley.

America has been made safe for Schwarzenegger (added that summer to the Reagans' birthday book) just in time to normalize the curious provenance of John Rambo, soon revealed as the spawn of the nation's two mortal foes, a man of mixed Native American and German descent.

Bitburg confused two Reagan narratives—one, that the Vietnam War had infected Americans with the idea of limited American power; the other, that victory in World War II represented America's limitless possibility.

Reagan saw the latter as a cure for post-Vietnam defeatism. But his failure to understand the symbolism of Bitburg compromised his connection to World War II. "In laying his wreath, the president was putting the wrong war behind him," Hendrik Hertzberg pointed out in the *New Yorker*. "It was the Vietnam War that people wanted to forget." The Bitburg debacle coincided

---

* Reagan's connection to the Holocaust was also based on movies. He'd been so disturbed by newsreels, showing liberated concentration camps that he imagined—and told Israeli prime minister Yitzhak Shamir—he had served in the signal corps and had actually shot the footage.

with the tenth anniversary of the Vietnam War's end, but the war's memory was stronger than ever. Both *Time* and *Newsweek* put the Vietnam memorial on the covers of their April 15 issues. Initial controversy had been laid to rest and, now the most visited site on the Washington mall, the memorial had taken on the trappings of a religious shrine.

Visitors brought personal artifacts to leave as offerings while a group called Veterans Vigil of Honor, founded shortly after the memorial opened, kept a twenty-four-hour watch demanding the repatriation of the 2,482 Americans thought missing or otherwise unaccounted for. Dressed in fatigue pants, jungle boots, and combat helmets, the veterans maintained a large army tent near the site. At dusk, the media scholar Harry Haines wrote, "an anonymous and mysterious figure in camouflage and cowboy hat steps out from a tree line near the Memorial and plays taps."

Local memorials proliferated. In the wake of *Uncommon Valor* and the euphoria produced by the Conquest of Grenada, subsequent Vietnam exorcisms grew increasingly fantastic and compensatory. The Chuck Norris vehicle *Missing in Action*, released in November and based on the same treatment that inspired *Rambo: First Blood Part II*, changed the emphasis from teamwork and esprit de corps to the glorification of a super-masculine principle, as well as the restoration of a lost national honor.

What *Newsweek* would later identify as a "Vietnam nostalgia industry" encompassed the media's nostalgia as well. The anniversary occasioned live television shows broadcast from the Vietnam memorial and Ho Chi Minh City (formerly Saigon). Then, just in time for Memorial Day, John Rambo returned to the scene of the crime.

Rambo begins with an explosion on a prison rock pile, and that voluptuous, rolling fireball—molten gold, lava orange—is reprised again and again during the fiery climax. The first detonation occurs at the camp where Rambo has been incarcerated after the rampage of *First Blood*. A hippie he-man who manages to keep his talismanic long hair even on a chain gang, Rambo is released to participate on a special assignment—the Green Beret extraordinaire parachutes back into Vietnam on a thirty-six-hour mission to find and photograph 2,500 MIAs. "Sir, do we get to win this time?" he plaintively asks his guru, Colonel Trautman (Richard Crenna), returning from *First Blood*.

Back in the Nam, Rambo strips down to his trademark tank top and sweatband. Before long he's discovered a tiger cage packed with POWs, sharing their miserable rations with rats and tarantulas. Trautman calls Rambo "a pure fighting machine"—which is to say, a Terminator—motivated by a "desire to win a war someone else lost." This stab in the back is recapitulated when the mission is aborted. Murdock (Charles Napier), the same nefarious government official who initiated the operation, terminates it precisely because it appears that it will be a success. "It was a lie, just like the whole damn war!" Trautman wails back at base, excoriating Murdock as "a stinking bureaucrat who's trying to cover his ass!" "Not just mine, the nation's," is the smarmy reply. Sweating, mud-caked heroic Rambo and his POW Exhibit A helplessly watch an American chopper reverse course and abandon them to the Vietcong horde slowly swarming over the rice paddy.

Although Rambo reinvents himself as a bare-chested Apache Übermensch incinerating battalions of Vietnamese soldiers with his special TNT-tipped arrows, it would seem that nonwhites are incapable of running a country (let alone winning a war). No sooner is Rambo captured than the Russians appear—his first words to them, a ripe Hell's Kitchen "Fuck You!"—and have him spread-eagled on an electric mattress with Steven Berkoff, the ranting Communist heavy of *Octopussy*, reprising his role with half-cracked gusto.*

Rambo escapes and runs amok, the ultimate Cost-Free Conquistador, wreaking havoc on Russians and Vietnamese alike. He single-handedly captures a chopper, blows up the camp, and frees the MIAs—returning to base to confront the treacherous Murdock. Not unlike the Terminator, Rambo rages against the machine. He destroys Murdock's computer bank and, as in *First Blood*, delivers a powerful statement regarding the war (whose only justification would seem that the U.S. happened to get itself involved). Permanently unreconciled, Rambo positions himself as the embodiment of unrequited patriot love, speaking for all Vietnam veterans and demanding unconditional admiration: "I want what they want—for our country to love us as much as we love it."†

---

* *Rambo* "draws on an older anti-fascist iconography," Russell A. Berman noted in *Telos*. "But now the political polarity is reversed: our former Soviet allies look like the hated Huns, and the Vietnamese Communists turn out to be nothing but 'Japs.' This revision of the twentieth-century past is clearly part and parcel of the same spectacular strategy that brought Reagan to Bitburg in the spring."

† *Rambo* naturally raised questions regarding the nature of Stallone's own service during the Vietnam War. "I went for my draft twice, and they wouldn't let me in," he told *Rolling Stone* writer Nancy Collins, "once for hearing and once for feet, I have flat feet. . . . I went there ready and willing to go."

In a *Time* magazine piece on "Rambomania," Stallone elaborated on the movie's appeal: "People have been waiting for a chance to express their patriotism. Rambo triggered long-suppressed emotions that had been out of vogue. Suddenly, apple pie is an important thing on the menu." So were Rambo collectibles—from the $150 aluminum replicas of the hero's mighty bow and custom-crafted, fifteen-inch "survival knife" ($2,250 in its special limited edition), to Rambo trading cards, action figures, and water pistols, along with T-shirts and bandannas.

Rambo's image reportedly displaced that of Uncle Sam in some Army recruiting sites. Stallone understood. "This is the point: frustrated Americans trying to recapture some glory," he explained. "The vets were told wrong. The people who pushed the wrong buttons all took a powder. The vets got the raw deal and were left holding the bag. What Rambo is saying is that if they could fight again, it would be different."

Rambomania gains momentum amid an upsurge of international terrorism that the president will blame on "a new, international version of Murder Inc.," Iran, Libya, North Korea, Cuba, and Nicaragua—five "outlaw states run by the strangest collection of misfits, Looney Tunes, and squalid criminals since the advent of the Third Reich."

June 14, two Arab terrorists hijack TWA 847 en route from Athens to Rome. The plane flies first to Beirut, then Algiers, then back to Beirut where one of the passengers, a U.S. Navy diver, is shot and dumped on the tarmac. After returning to Algiers, the plane flies again to Beirut on June 16, leaving thirty-nine Americans and crewmembers held captive by Shiite militants.

Three days later, Salvadoran guerrillas attack a San Salvador café, leaving thirteen dead—among them four marines and two American businessmen—and a bomb explodes at the Frankfurt airport, killing three and wounding forty-two. That weekend Reagan meets with the marine families and then at Camp David watches the new James Bond film, *View to a Kill* (two years ahead of its time in favoring détente and featuring a billionaire-capitalist, formerly KGB villain). Sunday night, an Air India flight carrying 329 people blows up over the Atlantic, presumably an instance of Sikh terrorism.

Saturday, June 29, Reagan monitors the impending release of the thirty-nine hostages—a deal partially brokered by Syrian dictator Hafez al-Assad, Shiite leader Nabih Berri, and speaker of the Iranian parliament Ali Akbar Hashemi Rafsanjani. The president also screens *Rambo*, apparently with guests, at the White House. As the hostages are freed, Reagan identifies himself as a spectator of his own presidency. "Boy, I saw *Rambo* last night," he jokes at a June 30 press conference. "Now I know what to do next time."

On July 5, Nancy and Ronald Reagan send Stallone birthday greetings. Later that summer, Stallone puts out a press release announcing that a "specially-requested color poster of Rambo" will be presented to the president at a $1,000-a-plate California Republican Party dinner. Shortly before the banquet, the gift is rescinded at the request of the White House (which denied that Reagan had ever asked for the poster).

Stallone's representatives explain that the star has postponed the presentation of the gift until fall. By then, posters that put Reagan's smiling face atop Rambo's nautilus-built body clutching an impressive automatic weapon, will be ubiquitous. Some posters include *Rambo*'s tag "No man, no law, no war can stop him." Others simply dub the cyborg "Ronbo!"*

Happy Daze

In early 1982, with the TV sitcom *Happy Days* in decline, the *New York Times* editorialized on "The Endless Fifties": "It is natural to look forward confidently to the future if it is flush with opportunity. But when it is not, what's also natural is to look back, to romanticize, to try to recreate it. It's not so much the 50's we're trying so ceaselessly to revive. It's happy days, small 'H,' small 'D.'"

However chaotic and confusing, and however strong the sense during the period of the Vietnam War that America had been conceived in sin (whether that of massacring the continent's original inhabitants or of institutionalizing slavery), the Sixties mentalité included a positive view of the future. This optimism was manifested in the moon landing (and its precursor, the movie

---

* A version of the image graces the cover of Susan Jeffords's 1994 *Hard Bodies: Masculinity in the Reagan Era*.

2001) as well as various other techno-utopian projects, the post–World War II baby boom belief in a generational manifest destiny, and the chimera of impending worldwide revolution. But, beginning with the dissolution of the counterculture in the early 1970s, futuristic utopianism was superseded by nostalgia—specifically for the presumed innocence of the mid-1950s.

The first stage of the Cold War ended, the Red Scare subsided, McCarthyism was passé. These imagined Fifties were initiated by the first baby boom festival, namely the Davy Crockett craze of 1955, the advent of Elvis Presley, and the popularization of rock 'n' roll. The period might well have ended on October 4, 1957, when the Soviets launched the first earth-orbiting satellite, Sputnik, but this national narcissistic wound notwithstanding, the nostalgized Fifties was imagined continuing for another five years through the edgier period of the Missile Gap, *The Twilight Zone*, and John F. Kennedy's Camelot, terminating, like *American Graffiti*, just before the Cuban Missile Crisis of October 1962.

The consensus was that the Eisenhower Era was the last age of consensus, the last time when America was America. Or perhaps it was really the first time, underscored by the sense that history truly began when television saturated the American market. The main thing was that the Fifties predated the upheavals of the Sixties. And so an airbrushed view of the Fifties became America's favorite theme park and official past. In *Reagan's America: Innocents at Home*, the first book-length analysis of Reagan culture, published in December 1986, Garry Wills called this magic kingdom Reaganland.

"Visiting Reaganland is very much like taking children to Disneyland, where they can deal with a New Orleans cut to their measure," Wills explained. "It is a safe past, with no sharp edges to stumble against." Reagan provided "the past as a present, America's 'remembered' self," an implanted memory, like those of the replicants in *Blade Runner*.

"If one settles for a substitute past, an illusion of it," Wills went on, "then that fragile construct must be protected from the challenge of complex or contradictory evidence, from the test of any evidence at all. That explains Americans' extraordinary tacit bargain with each other not to challenge Reagan's version of the past. The power of his appeal is the great joint confession that we cannot live with our real past, that we not only need but prefer a substitute." (The Bitburg fiasco brought Reagan's appeal into question. The movie *Das Boot* was not an adequate substitute for World War II.)

Reagan was only one successful Fifties impresario. Others included the television star Bill Cosby, prime mover of *The Cosby Show* (NBC, 1984–92), and the televangelist Pat Robertson, the son of Virginia senator Willis Robertson and the founder of the Christian Broadcasting Network. From modest beginnings, CBN had become the fourth-largest cable network by enlivening its religious programming with Westerns and sitcoms from the 1950s, including *The Life and Legend of Wyatt Earp* (ABC, 1955–61), *Wagon Train* (NBC, 1957–62; ABC, 1962–65), and *Bachelor Father* (CBS, 1957–59; NBC, 1959–61; ABC, 1961–62), and thus cancelling the spurious sex, drugs, and rock 'n' roll "revolution" of the Sixties with equally bogus counterrevolution.

Premiering the same month that *Happy Days* ended, *The Cosby Show* was a family sitcom featuring an upper-middle-class black family living in Brooklyn, New York, in which the father, Cliff Huxtable (Cosby), is a pediatrician and his wife, Clair (Phylicia Rashad), is an attorney. This celebration of the nuclear family and enlightened patriarchy was the last universal network television show before the triumph of cable. It was also the most popular TV program throughout Reagan's second term, equaling *All in the Family* (CBS, 1971–79) by finishing number one for five consecutive seasons between 1985–86 and 1989–90. While earlier sitcoms were implicitly didactic, *Cosby* was deliberately educational, and much was made of that fact.

As *Happy Days* might be said to have neutralized *All in the Family*, *The Cosby Show* supplanted *The Godfather* as an American success story, even as it served to complement the current president. A 1987 *Time* cover story on "Cosby, Inc." hailed Cosby as "a force in the national culture" who like Ronald Reagan ("another entertainer with a warm, fatherly image") exuded optimism and stood for traditional family values. That the Huxtable family was African American was "an encouraging sign of maturity in matters of race," with both white and black viewers taking *The Cosby Show* as "a weekly source of comfort and wisdom."*

---

* The same could not be said of *Cosby*'s main antecedent, *The Jeffersons* (CBS, 1975–85), a Norman Lear production spun off from and outlasting *All in the Family*. An irascible African American entrepreneur, the owner of a chain of dry-cleaning stores, George Jefferson leaves Archie Bunker's lower-middle-class Queens neighborhood for Manhattan's Upper East Side and a "deluxe apartment in the sky." The humor was largely predicated on

Still, as pointed out by the television historian David Marc, the show could be read in two ways:

Does *Cosby* offer a "color blind" vision of a successful family that redresses the images of African-American poverty and crime that otherwise saturate the mass media? Or is the exalted bourgeois lifestyle of the Huxtables being offered as congratulatory evidence to an America that has "fixed" its race problem and so can now get on with the business of unbridled consumerism?

Or, as might be said, taking the title of Hollywood's most elaborate superimposition of the Fifties over the Eighties, America could now get back to the future.*

Directed by Robert Zemeckis from a script written with Bob Gale, *Back to the Future* turned *American Graffiti* nostalgia inside out, transporting a present-day teenager to 1955, giving him the chance to alter history, change his 1985 conditions, and ensure his own birth.

Marty McFly (Michael J. Fox), a healthy high school boy living in suburban Hill Valley, saddled with a dipso mom (Lea Thompson, the virginal Valkyrie of *Red Dawn*) and a simpering, ineffectual dad (Christian Glover), is rendered carless through his craven father's abject cowardice and thus humiliatingly unable to consummate his big date with his extremely willing girlfriend.

The deus ex machina is also an automobile, namely a flashy DeLorean sports car converted into a time machine by the local eccentric inventor Doc Brown (Christopher Lloyd), using stolen plutonium that he has obtained from a Libyan "hit squad" under the pretext of manufacturing a bomb. Thanks to the Libyans' inadvertent intervention, the DeLorean conveys Marty from the parking lot of a suburban shopping mall to a 1955 cow pasture where, not

---

George's alienation, his simultaneous disdain of, and longing for acceptance from, the white phonies among whom he finds himself; unlike *Cosby*, it was all about race—including mixed marriages and biracial characters—as well as class. The Huxtable family, by contrast, lived in a sort of bubble, rarely leaving their house to experiencing such everyday racial inequality as might be found on the sidewalks of New York.

* The title was anticipated by a *New York Times* op-ed piece from early 1975, "Looking Backward into the Future," in which, addressing various aspects of the new nostalgia and the upcoming Bicentennial, history professor Martin E. Marty wrote that "a few years ago, the past had no future."

surprisingly, he's mistaken for a space alien. In a sense, Marty is his own E.T. (He will impersonate one to manipulate his young father, an aspiring science-fiction writer.) As dumbstruck as any immigrant to America, Marty looks on in wonder as a quartet of gas jockeys leap to their feet and, in an excess of service, briskly converge on a well-preserved De Soto while the Four Aces' 1954 hit "Mr. Sandman" blares on the soundtrack.

The Davy Crockett craze is also in evidence. The pawnshops, porn parlors, bail bondsmen, and graffiti present on Hill Valley's 1985 Main Street are not. A sign promoting the town's newly developed strip housing ("Live in the Home of Tomorrow . . . Today") suggests General Electric's "House of the Future," home to the Reagan family during the 1950s, while the Main Street movie theater that was showing *Orgy American Style* in 1985 now features the 1954 Ronald Reagan vehicle *Cattle Queen of Montana*. When, having located the young Doc Brown, Marty tells him that Reagan will someday be president, Doc sarcastically wonders if his vice president will be Jerry Lewis, adding a reference to Reagan's former spouse, "I suppose Jane Wyman is the first lady."*

Back to the Future's Fifties scenes revel in the enjoyably infantile drama of Marty's relative omnipotence (as when he flamboyantly eludes the town bully through his mastery of "futuristic" skateboard technology). He astounds his future mother and future grandparents by anticipating the jokes in the *Honeymooners* episode that we have seen in reruns in 1985—a joke that underscores the sense that *Back to the Future* is set neither in 1955 nor 1985 but on TV. He also has the distinct unpleasure of finding that his teenaged father is no less timorous or nerdy than the adult progenitor he knows.

No less than Disneyland or Reaganland, *Back to the Future* proposes the comforting past to improve the present and even frame the radiant future.

---

* Reagan screened *Back to the Future* at Camp David on July 26. According to former aide Mark Weinberg, Reagan enjoyed the reference to *Cattle Queen of Montana*, a Western in which he played an undercover army officer dispatched to Barbara Stanwyck's ranch to investigate an Indian cattle-rustling (and which would be the last movie he saw as president, shown at Camp David on January 14, 1989). But he didn't enjoy the reference to his first wife, who for much of Reagan's time in office enjoyed a resurgent visibility as the reigning matriarch of the primetime soap opera *Falcon Crest* (CBS, 1981–90). "The movie continued but for me—and, I suspected, those around me—it felt as if the air had gone out of the Aspen Lodge," Mark Weinberg recalled.

In *Hard Bodies: Masculinity in the Reagan Era*, Susan Jeffords notes that just "as Marty coaches his father from a wimp to a rescuer, Reagan set out to coach America from acting the part of the 'wimp' of the Carter years." At the same time, the film is fraught with comic psychosexual anxiety. Marty's Mac-Guffin is that he must bring together his teenage parents lest he jeopardize his future existence. This proves difficult not only because his future father is such a wimp but also because his future mother gets the hots for her future son—her ardor threatening to throw his entire genealogy out of whack.

"Apparently your mother is amorously infatuated with you instead of your father," Marty is sagely counseled by the young Dr. Brown. Marty parks with his mother—a ploy to ensure her rescue by Dad—only to get more than he bargained for. "Marty, don't be such a square," says Mom, lighting a cigarette, as her son looks aghast at the bottle of hooch she's swiped from grandma and starts quaking in terror at the prospect of violating the incest taboo. "You're beginning to sound just like my mother."

In short, Marty is an American Oedipus who, with Doc Brown as his therapist (Wilhelm Reich out of *E.T.*), learns to conquer his desire for his mother (projected, in the film's key scene, back onto her) and accede to the rule of the father (patriarchal wimpiness being in the eye of the beholder). His reward: an improved standard of living for the entire family plus a woman (and, as the film's closing makes explicit, eventually kids) of his own.*

As produced by Steven Spielberg, *Back to the Future* was characterized by his trademark innocence. While the Disney studio had found the movie too raunchy, Zemeckis and Gale worried that it was too tame—a sanitized version of the gross-out Fifties-set adolescent sex comedies *Porky's* (1981), *Porky's II* (1983), and *Porky's Revenge* (1985). "We're in a high school in this movie, and we never went into the girls' shower!" Zemeckis recalled.

So closely did the movie explicate the fantasy of Reaganland and illustrate Wills's thesis that Wills took it as the master metaphor for the last chapter of *Reagan's America*. As tied to the zeitgeist as *Back to the Future* was, conceived by Gale and Zemeckis during the summer of 1980 and germinating

---

* When I interviewed Robert Zemeckis in late June 1985, he professed what seemed a practiced surprise at this interpretation. In my *Village Voice* review I wrote that, whether consciously Freudian or not, *Back to the Future* could be seen as "an attempt to wrest Spielbergism away from its religious underpinnings (*Close Encounters*, *E.T.*) and ground it in the therapeutic."

throughout Reagan's first term, it also was the product of several fortunate accidents. The movie's first draft was rejected by every studio that saw it; its sole champion was Spielberg, but Zemeckis felt that he had to make a hit before he could allow his patron to sponsor the movie. With the success of *Romancing the Stone*, a commissioned Indiana Jones knockoff, which would be the eighth top-grossing film of 1984, Zemeckis was bankable.

There was, however, a rival movie involving time travel to the Fifties, namely Tri-Star Pictures' *Peggy Sue Got Married*, about to go into production and scheduled for a summer 1985 release. Fortunately for *Back to the Future*, the attached star, Debra Winger, objected to the prospective director—first Jonathan Demme, then Penny Marshall—with the result that all left the project. Francis Ford Coppola was brought in as a hired gun to direct Kathleen Turner, whose value had risen since *Romancing the Stone*; announced in October 1984, the movie opened two years later.

Back to the Future, which started shooting in early 1985, laid claim to the same summer spot intended for *Peggy Sue* but was thrown into some turmoil when, five weeks and $4 million dollars into production, the star Eric Stoltz was deemed unable to carry a comic movie and replaced by Michael J. Fox, the star of the hit sitcom *Family Ties* (NBC, 1982–89) and the original choice for the role. Zemeckis not only had to reshoot much of the film but fend off the Universal executive who insisted on retitling it *Spaceman from Pluto*. That same executive would be so excited by the finished product that he pushed the release date from August to July 4, causing the movie to be rushed into 1,100 theaters.*

Spielberg would memorably if somewhat misleadingly describe *Back to the Future* as "the greatest episode of *Leave It to Beaver* ever made." In fact, *Back to the Future* is the ultimate episode of *Family Ties* which, appearing shortly after *E.T.* and just before *First Blood*, provided a third icon for Reagan's first term in Fox's rebellious young Republican. Like *Happy Days* and *The*

---

* *Back to the Future* was not the only Spielberg production that summer. There was also *The Goonies*, which opened in June and shared a common theme—kids going into history to improve the lot of their respective nuclear families. All but pathological, *The Goonies* reduces the Spielberg style and its thematic obsessions to a virtual formula whose components include brand-name naturalism; lovable mutants and cute ethnic stereotypes; ten-year-old visionaries and tag-along girls; nudgy music keyed to a grandiose Sense of Wonder—all held together by old movie quotations and a fun-house structure.

Cosby Show, Family Ties was transparently modeled on the *Father Knows Best* sitcoms of the Fifties but with a twist. The show was predicated on a reverse generation gap.

Steven and Elyse Keaton (Michael Gross and Meredith Baxter) are former campus radicals trying to integrate their Sixties values into the Reaganite wonderland wholeheartedly endorsed by their cute obnoxious progeny Alex (Fox), a clean-cut kid who wears a tie, carries a briefcase, and has a poster of Richard Nixon in his bedroom. The situation struck David Marc as an inverted *All in the Family*, saddling Archie Bunker's progressive daughter and son-in-law with "a kind of demographically upside-down pint-sized Archie Bunker." Father didn't know best, but grandpa did!

On one hand, the parents' nascent yuppie values (and guilty betrayal of the counterculture) is projected onto their son. On the other, *Family Ties* anticipated *Back to the Future* in suggesting that the tension between the Sixties and the Eighties could be mediated by the comforting cultural forms of the Fifties, something Wills saw as the movie's essential significance: "The aim of *Back to the Future* is to unite the generations, to make the hero see his parents with new eyes, as not outmoded but still young." *Family Ties* would become the second-most popular show on TV save for *Cosby* (finishing just behind *Cosby* in 1985–86 and 1986–87), although it took off as a cult item for teenagers only after the emphasis shifted from Sixties parents to Eighties offspring. (The success of *Back to the Future* propelled it as well).

Fox's Alex was not only a teen idol but one endorsed by the president, who according to legend declared *Family Ties* his favorite TV show and was even rumored to have turned down an invitation to make a cameo appearance.

Back to the Future appeared amid two trends, time-travel movies and the comedies of yuppie angst. *Peggy Sue Got Married*—in which an unhappy forty-something mother of two attends her twenty-fifth high school reunion and is mysteriously returned to 1960, as well as to her teenage self, albeit with her mature mind—was both. (Marty uses his time trip to invent rock 'n' roll and inspire the civil rights movement; Peggy Sue can think of nothing better than introducing pantyhose.)

The comedy of yuppie angst became one way for movies to resurrect the Sixties. The protagonists in movies as disparate as Albert Brooks's *Easy Rider* parody *Lost in America*, Susan Seidelman's tastefully garish *Desperately Seeking Susan* (in which Madonna appeared as the personification of a one-woman counterculture), Martin Scorsese's *After Hours*, and John Landis's *Into the Night* (all released in 1985) were young professionals or their wives whose comfortable existences come unhinged.

Two distinct eras in American cultural history collided as a straight-arrow careerist had to cope with the menacing weirdos and baffling situations of some classless (fantasy) bohemia. Pitting a sense of petit bourgeois entitlement against a sense of existential risk—marriages and jobs typically on the line—the comedy of yuppie angst took the classic noir situation as the occasion for screwball farce.

Not quite *Happy Days*, *Back to the Future* was the lone yuppie (or proto-yuppie) comedy to acknowledge the Fifties' two great social upheavals—the African American struggle for civil rights and the youth culture initially embodied in Elvis Presley—both of which came to fruition in the 1960s. Aided by his backlog of future knowledge, Marty not only inspires a black soda jerk to dream of being mayor of Hill Valley but, more insultingly, introduces Chuck Berry's stage persona and sound (and thus rock 'n' roll) at a high school dance, although he loses the audience when, in a paroxysm of enthusiasm, he concludes with a burst of Jimi Hendrix dissonance.

As with the presence of the Monolith in *2001* or the von Däniken-ism of *Close Encounters*, with its suggestion that Einstein was a space alien, *Back to the Future* posits history (or human evolution) as a matter of divine intervention. The movie is a historical Möbius strip in which racial progress and rock 'n' roll are something like viral infections imported from the future. Conveniently set in 1955, rather than the following year of cultural revolution when Elvis Presley enjoyed his television apotheosis and the Reverend Dr. Martin Luther King became a national figure, *Back to the Future* ruled the box office all summer.*

Rock Hudson, a conservative Republican and Reagan supporter, died while *Back to the Future* was in release—and, as a result, the Reagans' worldview

---

* "If *Back to the Future* doesn't knock some of the box-office wind out of *Rambo*'s sails this July 4th weekend, nothing will," I began my *Village Voice* review. Even more than *E.T.*, the movie represented a complete surrender to Spielbergism, my own included.

was darkened with the knowledge of AIDS. (The epidemic had recently been on the cover of *Life* magazine which, offering pictures of a young woman, a soldier, and a family, warned that "Now No One Is Safe from AIDS." Hudson expanded that to include movie stars.)

The summer of *Back to the Future* was also the season that the rogue financier Ivan Boesky reassured a group of students at Berkeley that "greed is all right," and Reagan tacitly approved a plot hatched by his national security adviser Robert McFarlane and David Kimche, director general of the Israeli foreign ministry, to sell arms to Iran as a means of freeing the American hostages held in Lebanon. Reagan was told that contact had been made with moderates within the Islamic Republic. "Strange soundings are coming from some Iranians," the president noted in his diary on July 17.

A month later, Israel shipped ninety-six TOW (tube-launched, optically tracked, wire-guided) anti-tank missiles to Iran. This was around the time the Reagans celebrated their joint stardom by screening the anachronistic World War II submarine drama *Hellcats of the Navy* (1957), the only movie in which they appeared together (and also their last if one discounts the president's made-for-TV swan song *The Killers*.) "It was fun," Reagan wrote in his diary. Mark Weinberg remembered the screening as "a time-travel journey unlike any other."

The bad Fifties had returned as well. *Red Dawn* was a harbinger of things to come. The bluntly titled *Invasion U.S.A.* opened in late September to show the United States invaded by Russian-led Soviet-Cuban-Arab troops. Their leader, a red-eyed ghoul called Rostov, mocks Americans as "soft and ignorant," ripe for a takeover: "They don't understand the nature of their freedom or how it can be used against them. They are their own worst enemy."

America's enemies sow chaos through terrorist acts, including a Christmas season attack on families and children lead by the bazooka-wielding Rostov, but the invasion is thwarted by a big-jawed hippie (former karate champ Chuck Norris), once a CIA operative, now an alligator wrestler. Two days after the movie opened in late September, the *New York Times* critic Vincent Canby wondered whether the real attraction was action or politics. It was, he noted, necessary "to go back almost two years to find an intelligent, first-rate movie that, without apology, dramatizes a liberal position," namely Mike Nichols's 1983 portrait of a martyred whistle-blower, *Silkwood*.

Materializing the following week, the half-camp, studiously apolitical *Commando* starred Arnold Schwarzenegger—introduced biceps-first as John Matrix, a one-man army who declares war on the deposed Latin American dictator who has kidnapped his daughter. A perhaps parodic scene has Matrix and his lady friend (Rae Dawn Chong) shopping for mines, machine guns, and rocket launchers at a supermarket called Surplus World.

Later in October, ABC announced plans for *Amerika*, a $40 million, sixteen-hour miniseries imagining the U.S. under Soviet occupation. November brought Taylor Hackford's *White Nights*, a tale of two defectors, one American, the other Soviet (played by real-life defector Mikhail Baryshnikov). Canby dismissed it as "a modification of the basic design created for the Cold War movies of the 1950's."

Still, *Back to the Future* was the year's biggest moneymaker, grossing over $211 million, $60 million more than second-place *Rambo*. (*Rocky IV* would be number three.) Reagan acknowledged *Back to the Future* in his 1986 State of the Union speech, quoting the tagline "Where we're going, we don't need roads," prompting Robert Zemeckis to write a letter of thanks. A week later Ron Reagan Jr. hosted *Saturday Night Live*, danced in his underwear like Tom Cruise in *Risky Business*, and played Michael J. Fox in a *Back to the Future* skit.*

---

* Reagan was gone from the White House but a year when *Back to the Future Part II* opened in 1990. After reprising the punch line of the first *BTTF*—mad scientist Doc Brown returning to the "new, improved" 1985 from thirty years hence—*Part II* barely pauses for credits before pulling Marty away from his girlfriend and blasting off into the midair freeway frenzy of 2015. Lawyers have been abolished but sequels thrive. Marty receives his first future shock from a holographic advertisement for *Jaws 19*. The year 2015 is defined entirely in terms of consumer products—auto-Velcro Nikes, computerized down jackets, hovercrafts—and references to the original film.

In the first of several revisionist views of Reagan's New Morning, Marty visits Café 80's—the 2015 equivalent of the hyperreal '50s diners that first appeared in the early 1980s. Images of Reagan and the Ayatollah Khomeini partner as virtual waiters although it's a bit disappointing to find Michael Jackson's "Beat It" video dominating a TV wall barely worthy of a third-rate Tokyo department store. This, however, is in keeping with the film's media-centric, dystopian view: windows have been replaced by the Scenery Channel, teenagers watch six TV shows at once and wear telephone necklaces. The heart of *Part II* is a nightmare version of the original's now periodized "1985." This amounts to the dark side of the Reagan boom—although here, as in *BTTF*, social forces are conceptualized as something like viral infections imported from the future.

The presence of a black family in Marty's house (as well as the unconscious racism of

Top Ray-Gun

Hyped in trailers that, since late summer, had been preparing audiences to "get ready for the next world war," *Rocky* IV, written and directed by Sylvester Stallone, opens over Thanksgiving weekend, grossing $32 million in five days to surpass *Beverly Hills Cop* as the greatest non-summer opening of all time.

This time, in a cosmic struggle billed as "Us Against Them," Rocky fights Soviet superman Ivan Drago (Dolph Lundgren), an Implacable Alien Other so brutal that he actually kills Rocky's original nemesis Apollo Creed in the ring. In a sense, Creed paid the supreme price for Ali's refusal to fight the Vietcong by dying in the ring at the hands of the savage—and, of course, savagely racist—Russian beast. In his paperback bio *Stallone! A Hero's Story*, published to coincide with *Rocky IV*'s opening, Jeff Rovin provided a ready-made interpretation: "A few critics have applauded it as a fable of sorts in which the third world, represented by Apollo, is pounded down by the Soviets, only to be avenged by America."

America is taunted: "Perhaps the defeat of this little so-called champion will be an example of how pathetically weak your society has become," some Russian sneers. No matter, Rocky uses his triumph over Drago to plead for peace and understanding, thus winning what the *New York Times* described as "the screaming, tumultuous admiration of the entire Soviet Union, including the Communist Party's general secretary and the members of the Politburo"—one of whom is played by a Gorbachev lookalike.*

---

the premise) sets the scene for the more radical transformation of his suburban neighborhood into an inner-city wasteland of wrecked cars and chalk body outlines. Hill Valley is a cross between Watts and Reno, Main Street dominated by the skyscraper casino-cum-museum that marks the transformation of working-class villain Biff Tannen into the resident Donald Trump. Biff's triumph, which is explicitly a perversion of Marty's own echt-'80s drive towards wealth and power, further fuels the *BTTF* saga's Oedipal subtext. Acting out the desire that our teenage hero only barely repressed in the first installment, Biff has murdered Marty's father and married his mother. Again, Marty is compelled to return to the Golden Age. The Fifties will never die; as Marty exclaims, "This is heaven!"

According to Mark Weinberg, Reagan was offered (and turned down) the part of Hill Valley's 1885 mayor in *Back to the Future Part III* (1990).

* Having failed to present Reagan with a special *Rambo* poster, Stallone—or rather Jerry Weintraub, now CEO of United Artists—lobbied the White House to accept Stallone's

Not really. As noted by the White House, the Soviets have been pressuring ABC to reconsider *Amerika*, which had already been pared down to twelve hours and a $32 million budget. On January 9, ABC announced that it was postponing production of the miniseries. And after the publication of *Newsweek*'s late December cover story "Showing the Flag," subtitled "Rocky, Rambo and the Return of the American Hero" and emblazoned with the image of Stallone in the ring draped in the Stars and Stripes, the Soviets held a press conference to announce a new Soviet-American cultural exchange program. Making headlines in the U.S., Deputy Minister of Culture Georgi A. Ivanov accused Hollywood of promoting "a new type of hero, a killer with ideological convictions." Also present was the poet Yevgeny Yevtushenko, who coined a phrase to characterize *Rambo* and *Rocky IV*: "warnography." The name was well chosen in that the libidinal content of these belligerent films was much in evidence.

Noting the demand in Moscow for black-market VHS cassettes of *Rambo*, the *New York Times* subsequently ran an editorial on "warno-graphy," arguing these films had "less to do with nationalism than populism." *Rocky IV* "cedes science to the Russians," the editorialists pointed out. "It is the dreaded Drago who trains on Nautilus-like machines, whose vital signs pulse brightly on computer screens, whose performance is monitored by sophisticated sports doctors. It is Rocky, meanwhile, who becomes the peasant underdog, training in the rural snows, pulling sleds, pushing boulders and climbing icy ridges. . . . The losers are the educated, the elite, the high-tech intelligentsia of any society. The winner is the peasant, the child of nature, the little guy, the common man."

By whatever name, warnography was on the rise. Prompted by the conservative commentator Paul Weyrich, Pat Buchanan contacted Republican National Committee functionary Mitch Daniels to see if Reagan would be amenable to use Stallone to sell the Reagan Doctrine of "supporting Freedom Fighters world-wide in the war against the Soviet Empire." (Daniels declined.)

Rocky IV gloves and robe "in a suitable ceremony to be held in Washington and to be attended by dignitaries from the highest levels of all branches of the government," for display in the Smithsonian Institute. In an internal memo to White House lawyer Fred Fielding, future Supreme Court chief justice John Roberts called the offer "a rather transparent" stunt adding, "With the Rambo comments and White House dinner invitation, the President has already given Stallone more than his fair share of free publicity."

On January 17, the day after *Variety* screened the Finnish-American co-production *Born American* in Copenhagen, *Iron Eagle* opened. "Theaters may have to stay open from high noon to red dawn to handle the crowd," *Variety* predicted of this aerial extravaganza, which borrowed Israeli jets to fancifully rework the Gulf of Sidra incident.*

I had just written an article on this new trend and was eager to parse *Iron Eagle*, which I viewed with an audience and reviewed, some three weeks later, in the *Village Voice*—the paper not only indulged but encouraged my vulgar Freudian reading of the film.†

Directed by Sidney Furie, *Iron Eagle* is a relatively benign, or at least relatively abstract, example of the Hollywood genre the Soviets have, with more wit than one would expect, labeled "warnography." Their pun isn't even as facile as it seems: Archer Winsten's ironic (?) pull-quote—"Anyone who failed to respond to *Iron Eagle* has no red blood at all"—makes you wonder if the film he's touting isn't really *Spread Eagled (and Bodacious)*. *Rambo*, *Red Dawn* and *Rocky IV*, the key exhibits in the Soviet diatribe, purvey hypothetic wars the way porn films traffic in hypothetical sex. Indeed, the same arguments could be made as to whether such films are behavioral primers, pathetic substitutes, social symptoms, or all three in one. The only thing beyond question is that porno is a lot less respectable (and maybe even profitable) than warno these days.

Iron Eagle's premise, as any subway rider knows, has an American jet pilot (Tim Thomerson) shot down and placed on trial for "the crime of

---

* Another sort of spectacle occurred ten days into *Iron Eagle*'s run when the NASA space shuttle *Challenger* exploded seventy-three seconds after liftoff. Because the crew included a teacher, Christa McAuliffe, who would have been the first civilian in space, the disaster was watched live in many classrooms.

† Given the headline "Only Make Believe," the review was published in the February 11, 1986, issue. My somewhat less playful piece on Hollywood war movies was published in *American Film* (March 1986) as "The Fascist Guns in the West," and subsequently reprinted in the journal *Radical America*:

There is a strikingly solipsistic quality to current American patriotism. As the 1983 conquest of Grenada and the 1984 Olympics demonstrated, Reagan-era chauvinism celebrates itself; it thrives very well, and perhaps even better, in the absence of a clear-cut opposition. So it should come as no surprise that current action heroes exhibit an individualism bordering on the psychotic.

being an American." That is, he supposedly violated the airspace of a
North African nation that with a nod to the film's structuring absence—
this is, after all, a man's world—we might term "Labia." It's ruled by a
flaky military dictator whom, given the movie's fear of you know what,
I'll call "Colonel Cut-off-he."

Libyan strongman Muammar Gaddhafi had been cast as the personification of evil as well as Reagan's bête noire—and occasional punching bag.
After shooting down two Russian-made Libyan jets in the Gulf of Sidra in
August 1981, Reagan was told that Gaddhafi had sent a hit squad to take him
out: "It's a strange feeling to find there is a 'contract' out on yourself," he wrote
in his diary.

Reagan made at least one speech wearing a bulletproof vest, had his flights
to Camp David scrambled to avoid hand-launched heat-seeking missiles, and
for the rest of the year expressed concern that Gaddhafi was planning to as-
sassinate him and others, including Senator Howard Baker. To judge from
his diaries, Gaddhafi was often on Reagan's mind (although he could never
decide how to spell the Libyan dictator's name). Held responsible for massacres at the Rome and Vienna airports, Gaddhafi—whom Reagan referred
to as "Libya's top clown" and his "least favorite actor"—was the subject of several lengthy National Security Council meetings in January 1986.*

Faced with a do-nothing State Department, the pilot's sweetly hulking
teenage son, Doug (Jason Gedrick), teams up with the irascible yet
tenderhearted Chappy (Lou Gossett), a reserve pilot working as the
base mechanic, to borrow a pair of F-16s and bring back Dad themselves. [Thus] *Iron Eagle* blunders right into the disjunction between

---

* Writing some weeks later in *The Nation*, my former *Voice* colleague Alexander Cockburn analyzed Gaddhafi as a geopolitical Fu Manchu, the latest incarnation of the anti-
Western "superfiend." His "great contribution to the anatomy of superfiendishness,"
Cockburn wrote, "has been his deliberate and indeed joyous acceptance of the role thrust
upon him by Western fantasists, right down to the cultivation of sexual ambiguity. Sometimes he gives interviews only to women journalists or makes a pass at Imelda Marcos; at
other times he dashes about in campy military attire or unisex caftans."

Reagan and Rambo, the master of fantasy and the fantasy of mastery. No one in the movie even pretends to approve of the State Department's policy that leaves Doug's dad a helpless hostage. "Christ, we're holding all the aces!" one guy exclaims. "Why do they act like it's a pair of twos?" So tell me, who's "they"? When someone brings up Iran, Doug's friend—the only black person on the base besides Chappy and thus shamelessly exploited as a mouthpiece for the film's most jingoistic sentiments—becomes irate. "That was different," he explains. "Mr. Peanut was in charge then. Now we got this guy who don't take no shit from no gimpy country. That's why they call him 'Ronald Ray-gun.'"

Given this provocative use of the triple negative, it almost seems churlish to observe that, in the context of *Iron Eagle*, it is Ronald Ray-gun's government and not Mr. Peanut's that has wimped out by refusing to invade Labia. But who cares? The real point is: Would you rather be (i.e., have) a Ray-gun or a Peanut? In the real world, the real Reagan once resolved this contradiction by endorsing *Rambo*—identifying himself as a member of the audience just like everyone else, learning what he was supposed to do "next time." *Iron Eagle* is the mythological next time—it resolves everything with the happiest ending imaginable. Not only is Colonel Cut-off-he vaporized in man-to-gook combat, the fathers are resurrected, and Doug is even admitted to the Air Force Academy, bad grades and all.

By the time the review appeared, the Sixth Fleet had begun maneuvers off the Libyan coast.

The president screened *Iron Eagle* at Camp David on March 1. Two weeks later, he approved additional naval maneuvers in Libyan waters. "Will he (Qadaffy) open fire or not?" Reagan wrote in his March 23rd diary entry, answering the question a day later: "The real news was that Quadafy [sic] fired Sam missiles at our planes in the Mediterranean war games & sent a couple of missile ships out toward our naval vessels. Score—no hits on any of our craft but 2 Libyan ships sunk & our air missiles took out the radar without which the Sams can't be fired. Qudafi [sic] claims he shot down 3 of our planes—he lies." April 15, two weeks after accusing Libya of masterminding the bombing of a West Berlin disco in retaliation for the war games incident, the U.S. Air Force rained bombs on Tripoli and Benghazi.

The next day, Reagan noted that "in the last two 24 hr. periods the W.H. has taken 126,000 phone calls—15,000 couldn't get through—then 160,000 & 16,000 couldn't get through. They were more than 70 percent favorable. The sad note is that we have to assume the 2 missing airmen are dead." (That weekend at Camp David, the president watched himself as pitcher Grover Cleveland Alexander in the 1952 Warner Bros. production *The Winning Team*.)

Could there possibly be a form of socially responsible anti-Reagan warno?

Oliver Stone, a twice-wounded Vietnam veteran who had worked on the screenplay for *Conan the Barbarian* as well as writing Brian De Palma's *Scarface* remake, seemed to think so. Stone expressed the urgency of a documentary filmmaker. "My intelligence sources tell me that we're planning an invasion of Nicaragua as early as January," he informed the *Los Angeles Times* in December 1985. Stone had been planning a movie on the Salvadoran civil war for several years and hoped to shoot it on location there. "It would've been very inexpensive. You could stage *Apocalypse Now* down there for $5,000."

Stone visited El Salvador in early 1984 to confer with the nation's beleaguered centrist leaders. He also managed to woo military personnel connected with the right-wing death squads. "They loved *Scarface*. They kept telling me it was one of their favorite films." In the end, however, President José Napoleón Duarte turned them down: "He actually said that the film would hurt the country's tourist image." Even though the movie was shot in Mexico, aspects of a cut-rate *Apocalypse Now* were evident when *Salvador* opened to mixed reviews on February 28, 1985. In its shocking violence and freewheeling critique, Stone's movie, a British-Mexican co-production all but self-distributed, was the most reckless and confrontational of recent left-wing features depicting Latin American upheaval.*

Like its more temperate precursor *Under Fire*, as well as John Wayne's Vietnam movie *The Green Berets, Salvador* told the story of professionally

---

* Others include Costa-Gavras's *Missing* (1982), screened by the Reagans and much disapproved by the president as "a pretty biased slam at Chile and our own government"; Roger Spottiswood's *Under Fire* (1983); the British production *Beyond the Limit* (1983); and Haskell Wexler's *Latino* (1985). *The Year of Living Dangerously*, set in Indonesia and also screened at Camp David, is analogous.

skeptical war correspondents converted to a cause. Stone's models, however, were the photojournalist Richard Boyle (who co-wrote the script), gonzo *Rolling Stones* staff writer Hunter S. Thompson, and Francis Coppola's hallucinated *Apocalypse Now*. Although aspiring to docudramatic topicality, *Salvador* was a movie about the Sixties and specifically Vietnam, where Stone served.

Stone's dissolute, forty-ish protagonist, combat photographer Richard Boyle (James Woods), departs his squalid San Francisco pad, driving in a beaten-up Mustang to war-torn El Salvador with his pal, another countercultural relic who uses the DJ name "Captain Rock" (Jim Belushi). Once in the country, the movie turns wildly discontinuous, lurching from one atrocity to the next with Boyle a one-man platoon running around a tropical hell in an adrenaline-laced purple haze. Early incidents, like a death squad goon coolly shooting a kneeling student in the street, or a pile of corpses in a garbage dump outside town, evoke Vietnam or Cambodia. A few are humorous, as when Captain Rock spikes a supercilious female TV journalist's drink with LSD or Boyle manages to bribe his buddy out of prison. Others—like the assassination of Archbishop Romero in church or the rape-murder of four American churchwomen—are based on actual occurrences.

A brutal, unholy mess, *Salvador* impressed critics more than audiences. The liberal David Denby praised the movie in *New York* as "a nastier, crazier, hipper version of *Under Fire*." Writing in the *Washington Times*, the conservative David Brooks called it "one of the most rancid movies of the decade." Others were more detached. "The right has stolen all the special effects and heart-pounding rhetoric, leaving the liberals without a single stylistic trope to capture the attention of the easily bored MTV generation," Dave Kehr wrote in the *Chicago Reader*. *Salvador*, Kehr thought, was "a wholly new concept," namely "the first violent *left-wing fantasy*." Boyle, he suggested, was not so much an original character as "an original character to this genre"—an analogue to antiauthoritarian wise guys like Eddie Murphy and Bill Murray.

As such, *Salvador* was an attempt at shock didacticism. The key scene, set at a party in the American embassy, incorporates a cameo by the newly elected president Ronald Reagan, seen on television addressing the crisis in El Salvador. America, Reagan explains, must "halt the infiltration into the Americas by terrorists, and by outside interference and those who aren't just aiming at El Salvador but, I think, are aiming at the whole Central America and possibly later South America—and, I'm sure, eventually North America." The point is underscored by an appreciative military attaché who warns Boyle of "Cuban tanks on the Rio Grande."

The other side is heard when, after cleaning up his act in order to visit a rebel camp, Boyle undergoes a total personality change and becomes Stone's mouthpiece, albeit retreating a bit from his support of the Marxist revolutionaries when he sees them summarily execute some members of the death squads. The charge—"You've become just like them!"—is one that could have been leveled against Rambo. (By now, Lieutenant Colonel Oliver North, an associate of national security adviser Robert McFarlane, has come up with a scheme to bypass Congress and funnel money from the Iranian Deal to the Nicaraguan Contras.)

On April 26, the Chernobyl nuclear power plant, sixty-five miles north of Kiev, suffered an explosion and fire, sending radioactive material into the atmosphere for nine days in the most disastrous such accident in history. May 16 brought a Hollywood movie described by its producers, Don Simpson and Jerry Bruckheimer, as "*Star Wars* on earth."

Made at a time of record defense spending, *Top Gun* was partially subsidized by the Pentagon, which charged Paramount less than $2 million for the use of jets and aircraft carriers and the freedom to shoot several scenes at the actual Top Gun school. (In return, the Department of Defense got total script approval, including casting and line edits. One significant change had a major character's death altered from a midair collision to an ejection mishap.)

When the movie opened in mid-May, the *Voice* gave me extra space for my review, which began by observing that "*Top Gun* doesn't posit sex as aggression, it reformulates aggression as sex."*

A masterful packaging job—all chrome and close-ups—*Top Gun*'s ultimately depressing fly-boy saga comes complete with pre-sold hit songs (some of them twenty years old), military fashion accessories, and Reagan-friendly pull quote ("the best of the best"). There's also a ready-made

* "Phallus in Wonderland," *Village Voice*, May 27, 1988.

mythology of American male supremacy, nicely framed in high school terms. This nation (this football team, this guy) has something to prove and, as a cocky young fighter pilot given the soubriquet "Maverick," Tom Cruise is almost ferally avid to make the point. He'll flip an F-14 on its back just to give a Russian pilot the finger.*

Top Gun, which takes its title from the nickname given the navy's elite Fighter Weapons School, was directed by Tony Scott (Ridley's brother, best known for his Eurotrash bloodsucker *The Hunger*). Scott's advertising background is everywhere apparent, but the film's guiding intelligence is doubtless that of Don Simpson and Jerry Bruckheimer, producers of the megahits *Flashdance* and *Beverly Hills Cop. Top Gun* isn't about the right stuff, it's pushing the kid stuff. Like *Flashdance*, it's a high-tech fantasy recycling the talkies' most ancient clichés. (No less than success-oriented musicals, aviation films were a staple of the early '30s.)

Flashdance and *Top Gun* are teenage trance-outs; they give a new meaning to "go with the flow." Their protagonists are constructed as American winners—the cheerleader and the quarterback—at once sexual prototypes, erotic conquistadors, and paradigms of excellence. Making necessary adjustments in terms of demographics and topical background, the two films' formulas are quite similar. For Jennifer Beals's aerobicized body, read Cruise's no-less-synthetic aerodynamic F-14; for the 1982 Reagan Recession, substitute the post-Grenada new patriotism. In both cases, the spectacle of narcissistic performance (whether flash-dancing or dive-bombing) is underscored by a backbeat of nonstop rock 'n' roll.

From the Paramount logo through the end credits, *Top Gun* is fueled by an eclectic blend of Giorgio Moroder, Otis Redding, and the Righteous Brothers. (With one exception, the interpolated rock videos are visual heavy metal—portentous montages of machines and robotic humanoids.) The score gives the movie a kind of amoral insistence and subliminal history. As Herman Rappaport reiterates in *The 60s Without Apology*, Vietnam was the first rock 'n' roll war: "Introjected into the

---

* The movie was Cruise's first real hit in the three years since *Risky Business* and elevated him to number-one male star in the 1986 Quigley poll.

technology, the libidinal impulses of rock became the lure by which some men killed with pleasure . . . putting the weapon on 'automatic fire' was called putting it on 'rock and roll.'" Recycling the music of the Vietnam era, *Top Gun* goes beyond the similarly warnographic *Iron Eagle* in reenlisting rock for militarist ends, to evoke an utterly specious nostalgia. (Is this movie cynical? Interviewed by Alexander Cockburn in the June 1986 issue of *American Film*, co-producer Simpson brags of beating the draft during Vietnam by deliberately wrecking his motorcycle.)

Throughout, *Top Gun* practices a relentless displacement, both political and sexual. Maverick's father disappeared during the early stages of the Vietnam War, his F-4 bomber shot down under classified circumstances over some unspecified border. He's a heroic Viet victim unscarred by defeat and washed clean of our war crimes; still, his image is tainted in the eyes of an ungrateful nation. It's up to Mav to redeem Dad's memory—lucky for him that war is such a thrill. "This gives me a hard-on," one *Top Gun* undergrad cracks while watching a video-simulated dogfight. It's a joke, but later, in actual combat against Soviet MiGs, the line is repeated, seriously.

Given its taste for brash innuendo, *Top Gun*'s celebration of the male esprit de corps is so blatantly homoerotic you can imagine the dialogue as interpreted by the Cockettes: rival fly-boys taunt each other with cries of "You're mine!"; enraged officers brandish fat stogies and scream, "I want some *butts*!" Of course, as Freud is supposed to have said, sometimes a cigar is just a cigar. Still, there are moments in this movie when the screen is so packed with streamlined planes and heat-seeking missiles, wagging forefingers and upright thumbs that, had Freud lived to see it, he might be excused for thinking *Top Gun* an avant-garde representation of Saturday Night at the Saint Marks Baths.*

The academy in *Top Gun* is an even more programmatic bastion of machismo. If "dickhead" is the standard affectionate putdown, "pussy"

---

* A number of *Voice* readers thought I had gone too far here and that my delirious response to what I perceived as the movie's sexual delirium crossed into homophobia. Perhaps that's true. *Top Gun* did inspire a general phobic reaction that I would have then seen as more misandrist. (Some years later, Quentin Tarantino had considerable fun unpacking *Top Gun* as a "gay love story" with an apparently improvised riff in the 1994 movie *Sleep With Me*.)

is a moral insult. "This school is about combat. There is no second place," an officer admonishes his eager charges. Actually, there is—as one fly-boy points out, "The plaque for runner-up is in the lady's room." *Top Gun* isn't just a spectacle of pure aggression; it's a suppressed sob of terror. The atmosphere of macho anxiety is palpable.

Even the press book is in on the scam, emblazoned with a quote attributed to Cruise: "A Top Gun instructor once told me there are only four occupations worthy of a man: actor, rock star, jet fighter pilot, or President of the United States." (So much for movie-reviewing!) Given the pathos implicit in this statement—that it is virtually impossible for any male in the audience to achieve vocational manhood—it's almost poignant that *Top Gun*'s most prolonged striptease would be an endless scene of Mav fighting back tears after the death of his flying partner, Goose (Anthony Edwards).

What sort of woman, you might wonder, could represent her gender—and confirm Mav's sexual orientation—in this super-butch environment? Kelly McGillis, the Amish siren of *Witness*, plays *Top Gun*'s resident astrophysicist and romantic interest with a kind of sultry boredom. Outfitted mainly in leather and jeans and named "Charlie" (for our enemy in Vietnam?), she's the quintessential man's woman, a virtual penis in a wig—even if a little unhealthily fascinated by the forward thrust of the Soviet MiG . . .

The World War II of flirtations, Mav and Charlie's Moroder-powered staring contests are fun in a leaden sort of way, culminating midway through the movie in a blue-lit bout of slow-mo lovemaking. (This solitary sex scene was reportedly added by the studio after the film's initial previews; exhibiting an adolescent charm untempered by irony, it focuses on extravagant tongue-kissing rather than actual penetration.) In short, *Top Gun* is a movie where the locker room is more fetishized than the boudoir. The most sustained erotic tension is provided by the love-hate relationship between Maverick and his rival, Iceman (Val Kilmer), as they vie to be Top Gun's top gun.

This bellicose *2001* for the age of Reagan is designed as a roller-coaster-ride-cum-demolition derby through the upper stratosphere. But once Charlie's been pacified and the stunts start to pall, you're stuck with forty-five minutes of grating noise, spinning close-ups, and posturing beefcake. The film leaves you unpleasantly clenched. After a while, you're longing to see those orgasmic orange explosions—the "great balls of fire" Mav and Goose love to sing about. Miss Charlie notwithstanding, they're the only release *Top Gun* provides.

Even though Iceman wins *Top Gun*'s academic honors, in the context of the movie, only war can take the true measure of a man. Conveniently breaking out moments after the graduation ceremony, the real thing provides the requisite upbeat closer (complete with Iceman's Mav-induced thaw). In conjuring up a potential World War III scenario as the deus ex machina of a happy ending, *Top Gun* is far more alienated than the previous round of warnographic action flicks. Not only is the enemy totally dehumanized—a Darth Vader fusion of MiG and pilot—there's nothing personal at stake in the war, unless it's a matter of personal best.

Celluloid demagogues like Stallone and Milius exploit a sense of grievance, however misplaced. (Indeed, as a lump of human resentment, Sylvester Stallone may be just about perfect.) What Rambo lacks is cannon-fodder glamour; no one will ever mistake him for an officer and a gentleman. By contrast, Cruise and his cohort are looking good, having fun. Early on, *Top Gun* features a scene at a bimbo-rich pick-up bar. It's time for "target practice," Mav advises his buddy, but he's way off the mark. Make no mistake, draft-age spectator, *Top Gun*'s target is you.

Top Gun cashed the check that *Firefox* wrote. Enlistment spiked. The navy set up recruitment tables outside theaters and reportedly canceled a series of recruiting ads in favor of new ones modeled on *Top Gun*.*

---

* Building on the example set by *Flashdance*, also produced by Bruckheimer and Simpson, *Top Gun* was laden with interpolated music videos and would be a landmark example of what would later be termed "convergence culture." Aided by carefully timed singles and videos, the soundtrack went platinum—number one for three weeks during the summer of 1986. Helped by a quick release, low price, and massive advertising campaign, the VHS tape, released in March 1987, sold 2.5 million units, burying the previous record of 1.4 million held by *Indiana Jones and the Temple of Doom*. *Top Gun* was the first tape to include an ad (for Diet Pepsi, introduced during the 1987 Grammy Awards). The movie spawned a

The president screened *Top Gun*, which would gross $344 million worldwide, at Camp David over the Memorial Day weekend.

Cobra, Sylvester Stallone's latest, had already opened at 2,131 theaters (the largest opening ever) to crowds and derision. *New York* magazine critic David Denby was particularly outraged: "After deciding to distribute *Cobra*, how can Warners turn down any film as being unfit to carry the company name?" Arnold Schwarzenegger's new film, *Raw Deal*, opened two weeks later (the same day that the Reagans screened *Cobra* at Camp David). I had asked my editors to delay my review of *Cobra* for two weeks so as to bracket them.*

Sylvester Stallone must think he's making movies for the Flintstones—he's perfected the granite touch. Every shtick in *Cobra weighs* a ton; the bon mots fall like boulders. . . . *Rambo*, however witless, was reasonably exciting hackwork. For *Cobra*, director George P. Cosmatos has taken pains to recreate the screen-buckling cinderblock compositions and clunky cross-cutting of Stallone's lumpen Eisenstein style. Watching this film is like waltzing with an electric chair—when not crushing your toes, it gives a jolt to keep your attention.

Such Pavlovian stimuli actually precede the credits: *Cobra* opens with Stallone intoning a litany of U.S. crime stats, then firing a bullet straight into the camera. Clear enough. When not aggrandizing its star, the film is designed to intimidate the audience. All Los Angeles is being terrorized by the Night Slasher, a serial killer who "preys upon anyone." To reinforce the state of total terror, *Cobra*'s worst bloodbaths invariably occur in bland public spaces—a hospital, a motel courtyard, a supermarket. Like *Invasion U.S.A.*, the film is set during Christmas season.

According to Stallone's interviews, the script for this ponderous *policier* took him a mere sixteen hours to write. One reason, perhaps, that *Cobra* needed so little time is that the film is the Classic Comics version

---

series of video games in 1987 and, thirteen years later, was widely cited by pundits as providing a template for the televised reporting of the Gulf War.

* Bringing my warnographic studies to a close, the piece ran in the *Voice*'s June 10 issue under the headline "Planet of the Apes." The accompanying illustration, which matched complementary images of the two stars striking similar poses in matching leather jackets, was captioned, "Wanna dance?"

of *Dirty Harry*, with Stallone posing for Mount Rushmore in the role of the alienated supercop, here called Marion "Cobra" Cobretti. To symbolize the appropriation, Dirty Harry's partner (Reni Santoni) is recruited to be Cobra's straight man while the Eastwood film's nefarious Zodiac killer (Andrew Robinson) is resurrected as the smart-mouthed quasiliberal who serves as Cobra's intra-departmental nemesis. (At the end of the movie, Stallone gets to make his day and punch Robinson out.)

Actually, the unshaven, aviator-shaded Marion Cobretti bears a marked resemblance to Arnold Schwarzenegger's Terminator. Fear of Schwarzenegger seems a virtual subtext of *Rocky IV* (Drago being a blond Arnold), while the baddest guy in *Cobra* looks like a skinny Arnold (same lumpy face albeit without the muscular cheekbones).*

Even more than Stallone, Schwarzenegger comes across as a golem—a thing that talks, or at least recites phonetic English. "You should not drink and bake," he pleasantly advises his haggard wife early in John Irvin's *Raw Deal*. Unhappy with his job as a Midwestern sheriff, she's just hurled a cake inscribed "shit" at the ample target of his head.

Maybe Stallone does have reason to worry. Schwarzenegger not only has a more developed sense of irony, but better comic timing. "Who do I look like, Dir-tee Hahr-r-ree?" he sonorously joshes the FBI man come to lure him into undercover action against the mob in Chicago. One reason Clint Eastwood seems reasonable these days is that, as action heroes go, lunks like Stallone, Schwarzenegger, and Chuck Norris are so primitive they make Dirty Harry look like Adlai Stevenson. The least ideological, most purely functional of the crop, Schwarzenegger has carved out a career playing humanoid killing machines—first in *The Terminator*, then *Commando*. Thus, the climax of *Raw Deal*, signaled by many crashing guitar chords, has him dressing in leather and strapping on his grenades for war. Single-handedly decimating the mob, he accomplishes what one admiring cop calls "a hundred years of police work in a single afternoon."

---

* In a Sunday think piece, Vincent Canby pointed out that *Cobra*'s grand finale, set in an iron foundry, appeared to be a takeoff on the climax of *Commando*.

Not to exaggerate *Raw Deal*'s virtues, the film's sociopathic environment seems a veritable Tahiti after *Cobra*'s sullen psycho-ward chest-thumping. Compared to Sly's grimly apocalyptic firefights, the spectacle of Schwarzenegger wrecking a crooked gambling game to a heavy metal beat is positively wholesome. And when a group of shell-shocked gangsters drive off on flat tires in a hopelessly perforated limousine, the film achieves a certain simian savoir faire.*

---

* As a movie star and media personality, Schwarzenegger proved highly self-conscious, not unlike Madonna, who in her "Material Girl" video called attention to herself as a product, and elsewhere foregrounded her business savvy. Schwarzenegger's late '80s and early '90s interviews invited the public to share his inside analysis of career choices, admire his strategies, appreciate his real estate investments, and marvel at both his lifetime of hard work and uncanny sense of predestination. Schwarzenegger had a sense of himself as a historical being: "With *Rocky*, I think Stallone did a big service to my career because he opened up a whole new type of movie, where the body is accepted and people go to see the body." While Stallone was coy (or ambivalent), Schwarzenegger was open about his politics. Order and discipline were the stuff of his fantasy life: "I was always dreaming about very powerful people. Dictators and things like that," he recalled. Arnold's autobiographical accounts are unselfconsciously filled with reference to "the Master Plan," "iron discipline," and his own compulsive "neatness."

July 24, the *New York Times* reported from Moscow "Russians Strike Back with a Rambo of Their Own," citing *Solo Voyage* (Russian title: *Odinochnoye Plavaniye*), in which a "commando unit foils an attempt by agents of the American military-industrial complex to cause a war between the United States and the Soviet Union that would produce profits for American arms manufacturers." Filmed in Cuba, Czechoslovakia, Moscow, and the Crimea, *Solo Voyage* is unusually explicit in its violence, including close-up shots of bullets smashing into heads. After musing on "the unfortunate need to kill Americans to defend the 'moral and nonmaterialistic' Soviet Union," the hero is killed by a dying American who manages to squeeze off a final shot before collapsing.

The next day, Reagan wrote to the new Soviet leader, Mikhail Gorbachev, offering to abolish ballistic missiles and, in effect, lay the groundwork for what would be a new buddy team.

In Dreams: *Blue Velvet* and the New AmericanArama

Ronald Reagan's last great media extravaganza had been the four-day Liberty Weekend, July 3–6, 1986. A $32 million party produced by David Wolper and partially underwritten by ABC-TV, it was the Eighties equivalent of the Fifties' ancient-world PaxAmericanArama spectacles, and the antithesis of the Seventies' disaster films.

Reagan's co-star was the Statue of Liberty, newly refurbished and one hundred years old. His face melding with hers, the president pressed the button to launch a *Star Wars* laser beam and a zillion fireworks, proclaiming that "we are the keepers of the flame of liberty; we hold it high tonight for the world to see." With his approval rating at a near-peak 70 percent, Reagan presented medals to five naturalized citizens, including Elie Wiesel (no hard feelings). The talent included Elizabeth Taylor, Kenny Rogers, Andy Williams, Frank Sinatra, and Gregory Peck (later to become anathema to the right wing for lending his voice to the televised campaign against Reagan's pick for Supreme Court justice, Robert Bork). *Time*'s cover story, "Yankee Doodle Magic," hailed the president as "a Prospero of American memories, a magician who carries a bright, ideal America like a holograph in his mind and projects the image in the air," but some thought the magic was beginning to wear thin.*

Reagan's movie screenings that summer included Leo McCarey's 1937 screwball comedy *The Awful Truth*; the 1960 epic Western *The Magnificent Seven*; Roman Polanski's big-budget flop *Pirates*; James Ivory's E. M. Forster adaptation *A Room with a View*; the made-for-TV *Last Days of Patton*, with George C. Scott reprising his most famous role; and Gary Marshall's *Nothing in Common*, a comedy-drama in which the dying Jackie Gleason plays Tom Hanks's irascible father.

James Cameron's *Aliens*—which opened at number one and would be the

---

* Criticizing "the conventional wisdom that Reagan qualifies as the greatest leader to occupy the White House since Roosevelt," an unsigned editorial in the October 13, 1986, issue of the *New Republic* opined that the president's new morning was "giving way to the morning after," pointing out that "Reagan bought recovery from the 1981–82 recession with the fiscal equivalent of MasterCard," driving up the deficit with a three-year splurge of import buying and foreign credit: "When he retires, the charismatic spell will be over." Dream on!

seventh-highest-grossing movie of 1986—was not among them. Neither was the summer's most luridly outlandish production, David Cronenberg's lavish remake of the 1958 drive-in horror film *The Fly*. Garishly downbeat, these movies heralded the flowering of a pop counterculture that variously parodied, opposed, and ambiguously embraced Reagan's New Morning.

Directed by Ridley Scott, the original *Alien* had been the number-five hit of 1979, an interplanetary spawn of *Jaws* that took the Spielberg film's nominal anti-capitalism a giant step further: hardly set in a paradisiac beach resort, the movie was largely confined to a highly unpleasant, atomic-powered sweatshop, the rocket-freighter *Nostromo*. More radical than *Jaws* was the film's designated survivor. While the monster shark was slain by a middle-class family man (who happened to be a cop) and a hippie oceanographer, *Aliens'* no less terrifying creature, the ultimate Implacable Alien Other, was dispatched by warrant officer Ellen Ripley (Sigourney Weaver), the iconic equivalent of a single mom.

Recruited to make a sequel, Cameron reworked the original as a genre mash-up—a horror sci-fi war movie that was also a last-stand crypto-Western and a drama of maternal love—multiplying the monsters while maintaining the original's anti-corporate attitude. Ripley is dispatched, along with a squad of marines, on behalf of "the Company" to investigate the disappearance of settlers on the alien planet. The Company has no difficulty writing off human life in the service of profit, while Ripley is innately nurturing. Significantly, it's the revelation that innocent pioneer families are in danger that helps sends her back—and Cameron ups the ante. The cat Ripley looked after in *Alien* is here a traumatized nine-year-old girl.

The original *Alien* was set almost entirely on the *Nostromo*. *Aliens* is scarcely less claustrophobic once it gets to the abandoned settlement, a derelict factory that is basically a giant fusion reactor. The marine hardware has an uncanny resemblance to Ghostbusters weaponry. Thus, the threat of a nuclear holocaust hangs over much of the movie. Ripley battles the aliens amid panic and confusion under threat of a nuclear meltdown even as she contrives to have the factory site nuked.*

---

* Motherhood is at once macho and monstrous and, in her all but single-handed conquest, Ripley can lay claim to be the greatest Reagan-era hard body of all. The protagonist of *The*

Ripley's struggle with the Implacable Alien Other is an instance of species-to-species combat in which the enemy is not an allegorical stand-in for Communists but rather a life-form with its own imperative to reproduce and thrive, not unlike a virus. A similar conflict is at the heart of David Cronenberg's soulful and disgusting philosophical love story *The Fly*. Rich with gross-out special effects and intimations of Kafka's *Metamorphosis*, *The Fly* opened in mid-August, replacing *Aliens* as the nation's number-one movie (a spot the Cameron movie held for four weeks) and reigning there for the rest of the month.

Like *Aliens*, *The Fly* had a marked Darwinian component, pitting one species against another. An eccentric scientist (Jeff Goldblum), working on a process of teleporting that will "change the world as we know it," winds up changing himself into a monstrous, monstrously strong human fly with an extraordinary sex drive and equally powerful sweet tooth—"a creature so repulsive," Caryn James wrote in her *New York Times* review, that "he makes the monster in *Aliens* look like Grandma in a Norman Rockwell painting."

Beginning with the transformation of a teleported baboon into a puddle of twitching goo, Cronenberg orchestrates a series of changes, mostly to the scientist, whose body grows stronger even as it disintegrates and ultimately deliquesces. In his moments of lucidity, he attempts to diagnose his condition. Is it a bizarre form of cancer, a contagion, a form of evolution? That his girlfriend (Geena Davis) is pregnant with his post-mutation baby introduces an additional component to the movie's already hysterical body-loathing and sense of sexually transmitted disease.

Like *Gremlins* and *The Terminator*, *Aliens* and *The Fly* broke with Spielberg-Lucas anti-camp naturalism to revel in their identity as hyper-real live-action comic books. Both movies also used insects as manifestations of absolute Otherness. Both suggested metaphors for actual terrors. *Aliens* had intimations of the nuclear meltdown at Chernobyl; *The Fly* could not help but evoke the AIDS plague. Having its first screenings that summer was a third horror film, Tim Hunter's *River's Edge*. Directed from a script by UCLA student Neal Jimenez, it had affinities to the most poetic (and archetypal) of high school social problem pictures, *Rebel Without a Cause*.

Fly, by contrast, was the negation of hard-body cyborgs from *Blade Runner*'s replicants and Schwarzenegger's *Terminator* to the machine-man Rambo.

Here the monsters were all too human and the story based on an actual 1981 incident. Spawn of a suburban wasteland, a group of post-punk, stoned-out teenagers are too vacant to register any emotion when one of them rape-murders his girlfriend and leaves her body unburied by the river. "There's no-one in *River's Edge* for the audience to identify with; just about every character is repulsive," *Variety* complained upon seeing the movie at the Montreal Film Festival. Dennis Hopper plays a one-legged ex-biker who lives alone with an inflated sex doll, selling loose joints and reminiscing about his colorful past: "I ate so much pussy in those days, my beard looked like a glazed donut." (According to Hopper, Harry Dean Stanton read the script and called him, explaining, "This is too weird for me. You should do it.")

Not obviously commercial—financed like Oliver Stone's *Salvador* by the British company Hemdale—*River's Edge* would not open theatrically until the spring of 1987. It was hailed by David Denby in *New York* magazine as "the most disturbing movie I have seen in the nearly nine years I have held this job."

Warnos, photo ops, and remakes were not the sole instances of Reagan-era culture. Nor was Spielbergism the lone source of cinematic fantasy. By 1986, an avant-pop version of American self-absorption had become common currency.

Whereas the spectacles of the 1950s projected imperial America back into the ancient world, imperial majesty was found—three decades later—in the hermetic solemnity of photographer William Eggleston's color images of Elvis Presley's Graceland home, published in *Artforum* in 1984, the vacuum-sealed vacuum cleaners of Jeff Koons's commodity art, or Errol Morris's 1978 *Gates of Heaven*, a documentary account of two California pet cemeteries that constructs each frame as a sarcophagus all its own.

American greatness was perversely celebrated by the publication of Thomas Hine's *Populuxe*, a lavish compendium of American product design between the Korean and Vietnam wars, and confirmed twenty minutes into Jim Jarmusch's independent film *Stranger Than Paradise* (1984) when, interrogated by his greenhorn cousin, one character launches into an impassioned defense of the TV dinner—a gag leaving the viewer to wonder if the meal in question was not simply defrosted from the freezer but exhumed intact from a pharaoh's tomb.

Artistically ambitious independent movies adopted souvenir-stand iconography, pondering the pathos of received ideas, the triumph of the ersatz,
and the wonder of bad taste. While *Stranger Than Paradise* recreated the
once-exotic wasteland of Robert Frank's mid-1950s photographs as a nostalgic pastoral and the Coen Brothers' triumphantly snide *Blood Simple* (1984)
reanimated the dead form of film noir as a baroque caricature, David Byrne's
ostentatiously benign *True Stories* (1986) celebrated small-town American life
with an exaggerated, shadowless clarity.

Welcome to Reaganland! The sense of the U.S. as a kitsch theme park was
promoted by television and theorized by the French philosopher of simulation Jean Baudrillard, who wrote in his delirious, late-1980s manifesto *America* that, with Reagan, "a system of values that was formerly effective turns
into something ideal and imaginary." Baudrillard visualized the continental
U.S. as an awe-inspiring planet of freeway deserts, urban jungles, and monumental enigmas, where California oil-drilling platforms stand sentinel till
dawn "like grand casinos or extraterrestrial spacecraft." The *E.T.* metaphor
was irresistible: the Mormon tabernacle in Salt Lake City was "straight out
of *Close Encounters*," the museums of Washington, DC, suggested an attempt
"to gather all the marks of earthly endeavor and culture . . . for the benefit of
a visitor from outer space."

In 1981, Baudrillard had conceptualized Disneyland as an inoculation,
an official fantasy designed to make the rest of America seem authentic by
comparison. By the mid-1980s, he had moved on to a higher truth, one implicit in the movies *Videodrome* and *The King of Comedy*, that Disneyland
was authentic: "The cinema and TV are America's reality!"

Less dissident than dissonant, more deadpan than ironic, not in the least
nostalgic however interested in recuperating a usable past, this manifestation of the new imperial, triumphantly fake AmericanArama was (like Reaganism and Spielbergism) rooted in the Happy Daze of the 1950s. In part a
revolt against suburban alienation that drew on the more disreputable aspects
of Fifties mass culture (Top 40 pop, drive-in monster movies, TV reruns), it
was pleased to imagine American life as a mirror of the Reagan administration, namely a costume drama predicated on the recycling of familiar artifacts in new and inappropriate contexts. First manifest in New York City's
crumbling East Village in the late 1970s, this vulgar postmodernism was manifest in punk and post-punk rock bands like the Ramones and the B-52s as

well as the art students who collected lurid tabloid headlines ("Headless Body in Topless Bar") and flocked to riff on 1950s monster movies at Club 57.

Beginning at the margins, aspects of this Eighties sensibility found its way to a mass audience in music videos like Michael Jackson's "Thriller" and Madonna's "Material Girl" that used Fifties iconography to cast their stars as sacred monsters. It can also be seen in *Blade Runner's* evolution from big-budget flop to visionary cult film; in the flaming cool of the TV show *Miami Vice*; the neo-Pop Art paintings of Jean-Michel Basquiat, David Salle, and Kenny Scharf; and the work of performance artist Pee-wee Herman (Paul Reubens), who used a regular television show as a vehicle for his invented personality: a manic, nerdy man-child in a too-small gray suit, red bow tie, and lipstick.

Broadcast in the Saturday-morning cartoon ghetto, *Pee-wee's Playhouse* (CBS, 1986–90) was a fully realized private universe—a candy-colored world of sexual ambiguity and a realm of total anthropomorphism. Every object was potentially alive: the window, the chair, the floor. The creatures who called the Playhouse home included miniature dinosaurs, sentient machines, and a refrigerator of foodstuffs that enjoyed an ongoing fiesta—truly the United States of America.*

River's Edge was only one of several current films made on the margins that appeared to engage and critique the New Morning promised in Ronald Reagan's 1984 campaign ads—or, in at least one case, mimic it. *True Stories*, written and directed by, as well as starring, the leader of the new wave rock band Talking Heads, is so unambiguously patriotic as to be the avant-pop analogue to *A New Beginning*.†

---

* *Playhouse* had a remarkable capacity to be both progressive and regressive, sweet and risqué. As Pee-wee was an adult who acted like a child, so the Playhouse aesthetic blended high and low tech, the avant-garde and the vulgar. The Playhouse was further distinguished by its racial diversity and frisky gender-bending. Jambi the blue-faced genie (John Paragon) and the elaborately be-wigged Miss Yvonne (Lynne Marie Stewart), "the most beautiful woman in Puppet Land," each in their way evoked drag performers. Dixie the cabdriver (Johann Carlo) and Reba the mail lady (S. Epatha Merkerson) were notably assertive women, while Cowboy Curtis (Laurence Fishburne) and the various hunky beach boys who drifted in and out of the Playhouse were bashful and flirtatious.

† Both *True Stories* and *A New Beginning* have the texture and structure of a TV special built around a particular star, even as they share a concern with universal representation. Both are paeans to communication technology set in a pastoral mode, filled with positive

Indeed, *True Stories* goes even further than *A New Beginning* in endorsing corporate America—nobody seems to mind that an entity called Varicorp controls the town. On a gee-whiz trip to a mall, David Byrne waxes enthusiastically on consumer pathology: "They're wise to advertisers' claims. . . . They go where the bargains are. . . . Here they can comparison shop!" At once the observing alien and the voice of normality, he may be the movie's resident mad artist, but the other characters are all patently crazier them him.

Significantly, *True Stories* has no yuppies, a not inconsiderable segment of the Talking Heads fan base. Appearing that season, two dark comedies of yuppie angst, David Lynch's *Blue Velvet* and Jonathan Demme's *Something Wild*, evoked a divided America with a buried past and were predicated on crashing through the façade into some other reality. Both films confounded genre. *Something Wild* begins as screwball romantic comedy, becomes a road film, and swerves into thrilling violence, all the while presenting a Middle American landscape of 7-Elevens and theme restaurants as intrinsically exotic, populated by a teeming, romanticized yet marginal Third World of gypsies, rappers, bikers, and African American bit players. But where *Something Wild* discovers another more diverse and human America, *Blue Velvet* lifts up the rock on Middle American "niceness." Are there maggots in the apple pie? Generically a teen coming-of-age film crossed with a noir, it is a unique blend of raw pathology and icky sweetness, in which innocence is no less perverse than experience.*

Weirdest precisely when attempting to be normal, *Blue Velvet* opens

---

platitudes and national anthems. Both emphasize traditional family values and show a corresponding concern with home construction. Both exude a sense of positive transformation. In *A New Beginning*, a black man maintains that "we're gonna be better off in the long run"; in *True Stories*, the narrator (Byrne) asserts that "something is happening . . . the world is changing," seemingly for the better. Byrne's City of Dreams is Reagan's New Beginning. The market functions perfectly. There's no ugliness, no sexism, no class warfare, no racism, although a special nod is given to the significance of African American support and approval.

* As filmmakers, Demme and Lynch developed outside the Hollywood mainstream. Demme started directing exploitation or drive-in movies in the 1970s, a decade when Lynch made the greatest of all midnight movies, *Eraserhead*. Although they were products of the Sixties, their politics were quite different—Demme being a diversity-minded liberal activist who would later make a sympathetic documentary portrait of Jimmy Carter, and Lynch an eccentric conservative who, although he eschewed interest in politics, strongly supported Reagan.

with a literal collapse of authority as the protagonist's father suffers a seizure—or is it a bee sting?—while watering the front lawn. Even before the hero discovers a severed ear in an open field, Lumberton is a place of latent menace. "It's a sunny, woodsy day—so get those chainsaws out," the radio weatherman advises. *Blue Velvet* is an American dream. Its mutable geography suggesting the fluctuating size of the giant ape in the Surrealist favorite *King Kong*, Lumberton is variously a small, somewhat depressed city; an idyllic town out of *A New Beginning*; and a pleasant suburb with a sinister apartment building mysteriously planted on the wrong (which is to say the right) side of the tracks. Indeed, Lynch himself was a Reagan fan and evidently horrified by the idea that *Blue Velvet* might be taken as a critique.

Oedipal stories of male initiation, *Blue Velvet* and *Something Wild* were anticipated by *Risky Business* in some ways and by *Back to the Future* in others. Both concern innocent men, Jeffrey (Kyle MacLachlan) in *Blue Velvet* and Charlie (Jeff Daniels) in *Something Wild*, who struggle with their repressed urges and are victims of their own passivity. Each must contend with a demonic outlaw, Frank (Dennis Hopper) and Ray (Ray Liotta), who is in some sense an alter ego. As the hero of *Risky Business* manages to wrest a winsome prostitute away from her pimp, Jeffrey and Charlie each steal—or rescue— the outlaw's girl, although to different effect. These enigmatic women, bewigged and suggestively named for movie protagonists—Dorothy (Isabella Rossellini) and Lulu (Melanie Griffith)—are simultaneously the victims and engines of desire.

Everything repressed in Reagan's "Morning in America" is here apparent. *Blue Velvet* and *Something Wild* are filled with sexual violence. However, the primal scene in *Something Wild*, wherein the free-spirited Lulu seduces the repressed Charlie after introducing him into a life of petty crime, is more playful than that in *Blue Velvet*—an astonishing sequence in which, hiding in a closet, Jeffrey spies on a bizarre sexual interaction between Dorothy and Frank and then, discovered by Dorothy after Frank's departure, is forced by her at knife-point to disrobe.

"I'm seeing something that was always hidden. I'm in the middle of a mystery and it's all secret," Jeffrey excitedly tells his innocent girlfriend Sandy (Laura Dern), who happens to be an FBI man's daughter. Is her father, who wears his gun and badge in the house, a crooked cop or an incorruptible one?

Either way, he's a Fifties icon and, for all the help he provides, the movie's resident Reagan.

In dealing with the buried past, both *Blue Velvet* and *Something Wild* address *Back to the Future*, the movie which most obviously superimposed the Fifties over the Eighties. Unfolding beneath the banner "Spirit of '76," the ten-year high school class reunion in *Something Wild* is a version of *Back to the Future*'s aptly named "Under the Sea" dance—rich with instances of voyeurism, exhibitionism, and sexual assault as Marty's father spies on Marty's mother undressing, Marty performs on stage, and Biff attempts to rape Marty's mother, who has already expressed her interest in Marty.

Played mainly for humor in *Back to the Future*, these issues are brought to the fore in *Blue Velvet*, which constructs a lurid Oedipal triangle between Jeffrey, Dorothy, and Frank—transposed by some viewers to their own high school experience. Some weeks after *Blue Velvet* opened, *Newsweek* reported that the movie was dividing audiences and inspiring a cult following. "Whatever your reaction, once you see *Blue Velvet*, the sappy old Bobby Vinton song that echoes through the sound track will never again remind you of your senior prom." (The song, which went to number one on September 21, 1963, and held that position for three weeks, was a part of the national soundtrack on the eve of the Kennedy assassination.)

Ostensibly set in the present, *Blue Velvet* evokes the Fifties and, even more than the actual era, its florid melodramas. Lynch both celebrates and defamiliarizes a comfortable, picture postcard façade of malt shoppes, football fields, and rec-room basements—as well as Roy Orbison, whose morose ballad "In Dreams" is lip-synched by the androgynous proprietor of a shabby brothel (Dean Stockwell).*

Given its originality, *Blue Velvet* received a mixed response. The movie was rejected as "pornographic" by the Venice Film Festival even though it was produced by the Italian mogul Dino De Laurentiis and starred native daughter Isabella Rossellini. On the other hand, the critic for the mainline

---

* For Lynch, Jeffrey was the Fifties: "The boy is an idealist. He behaves like young people in the '50s, and the little town where I filmed is a good reflection of the naïve climate there was back then. The local people tended to think the way people did 30 years ago. Their houses, cars and accents have remained the same." As the quintessential Hollywood hippie, creator of *Easy Rider* Hopper personifies the Sixties, as he did, even more explicitly, as the one-legged biker in *River's Edge*.

Protestant journal *Christian Century* declared it the best film of 1986, "probing the depths of evil." Writing in the *National Review*, John Simon called
Lynch "a naïf from Montana who wants to be deep, but whose depth consists of drawing huge sexual organs on a Norman Rockwell painting." Dis-
missing the movie's "sophomoric satire and cheap shots," Roger Ebert gave
it one star in the *Chicago Sun-Times*.

The critic Howard Hampton seems to have been the first to link *Blue Velvet* with the 1942 movie *Kings Row*. Quoting from Pauline Kael's capsule
description of *Kings Row*, Hampton pointed out that she might have been describing *Blue Velvet*: "Tranquilly accepting the many varieties of psycho-
pathic behavior as the simple facts of life," *Kings Row* offers "the typical
nostalgic view of American small-town life turned inside out: instead of
sweetness and health we get fear, sanctimoniousness, sadism, and insanity,"
not to mention hysteria, incest, suicide, torture, murder, and Ronald Reagan—
whom the movie provided with his favorite dramatic role and the title for
his ghostwritten 1965 memoir, *Where's the Rest of Me?*

Adapted from a racy best-seller, the script for *Kings Row* had a difficult time
securing approval from the Production Code, which not only objected to copi-
ous suggestive dialogue ("the general suggestion of loose sex [and] gross sexual
abnormality") but also an instance of euthanasia and a scene of children bathing nude. (References to homosexuality and nymphomania had already been
eliminated.) Still, the movie managed to keep enough sensational material,
most famously the gratuitous amputation of the Reagan character's legs by a
sadistic doctor who resents his daughter's infatuation with him, to be one of
the top-grossing films of 1942, nominated for best picture, best director, and
best photography, and the basis for a 1955 TV series that rotated episodes
drawn from two other Warner Bros. films, *Casablanca* and *Cheyenne*.

On the surface, *Kings Row* is "A Good Town to Live In and a Good Place
to Raise Your Children" (as might be said of the domain mapped in *A New
Beginning*). Reagan, then thirty years old, is sharp-featured and slightly feral
as the town rake. He plays off the blandness of nominal star Robert Cum-
mings, his best friend who goes off to Vienna to study "psychiatry" with an
irascible stand-in for Sigmund Freud and, upon returning, must ultimately
come to grips with the town's dark secrets.

Despite its bizarrely sunny tone, *Kings Row* is not so different from daytime soap operas or even *Dynasty*. The pathology normalized by Reagan's

own lack of introspection makes his fondness for the film's primitive faith in psychotherapy all the more fascinating—as though there had been a sinister Lumberton that haunted his presidential dreams.*

The summer of 1986 brought a third avant-pop masterpiece projecting an America at once crazier and more rational than that of David Lynch or Pee-wee Herman—the twelve-issue epic comic book series *Watchmen*.

Written by Alan Moore and illustrated by Dave Gibbons (and anticipated by revisionist superhero comics like *The Dark Knight Returns* and *American Flagg*), *Watchmen* was, according to Moore, a thought experiment imagining the political and psychological impact that actual superheroes might have on the world. Thus, although he never said so, his apocalyptic pulp-fiction sci-fi murder mystery is a nod to the regime of Rambo, the Terminator, and Ronald Ray-gun.

Watchmen is replete with intertextual integration of printed matter ranging from other comic books and pornographic eight-pagers to newspaper articles, letters, and excerpts from fictional books providing back stories for the major characters, as well in its medium-specific juxtaposition of simultaneous time frames. It's a demonstration of comic book modernism that could be described as an epic, imaginative version of *The Big Chill*, set in an alternate universe where masked superheroes are real, albeit largely retired (thanks to a 1977 congressional bill banning vigilantism) and consequently nostalgic for their youth.

Moore's novelistic narrative provided an alternate history of the Cold War in which Richard Nixon is enjoying his fifth term as president—in part because the most awesome of superheroes, Dr. Manhattan, a mutated atomic scientist who glows like blue kryptonite and possesses unlimited cosmic powers, settled the Vietnam War with an American victory in 1971. When the story begins, some fourteen years later, however, the increasingly alienated Dr. Manhattan has retreated to Mars and thus shifted the balance of power away from the U.S., encouraging the Soviet Union to invade Afghanistan and increasing the likelihood of nuclear war.†

---

* *Blue Velvet* was still in its first release when Reagan revisited *Kings Row*, screening it at Camp David over the same mid-October weekend that he ran *Peggy Sue Got Married*. "I'd forgotten how really good that pic. was," he wrote in his diary.

† *Watchmen* had intimations of the Fifties as well, as noted by Bhob Stewart in the *Comics*

As the U.S. and Soviet Union face off over Afghanistan, the irascible renegade "mask" Rorschach discovers that an even more asinine colleague—and government agent—formerly known as the Comedian has been murdered. A paranoid loner who keeps a Travis Bickle–style journal, Rorschach jumps to the conclusion that someone is plotting to kill all surviving masks. He is not entirely wrong. It gradually becomes apparent that the mask formerly known as Ozymandias, now a super-yuppie entrepreneur (merchandizing Nostalgia-brand perfume, among other things) and master political manipulator, has contrived a messianic Fifties strategy to forestall nuclear war by staging a phony extraterrestrial attack on New York, sacrificing the city so as to unite America and the Soviet Union against an imaginary common foe.

Indeed, this possibility was part of Ronald Reagan's worldview. He expressed it to Mikhail Gorbachev on the occasion of their first meeting in Geneva in November 1985. Gorbachev was evidently nonplussed—as Lou Cannon drily noted, the Soviet leader "did not have at his fingertips the Marxist-Leninist position on the propriety of cooperating with the imperialists against an interplanetary invasion." Although the subsequent summit in Reykjavik foundered on the rock of Reagan's stubborn attachment to his Star Wars scenario, it did set the stage for a later agreement on limiting the arms race.

Watchmen does not have so positive a denouement. The story ends with the surviving masks in existential crisis. Do they reveal their erstwhile colleague Ozymandias as a mass murderer or tacitly support his ruthless scheme? *The New Frontiersman*, a right-wing publication that—although unaware what Rorshach's explosive diaries contain—seems poised to print them as filler, turns the narrative back on itself by noting Robert Redford's presumed

---

Journal: Dave Gibbons's art and page layouts recalled those of the EC horror comics, something that Gibbons would later acknowledge as a deliberate choice; it also anticipated the digitally fabricated superhero movies that came to dominate and define Hollywood production in the post-9/11 twenty-first century. Although unequal to the material, Zach Snyder's 2007 film adaptation enriches the mix by riffing on an alternative-'80s periodicity—a simulated *McLaughlin Group* with Pat Buchanan opining on the nature of Dr. Manhattan is particularly funny—and employing a strategic '60s soundtrack. Indeed, the credit sequence, which scores a frozen-tableaux history of the Watchmen and their precursors the Minutemen to the young Bob Dylan declaiming, "The Times They Are A-Changin'," is far wittier filmmaking than any of the movie's excessively juicy fisticuffs or the escalating pandemonium Snyder orchestrates as *Watchmen* staggers toward its climactic Armageddon.

campaign for president in 1988: "Who wants a Cowboy Actor in the White House?"*

The real Robert Redford sat on the sidelines, but Ronald Reagan campaigns during the 1986 midterm elections as though it were still 1984, at times chanting the words to "God Bless the U.S.A." His mantra fails. Hours before Americans go to the polls, the speaker of the Iranian parliament reveals the national security adviser Robert McFarlane's late May mission to Tehran and the Deal struck to exchange weapons for hostages.†

Two days after the Democrats regain control of the Senate, the story breaks in the American press, causing outrage in Congress and confusion in the White House. Reagan denies knowledge of the Deal while insisting that it had been approved by Secretary of State Caspar Weinberger and Secretary of State George Shultz. In his diary, Reagan refers to the news report as "wild" and "unfounded" and, as if writing for posterity, haplessly reports, "We've tried 'no comment.'" As congressional leaders call for an investigation, the president uses a televised Rose Garden photo op to hide behind one recently freed, evidently traumatized hostage before flying to Camp David. That weekend, the Reagans watch John Wayne battle his surrogate son Montgomery Clift in *Red River* and their own son in a more recent film. (Ron had a bit part in the controversial comedy *Soul Man*, in which a well-off white student passes for black to win a college scholarship.)

Monday morning, Reagan meets with his top advisers to discuss, as he writes in his diary, "the press storm charging we are negotiating with terrorists [and] kidnappers for the release of hostages using sale of arms as ransom." He notes, "I ordered a statement to effect we were <u>not</u> dealing in ransom etc." Thursday night, the president delivers a televised twelve-minute speech on what he calls "the Iran incident" in order to, as he writes in his diary, "re-

---

* In 1972, Robert Redford told the journalist Richard Reeves that "actors are suckers for politics. . . . Ronald Reagan is only the beginning." Made the same year, *The Candidate* starred Redford as a young reformer who unexpectedly defeats California's sitting senator, a veteran politician whose speeches were largely drawn from Governor Reagan.
† The downing of a cargo plane over Nicaragua on October 5, along with the capture of former marine crew member Eugene Hasenfus, resulted in the revelation that the CIA had been secretly arming the Contras. That the project was funded by money from the Iran Deal would soon be apparent.

fute the firestorm the press is raising based entirely on unsubstantiated rumors & out right inventions."

Sunday morning, Shulz appears on the CBS news show *Face the Nation* to publicly disassociate himself from the Deal. Three days after that, the president has a disastrous televised news conference in which he acknowledges that the Deal ("our own 'Dreyfus' case") had been opposed by unnamed top advisers and haplessly obfuscates his way through a barrage of questions regarding the details. "They were out for blood—every Q. had a sharp barb," he writes, hopefully adding, "Our gang seems to feel 'I done good.'"

As the president watches himself as a wounded GI in *The Hasty Heart* (1949) at Camp David, the Deal's architects, CIA head William Casey and MacFarlane's successor as national security adviser, John Poindexter, huddle to coordinate their stories while their associate Lieutenant Colonel Oliver North holds a weekend document "shredding party." November 25, Reagan appears at an unscheduled press conference with Attorney General Edwin Meese to deny he made a mistake sending arms to Tehran. Poindexter has resigned. Meese puts the blame on North (who, watching on TV, realizes it is time get a lawyer.)

"The press was like a circle of sharks," Reagan writes. Almost overnight, his approval rating dives from 67 to 46 percent—a free fall some think unequalled in American history.[*]

Platoon Time (from *Heartbreak Ridge* to *Hamburger Hill*)

On December 2, 1986, as the arms-for-hostages Deal continued to roil the Potomac, Ronald and Nancy Reagan—or rather, their video images—paid effusive homage to their longtime agent and mentor Lew Wasserman, a major Democratic fundraiser not least in the 1986 election, on the occasion of his fiftieth year in show business.[†]

---

[*] Also in mid-November, the Securities and Exchange Commission and New York District Attorney's office announced the arrest of financier Ivan Boesky for insider trading.

[†] Material in the Reagan Library suggests considerable work went into producing the Reagans' taped comments, which were the subject of White House memos throughout the turbulent month of November 1986. A rehearsal tape was made on November 18, the day before the president's disastrous televised news conference, along with short pieces to be

Three days after that, Clint Eastwood celebrated the Conquest of Grenada with *Heartbreak Ridge*, his first combat movie since he appeared in the misbegotten 1968 spectacle *Where Eagles Dare*. (Unlike John Wayne, Sylvester Stallone, and Arnold Schwarzenegger, Eastwood was a veteran. Drafted by the army during the Korean War, he spent two years as a swimming instructor at Fort Ord.)

As Reagan followed Eastwood's career, so Eastwood, a Reagan supporter since 1965, followed the president into politics, successfully seeking the mayoralty of Carmel, California, in April 1986. (That month, *Time* magazine reported that the singer-actor-activist Harry Belafonte was pondering a run against New York senator Alfonse D'Amato, while Charlton Heston and Fess Parker, Disney's Davy Crockett, considered running against California senator Alan Cranston.) Eastwood was said to govern in character, wearing his Dirty Harry tweed sports jacket to city council meetings, acting "mean and hostile," per one political opponent, and employing his gavel to interrupt those in disagreement, whom he would sometimes compare to wolves or coyotes.

Such nastiness is evident in the character of Tom "Gunny" Highway, the old-school marine sergeant Eastwood played in *Heartbreak Ridge*—in production during the summer break he took from browbeating the Carmel City Council. The script, by a then thirty-eight-year-old Viet-vet, James Carabatsos, had been optioned by Warner Bros. in 1984 and offered to Eastwood. The star, now fifty-six, appreciated Gunny as a sort of flawed, middle-aged military version of Dirty Harry—an authoritarian who hates authority, with a self-parodic sensitive streak. (He cluelessly studies *Vogue* magazine in order to understand his ex-wife.)

Eastwood was not unaware of his competition. After two years atop the Quigley list, he had been ousted by Stallone, who remade *Dirty Harry* in the egregious *Cobra*. Schwarzenegger had also paid homage to Eastwood's most famous role in *Raw Deal*, and in *Heartbreak Ridge*, Gunny beats up an oversized hunk with a marked resemblance to Arnold. Eastwood did cling to number seven (right behind Stallone) in 1986, when Tom Cruise topped the list. The number-one movie of 1986, *Top Gun* was riding high when *Heartbreak*

---

shown at the West Coast Ireland Fund Dinner, the International Conference on Private Sector Initiatives, and the Macy's annual Thanksgiving Day Parade. The final tape was produced on December 1, one day before Universal Studios hosted a banquet in Wasserman's honor.

Ridge went into production and at times suggests itself a crabby, geriatric riposte, as Gunny abuses his men with a nonstop stream of homophobic innuendo, even as he successfully bridges the chasm between urban black rock 'n' roll and redneck country-western. *Top Gun* ended with a fake victory over the Soviets (something Eastwood had already achieved in *Firefox*). *Heartbreak Ridge* ends by staging a real victory—the Conquest of Grenada.

Eastwood insisted on using Grenada as the climax of the movie, yoking his claim as still the nation's preeminent action star to Reagan's greatest triumph. The ploy struck some as absurd. "Desperate for action," the *Fort Wayne News-Sentinel* opined, the film involves Eastwood's men in "a pathetic little skirmish that looks more like another training exercise than a real battle." Had a Hollywood Freedom Fighter ever given himself to so paltry an event? *Heartbreak Ridge*, named for an American army victory in Korea, seems to suggest that the operation is the greatest tactical success since D-Day. Gunny declares that after a tie in Korea and a loss in Vietnam, the United States had finally won one.

That *Heartbreak Ridge* made no mention of the 241 marines blown to bits in Beirut two days before the invasion, even as a subject for barracks jitters or maudlin flag-waving, struck some critics (myself included) as evidence of Eastwood's bad faith. In fact, the Department of Defense had requested that the filmmaker remove an existing reference. The movie's greatest battle was behind the scenes.

Eastwood had counted on Pentagon support, not least to save money on equipment. After all, hadn't the brass gratefully promoted his blatantly absurd *Firefox*? But early on, the deputy secretary of defense, Robert Sims, objected to certain aspects of the script, citing, among other things, the abundance of profanity, absence of uplift, and generally retro nature of the protagonist. Worse, he further suggested that the climax might better concern a fictional liberation. Eastwood thanked Sims but ignored his requests, perhaps because he was encouraged by his adviser Lieutenant Colonel Fred Peck (a former marine, briefly an aide to President-elect Reagan), who thought the movie would be a great recruiting poster, doing for the marines what *Top Gun* did for the air force.*

---

* Peck's strategy added fuel to the fire. Under the headline "Vets in Battle over Clint Film's Accuracy," the July 3, 1986, *New York Post* reported, "Korean War veterans are fighting

When, on November 14, the Pentagon screened the finished film, Sims was appalled. "Little was done to incorporate the requisite changes," he wrote to producer Fritz Manes. Moreover, Eastwood had added a scene in which Gunny shoots a wounded, incapacitated enemy soldier twice in the back, a violation of the Geneva Convention (mention of which was included in the letter). Sims recommended that the Marine Corps disassociate itself from the film, sending memos to that effect to both the corp's director of public affairs and the secretary of defense, Caspar Weinberger.

Sims's letter prompted an angry response from Eastwood, who insisted that his stated concerns had been addressed in their entirety. "All references to Beirut were removed from the script even though we thought it was a rather silly request to ignore a fact of history," he wrote, further accusing Sims of disrespecting "the military who served in World War I, World War II, Korea and Vietnam" and especially the Marine Corps: "It is a crime you have forbidden us to give [them] credit where credit is due on this project."

The letter was copied to Reagan, who likely had other things on his mind. The day Eastwood issued his missive, the president held the disastrous press conference at which he lied repeatedly about the facts of the Iranian Deal, declaring, "We will never pay off terrorists because that only encourages more of it." The day before *Variety* announced that the marines had withdrawn support from *Heartbreak Ridge*, refusing Eastwood to have his benefit world premiere at Camp Pendleton in Southern California, Reagan and Attorney General Edwin Meese held an unscheduled press conference to announce the resignation of national security adviser John Poindexter and the firing of National Security Council staffer Oliver North.

Before the movie's December 5 opening, the president's approval ratings had plummeted. That evening at Camp David, the presidential couple screened the hit Australian action-comedy *Crocodile Dundee*, the surprise number-two movie of 1986. The next week, CIA director William Casey— scheduled to appear before the Senate Intelligence Committee—would suffer

---

mad about Clint Eastwood's upcoming film *Heartbreak Ridge*, claiming it unaccurately [*sic*] gives the Marines credit for winning one of the Army's bloodiest battles. . . . Because of the controversy, the Department of Defense plans to ask [Eastwood's company Malpaso] to consider changing the film's title."

a seizure in his office, dying six months later on May 6, the day after Congress began public hearings on the Deal.*

Heartbreak Ridge received mixed, mainly negative, reviews.

Chicago Tribune critic Dave Kehr was enthusiastic, writing that "Eastwood has created his most complex, fully dimensional characterization in Tom Highway; as a director, he has worked to put that characterization in a remarkably mature, self-critical context. *Heartbreak Ridge* is a film of genuine substance and courage." Pauline Kael, a reliable Eastwood disparager, wrote that "it would take a board of inquiry made up of gods to determine whether this picture is more offensive aesthetically, psychologically, morally, or politically."

Heartbreak Ridge wound up grossing $43 million (finishing number eight for 1986) but, as a paean to the American military, it was obliterated two weeks later with *Platoon*, written—as well as directed—by another Viet-vet, Oliver Stone, who served a fifteen-month tour of duty with the 25th Infantry Division from September 1967 through November 1968.

Despite a measure of success in literature and politics, and despite the popularity of such Nam-identified figures as Stallone and Bruce Springsteen, no actual Viet-vet had established a beachhead on the shores of American popular culture. Thus, even more than John Ford, who came back from World War II to pay tribute to U.S. PT boats with *They Were Expendable*, Stone was portrayed as a returning warrior. *Platoon*'s early print ads used an old photo of a uniformed Stone with fellow grunts and included biographical information:

> In 1967, a young man named Oliver Stone spent 15 months in Vietnam as
> an infantryman in the United States Army. He was wounded twice and re-
> ceived a bronze star for gallantry. Ten years later Stone was a screenwriter in
> Hollywood, author of *Midnight Express*. It made him the only man in Holly-
> wood with both a purple heart and an Oscar.

In fact Stone was not—Lee Marvin received a purple heart for his service during World War II and an Oscar for his performance in the 1965 Western comedy *Cat Ballou*. Still, *Platoon* was positioning itself as a corrective to the fantasies of noncombatants John Milius and Sylvester Stallone.

---

* Humiliated by his exposure, McFarlane—who had resigned as national security adviser in early 1986—attempted suicide on February 9, 1987.

Released in the late 1970s, the first wave of Vietnam films, notably *Apocalypse Now* and *The Deer Hunter*, were self-important epics that sought to provide a narrative for the America's most unsatisfying war; the second wave, clustered in the mid-1980s, were essentially compensatory, focused on hero-building and restoring national honor through the rescue of American captives; the third, longest, and most varied wave sought, with mixed success, to tell it like it was. *Platoon* was the first of these—experienced and subsequently presented as a form of national therapy.*

"People are lining up all over America to hurt themselves," Jack Mathews wrote under the headline "Hollywood Steps on a Gold Mine" in the *Los Angeles Times*, which published five articles on *Platoon* in its January 25th Calendar section. "They're standing in lines that run around the block, often in sub-zero temperatures, waiting for the opportunity to pay from $4 to $6 for a ticket to a movie that may be more violent, more frightening and more depressing than anything they have ever seen before." But also more transparent.

Cannily ignoring conventional wisdom, Orion Pictures had given *Platoon* a limited Oscar-qualifying opening in six theaters in three cities (Los Angeles, New York, and Toronto). Starved for substance, local critics praised the film and, considering it newsworthy, their editors gave it considerable space while radio talk shows were flooded with calls. Amid the discourse, according to Mathews, the select movie houses "overflowed mostly with Vietnam vets, many of whom were showing up in combat jackets with their years of service sewn on the sleeves." Thus, by the time *Platoon* was rolled out in an additional twenty-five more cities, having already made its money back and landed *Time*'s cover: "Platoon, Viet Nam as It Really Was," Stone had succeeded in transforming the longest, least popular American war of the twentieth century into a mass cult film—the first such in the near decade since *Rocky* and *Star Wars*.

Platoon was taken as a corrective. Mixing arty detachment and vivid detail, it provided a visceral representation of physically demanding and fearful troop movements through dense jungle, as well as extensive scenes of base-camp life. The movie emphasizes physical discomfort; no one is vermin-free, everyone's feet are in some stage of rot. *Platoon*'s power resides in its

---

* The movie's first telecast on the cable station HBO would be heralded by print ads stating, "It's not too late to do something about the Vietnam War—see *Platoon* and understand."

specifics—the grunts talking about their "bad feelings," the bandannas and fetishes of the men who've gone native, the base psychedelicatessen furnished with gas mask candelabras and a poster of Ho Chi Minh.

At the same time, Stone's solemnity rivaled that of Francis Ford Coppola and Michael Cimino—opening his movie with a quote from Ecclesiastes and burst of Samuel Barber's "Adagio for Strings" as green recruits are discharged from the belly of a transport plane. (The dirge is reprised at the conclusion of the movie's My Lai sequence, played over a long shot of a torched Vietnamese village.) Rather than focusing on a heroic individual, *Platoon* is, as its title makes clear, an ensemble film—with a divided ensemble.

The education of Stone's alter ego, Chris (Charlie Sheen), a volunteer as he had been, proceeds in the context of an American civil war. Set in late 1967 but projecting the domestic "1968" into Vietnam, Stone draws a sharp line between white and black, "smoke-heads" and "whiskey-heads," lifers and draftees, as well as the two sergeants who battle for the platoon's soul, saintly Elias (Willem Dafoe) and dastardly Barnes (Tom Berenger).

To the insinuating strains of Jefferson Airplane's trippy "White Rabbit," Chris is inducted into the "smoke-heads" as Elias invites him to suck marijuana fumes shotgun-style through a rifle barrel. Already rich in homoeroticism, the sequence reaches its climax with a dance party worthy of *The Big Chill* as the dopers, blacks and whites, equally stoned, groove together to Smokey Robinson singing "The Tracks of My Tears." Meanwhile, the "whiskey-heads" unwind by gnawing beer cans, chucking knives, and ruminating, somewhat anachronistically, on Merle Haggard's 1969 hit "Okie from Muskogee."

Platoon eschews analysis, even on the primitive level of *Rambo*'s accusation of political treachery or back-stabbing to present Vietnam as a generational experience. In part through Charlie Sheen's uncanny resemblance to his father, *Platoon* continually engages *Apocalypse Now*. Stone, however, is more concerned with the chaos of combat than the overall spectacle of technological war. More harrowing than Coppola's, Stone's evocation of My Lai leads the viewer step by step into the terrifying breakdown of restraint. Combat is a mixture of incredible confusion—panics, shrieks, men dying with their eyes open—and shrill hyper-excitement. A lethal shadow play in which fires and parachute probes scoop a shallow, deadly proscenium out of the hellish jungle night, the climactic battle scene has the base camp itself under assault, with men in the field haplessly retreating from foxhole to foxhole until air support arrives. The shocking aftermath has survivors return to consciousness in an enormous crater, some deliberately wounding themselves, others cutting the ears off dead enemies or rifling their corpses. Chris's most heroic act is fragging Barnes.*

Jane Fonda told the *Los Angeles Times* that Stone's movie made her weep, explaining that *Platoon* might be the central panel of a Vietnam triptych that culminated with her Oscar-winning vehicle *Coming Home*. Although there was as yet no first film explicating the Vietnam War's origins, *Platoon* explained *Coming Home*: "I don't mean to be self-congratulatory or anything like that," Fonda said. "It's just that our movie was very cathartic."

Not everyone agreed. Writing in the *Washington Times*, John Podhoretz called *Platoon* "one of the most repellent movies ever made in this country," in that Stone sought to "win over the critics by denouncing the war experience while at the same time making violent goo of everybody on the screen." Still, *Platoon* went to number one in late January and remained atop *Variety*'s box-office chart for another five weeks through February, remaining in the top three slots into April.†

As *Platoon* marched toward box-office glory—the third top-grossing movie of 1986—and presidential candidates began making their moves, the Iran Deal, now called Iran-Contra, continued to dominate national politics.

The Tower Commission report issued on February 26 concluded that William Casey should have assumed responsibility for the Deal, explained the risks to the president, and notified Congress. Within the week, Reagan appeared on television to take responsibility for using arms to ransom hostages,

---

* Teaching a course on Vietnam movies at NYU in 1990, I projected a 16mm print of *Platoon* over a print of *Rambo*. A suffering Stallone appeared superimposed on a torched Vietnamese village; Rambo liberated American POWs as, in another part of the jungle, the men of *Platoon* marched into an ambush. Betrayals occurred simultaneously: Elias's slow-motion death agony coincided with Rambo's water torture. (Rambo, however, repeatedly escaped death.) Ultimately, *Rambo Platoon* became one exciting near-continuous action film.

† On Oscar night, *Platoon* won best picture and best director (plus sound and editing), receiving two nominations for supporting actor, as well as for original screenplay and cinematography. *Top Gun* won best song, with a nomination for editing; *Blue Velvet* was nominated for director; *Heartbreak Ridge* was nominated for sound. Stone's other film that year, *Salvador*, got a nomination for actor (James Woods) and original screenplay. Stone accepted his Oscar on behalf of the Vietnam veteran: "I think that what you're saying is that for the first time, you really understand what happened over there."

or rather, with magnificent obfuscation, take responsibility for his well-meaning objectives: "A few months ago I told the American people I did not trade arms for hostages. My heart and my best intentions tell me that's true, but the facts and the evidence tell me it is not." The press conference was considered a triumph, Elizabeth Drew wrote in the *New Yorker*, "in that Reagan simply got through it without too much faltering and mental wandering (though there was some). He turned in a relatively good performance as Ronald Reagan, but it was obviously a performance."*

Platoon opened the door through which a crowd of Vietnam films and TV shows would follow. An early March episode of the detective show *Simon & Simon* (CBS, 1981–89) featured a prolonged flashback to Vietnam. In early May, Francis Ford Coppola returned to the Nam, after a fashion, with his inert, ponderous *Gardens of Stone*—essentially a revisionist second-wave Vietnam film making heroes out of the elite home-front officers in charge of burials at Arlington National Cemetery. Like *The Hanoi Hilton*, which had a brief run in March, and *Hamburger Hill*, still in previews, *Gardens of Stone* vilified the peace movement, reaching its nadir at a Georgetown lawn party where one of Coppola's protagonists (James Caan) beats up and stomps on a pugnacious peacenik (the hippie-entrepreneur Bill Graham in a Nehru suit). In late June, Stanley Kubrick's much-heralded *Full Metal Jacket* appeared, a belated first-wave film, designed to challenge *Apocalypse Now*. As Coppola had restaged Vietnam in the Philippines, Kubrick more outrageously brought Vietnam to London, using an abandoned gasworks southeast of London to stand in for Hue during the Tet Offensive of 1968.

The non-victory parade gathered momentum during the summer. "Is It Prime Time for Vietnam?," asked the August 2nd *New York Times*, in an article previewing the upcoming CBS series *Tour of Duty*, scheduled against *The Cosby Show* and HBO's *Vietnam War Story*: the piece identified what seemed to be "the storyline of choice in the new Vietnam nostalgia, the grunt's-eye-view approach that considers the political and moral questions of the war implicitly and only secondarily to the first purpose, which is capturing the 'feel' of the war."

---

* Reagan and his handlers had been using his forgetfulness so frequently as an excuse that some commentators, notably Drew, voiced suspicions about his mental capacity, although only Alexander Cockburn in *The Nation* was rude enough to suggest that the president was suffering from incipient Alzheimer's.

A follow-up to *Platoon* and epitome of the "new Vietnam nostalgia," *Hamburger Hill* opens with shots of the Vietnam memorial. The movie was directed by John Irvin (who, in addition to working with Arnold Schwarzenegger, had made a TV documentary in Vietnam during the war) and drew from Viet-vet Jim Carabatsos's script, based on a May 1969 incident during which U.S. forces made eleven incredibly costly attempts to take a mountain near the Laotian border.*

Resembling *Platoon* in its grim, combatant's view of the war, *Hamburger Hill* went for grit rather than hallucination, esprit de corps over Übermensch. It is a group portrait of a dozen or so recruits—fresh-faced, well-meaning, sensitive, tormented, black, white ethnic, innocents all—and their gruff camaraderie on a muddy field of flaming choppers and screaming medics where gut-hemorrhaging bodies drop from the trees. "*Hamburger Hill* treats combat in the Vietnam War with a candor that equals that of *Platoon* and in some ways goes past it," Stanley Kauffmann wrote in the *New Republic*.

Like *Platoon*, *Hamburger Hill* gave no sense of the army brass or the larger trajectory of the war; even more than Stone, Irwin and Carabatsos portrayed U.S. soldiers as victims, in this case, of the peace movement and the media. (*Hamburger Hill*, unlike *Platoon*, did receive assistance from the Pentagon.) The counterculture has no place in this platoon. The villains are not the Vietcong but the antiwar movement and the media. When the grunts aren't grimly regaling each other with apocryphal tales of college coeds pelting returning soldiers with bags of dogshit, they torment themselves with the idea of hippie "hair heads" stealing their wives. (Even worse are the anti-condolence letters that rabid war opponents supposedly sent to bereaved parents, saying they're glad their boy was killed.)

Vietnamese women are intrinsic to the film's libidinal economy—sex with prostitutes is the most evident signifier of grunt power. Still, as if to remind

---

* Carabatsos's first produced screenplay, *Heroes* (1977), starring Henry Winkler as a disturbed vet, was among the first postwar movies to address Vietnam. Carabatsos described it as a film "about a guy who had trouble adjusting after Vietnam, falls in love and was able to realign his life," adding, "I was hoping myself to fall in love." *Hamburger Hill* was produced by Marcia Nasatir, whose credits include *The Big Chill* and who encouraged Carabatsos to write the script. Interviewed by the *Los Angeles Times* in February 1985 before *Hamburger Hill* had financing, Carabatsos criticized *Apocalypse Now* ("Stupid—made us look like idiots, all doped up on the line") and *The Deer Hunter* ("A Green Beret with a goatee? Come on, who are they kidding?").

the men of their actual impotence, a scene of relatively carefree whorehouse hot-tubbing is immediately followed by one featuring the Vietnam War's enduring class, sex, angst, and revenge ballad, "Ruby, Don't Take Your Love to Town," first recorded by Waylon Jennings in 1966. Caught in an unexamined psychosexual rut, *Hamburger Hill* broods anxiously over the peacenik mantra "Make love, not war." (Similarly, the movie acknowledges micro-incidents of racial tension without recognizing the war's essential racial nature.)

Hamburger Hill is as sanctimonious as *Platoon*, albeit in a different way. There's no cosmic struggle between good and evil. The idealization exists on a grungier level. The grunts have a dirty job that somebody has to do. The best the filmmakers can do is to celebrate situational loyalty and show the men in touch with their feelings—war as a kind of gritty group therapy punctuated by horrendous violence. The grunt mantra, delivered in the face of any catastrophe, is "It don't mean nothin'."

In the absence of patriotic platitudes, the movie has no choice but show war as existential madness and awesome stupidity. Heads get blown off and there's even a scene in which the platoon is attacked by American choppers. Most crucially, the battle for control of "Hamburger Hill" seems to have no intrinsic meaning, strategic or otherwise. (This Sisyphean exercise would have made a worthy second half for the absurdist *Full Metal Jacket*—providing an appropriate arena for Kubrick's misanthropic sense of the absurd.). Driven by the exigencies of the marketplace and their own desperate brand of positive thinking, however, Irvin and Carabatsos are forced to find inspiration. The film ends with vignettes of the survivors looking like so many El Greco Christs on the smoky Golgotha of Hill 937. The wind is blowing, the choppers are hovering, and tears are welling up in some dazed grunt's eye. They took the hill—but for what?

Far more despairing than *Platoon*, *Hamburger Hill* celebrates what David Denby called "the glory of unquestioning devotion," which is to say it makes a virtue of being cannon fodder. Opening number five for its week, *Hamburger Hill* would gross $14 million—about one-tenth of *Platoon*'s domestic box-office.*

---

* Released in mid-June was the season's most bizarre war movie, *Predator*. This all-purpose anti-Vietnam, anti-*E.T.*, *Aliens* knockoff set in a Central American war zone was directed by John McTiernan from a script by Jim Thomas and John Thomas, and starred Arnold Schwarzenegger as U.S. Army commando "Dutch" Schaefer. Sent on a rescue mission

Ronald Reagan watched only one Vietnam movie that season, Lionel Chetwynd's *The Hanoi Hilton*, screened at Camp David on July 17.*

Although a major third-wave Vietnam film, *The Hanoi Hilton* predates the first wave. Chetwynd, one of Hollywood's best-known right-wingers, first submitted a version of his script to the Pentagon the year the war ended in 1975. Originally, the movie was to focus on a single POW, the downed navy pilot and future senator John McCain, and also dramatize the failed 1970 raid on the Sontay prison.

Pentagon preapproval notwithstanding, the initial version of the project failed to attract funding. A three-hour telefilm, scheduled by ABC for the fall of 1978, fell through. Chetwynd's revised script languished—in part, he felt, because he refused to excise a scene in which Jane Fonda and other antiwar activists visit Hanoi—until the success of *Rambo* made it commercially viable. He directed it himself for the independent studio, Cannon.

Opening in New York and Los Angeles shortly before *Platoon*'s Oscar coronation, *The Hanoi Hilton* was greeted by a fuselage of negative reviews. Vincent Canby blew it off as "an earnest but clumsy tribute to the heroism of the American servicemen—mostly officers—who were captured and held prisoner by North Vietnam," comparing it to World War II anti-Japanese propaganda. David Denby called it "hell to sit through . . . not because the material is repetitive and sadistic but because the filmmaking is colorless and unimaginative."

Denby took issue with the movie's politics as well, arguing against the idea that "the prisoners held in Hanoi were as much victims of the anti-war

---

after an American chopper has gone down behind Soviet-supported guerrilla lines, Dutch must contend with the duplicity of his CIA controllers as well as that of an apolitical Implacable Alien Other—a shape-shifting, dreadlocks-wearing, laser-firing cyborg slime lizard from outer space. Schwarzenegger's character not only shares a nickname with Ronald Reagan but, as noted by *Variety*, spends the movie's first half looking and acting like Tom Highway and ends up as a bare-chested super-grunt Rambo, complete with bow and arrow. *New York Times* critic Janet Maslin called the movie "grisly and dull"; writing in the *Village Voice*, Juliann Garey noted the warnographic innuendo: "The movie is underscored by the melodic whir of machine guns that never stop firing . . . even under pressure . . . even when they run out of bullets." *Predator*, which featured former wrestler and future Minnesota governor Jesse Ventura as one of Dutch's comrades, opened number one for the week and finished number twelve for the year.

* The only other film with an Indochinese setting shown at Camp David was *The Killing Fields*, screened January 4, 1985. Ronald and Nancy did not favor war films, although, on September 7, 1985, they treated their staff to *Hellcats of the Navy*.

movement as of the North Vietnamese." Chetwynd, Denby writes, "pursues the sour right-wing sophistries of fifteen years ago. *The Hanoi Hilton* has the grinding vindictiveness of an old Patrick Buchanan column." Stanley Kauffmann was even more emphatic, beginning his review with the assertion, "*The Hanoi Hilton* is filth. It exploits the sufferings—and deaths—of American POWs in North Vietnam in order to promote a distortion of history: that the peace movement in the United States and elsewhere prolonged the imprisonment of those men by impeding American victory." Cannon yanked the film, which subsequently became a right-wing cause célèbre— repeatedly defended in the *Washington Times* with liberal animus ascribed to the backlash against the movie's parodic representation of Jane Fonda.*

Neither *Hamburger Hill* nor *The Hanoi Hilton* offered the healing that Hollywood ascribed to *Platoon*. A 1989 *New York Times* article credits *Platoon* with inspiring the first Viet-vet "therapy" returns to Vietnam. The initial VHS release would include an advertisement-cum-public-service announcement in which Chrysler chairman Lee Iacocca walks through the woods to pose beside an army jeep and explain that *Platoon* is "a memorial— not to war but to the men and women who fought in a time and a place no one really understood."

Here, in an example of post-Reagan Reaganism, the trauma of Vietnam is merged in memory with World War II under the aegis of corporate America. The image dissolves into a red, white, and blue Chrysler logo with the words "Jeep Eagle."†

---

* Re-released to little effect in June, *The Hanoi Hilton* wound up grossing less than a million dollars but garnered a devoted following on VHS. A special DVD edition, including an interview with Senator John McCain, was scheduled for release during the 2008 presidential campaign but was withheld until after the election was over.

† The third wave of Vietnam films continued into 1988 and beyond, capped by two problematic tours de force—Brian De Palma's showy, disturbingly sensual *Casualties of War*, which opened during the summer of 1989, and Oliver Stone's second tour of duty, *Born on the Fourth of July*, held for Christmas 1989. "Cashing in on Vietnam," an article published in *Newsweek* during the last month of the Reagan's presidency, described the war as "a highly profitable nostalgia franchise," citing Vietnam commemorative shotguns, ashtrays, condoms, X-rated movies, neckties, customized medals, pewter sculptures of a vet kneeling before the Vietnam memorial, and $2,600 granite tombstones engraved with name and combat unit, a map of South Vietnam, and a scene of marines evacuating a body to a Huey chopper.

Ishtar, Moment of Truth

The race for president was on and the Democratic nomination was Gary Hart's to lose. The Colorado senator was the anointed front-runner when he declared his candidacy on April 13. Prominent supporters included Warren Beatty, his comrade from the 1972 McGovern campaign that Hart had managed.

But as the post counterculture yuppie candidate, Hart was susceptible to the merger of the political and the personal. Three weeks after his declaration, the *Miami Herald* published pictures of the foolish-looking senator sitting on the deck of a boat—incredibly named the "Monkey Business"—with model Donna Rice perched in his lap. After five days of media bludgeoning, Hart withdrew from the race. "My approval rating holds at 53%," President Reagan noted smugly in his diary entry for May 14.

The next day, a week after Hart ended his twenty-five-day candidacy, Beatty suffered another blow: *Ishtar,* a $51 million comedy produced by Beatty—who also co-starred with Dustin Hoffman—and directed by Elaine May from her own screenplay, opened some $23 million over budget, to reviews that ranged from the underwhelmed to the savage. Roger Ebert called it "a truly dreadful film, a lifeless, massive, lumbering exercise in failed comedy."

Widely ridiculed as Hollywood's greatest debacle since *Heaven's Gate,* *Ishtar* (named for an imaginary North African kingdom) was something of a retro mash-up. According to Beatty, May was inspired by the Hollywood movies of her girlhood. *Ishtar* updated the series of Bob Hope–Bing Crosby comedies that began in 1940 with *Road to Singapore,* using two stars redolent of the 1960s and a North African location that was in some ways reflective of the 1980s—or at least 1980s movies.

Rogers and Clarke (Beatty and Hoffman) are a pair of dim, talentless singer-songwriters, haplessly aspiring to the status of Simon and Garfunkel. "You're old, you're white, and you got no shtick," according to their bottom-feeding agent, who nevertheless offers them a choice of gigs, Morocco or Honduras—which is to say, "Libya" or "El Salvador." The guys opt for North Africa over Central America and, minutes after their plane lands in Ishtar en route to Morocco, are mistaken for two prophesized messengers of God.

Competing for the affections of the same woman of mystery (Isabelle Adjani) while playing an engagement in Marrakesh, the pair becomes embroiled in a lethal war in neighboring Ishtar between left-wing Shiite revolutionaries (led, in part, by Adjani) and the CIA (personified by Charles Grodin).*

That the former are the good guys and the latter, identified with the Reagan administration, are comic villains serves to foreground the political criticism implicit in the movie's prescient opening and closing theme, the Rogers and Clarke signature song that begins, "Telling the truth can be dangerous business. 'Honest' and 'popular' don't go hand in hand."

The notion was hardly inappropriate given that *Ishtar*, largely predicated on the spectacle of two American idiots wandering cluelessly through the Arab world, was weirdly timely, opening as it did ten days into the joint hearings of House Select Committee to Investigate Covert Arms Transactions with Iran and the Senate Select Committee on Secret Military Assistance to Iran and the Nicaraguan Opposition.

Like the Iran-Contra fiasco, *Ishtar* had been conceived during the heady Rambo to the Future summer of 1985, even as Robert McFarlane and David Kimche cooked up their scheme to barter arms for hostages.

Oliver North made his first secret mission to Iran on September 15, something Reagan all but confirmed in a *700 Club* interview with Pat Robertson, who seemed surprisingly well-informed with regard to the doings of the president's "official family." Even before the *Ishtar* shoot opened in October, Iran had received another 408 TOWs and, in return, freed a single hostage. A number of Hawk surface-to-air missiles and a thousand additional TOWs were shipped to Iran during the shoot, without another American released. While the president was preoccupied with the hostages, McFarlane and North

---

* The filmmakers themselves felt they were working in a dangerous neighborhood. The Moroccan government was involved in an ongoing struggle with guerrilla forces in the Western Sahara. After Israeli warplanes bombed the headquarters of the Palestine Liberation Organization in Tunisia, the PLO responded by hijacking the cruise ship *Achille Lauro* and then dumping a Jewish-American passenger, Leon Klinghoffer, into the Mediterranean. There was apprehension on the set. "We heard there were armed Palestinians headed our way," the production designer Paul Sylbert later recalled. According to Peter Biskind, there were rumors that Palestinian terrorists might try to kidnap Hoffman, and some locations had to be checked for land mines before shooting could begin.

derived enormous satisfaction from overcharging the Iranian "rug merchants" they imagined they were dealing with and using the windfall profits to secretly fund the Nicaraguan Contras.

North Africa was even more in the news during the spring of 1986 when *Ishtar* began postproduction. After the bombing of a West Berlin discothèque popular with American soldiers, Reagan ordered air raids over Tripoli and Benghazi. The retaliation was a popular success and the president's ratings were approaching their zenith when, in a bizarrely *Ishtar*-like mission, McFarlane and North flew to Tehran using false names and fake passports, bringing a load of Hawk spare parts, along with a cake and—*Top Gun* time— suicide pills (just in case).

Another American hostage was released that summer (although another two were kidnapped). Even as rumors of the secret arms Deal spread in Washington, North soldiered on. Meeting with Iranians in Germany, he presented them with a Reagan-inscribed Bible, explaining that the American president had received divine instructions to accept the Iranian Revolution. It is not clear whether the Iranians mistook Reagan (or North) for a messenger from God.

Had *Ishtar* opened in December as originally planned, it would have coincided with the dramatic decline in Reagan's approval rating from 67 percent to 46 percent and might have provided a one-two punch with *Platoon* in assaulting U.S. foreign policy.

But postproduction dragged on as May squabbled with Beatty and Hoffman, and thus *Ishtar* did not open until that May, well after the Academy Award ceremony that saw *Platoon* win four Oscars, not to mention Reagan's March 14 televised apology for the Deal, a sincere expression of befuddlement that helped push his ratings back several points above 50 percent. Reagan got a further boost over *Ishtar*'s opening weekend when an Iraqi jet fired two missiles at an American frigate in the Persian Gulf. Several days of saber rattling resulted in an Iraqi apology and promise of compensation.

Few if any reviewers remarked on *Ishtar*'s connection to the Iran-Contra hearings then in progress—almost as if any disgust with the Reagan administration's chicanery was sublimated into anger with May's extravagance. Still, the movie won its first weekend (barely edging out a low-budget horror film, *The Gate*, about three boys who find the portal to hell in their backyard) even as critics pronounced it dead on arrival. Reporting in the *New York Times*, Aljean Harmetz wondered how such talented entertainers could make a movie that critics were deriding as "colossally dunderheaded," "a runaway ego trip," and overpriced "piffle."*

Andrew Sarris felt compelled to give *Ishtar* a second negative review in the *Village Voice*. "People have been stopping me on the street to tell me how unbelievably awful *Ishtar* is," he wrote a few weeks after the movie opened, asserting that "the dimensions of the disaster are so staggeringly vast and varied that some of this stinker's most obvious flaws have been overlooked." Indeed, *Ishtar* was not only a quasi-allegorical satire of inept American foreign policy but, perhaps more insultingly, a sustained blizzard of clichés that parodied the assumptions of American heroism, from the neo-adventurism of Indiana Jones to *Rocky's* feel-good inanity.

A movie that's all too aware of its existential pathos, *Ishtar's* image of two clowns crawling around the Sahara in the company of a blind camel is worthy of Samuel Beckett. The opening line from one of their songs—"Life is the way we audition for God"—is a bleak, cosmically banal restatement of the notion that show business is a tale told by an idiot. The very nature of American entertainment was derided. The desultory firefight May staged as a climax, with Adjani's character manning the artillery, may have been more offensive to critics than her identification of the movie's dim-witted protag-

---

* May would blame the movie's poor reception on the Columbia's new (and short-lived) studio head, the British director David Puttnam, explaining in a 2011 screening at the 92nd Street YM-YWHA in New York that Puttnam resented Warren Beatty because *Reds* had competed for Oscars with Puttnam's *Chariots of Fire*. Puttnam, she recalled, wrote a piece before the Academy Awards saying that Beatty was "self-indulgent and should be spanked. . . . He then had a falling out with Dustin, and he said that Dustin was a brat and was troublesome and also some childlike person. And this is a guy who then became head of our studio!" *Ishtar's* initial previews went well, she explained, "so I went to Bali, because I thought everything was fine."

> [Then] Warren calls and tells me that the day the press came, an article came out in the *Los Angeles Times* in which the head of Columbia wiped us out—David Puttnam. It was the same thing he said before: That we should be spanked, that there was too much money, that he was going to reform Hollywood. It was really sort of unforgivable what he did. He attacked his own movie. . . . So when the press junket came, the next screening of this movie, which had sort of gotten really good word-of-mouth, there were no laughs, and people kept saying how much money it cost. Because [Puttnam] had done something that no studio had ever done: He actually released the budget, or his version of it.

onists as "true Americans." The happy ending, with Rogers and Clarke's debut album going from massive window display to the bargain bin, is as pointed a parody of the film's triumphant *Rocky*-style denouement as the single image of Ronald Reagan presiding over an inept U.S. government office is of American cluelessness.

According to May, the connection was significant. "At that time, Reagan was president, and I met him," she told the audience at the 92nd Street Y.

> And he's an amazingly naïve, innocent, charming guy who really, really cared about show business! In the nicest way, really.
>
> He knew Mike [Nichols]'s and my albums. He could quote them—he memorized them! He did our "Telephone" routine. So he was the president. And nobody really knew what was going on, actually. I thought, "Really, there's something very endearing, if terrifying, about this kind of innocence, this kind of naiveté."

The weekend following *Ishtar*'s opening, the Reagans watched *Harry and the Hendersons*, a Spielbergian fable about a Seattle family's encounter with the legendary creature Bigfoot (Kevin Peter Hall, who played the title monster in *Predator*), directed by William Dear for Spielberg's company Amblin Entertainment. "Saturday night as usual. Ran a movie about Big Foot & to my surprise I was in it—a shot of me & Bonzo on a TV set," the president noted in his diary.*

---

* Writing in the *Chicago Tribune*, Dave Kehr observed that "like Spielberg's richest creation, *E.T.*, *Harry* is a wish-fulfilling unification of opposites." Kehr might almost have been acknowledging the president when he added that "Spielberg's commercial potency lies precisely in his ability to construct such deliberately ambiguous images, which symbolically reconcile the apparently irreconcilable, providing simple, fantasy solutions to complex emotional and ideological problems." The movie finished number forty-three for 1987, behind *Revenge of the Nerds II: Nerds in Paradise* and ahead of *Police Academy 4: Citizens on Patrol*.

VI

ONCE UPON A TIME IN THE EIGHTIES, 1987–88

June 12, 1987, Ronald Reagan stopped off in West Berlin en route back home from an economic summit in Venice and, speaking mainly to his domestic critics, stood before TV cameras near Brandenburg Gate to declare, "Mr. Gorbachev, tear down this wall."

With eighteen months left in his presidency, Reagan was in eclipse. A new star twinkled in the political firmament: forty-three-year-old Marine Corps Lieutenant Colonel Oliver North. The first couple spent July 4th weekend watching two Fred Astaire musicals, *Swing Time* and *Funny Face*. The following Tuesday, North was sworn in for four days of testimony before the joint hearings of the House Select Committee to Investigate Covert Arms Transactions with Iran and the Senate Select Committee on Secret Military Assistance to Iran and the Nicaraguan Opposition.

Spectators had begun lining up at 5 a.m. All three networks preempted their daytime schedules to broadcast North's appearance—it was estimated that over 70 percent of the nation saw or heard parts of North's performance live. What goes around comes around: North had learned last November that he'd been fired from the National Security Council while watching the president's televised news conference. However, as would be reported a few days later, he was "heartened by a telephone call of gratitude from Mr. Reagan, who, according to one acquaintance, began the conversation by suggesting that the revelations of recent days would make a great movie."

Message received: North appeared before Congress bedecked with medals in the marine uniform he had seldom worn while at the NSC. He began by evoking a vintage Clint Eastwood vehicle. "I came here to tell you the truth—the good, the bad and the ugly." Accordingly, *New York Times* reporter Maureen Dowd would begin her front-page story with the observation that "through the smirks and winks and teary eyes, through the 'Peck's Bad Boy' grins and earnest altar-boy gazes, Oliver North seemed, as always, to be starring in his own movie." So everyone thought. "He's a lot more compassionate man than Rambo," the future Republican congressman Nick Thompson, then a twenty-one-year-old student at Washington and Lee University, told Dowd in a line she used for her kicker.*

When it came to self-pity, even Rambo might learn from North, who managed to simultaneously blame Reagan and defend him, maintaining that as a good soldier he was simply following orders, and as a patriotic American he naturally did the right things. Congress, which had shirked its duty to support the Contras, was cast as the bad guy. But while Dowd was present at the event, everyone else was watching it on TV. As *People* magazine would explain, "North won his battles with a barrage directed over the heads of the committees and into the living rooms of America."

Dowd herself had reported back in December that North was already recognized as "the most marketable character in the Iran affair" (which was itself being taken for another Watergate). The veteran Hollywood agent Irving Paul "Swifty" Lazar had offered to represent North. Jay Weston, a producer on *Heartbreak Ridge*, was bidding for a North biopic. The best scenario was one pitched to Dowd by an anonymous New York literary agent: "It would make a tremendous movie scene with the president and this sort of Rambo sitting by the fire in the Oval Office."

> Imagine North telling the president, "I'm the guy who got the fellows off the *Achille Lauro* for you. I'm the guy who got the Arab terrorists captured for you. Now I have an even better stunt to help the hostages and the Contras. Don't worry, just leave it to me."
>
> And the president sits there chortling, saying "Hey, I'm getting this done and I'm getting it done my way."

Polls reported that an overwhelming majority of Americans found North credible and most believed the president lied in disavowing any knowledge

---

* North was also more impressive. Having helped coordinate the invasion of Grenada and orchestrate the capture of the Palestinian terrorists who hijacked the *Achille Lauro*, he functioned as an alternative secretary of state, instructing diplomats and even generals, imagining he might win the Nobel Peace Prize for Reagan as the president who reestablished ties with Iran.

of the Iran-Contra Deal—North was an honorable patriot who acted with Reagan's approval and, not unlike Rambo, was hung out to dry. Back in February, after the Senate Intelligence Committee released the *Preliminary Inquiry into the Sale of Arms to Iran and Possible Diversion of Funds to the Nicaraguan Resistance*, North's polling numbers were 6 percent favorable, 35 percent unfavorable. Now they had reversed—43 percent favorable and only 14 percent unfavorable.

Unsurprisingly, North reportedly enjoyed greater recognition and more positive ratings than the current field of presidential candidates. These were Reagan's vice president George H. W. Bush, Kansas senator Bob Dole, New York congressman Jack Kemp, religious broadcaster Pat Robertson, and the Democrats derisively known as "The Seven Dwarfs": former Arizona governor Bruce Babbitt, Delaware senator Joe Biden, Massachusetts governor Michael Dukakis, Missouri congressman Richard Gephardt, Tennessee senator Al Gore, civil rights leader Jesse Jackson, and Illinois senator Paul Simon.

The Democrats, who controlled both the House and Senate, were flummoxed. "I believe during the past week we have participated in creating and developing very likely a new American hero," committee chairman Senator Daniel Inouye said in his closing statement. Despite—or perhaps because of—the ranking Republican member of the House Committee Dick Cheney's assertion that the members of the press were spreading lies about North and Reagan, the media went wild. North made the covers of *Time* and *Newsweek* two weeks in a row and was prominently featured by *People*, with a story titled "Ollie-Oop!" that began by confessing, "We had him pegged."

> Even hard-shell conservatives suspected that Lieutenant Colonel Oliver North was a real-life Rambo who had run amok in the Reagan White House. He was seen as a power-mad Marine who had engineered Contragate behind the President's back. . . . [But seen on TV] he looked remarkably like Mel Gibson and spoke with a persuasive air of sincerity that evoked a young Jimmy Stewart [albeit] a Jimmy Stewart with smart-aleck humor, virile charm and forceful eloquence.

"The guy's a star!" *People* quoted the popular casting director Mike Fenton (responsible for *Indiana Jones and the Temple of Doom*, *Back to the Future*, and most recently *Harry and the Hendersons*). "He's a lieutenant colonel acting like a five-star general."*

North reportedly received 120,000 supportive telegrams, as well as carts of flowers during his six days of testimony. Planes towed banners in the sky overhead. "Radio call-in shows were besieged," according to *People*. Listeners "sang, shouted, and babbled" North's praises. Some spoke of a Jack Kemp–Oliver North ticket for '88. Others formed "Ollie for President" committees. There were Oliver North haircuts, hamburgers, dolls, and, of course, T-shirts. The one in *People* was modeled by George Bush's Michigan campaign co-chairman L. Brooks Patterson, notorious years later for proposing to turn Detroit into an Indian reservation "where we herd all the Indians into the city, build a fence around it, and then throw in the blankets and corn."

Of course, there would be a movie starring Harrison Ford, Mel Gibson, Dennis Quaid, or maybe North-lookalike Treat Williams. (Sean Penn was deemed too crazy and Dustin Hoffman too ethnic.) Three former Spielberg actresses—Kate Capshaw, Karen Allen, and Dee Wallace—were bruited for the role of North's wife, Betsy. North's glamorous secretary, Fawn Hall, could only be played, *People* joked, by Fawn Hall herself. Even before North finished testifying, the *Philadelphia Inquirer* film critic Carrie Rickey published a long piece arguing that with his "uplifted eyes" and "halting, hoarse voice," the lieutenant colonel had inserted himself into the *Mr. Smith Goes to Washington* scenario. Others noted the stack of congratulatory telegrams and adoring assistant as *Mr. Smith* props.

The most thorough movie analysis was David Denby's piece in the *New Republic*. North, Denby wrote, turned "the event into an appreciation of his 'sincerity.'" At various times and in various ways, the colonel resembled James Cagney, Clark Gable, Gary Cooper, and Paul Newman. He was "more serious than Joan Crawford"; his ironic politeness was "an obvious imitation of Clint Eastwood." North recalled Henry Fonda, John Wayne, and "more centrally," James Stewart. "But most of all," Denby concluded, North was "a chip off the old block."

---

* North was also something of an impresario. His slide-show briefing on the Contras garnered considerable word of mouth among the reporters who saw a special evening presentation. "If Ollie North could make a quick deal with a home video firm, his slide show might prove to be the hottest seller since Jane Fonda last wore tights," Tom Shales wrote in the *Washington Post*.

The model is not so much Ronald Reagan the star of *Kings Row* as it is Reagan the President. The superbly timed catch in the voice, the mixture of truculence and maudlin self-pity; the anecdotal view of world politics. . . . Faced with a star turn like North's, reporters and media personalities with a reputation for critical acumen either kept their mouths shut—as if suddenly their opinions had become worthless—or jumped on the bandwagon, connoisseurs of the image-maker's success. The man was a hit, and that was all that mattered.

At least for the moment.*

Iran-Contra had been for all purposes resolved, and Ollie-mania was still raging when an even more perfect hero appeared: RoboCop.

Like its most obvious precursor *The Terminator*, Dutch director Paul Verhoeven's first English-language hit, written by Edward Neumeier and Michael Miner, brought forth an original full-blown comic-book character—a cyborg lawman produced by, yet somehow driven to oppose, a rapacious capitalist system. This attitude was embodied in the movie itself. "There's no better way to steal money than free enterprise," one career criminal gratuitously exclaims.

Like *The Terminator* as well, *RoboCop*—set in Detroit in the very near future—answered a need that the audience had yet to articulate. Featuring monumentally aggressive cartoon violence and made from a script inspired,

---

* "As Oliver North's Story Fades, 'People Are Ready for a New Controversy,'" the August 7 *New York Times* reported from Anniston, Alabama. Five weeks later, the *Times* ran a piece headlined "North Souvenirs Draw Few Takers," noting that "scores of Oliver North T-shirts, buttons, stickers, books, videocassettes and even dolls remain unsold." North ran for the Senate from Virginia in 1994, invoking *Rocky* when he won the Republican nomination and *The Terminator* after he lost the general election, telling the *New York Times*, "I've taken this line from Schwarzenegger—'I'll be back.'" By that time Fawn Hall, who had moved to Los Angeles to pursue a modeling career, was married to the manager of the post–Jim Morrison Doors, Danny Sugerman, who turned her on to crack cocaine. She became addicted, and following a 1994 overdose, entered rehab.

After the summer of 1987, Hollywood showed relatively little interest in North or Iran-Contra. Thirty years later Doug Liman, the son of Arthur L. Liman, chief counsel to the Senate committee during the Iran-Contra hearings, directed a comic thriller, *American Made*, starring Tom Cruise as Barry Seal, a real-life smuggler with ties to the CIA, among other government agencies, who may have had a supporting role in North's arms-for-hostages deal.

according to Neumeier, by a poster for *Blade Runner*, Verhoeven's film advanced a completely cynical view of American entertainment. Praising the movie's "healthy contempt for the culture that gave birth to it," *Village Voice* critic David Edelstein saw *RoboCop* as "a satire of the Reaganaut present"—social services cut or privatized; unregulated corporations buying politicians and controlling devastated cities.

The landscape has been despoiled (one of RoboCop's adversaries memorably deliquesces in a pool of toxic waste) while, as Edelstein notes, "billions are poured into high-tech boondoggles that continually screw up." The latter is a source of brutal comedy: A RoboCop prototype, the lumbering Enforcement Droid, loses control during a demonstration and massacres half a boardroom. A TV news program reports that a malfunctioning Strategic Defense "Peace Platform" has fired on America from space, obliterating Santa Monica with two retired U.S. presidents as collateral damage.

Verhoeven was a fan of the media spectacle, telling *American Film* that he "spent every minute [he] could spare watching those Iran-Contra hearings."

> I am fascinated by these people—the change in mood when Oliver North testified and how the senators tried to get some of that wonderful charismatic quality to rub off on them. I also followed the aftermath of the *Challenger* disaster—the same spectacle of people reproaching each other and lying and cheating. It was wonderful!

Originally rated X for violence, *RoboCop* struck a nerve—it was the number-one new movie the week it opened (edged out by a reissue of *Snow White and the Seven Dwarfs*) and, grossing over $50 million on a budget of $13 million, went on to be the year's sixteenth-highest box-office attraction—despite, or perhaps because of, its depiction of the American people, per Edelstein, as "illiterate clods who watch three-minute news shows and apparently endless sitcoms featuring big-breasted blonds and a salacious little man who leers into the camera and quips, 'I'd buy *that* for a dollar!'"

On one hand, *RoboCop*'s TV news is totally concerned with social chaos and physical danger. On the other, the commercials that punctuate these grim reports of disasters abroad (nuclear war in South Africa, revolution in Mexico) are all about prolonging human life through buyable remedies (like a new heart). Thus, RoboCop, the technologically resurrected police casualty, reborn from the ashes of the Vietnam War (or the Detroit riots), synthesizes threat and antidote. With his reconstructed, superior body, he is impervious to bullets and emotion (although he does prove susceptible to traumatic memories).

Programmed to be a helpful Terminator, RoboCop is more humane, because more rational, than the legal vigilante Dirty Harry. That the cyborg lawman is also fully at home in the robot world is demonstrated by his facility in making an arrest at a techno-punk nightclub whose patrons regard him as part of the freak show. Naturally charismatic and repeatedly told that he's a "product," RoboCop is Verhoeven's satirical view of the ideal American leader—a dispassionate, perfectly packaged technocrat maintaining order and enforcing the law against criminal enemies of all sorts.*

Unfortunately, none of the candidates fit the bill. A Gallup poll in early August discovered that, four months after his candidacy imploded, the Democrat front-runner was still, by a two-to-one margin, Gary Hart. Not one of the Seven Dwarfs was close, although Massachusetts's technocratic governor Michael Dukakis had a notably robotic personality, and some detected promise in the gregarious campaign of Senator Joe Biden who, not yet forty-five, might have credibly inherited a bit of Hart's youthful luster. By mid-September, however, Biden was exposed as a plagiarist, having cribbed chunks of his stump speech from one by British Labour Party leader Neil Kinnock. The same week brought Adrian Lyne's *Fatal Attraction*—the slickest Hollywood genre film in the tumultuous year since *Top Gun* crowned the Reagan presidency.

Bedroom horror rather than bedroom farce, *Fatal Attraction* applied Murphy's Law to the extramarital fling. Working overtime through the weekend, yuppie-man lawyer Michael Douglas is unexpectedly reunited with single-gal, crypto-feminist publishing exec Glenn Close, the intriguing, frizzy-permed Medusa with whom he'd recently exchanged pleasantries at a job-related book party. A drink expands into dinner and dinner becomes the weekend. But the ostensibly sophisticated Close refuses to obey the

---

* *RoboCop*'s appeal would prove as indestructible as he. Starting in 1988, the cyborg lawman was the protagonist of multiple comic books (including one by *The Dark Knight Returns*' Frank Miller), TV shows (both live action and animated), video games (including "RoboCop versus The Terminator"), and two sequels, as well as a 2014 remake. A campaign to boost Detroit's morale with a RoboCop statue was announced in 2011, while RoboCop's Ford Taurus was put on display at the auto museum in Branson, Missouri.

conventions of the casual affair—when Douglas politely loses interest, she becomes unpleasantly obsessed and then positively vengeful, an implacable threat to him and his family.

An astonishing success, *Fatal Attraction* topped *Variety*'s weekly chart for eight consecutive weeks—finally deposed by Arnold Schwarzenegger in *The Running Man*—en route to finishing number two among the year's releases (behind the comedy *Three Men and a Baby* but ahead of *Beverly Hills Cop II*). The movie inspired an extraordinary degree of viewer participation—spectators typically exhorting Douglas to "kill the bitch!" as he defended his family against the crazed assault launched by a jilted one-night stand—as well as much discussion. It was taken by some as an expression of misogyny and by others as a metaphor for the AIDS crisis.

Sex was dangerous. "If Gary Hart had seen *Fatal Attraction* in 1983, he would be president today," rival Democratic candidate Bruce Babbitt is said to have quipped. Douglas himself promoted the movie as a form of sexual backlash: "If you want to know, I'm really tired of feminists, sick of them. They've really dug themselves into their own grave. It's time they looked at *themselves* and stopped attacking men."

The Crash

Star Wars was not the only science-fiction scenario on Ronald Reagan's mind. On September 15, the president stumped those attending a ceremonial meeting with the Soviet foreign minister Eduard Shevardnadze by musing, "If suddenly the earth's civilizations are threatened by other worlds, the USA and the Soviet Union will unite. Isn't that so?"

This was not the first time Reagan advanced the notion that extraterrestrial invasion would trump national differences. (The president was more likely recalling the U.S.-Soviet alliance of World War II than referencing *Watchmen*.) He had floated the idea upon first meeting Mikhail Gorbachev at Geneva in 1985, in a departure from script that flummoxed both the Soviet general secretary and Reagan's staff. Already acquainted with what he called the president's interest in "little green men," national security adviser General Colin Powell was convinced that the proposal had been inspired by the 1951 movie *The Day the Earth Stood Still*, an obviously (and then unfashionably) progressive film that, thanks to its proliferation on television and an underlying message favoring what the Soviets termed "peaceful coexistence," became the best-loved science-fiction film of the early Cold War—a precursor to, if not an inspiration for, *Close Encounters* and *E.T.*

Feeling the heat for his new accommodation with the Soviets, Reagan went public with the *Day the Earth Stood Still* scenario less than a week after the Shevardnadze meeting in a speech at the United Nations: "I occasionally think how quickly our differences worldwide would vanish if we were facing an alien threat from outside this world." The president was living in a new movie, although the following weekend, he watched himself in his favorite role as George Gipp, the gallant, doomed college halfback in *Knute Rockne, All American.* ("It's like seeing a younger son I never knew I had," Reagan would say.)

It was not Reagan's strength but his weakness that was rubbing off on heir apparent George Bush. In mid-October, *Newsweek* put Bush on a cover with the headline, "Fighting the Wimp Factor." The vice president "enters the nomination fight with enviable advantages—high name recognition and stronger voter ratings for experience and competence," *Newsweek* allowed.

> Yet Bush suffers from a potentially crippling handicap—a perception that he isn't strong enough or tough enough for the challenges of the Oval Office. That he is, in a single mean word, a wimp. . . .
>
> The epithet has made its way from the high-school locker room into everyday jargon and stuck like graffiti on Bush. What's come to be known as the vice president's "wimp factor" is a problem, concedes Bush pollster Robert Teeter, "Because it is written and talked about so much."

Truly, Ronald Reagan was a tough act to follow. If womanizing Gary Hart self-destructed for being overly or uncontrollably masculine, the well-bred, Yale-educated George Bush was deemed insufficiently masculine, mainly for being Reagan's good soldier. "Adding muscle to Bush's image won't be easy," *Newsweek* thought. "'Fairly or unfairly, voters have a deep-rooted perception of him as a guy who takes direction, who's not a leader,' says Democratic pollster Peter Hart."

The first Republican debate, a special two-hour edition of William Buckley's *Firing Line*, was held a week after Black Monday, October 19, 1987, when two American warships shelled an Iranian oil platform in the Persian Gulf and the Dow Jones Industrial Average dropped a record 508 points, losing almost 23 percent of its value in a single day. The Crash, however, was a secondary issue.

As the only Republican candidate supporting Reagan's prospective treaty with the Soviets, Bush had to endure former secretary of state Alexander Haig's slyly contemptuous recollection of the discussion of the treaty back in 1982: "I never heard a wimp out of you, not a word." Bush, however, grabbed an opportunity to counterpunch when his most patrician rival, former Delaware governor Pierre "Pete" du Pont IV, piled on, suggesting that the vice president was merely Reagan's lap dog. Patronizingly, Bush addressed du Pont by his given name: "Pierre, let me help you." "Round 1 Goes to George Bush," the *Washington Post* reported: "It was fast, it was surgically neat, and it was a political execution."*

Such executions, staged for an audience on live TV, were the subject of Arnold Schwarzenegger's latest vehicle, *The Running Man*, from Tri-Star. Schwarzenegger, who would end 1987 as the fourth-ranked star on the annual Quigley poll and would later be a prominent Bush supporter, had fine-tuned his image—playing an anti-fascist hero in what Vincent Canby called "an engagingly mean, cruel, nasty, funny send-up of television."

The Running Man, which opened November 13, ousting *Fatal Attraction* from the top spot and maintaining box-office dominance for a second week, was based on a pseudonymous novel by Stephen King. Although set thirty years in the future, many Eighties styles (big hair, women in power suits) are still in vogue. Big government is synonymous with big TV. The world economy has collapsed; its population is kept stupefied by an unending series of gladiatorial game shows; and the United States is a totalitarian state dominated by show business. "Get me the president's agent," the ruling game show host (Richard Dawson, the former emcee of the popular show *Family Feud*) says at one point.

Schwarzenegger, an honest cop who refused to fire on food rioters and was consequently framed for the ensuing massacre, is given a chance to survive as a participant in the most popular game show, *The Running Man*, and essentially turns Spartacus, leading a rebellion with a disco-MTV backbeat.

---

* Three days later, the administration suffered a defeat when the Senate rejected Robert Bork's nomination to the Supreme Court, 58–42.

The year ends with two remarkably well-timed movies featuring two all-American villains: *Walker*, Alex Cox's scurrilous takedown of the nineteenth-century adventurer William Walker, a crypto–Oliver North, and *Wall Street*, Oliver Stone's exposé of a corporate raider partially inspired by the arbitrageur Ivan Boesky. Both were produced by Edward Pressman with the backing of a major studio (Universal and 20th Century Fox, respectively) and both enjoyed a good measure of pre-released publicity.

Walker, which opened December 4, was as much a punk gesture as Cox's previous films, the scuzzy American picaresque *Repo Man* (1984) and the grotesque romantic tale of the Sex Pistols' stunted bassist and his abrasive groupie lover, *Sid and Nancy* (1986). Cox—who had regretfully turned down the chance to direct *The Running Man*—adopted the cartoon sensationalism of *Red Dawn* and *Rambo* to go beyond the tasteful liberalism of *Under Fire* or even *Salvador*. Shot during the spring of 1987, even as the Iran-Contra hearings were gearing up, *Walker* was made partially on location in Nicaragua with the support of the Sandinista government. *The Wild Bunch* scaled down for the Contra war, *Walker* feels cheap and looks disposable, refusing to recreate the past or even dignify it. History is a bloody farce. Every battle is the same—cruel and ridiculous.*

Ed Harris, who played a cynical mercenary in *Under Fire* and John Glenn in *The Right Stuff*, brought the full weight of blue-eyed craziness to Manifest Destiny, declaring, "It is the God-given right of the American people to dominate the Western Hemisphere." If Walker is the Ugly American, the anti–Indiana Jones, his Immortals are pure rabble, a bunch of grunting pirates who start brawling the moment his back is turned and, kept away from the local senoritas, end up storming the local sheep pen. Harris plays Walker as a performer who, like Reagan or North, is hypnotized (and convinced) by his own rhetoric. To make it unmistakably clear, a parting shot, under the

---

* For half a dozen years before the American Civil War, William Walker was a popular hero, considered by many to be a Man of Destiny and even another George Washington. His exploits were followed by millions; in 1855, Walker, then thirty-one, led his fifty-eight "Immortals" to Nicaragua at the behest of the local Democrats, defeated the Nicaraguan Army, and took over the country. Walker ruled Nicaragua from 1855 to 1857, when he was chased out by the combined armies of the surrounding nations; he was killed by Honduran troops three years later, trying to stage a comeback.

credits, has the official portrait of the president's smiling face. *Walker* ended Cox's Hollywood career.*

The following Friday, one day after the Washington Summit closed—with Mikhail Gorbachev eclipsing the popularity of his co-star Ronald Reagan—*Wall Street* was released. The timing was miraculous, less than two months after Black Monday and a week before Boesky was fined $100 million and sentenced to prison for insider trading.

Wall Street—which Stone co-wrote with Stanley Weiser—was intended to lay waste to the rampant speculation and excesses of the Reagan boom. Also merging with the Crash, Tom Wolfe's novel *The Bonfire of the Vanities* was a best-seller. "If, in fact, the great ride is over, I don't know how the skills of investment manipulation will translate to anything else," Wolfe told one journalist. "Most of these people can't even explain to their children what they do. They're not producing anything. It's difficult to argue even that they're providing a service."

The fall guys were the yuppies—a convenient target in that, as a lifestyle vanguard, the yuppie was the heir to the hippie. Yuppie narcissism, libertarianism, and contempt for polyester were implicit in hippie self-absorption, do-your-own-thing, and back-to-naturism. The Sixties suggestion that "You are what you eat" was not only taken literally but globalized. Yuppies were defined exclusively by what they consumed. In short, yuppie was an extension of the counterculture by other means—a stage in the eventual transformation

---

* *Walker* had been in competition at the 1987 Havana Film Festival, which is largely devoted to the promotion of Latin American film. Given the movie's highly original agitprop vision of U.S. intervention in Nicaragua, as well as the production assistance provided by Nicaragua's film agency, INCINE, it would have been a very good bet to win—an accolade that would likely have shamed Universal, the studio that partially bankrolled and distributed *Walker*, into giving the movie a Latin American release. In his book *X Films: The True Confessions of a Radical Filmmaker*, Cox described the enthusiastic audience reception the movie received on its public screenings in Havana; in 2012, at the Pacific Film Archive, he recalled his amazement upon arriving at the festival to discover that the movie had been removed from competition. Universal had offered Cuban officials an alternative—Cheech Marin's *Born in East L.A.*—with the tacit, tantalizing possibility that further Universal movies would be released in Cuba. The festival's first prize went to an obscure Argentine comedy, *A King and His Movie*. *Born in East L.A.* was rewarded with third prize as well as prizes for best screenplay and best production, plus the special Glauber Rocha Award for "innovation and originality." *Walker* never got a Latin American release. Universal has yet to present another movie in Cuba, although *The Fate of the Furious* was partially filmed there in 2017.

of hippie to flabbie (fifty-something lawyer-accountant-broker) or grabbie (graying, retirement-bound baby boomer).

One day after the Crash, the *New York Times* reported that marketers now predicted "the beginning of the end of yuppies and the free-spending ways that have endeared them to real estate agents, car dealers and fashionable clothiers." Rampant "yuppie bashing" was again documented two weeks later in a second *Times* article that began, "In the harsh denunciations and glee-fully venomous jokes, one sentiment has surfaced with startling frequency in the wake of the stock market plunge: now the yuppies will get theirs." The Crash "brought yuppies face to face with something worse (in their eyes) than dishonor: failure," Hendrik Hertzberg wrote in a yuppie postmortem pub-lished by *Esquire* in early 1988.

Hertzberg, who happened to be interviewing Michael J. Fox, America's most beloved yuppie, in the days following the Crash, asked the actor how his *Family Ties* character would have taken the blow. "I can see Alex coming down the stairs and saying grimly, 'Well, I guess you've heard the news,' and everybody saying yes, and then everybody looks concerned and sympathetic." Fox told him. "And then Alex breaks into a big grin and says, 'I got into real estate three weeks ago!'"*

Time magazine declared that the emperor had no clothes. The real crash was "the Reagan Illusion: the idea that there could be a defense buildup and tax cut without a price, that the country could live beyond its means indef-initely." Until then, the titans of finance had been lionized. Throughout 1986, the Chrysler Corporation's CEO Lee Iacocca had been bruited as a possible Reagan successor, ultimately telling reporters that he would not want to be president because the economy was due for a crisis that "I'd be damned if I know" how to fix. House Speaker Jim Wright invited Iacocca's protégé, the brash forty-one-year-old real estate magnate Donald J. Trump to host the twenty-fifth annual Democratic congressional dinner. Trump, whose own ghostwritten book *The Art of Deal* would soon join *Bonfire* on the best-seller list, declined. He also dismissed talk of entering the New Hampshire primary

---

* Yuppies had matured. Inspired by *The Big Chill*, the hour-long family drama *thirtysome-thing* (ABC, 1987–91) appeared the same season as the stock market crash, while the sitcom *The Wonder Years* (ABC, 1988–93) superimposed the Eighties over the Sixties through the narration and point of view of the young protagonist's older self.

as a Republican, while assuring the *New York Times*, "I believe that if I did run for President, I'd win."

Wall Street was a buzz generator from the moment it was announced by 20th Century Fox. Coming off *Platoon*'s multiple Oscars, Stone's latest was hyped as a new kind of war film that, the *Los Angeles Times* predicted, would "make the airstrip at Khe Sanh look like Club Med." Stone was himself a stockbroker's son. No less than *Platoon*, the story was personal and nothing if not ambitious. (With a nod to Erich von Stroheim's mutilated silent masterpiece, its working title was *Greed*.)

Both detractors and proponents called *Wall Street* a documentary. Indeed, an exclusive preview for a generally appreciative cabal of bankers, financiers, and sundry economic power brokers was described by the *New York Times* as an evening of "home movies." Evidently, the invited audience believed it too. Some at the preview thought the masses wouldn't get *Wall Street*—it was too arcane and too "New York." But, although not nearly as remunerative, *Wall Street* complemented *Top Gun* as a self-conscious embodiment of the Eighties zeitgeist, particularly in its male principle. *Wall Street* was coded as "grown-up" (opening with Frank Sinatra swinging "Fly Me to the Moon" rather than Kenny Loggins or the Miami Sound Machine), but the movies shared parallel excitements—making money and flying jet planes, activities both characterized as "better than sex."

Wall Street is not an action movie (even if the name "Rambo" is evoked to characterize one aggressive broker) so much as a movie about those who control the action. Whereas *Top Gun* fills the screen with $30 million fighter jets, *Wall Street* defines success as being "rich enough to have your own jet." Even more than *Top Gun*, *Wall Street* is a father-story. As he did in *Platoon*, Charlie Sheen plays an unformed American boy, Bud, caught between good and bad fathers. The good dad is a salt-of-the-earth machinist and union rep (Sheen's actual father, Martin Sheen), the bad one is Gordon Gekko (Michael Douglas), all slicked-back hair, red suspenders, and outrageous sneering pronouncements: "Lunch is for wimps." (Did George Bush groan?)

A downsizer and a union buster who refers to his trusted assistant as the Terminator, this flamboyant corporate raider doesn't need food—he devours entire companies. Played by Douglas with vulpine, Oscar-winning gusto, Gekko was at once the genius of the system, exhibiting what Karl Marx called capital's "werewolf-like hunger for surplus labor," and a new version of the

Ugly American. Not everyone thought so: by mid-January 1988, *New York Newsday* reported that Gekko's outfit offered a new "look for the successful man." (Some twenty-two years later, a fashion writer for the *Washington Post* imagined that this peacock was something of a drag act: "The 1980s boom years required women to look like curvy Gordon Gekkos.")

"I think of *Wall Street* as a *Scarface* of business," Stone would write, with "Gekko replacing Tony Montana." Of course, *Scarface* was the "*Scarface* of business," but, as with Tony and, as in *Paradise Lost*, the Devil got the best lines. Gekko's infamous "greed is good" speech combined a warning against America's decline with an attack on unaccountable, overpaid corporate managers, arguing that in a system that promotes "survival of the unfittest," naked self-interest is an evolutionary positive.*

Gekko elaborates on his worldview when he tells his protégé that the richest 1 percent in America control half the wealth and consequently make the rules: "You're not naïve enough to think we're living in a democracy?" Thus did the movie's arch-capitalist offer the movie's most stinging attack on capitalism. Despite mixed reviews, *Wall Street* proved to be a moderate hit, finishing twenty-sixth for 1987 with grosses of $44 million. "It's thrilling left-wing trash," *Village Voice* critic David Edelstein ended his review, "and it's more or less disposable." True enough, but by the time Douglas

---

* Gekko has always been regarded with ambivalence. At first, he was a bona-fide movie monster. Yet, by the time that the economy turned around in the mid-1990s, comparison to Gekko in competitive fields became almost complimentary. New York Knicks coach Pat Reilly was admired for his Gekko drive (and Gekkonian look). With his cigars and bling, the pre-gubernatorial Arnold Schwarzenegger was characterized as "Tony Soprano meets Gordon Gekko."

More than twenty years after *Wall Street* went into production, amid another bull market, Fox announced a sequel allowing Gekko to "resume his machinations on a global scale." Stone had initially declined to revisit his greatest creation, but with the crash of 2008 he changed his mind. *Wall Street: Money Never Sleeps* found Gekko released from prison and flacking his memoir with a batch of new homilies: "Greed got too greedy," "Speculation is the mother of all evil." This time, the bad guy was Josh Brolin, a cardboard stand-in for Goldman Sachs, given the fatal words, "We're too big to fail." Donald Trump's cameo wound up cut from the movie but, in a switch not unlike that in the 1945 *House of Dracula*, wherein the Wolf Man helps rid the world of Dracula and the Frankenstein monster, Gekko emerged as the clear-sighted prophet of doom. Douglas was also recruited for an FBI public service ad meant to discourage insider trading: "The movie was fiction," Douglas maintained, "the problem is real."

won his Oscar, *Wall Street* had assumed its position, alongside *The Bonfire of the Vanities* as an epitaph for the boom-boom Eighties.

Greeted in his travels through haute Manhattan with shout-outs and enthusiastic high-fives, Douglas was a hero on the real Wall Street. Years later, the actor told the *New York Times* how pleased he'd be to never have another "drunken Wall Street broker come up to me and say, 'You're the man!'" In 1988, however, Douglas fully identified with the character. "I don't think Gekko's a villain. Doesn't beat his wife or his kid. He's just taking care of business. And he gives a lot of people chances." Nevertheless, it was Martin Sheen who, as the central figure in the television drama *The West Wing* (NBC, 1999–2006), was elected a future president in the Dream Life.*

Roger Rabbit's Last Temptation: "Read My Lips"

Although the failures of Reaganism—the exploded deficit, the AIDS epidemic, crumbling infrastructure, homelessness, farm foreclosures—are apparent, thanks to the Washington Summit, the president is rising like a phoenix in the polls.

"For the first time in four years a majority of Americans disapproved of the way he was handling the economy," *Newsweek* reports. "Forty-nine percent disapproved of his handling of foreign policy" and yet, the magazine marvels, Reagan's "personal popularity remained high."

Gary Hart, who had long argued for an understanding with Mikhail Gorbachev and even visited Moscow, imagines he too might be ripe for resurrection. Hart, Sidney Blumenthal will write, "had been interred like a barrel of toxic waste"—invoking one of the most memorable images in *RoboCop*—"but the disturbing events in the campaign shook loose the cover of his crypt."

Appropriate for an election year with the president poised to depart the scene, the movies are rife with odd, almost free-associative intimations of the counterculture that had been Reagan's enemy. Christmas brings a

---

* Having played a beleaguered yuppie in *Fatal Attraction* and won an Oscar for *Wall Street*, Douglas staked a claim as Hollywood's preeminent male star—although he would not emerge as such until the Clinton era with successive appearances in *Basic Instinct, Falling Down, Disclosure*, and crucially, *The American President*, where he played something like an idealized, single-dad Bill Clinton. Politically, Douglas was a liberal Democrat.

blockbuster flashback to 1965, the year he was elected California governor: Robin Williams, the friendly alien of the sitcom *Mork and Mindy* (ABC, 1978–82) and the 1984 movie *Moscow on the Hudson*, is calling the hogs to table, "Good morning, Viet-naaammmmmm!!!!" His mission is to liberate armed-forces radio from the tyranny of easy listening. Rock 'n' roll comes to the Nam and thus makes Vietnam movies possible. That the DJ is the first man in armed-forces radio history to get fan mail suggests that the war really is being fought for audience share. Written by Mitch Markowitz, a veteran of the TV sitcom *M*A*S*H*, *Good Morning, Vietnam* is the number four box-office film to open in 1987 (with grosses of $124 million that nearly equal those of *Platoon*).

Reagan's renewed popularity notwithstanding, the House of Representatives rejects his request for $36 million in aid to the Contras. During the Senate vote, candidate Bob Dole twice confronts candidate George Bush, denouncing him for campaign statements impugning his wife. Wimp no more, Bush is reported to be in "high spirits," still basking in the glow of his on-air shouting match with CBS news anchor Dan Rather as the newsman attempted to make the Iran-Contra affair into Bush's problem. (*Washington Post* columnist Mary McCrory writes that, thanks to Rather, Bush has not only cinched the Republican nomination but the election as well.)

For the moment, Reagan is neutral in the battle to succeed him. After three weeks of Christmas releases, the first couple revisit the past with a weekend double-bill of *Santa Fe Trail* (1940), a cavalry movie in which the president played the young George Custer, and *Bad Day at Black Rock* (1955), a movie exposing the internment of Japanese-Americans during World War II. (Some months later, Reagan will sign a bill providing reparations for the internees.)

After two Midwesterners, Dole and Representative Dick Gephardt of Missouri, top the Republican and Democratic Iowa caucuses, Bush lands in New Hampshire, just across the border from his summer home in Kennebunkport, Maine, with a new message: "He's one of us!" (During the course of the campaign he will defend Reagan's opening to the Evil Empire by quoting John Lennon and Yoko Ono: "Give peace a chance.") February 12, Alexander Haig drops out the race for the Republican nomination, and Sidney Poitier returns to serve the American people as a trim, workaholic G-man. Handling the stakeout that opens *Shoot to Kill*, Hollywood's designated civil rights icon is the ultimate in crisp crisis management. (The Reagans will screen the movie on March 11.)

February 16, Bush beats Dole in New Hampshire, 38 percent to 29 percent and then again, two days later, in Nevada, 27 percent to 22 percent. On February 21, televangelist Jimmy Swaggart tearfully confesses to an unnamed sin (which turns out to be consorting with prostitutes). Later that week, Dole takes primaries in Minnesota, Wyoming, and South Dakota. Bush finishes third in South Dakota, behind Dole and televangelist Pat Robertson, who like Bush is the son of a U.S. senator, and fourth in Minnesota, behind Dole, Robertson, and the former Buffalo Bills football star, now New York representative Jack Kemp. March 5, Robertson finishes third in South Carolina—where he has identified himself with Rocky—but unexpectedly wins Washington on Super Tuesday. Bush, however, is the big winner, taking every other one of the seventeen primaries. On the Democratic side, Massachusetts governor Michael Dukakis wins seven primaries; Senator Al Gore of Tennessee, six; and Jesse Jackson, five.

Deciding that "the people have decided," Gary Hart withdraws a second time from the race and the action-thriller *Off Limits* returns to the scene of the crime: a rainy night in Saigon, a dreamy pan past the lava lamp, a forgotten Top 40 hit by the Left Banke, previously recycled in *Apocalypse Now*. The camera finds a naked woman fetchingly sprawled across her fetid cot—and so does an American army officer. He gets up, gets dressed, and blows her brains out. It's Vietnam in the light of *Blade Runner, Blue Velvet*, and *Salvador*. Willem Dafoe, making his second tour of duty, and Gregory Hines play a pair of plainclothes detectives assigned to the Criminal Investigations Detachment of the U.S. Army; the two toughest ballerinas in the Bolshoi pirouette through the neon slime to catch a ritualistic murderer of Vietnamese prostitutes.

Directed by the prolific television writer Christopher Crowe, the movie offers no comforting illusions about America's impact on the nation it was trying to protect. The war is beyond the law, an obscenity waged by characters nicknamed Drippy Dick and Preacher. Saigon is a cultural garbage dump, "the cesspool of the world," a foggy, smoldering disco inferno where dope is peddled in pidgin English, an irate hophead quotes *Mod Squad* as scripture ("Those are my terms: nonnegotiable, power-to-the-people"), Vietnamese hustlers entertain American officers with lascivious renditions of "Dang Me," a nun details the erotic specialties of dead whores, and Jack the Ripper has been reincarnated as a U.S. Army officer.

March 15, favorite son Senator Paul Simon defeats Jesse Jackson in Illinois, while Bush wins over Bob Dole. March 23, Reagan announces a late May visit to the Soviet Union, for his fourth summit with now co-star Mikhail Gorbachev. March 26, Jackson trounces Dukakis in Michigan; Gephardt, who finished third, ends his campaign. A CBS newsman makes the apocalyptic pronouncement that "Jesse Jackson has become the front-runner," but on April 5, Dukakis takes out Jackson in Wisconsin. April 14, Afghanistan, Pakistan, the U.S., and the Soviet Union sign an agreement for the withdrawal of Soviet forces from Afghanistan. More toxic waste: the next day brings *Colors*, the first film Dennis Hopper has directed since declaring his sobriety, as well as his first studio project in the sixteen years since *The Last Movie*.

Indeed, as bilious as it is, *Colors* could almost be mistaken for community service, celebrating the Los Angeles Police Department's war against the crack-dealing teenage killer zombies of East L.A. and Watts although, loath to honor the pigs, Hopper posits three gangs—the Crips, the Bloods, and the Cops. Los Angeles is an infinite expanse of seedy stucco, the two white cops (antithetical stars Robert Duvall and Sean Penn) wading through graffiti rubble as lush as tropical foliage, dogged by the incantatory rap beat. The slums of L.A. are a kind of zoo without walls. The city is a chunk of the Third World—not until the movie is almost over is there even a glimpse of a "civilized" skyscraper. A gang member's funeral is peppered with machine-gun fire; four squad cars pursue the perps through garbage-strewn back alleys where derelicts relax in cast-off easy chairs, then up onto the sidewalk, and finally, several aerial cutaways later, to the crumbling Watts Towers.

The first stage of the presidential race is all but over. April 19, Bush and Dukakis win New York's presidential primaries. Two days later, Gore gives up and Jackson starts campaigning for vice president. The following Tuesday, Bush locks up the nomination with an easy victory in Pennsylvania. After a two-month stretch of recent movies, the president and first lady are again plumbing the past, following the body-switch comedy *18 Again!*, a vehicle for ninety-two-year-old George Burns, with *Butch Cassidy and the Sundance Kid*. The next weekend, they watch Fred Astaire and Ginger Rogers in *Follow the Fleet* and John Wayne in *The Searchers*. Reagan waits until after Pat Robertson suspends his campaign on May 12 to endorse Bush.

On May 25, ten days after the Soviet Union begins withdrawing 115,000 troops from Afghanistan, ending a futile eight-year-long struggle, Sylvester Stallone's monstrously expensive *Rambo III* opens. The same day, Reagan leaves for Moscow and his fourth summit meeting with Mikhail Gorbachev. Would that Stallone were there. According to his security chief, Stallone is, after Reagan and Gorbachev, "the third best known personality in the world" and, under constant threat of a terrorist attack—particularly in Israel where most of *Rambo III* was shot—is constantly accompanied by Uzi-packing bodyguards.

"My war is over," Rambo tells Colonel Trautman when his old commander tries to recruit him for some commando work in Afghanistan. Of course, once Trautman is captured by the Soviet army of sadists, Rambo hastens to the marketplace of Peshawar, warning his guide that he is not a tourist. Many chopper attacks, numerous explosions, and much numbskull dialogue later, the movie builds up to a classic confrontation: Trautman and Rambo versus thirty Russian tanks. "What do you say, John?" Trautman wants to know. Rambo clenches his chin like a fist. His dreamy, benign smile curls into the juiciest sneer since Elvis Presley. "Fuck 'em!" he answers, whipping out his bazooka.*

As summer approaches and the political parties prepare to anoint their respective leaders, two wildly ambitious movies—each, in its way, a crazy miracle—slouch toward Bethlehem. Robert Zemeckis's *Who Framed Roger Rabbit* and Martin Scorsese's *The Last Temptation of Christ* are themselves the subject of extensive antithetical campaigns, one of merchandising and the other of vilification.

Roger Rabbit is the first to appear, opening on June 22. A majestic animation–live action synthesis, a cartoon film noir substituting hardboiled nostalgia for Disney's traditional saccharine tone, the movie is heralded by

---

* Trautman warns the sadistic Soviet commander, one imperialist colonel to another, that Afghanistan will be Russia's Vietnam, thus sending the movie's moral schemata completely through the looking glass. Although it's unclear exactly who's the cavalry here—the Russians or the Mujahedeen—the movie's Western subtext comes full circle when the Afghan settlers plead with Rambo to stay. There's a long ideological pause before he responds, "I've got to go." Fifteen years later, we were back for a stay that would surpass the length of our participation in the Vietnam War.

newsweekly covers and tabloid front pages. It is the apparent premise of *Roger Rabbit* that, once upon a time, specifically 1947, Hollywood was populated by cartoon stars as well as flesh-and-blood ones, and that these Toons had their own studios, their own neighborhood of Toontown, and their own peccadillos. But it is the movie's true premise that, in the age of all media, we live our lives in a thicket of cartoons and trademarks.

Not just the present but the past has become elastic. The real 1947, as the president may or may not remember, was arguably the most traumatic year in Hollywood history, opening with the ghoulish murder of the Black Dahlia, continuing with a steep decline in box-office revenues and a rise in studio lay-offs, and ending with congressional hearings into Communist subversion of the motion picture industry, at which Ronald Reagan had been a friendly witness. *Roger Rabbit* is a show of strength, Hollywood's belated triumph over the era's bad vibes. The Reagans thus create their most epic Camp David double-bill, preceding a Saturday night *Roger Rabbit* screening with a Friday night showing of the 1943 spectacular *This Is the Army*, a star-studded showcase for . . . the young Ronald Reagan. For a weekend at least, the glorious Forties live again.*

While *Who Framed Roger Rabbit* projects a cheerful form of retro social realism, *The Last Temptation of Christ*, an unpleasant flashback to the counterculture, meets far greater animus than did the flower-child rock opera *Jesus Christ Superstar* (the number ten top-grossing film during the year of *The Exorcist*, 1973), which similarly, if less explicitly, suggested a sexual relationship between Jesus and Mary Magdalene. The movie is scheduled to open on August 12, but organized protests against Scorsese's passion project— adapted by Paul Schrader from the novel by perennial Nobel Prize nominee

---

* Just as the Moscow Summit might be considered the Great Communicator's last hurrah, so *Who Framed Roger Rabbit* suggests the last efflorescence of Spielbergism—that is, the process by which the subversively self-reflexive practice of the French new wave was recuperated in the service of building bigger, better, and blander entertainment machines. At one point in *Made in U.S.A.* (1966), Anna Karina describes the movie she's in as "a Walt Disney film with Humphrey Bogart." *Roger Rabbit* is that Disney film—belatedly but literally. One of the few critics to grasp the movie's political implications, Jonathan Rosenbaum noted that "what *Roger Rabbit* shares with the other Spielberg/Lucas blockbusters of the Reagan era, for better and for worse, is an inability to view history as anything other than a reflection of film history (rather than the other way around)," calling it "as succinct an expression of the Reagan legacy as I can think of."

Nikos Kazantzakis, and starring Willem Dafoe as Jesus Christ—have been building for weeks.*

Ignoring Universal's offer to preview *The Last Temptation of Christ* in mid-July, a number of religious leaders base their animus largely on hearsay and an early draft of Schrader's script. Their major target, however, is not Kazantzakis, Scorsese, or Schrader, but Lew Wasserman, Reagan's former agent, chief executive of Universal corporate owner MCA, and a prominent Democrat. After the Reverend Bill Bright, president of the Campus Crusade for Christ and a longtime Reagan associate, offered to buy the movie from Universal in order to destroy it, the Reverend Robert L. Hymers Jr. and two hundred members of his Fundamentalist Baptist Tabernacle picket Universal studios. "These Jewish producers with a lot of money are taking a swipe at our religion," Hymers explains as a small aircraft flies over the demonstration, pulling a banner that reads "Wasserman Fans Jew-Hatred w/ 'Temptation.'"

July 20, one day before the nomination of Michael Dukakis, Hymers and his church members demonstrate outside Wasserman's Beverly Hills home. A man dressed as Jesus kneels before a wooden cross and is lashed by a "movie producer" in a business suit. Other protesters carry banners reading "Universal Is Like Judas Iscariot," and "Wasserman Endangers Israel." That same week, the Reverend Donald Wildmon, a United Methodist minister from Mississippi, mails a half-million fliers characterizing Universal as a "company whose decision-making body is dominated by non-Christians," and the Reverend Jerry Falwell predicts *The Last Temptation* will "create a wave of anti-Semitism." Pat Robertson has written a letter to Anti-Defamation League head Abraham Foxman, warning that the movie will be seen as "a Jewish

---

* Scorsese has traced his ambition to make a movie on the life of Christ back to his seeing the Biblical extravaganza *The Robe* (1953) as an eleven-year-old altar boy. In 1972 he read Kazantzakis's 1955 novel and optioned the screen rights. (The novel, which portrays a human Christ unsure of his divinity, was already controversial, having been placed on the Papal Index of Forbidden Books soon after its publication.) Paramount Pictures agreed to finance the production, to be shot in Israel, following the release of *The King of Comedy* in early 1983. Soon after the movie was announced, a Protestant group called the Evangelical Sisters began organizing protests directed against Paramount's parent company, Gulf+Western and, by the end of the year, Paramount cancelled the project. Four years later, Scorsese's agent Mike Ovitz managed to place a revised (and less expensive) version of *The Last Temptation of Christ* at Universal. The picture was shot on location in Morocco in late 1987.

affront to Jesus Christ," and syndicated columnist Pat Buchanan has accused Hollywood of "assaulting the Christian community in a way it would never dare assault the black community, the Jewish community or the gay community."

Demonstrations continue into August, including one staged outside a synagogue to which Wasserman was thought to belong. August 9, the same day Wildmon characterizes *The Last Temptation* as "blasphemous" on *Nightline* and Hymers stages a demonstration in which Wasserman is represented nailing Jesus to the cross, the American Catholic Church officially condemns the film, rated "O" for morally offensive. In Calcutta, Mother Teresa issues a statement suggesting that if U.S. Catholics intensified their prayers, "Our Blessed Mother will see that this film is removed from your land."

August 11, on the eve of the movie's opening, some 25,000 evangelical Christians and Catholics rally outside Universal Studios. Among the speakers, Wildmon tells the crowd that "Christian-bashing is over. . . . We demand that anti-Christian stereotypes come to an end." Universal opens the movie under tight security in nine cites. There are pickets but no incidents, although several Republican members of Congress called the movie "blasphemous" on the floor of the House. Despite all the publicity, the movie will barely turn a profit, ultimately grossing only $8.3 million.*

August 15, the first night of the Republican National Convention, Ronald Reagan who had resisted requests that he chastise his friend Wasserman, bids a sentimental farewell to his party and the nation, declaring in a spectacular Freudian slip that "facts are stupid things." Accepting the nomination, George Bush makes the truculent promise, "Read my lips—no new taxes," and leads the delegates in the Pledge of Allegiance.†

---

* Although no attempt was made to link Dukakis, the most ethnically identified major presidential candidate since John F. Kennedy, to Kazantzakis, an undated flyer distributed in Los Angeles by a group called the Christian Anti-Defamation League wondered what the candidate's "Jewish wife [thought] of this effort to slander and defame Christ." Meanwhile, outside the Republican convention, Jerry Falwell distributed a crudely drawn comic book caricaturing Dukakis in drag as a "women's libber" and as a vacuum-wielding "pro-abortionist."

† It is scarcely noticed in the post-convention excitement that Iran and Iraq have declared a cease-fire, ending eight years of war.

Running on Empty, *They Live* Again

There was a temporary glitch. George Bush's vice-presidential nominee, Senator J. Danforth Quayle, the scion of an influential Indiana family and the first baby boomer put on a national ticket, has been compelled to defend the favoritism that secured his Vietnam War service in the National Guard. Democrats had imagined they would play the generational card, but Bush beat them to it. More significant than Quayle was the presence of thirty-seven-year-old Atlanta-born political strategist Lee Atwater, a onetime rock guitarist and student of MTV, who largely created Bush's new populist, down-home persona.

Quayle is a reminder that the Sixties cannot live but will not die. Movies in release are correspondingly rife with morbid symptoms. Back in the spring there was the exploitation film *Bad Dreams*: Thirteen years after the Unity Fields commune committed collective suicide, the sole survivor (Jennifer Rubin) wakes from a coma; she's transferred to a mental hospital and given group therapy to help her adjust to the Eighties. The group is amazed by her utopian hippie rap—this somber ditz wants nothing more than to find another Unity Fields. Before long, however, Unity Fields finds her—and them—with the cult's charismatic leader bumping off the group members, one by one, from beyond the grave.

The trend had been presaged by Kathryn Bigelow's *Near Dark* which, opening in late 1987, was a road film set in the Southwest with a "family" of vampires who strongly suggest a Mansonesque hippie cult driving through *Bonnie and Clyde* country in a succession of stolen vans. Even more explicit, *River's Edge* (released in May 1987) juxtaposed various forms of Sixties activism with Eighties anomie. Janet Maslin's *New York Times* review began by citing "the generation gap" between Dennis Hopper's echt-Sixties character and a vacant high school killer. Peter Rainer opened his notice in *Premiere* by asserting, "The ragamuffin dopers in *River's Edge* loom before us like the Curse of the Sixties. They're the strung-out progeny of the hippies."

Jittery police officer aside, the three adult authority figures in *River's Edge* are all counterculture burnouts. Hopper's biker is the Sixties incarnate; the high-school history teacher who brags "we stopped a war, man!" is a self-righteous former protester; and the protagonist's frazzled mother, as described by David Edelstein, is "an ex-flower child who got knocked up and came crashing down to earth." (Confounded by her three children, she blurts out, "You're all mistakes, anyway!")*

Premiered at Cannes in May, Paul Schrader's biopic *Patty Hearst* visualized the counterculture as a grotesque acid trip that inexplicably disrupts the life of a blandly privileged post-debutante when she is kidnapped by the terrorist cult that called itself the Symbionese Liberation Army. In maximizing Patty's subjective point of view, *Patty Hearst* offers little to no context. There are no references to Nixon or Vietnam. The connect-the-dots narrative, which had itself been a high-speed, highly theatrical replay of the entire Sixties debacle, proceeds from one media epiphany to the next: the SLA's taped messages, the group's compelling Patty's father to undertake free food distribution as evidence of good faith, the picture of Patty (now "Tania") posed in battle fatigues before the SLA's seven-headed cobra, the automatic surveillance photos documenting the Hibernia bank robbery, the televised firefight in which the Los Angeles SWAT team incinerated most of the gang, Patty's arrest and self-description as an "urban guerrilla."

In Sidney Lumet's *Running on Empty*, the Sixties is precisely that historical nightmare from which its young hero tries to awake, although the movie has obvious parallels—including the protagonist's name—to Lumet's treatment of early Cold War political martyrdom, *Daniel*. Opening to paltry numbers on September 9, *Running on Empty*, no less than *Back to the Future* or *Fatal Attraction*, is a family film—except here the beleaguered nuclear family is a quasi-military "unit." Some fifteen years ago, Annie and Arthur

---

* The juxtaposition of the Sixties and Eighties might also be seen in the filmmaking. Writing about *River's Edge* ("the year's most riveting, most frightening horror film") in a Sunday think piece, Vincent Canby issued a remarkable j'accuse: "After seeing *River's Edge*, it's difficult to sit through (as I did) *Harry and the Hendersons*, the latest production from Steven Spielberg's movie factory, without wanting to blame Mr. Spielberg and his associates for Western Civilization's imminent decline and fall."

   That's putting a possibly unfair burden on situation comedies in general and, in particular, on the Spielberg-factory film. *Harry and the Hendersons* is, after all, an apparently harmless *E.T.* ripoff about an idealized Middle American family that attempts to make a house pet of Bigfoot, the legendary half-man, half-beast who's supposed to stalk the mountains of the Pacific Northwest.

   However, *Harry and the Hendersons*, which reduces the mysteries of life to soothing, sitcom dimensions, could be just the sort of movie that would have contributed to the dread sense of aimlessness that afflicts the kids in *River's Edge*.

Pope (Christine Lahti and Judd Hirsch) blew up a napalm-producing re-search lab, inadvertently blinding and paralyzing an innocent janitor.

The couple went underground with their baby son Danny (River Phoe-nix, himself the offspring of hippie parents) and, producing a second child, has remained in a pseudonymous netherworld of rented rooms and menial jobs without entirely losing their counterculture joie de vivre. When Danny, who happens to be a musical prodigy, brings home a schoolmate (Martha Plimpton, daughter of a *Hair* original cast member), she's stunned by the Popes' out-front relating and offhanded LSD jokes. In the movie's bizarre *Big Chill* moment, the family dances the twist to James Taylor's "Fire and Rain." Although archetypal New Left foot soldiers, the Popes are still American enough to set their oldest child free.

On October 8, the Reagans screened Lumet's second "Book of Daniel" at Camp David. So far as known, they did not see *Patty Hearst*. Perhaps it re-minded them of their own Patty. Or maybe of then governor Reagan's taste-less one-liner, delivered in response to the SLA's forced food distribution: "It's just too bad we can't have an epidemic of botulism." The movie was too close to home.*

The last sitting vice president elected president was Martin Van Buren in 1836, but George Bush was born lucky. His Republican opposition imploded and potential Democratic challengers like senators Gary Hart and Joe Biden com-mitted political hara-kiri.

Moreover, the zeitgeist stalled. Ever since *The Godfather*, the movies had been proposing Italian-American city kids as masculine icons. Yet the most formidable of these, New York governor Mario Cuomo, the man who mem-orably lambasted Ronald Reagan at the 1984 Democratic convention, had un-accountably decided not to run for president. Instead, Bush had the pleasure of facing another, far weaker, white-ethnic northeastern governor, Michael Dukakis.

Early polls showed that, given the unequal economic gains of the 1980s, the mounting deficit, and the loss of jobs overseas, Republicans would have a difficult time. In late May, Gallup put Dukakis ahead of Bush 54 percent to

---

* After one screening, Schrader remarked that "Patty Hearst is today as you would think she'd be if this never happened"—a George Bush Republican.

38 percent, but Bush's operatives—including Roger Ailes, who coached Bush's on-air shouting match with Dan Rather, and Lee Atwater—had devised a strategy to cast the straight-laced Massachusetts governor with the foreign-sounding name as the most liberal of liberalistic liberals. Their targets would be his veto of an unconstitutional bill requiring that the Pledge of Allegiance be recited in classrooms, his approval of a prisoner furlough program that allowed a black convicted murderer named Willie Horton to rape and murder a white woman on a weekend pass, and his self-proclaimed "card-carrying" membership in the American Civil Liberties Union.*

By early September, when Horton began turning up in Republican TV ads, Dukakis's early advantage, if not his frosty reserve, had melted away. His RoboCop decision to run on competence was a non-starter, not least because Bush's people helped spread a rumor that Dukakis had twice consulted a psychoanalyst. Bush further benefited from his own anti-wimpery, relentlessly attacking Dukakis as a weak-on-defense, criminal-coddling liberal. Wrapping himself in the American flag, Bush charged his opponent with promoting class warfare even as he impugned his patriotism. Meanwhile, Dukakis did himself no favors with a photo op wearing an oversized combat helmet and peering out of a tank, foolishly grinning and absurdly accompanied by the theme from *Patton*. This ridiculously wimpish maneuver provided the basis for the most satiric Republican TV spot.

"Poll Shows Bush Sets Agenda for Principal Election Issues," the *New York Times* reported on September 14. Bush now held a clear lead, 47 percent to 39 percent. To some degree, this was due to Reagan's post-Gorbachev bump as well as the president's skill as a wingman. "I must tell you that everything we have done these last eight years, everything could be lost faster than you can say the Pledge of Allegiance," Reagan jokingly warned an audience at Southeast Missouri State University before returning to Camp David to watch himself as an amiable adman with an eye for feminine pulchritude in the feeble

---

* Sidney Blumenthal's furious account of the 1988 campaign, *Pledging Allegiance*, frames it as a virtual replay of Cold War thematics, held in the absence of the Cold War: "Bush's campaign was the continuation of the Cold War by metaphor. What was slipping away—the monolithic dualities, the easy moral rivalry—was what he sought to sustain." Bush "attempted to revive [the Cold War's] earlier draconian atmosphere through repetition of certain themes that had occurred since even before the Cold War's beginning. His campaign, of course, failed to sustain the Cold War, but, for a few months, he succeeded in creating its illusory equivalent."

1949 comedy, *The Girl from Jones Beach*. Two nights later, after his last sitting for his official portrait, the president hosted forty guests for a White House screening of the grand old 1942 flag-waver, *Yankee Doodle Dandy*: "It was great & everybody enjoyed it."*

Carefully coached by his advisers, Bush insisted that despite pummeling Dukakis for his failure to honor the Pledge or respect the flag, he was running a positive campaign, recycling elements of Reagan's "Morning in America" in his TV ads in his quest for a "gentler, kinder" America. ("Kinder and gentler than who?" Nancy Reagan was said to have asked.) In an interview with Maureen Dowd, the candidate savored his double personality: "'I like the mix,' Mr. Bush said, as though he had just sipped a martini or tasted a pasta sauce and found the ingredients properly blended." Bush salted his speeches with a few vaguely liberal ideas even while excoriating Dukakis's liberalism. But mainly, the patrician Bush was sold as the American candidate, one who brought back patriotism ("Flag sales have taken off!"), ate pork rinds, and loved country music.

The risk-adverse Dukakis was portrayed as a "risk" for America, as well as an un-American Other. "Why I can't even pronounce his name," country singer Loretta Lynn said of Dukakis at a Bush rally in downstate Illinois while, one day after Bush defended Quayle's patriotism (he "did not go to Canada, he did not burn his draft card and he damned sure didn't burn the American flag"), a Republican senator from Idaho claimed to have seen photographs of the candidate's wife, Kitty Dukakis, incinerating the Stars and Stripes.†

Post-Reagan, the presidential debates were understood to be meta-debates. "What gets said about the debate is often more important than what gets said at the debate," the *New York Times* explained to its readers. "Is this the time to unleash our one-liners?" was Bush's rhetorical question, a virtual

---

* Along with *Knute Rockne, All American*, screened on October 24, 1982 and October 2, 1987, *Yankee Doodle Dandy* appears to be the only movie Reagan screened twice during his presidency, having previously shown it at Camp David on February 19, 1988.
† Pee-wee Herman served the Republicans as an occasional Dukakis substitute. Delivering the keynote address at the Republican National Convention, New Jersey governor Thomas Kean warned that "the Dukakis Democrats will try to talk tough but don't be fooled. They may try to talk like Dirty Harry. But they will still act like PeeWee Herman." And, five days before the election, Bush surrogate Arnold Schwarzenegger claimed to have seen Reagan and Bush "take over an economy that looked like PeeWee Herman" and turn it around to "look like Superman."

reading of his cue card, before making his first joke about polluted Boston Harbor (another TV ad trope). The debate was deemed to be a draw and *Time* magazine's postmortem cover story was "Battle of the Handlers."

Cast by Republicans as Jimmy Carter redux, Dukakis was being encouraged to rather identify himself with the last Democratic icon, John F. Kennedy. Some believe that the Massachusetts governor chose Lloyd Bentsen, who had defeated Bush in the 1970 race for Texas senator, as his running mate in order to geographically mirror the 1960 Kennedy-Johnson ticket. But it was Dan Quayle who chose to invoke JFK in the vice presidential debate, thus setting himself up for the campaign's best remembered riposte: "Senator, I knew John F. Kennedy. I served with John F. Kennedy. John F. Kennedy was a friend of mine," Bentsen told Quayle and the television audience. "Senator, you're no John F. Kennedy."

The night of the vice presidential debate, the Republicans premiered the grim "revolving door" ad that subliminally suggested Dukakis had personally furloughed Willie Horton, and Horton made another ghostly appearance early in the second Bush-Dukakis debate—recalled mainly for Dukakis's bizarrely unemotional response to a question which posited his wife as the hypothetical victim of a rape-murder. Bush, however, described the debate as a Western shoot-out (even as Charlton Heston was attacking Dukakis for his position on gun control).

"We came at each other pretty hard, and when the smoke cleared it was pretty clear where we stood," Bush bragged. This time, the vice president was declared the winner. Two days before the Reagans screened *Running on Empty* at Camp David, Bush boastfully told a conclave of Texas police officers that the Reagan administration changed the nation's movie preference from *Easy Rider* to *Dirty Harry*. He had begun quoting Dirty Harry himself ("Go ahead, make my day") and joking that, in a reference to Massachusetts's now notorious prison furlough, Dukakis's motto was "Go head, have a nice weekend."

As Bush took to giving Gorbachev a cameo as a figure of menace in his TV ads, Dukakis's popularity fell below that of Jesse Jackson. Moreover, Bush was perceived as the more likeable candidate—another post-Reagan requirement for an American president. The manufacturers of novelties and dealers in memorabilia were already mourning Reagan's departure. The president's "charms and foibles have been depicted on buttons, postcards, candy jars and dolls, and in comedy routines and musical theater. Bright moments or dark, he has been a money-maker," the *New York Times* reported. "Sales of Presidential novelty items tripled after Mr. Reagan took over from Jimmy Carter."

A week before the election (and a day after Dukakis finally decided that he really was a liberal), the *New York Times* ran a front-page article that, just as if 1984 had never happened, made the obvious point that "the next President will have been chosen in a campaign dominated as never before by television. . . ."

> Voters are telling pollsters that ads matter. More money is being spent on them than ever before and, campaign officials contend, the dictates of television have led the candidates to attack each other from the stump with uncommon frequency for a modern Presidential race. . . .
>
> Experts on Presidential campaigns say this is the first time in a Presidential race that candidates have used advertising at least as much to bash the other side as to promote themselves.

On the Friday before the election, a movie appeared to explain it all, advertised with a suitable paranoia: "You see them on the street. You watch them on TV. You might even vote for one this fall. You think they're people like you. You're wrong. Dead wrong."

John Carpenter's *They Live* was a low-budget social science–fiction film in the tradition of *Wild in the Streets* and the original *Invasion of the Body Snatchers*. It also revisited *The Next Voice You Hear* in the Age of Rambo and Reagan. Where the 1950 movie channeled sociological propaganda via God through the radio, it was the premise of Carpenter's far more scurrilous release that the Reagan revolution was masterminded by TV-savvy creatures from outer space who used the medium to create a world of subliminal sociological propaganda.

Reality, which in *They Live* can only be seen through demystifying sunglasses, is worse than Adorno and Horkheimer could have imagined—a grim black-and-white world where invisible surveillance-saucers hover in the polluted air, and every billboard or page of *Time* is a single Orwellian exhortation to "Obey," "Consume," or "Marry and Reproduce." Eschewing the soft sell, this all-pervasive mind control is as subtle as generic packaging: dollar bills are simply emblazoned, "This Is Your God." Going from a phony color world to an actual black-and-white real world, *They Live* inadvertently paralleled Bush's TV ads, which went monochromatic whenever they showed the horror of a Dukakis future: polluted harbors, grim prisons, menacing criminals.

"Just in time for election day, director John Carpenter has released into the nation's movie theaters the most anti-Reagan film ever to come out of Hollywood," Lewis Beale wrote in a widely syndicated profile. According to Carpenter, the movie reproduced his own revelation. "The whole idea came about when I disengaged myself from major Hollywood filmmaking in 1986," he told Beale.

> I took about six or seven months off, started reading newspapers and watching offbeat cable TV shows. I looked at the country and thought we were in really deep trouble. This seems like fascism to me, the rise of the fundamentalist right and the kind of mind control they're putting out, the kind of presidency Reagan has had. I sort of never picked up on it on a soundstage where you're really insulated from the outside world.

For Carpenter, *They Live* was made at a moment of crisis in response to an actual problem. He assigned himself a mission that he had to work outside of Hollywood to fulfill. Like *The Next Voice You Hear* or the original *Invasion of the Body Snatchers*, intended as a critique of conformity, *They Live* was designed to alter the viewer's perspective—which is, in fact, its subject.

Carpenter was even more explicit in another interview, detailing his message that the Reagan Revolution was "controlled by free-enterprising aliens from outer space. . . . They're dismantling the middle class, the rich are getting richer, the poor are getting poorer. Planet Earth is the Third World to these people." The filmmaker identified his Implacable Alien Others as Republicans.*

Carpenter, it would seem, expected too much of the 1987 Crash. Still, Michael Dukakis could have used him as his media guru. *They Live* was full of crude characterizations and lumbering dialogue but, for all its laughable cloddishness, it does articulate an alternative Democratic strategy—mixing

---

* Although the aliens—rapacious "free enterprisers" for whom the earth is "just another developing planet"—are even depleting the ozone to suit their own metabolisms, not everyone found that a problem. Reviewing the movie in the UCLA *Daily Bruin*, student Jim Pickrell wrote, "I was with them until they said the aliens were really free-market slime balls, at which point I changed sides and was rooting for the aliens."

Dick Gephardt–style protectionist populism with Jesse Jackson's more altruistic, left-wing brand and a lump of Stallone-esque resentment. (The penultimate sequence includes the quintessential Rambo image of Uzis in the computer room.) Indeed, the movie—in production in the early spring of 1988, around the time that, having beaten Dukakis in Michigan, Jackson was the front-runner for the Democratic nomination—unfolds in a depression landscape-cum-Rainbow Coalition of skid rows, shantytowns, and moldering community centers. Los Angeles for people without cars.

The protagonist of *The Next Voice You Hear* is a family man with a factory job, a regular Joe (which is in fact his name). In *They Live* he's become unmoored. John Nada, the movie's dumb but honest protagonist (played by sub-Stallone former professional wrestler Roddy Piper), is a sort of post-hippie lumberjack who believes in America yet, along with his comrade unemployed workers, is wont to invoke closed factories, rail against auto imports, and cite a divisive new Golden Rule: "He who has the gold, rules." (Curiously, Carpenter missed a beat by not making Nada a Viet-vet.)

This acid-ripped Woody Guthrie worldview offers the most viscerally paranoid theory imaginable for consumer greed, industrial pollution, and media narcosis. The warnings, meanwhile, come from an underground alliance of black street preachers ("They control us—wake up!"), disaffected do-gooders ("They are dismantling the sleeping middle class!"), and middle-aged video freaks, who break into the televised signal to warn that alien TV transmissions "keep us sedated." Still, thanks to his newfound powers of analysis, Nada can see the creatures with ball-bearing eyes walk among us, recruiting unscrupulous yuppies to their nefarious cause.

They Live picks up immediately whenever Nada dons the magic sunglasses. Carpenter was too prudent or lacked the guts to turn the lenses on the American flag. Nevertheless, the glasses that dispel the mists clouding human minds are a perfect metaphor for the tool of scientific socialism. Nada's epic back-alley fight with his black buddy (*Platoon* vet Keith David), whom he is attempting to persuade to don the shades, is six or seven minutes of gurgling, kicking, and kneeing to the groin, an impressively cosmic illustration for the inherent difficulty in getting someone to see your point of view.

Well received by anti-Reagan film critics, *They Live* was later championed by the leftist political theorist Slavoj Zizek, who saw the movie as an allegory about omnipresent ideology, and the fight between Nada and his buddy as representing the struggle required to recognize unpleasant truth: "The violence staged here is a positive violence, a condition of liberation."*

They Live was the top-grossing movie in the U.S. on November 8, when Bush carried forty states, receiving nearly 54 percent of the vote in the lowest turnout since Calvin Coolidge was elected in 1924. After that *The Live* quickly faded, as did the sort of topical, metaphoric genre film it represented. The premise of *The Next Voice You Hear* is that everyone can receive the same divine message; in *They Live*, truth is available only to those who wish to see it.

Thus, *They Live* acknowledges what *The Next Voice* can't, namely the end of Hollywood universality. Like its protagonist, it knows itself to be marginal. The last Reagan movie suggests that when Reagan goes away he will take Hollywood's Dream Life with him.

Morning After in America

The cover of the January 3, 1989, issue of the *Village Voice* was a photograph of a laughing Reagan beneath the headline "So Long, Suckers!" The feature-well that week was devoted almost entirely to essays on the "End of the Age

---

* Zizek, who has several times characterized *They Live* as a "neglected masterpiece of the Hollywood Left," returned to it again during the 2008 election:

> What would we see if we were to observe the Republican presidential campaign through such glasses? The first thing would be a long series of contradictions and inconsistencies:
>
> • Their call to reach across party lines—while waging the cultural war politics of "us" against "them."
> • Their warning that the candidates' family life should be off limits—while parading their families on stage.
> • Their promise of change—while offering the same old programs (lower taxes and less social welfare, a belligerent foreign policy, etc.)
> • Their pledge to reduce spending—while incessantly praising President Reagan. (Recall Reagan's answer to those who worried about the exploding debt: "It is big enough to take care of itself.")
> • Their accusations that Democrats privilege style over substance—which they deliver at perfectly staged media events.
>
> The next thing we would see is that these and other inconsistencies are not a weakness, but a source of strength for the Republican message. Republican strategists masterfully exploit the flaws of liberalism.

of Reagan," including mine, titled "The Last Picture Show," reproduced here, with annotations and minor adjustments.

---

1. Who Was That Masked Man?
Facts are stupid things.

—RONALD REAGAN, 1988 Republican
National Convention

In the end, he told us the truth. Let's face it, facts *are* limited, tedious, stupid things. Facts affront the imagination. You don't have to tell Steven Spielberg that documentaries don't gross a hundred million bucks. Fantasies are box office—or were.

Jimmy Carter had promised never to lie to us—his mistake, even worse than walking to his own inauguration. Why should anyone want the facts? Shared fantasies are what hold a people together, provide their brightest symbols and most cherished assumptions, their narratives and dreams. With all due respect to George Bush and his speechwriters, Ronald Reagan was the man who "lived the American Dream."

Reagan was the first American president to emerge from Fantasy Central [aka the Department of Amusement]. He lived and loved in the utopia of mass entertainment: its heroes and villains, handkerchief scenes and happy endings, props and costumes, thrills and bromides. Trademarks and sell lines were his stock-in-trade. There is no need to rehearse the Reagan résumé; suffice it to say that he did everything from protect top secret "inertia projectors" and romance Shirley Temple to pitch in the majors and command a submarine before he settled down to become a TV personality and corporate spokesman.

The story of Ronald Reagan is the story of his image—how he developed it, refined it, layered it, solved its problems. . . . In the sine qua non of American tele-politics, he was the best-trained candidate who ever lived. As lifelong media junkies, we were the best-prepped audience he ever had. Even as Reagan changed the rules of the game, his will be one tough act to follow.

It is precisely because Reagan was himself a text that he became as much a master of intertextuality as any movie brat—quoting lines from

State of the Union, reliving scenes from *A Wing and a Prayer*. Who can blame him for inadvertently calling his dog "Lassie" (reporters were watching) or telling Shimon Peres that his Culver City–based film corps had liberated a concentration camp or screening *Moscow Does Not Believe in Tears* before meeting Gorbachev (who was briefed to ask him about *Kings Row*). The dream was all of a piece. Perhaps it is misleading to say that Reagan emerged from mass entertainment. Let us say that he materialized—a magic bubble shimmering around him—like the good witch in *The Wizard of Oz*.

Reagan had been the master of ceremonies for the televised opening of Disneyland in 1955. Twenty-five years later, in the tradition of Henry Ford and Hugh Hefner, Walt Disney and Howard Hughes, and America itself, Reagan created his own Magic Kingdom: a nostalgic, enchanted realm without poverty and racism, ozone depletion, or dead dolphins. The Third World was a picturesque backdrop and your American Express card was always welcome. Mediated by the media, that past became a present—a perfect remake; Reagan led us not Back to the Future but rather backing into the future, eyes on some imaginary Golden Age.

These were the good old days, come around once more. It was as that poet of simulation, Jean Baudrillard, wrote of Peter Bogdanovich's early nostalgia film, *The Last Picture Show*:

> You need only be sufficiently distracted, as I was, to see it as a 1950s original production: a good film of manners and the ambience of small-town America, etc. A slight suspicion: it was a little too good, better adjusted, better than the others, without the sentimental, moral, and psychological tics of the films of that period. Astonishment at the discovery that it is a 1970s film, perfectly nostalgic, brand new, retouched, a hyperrealist restitution of that period.

Like some supernatural suburban patriarch or benign TV impresario, Reagan conjured up the themes and creatures of the '50s—anticommunist paranoia, science-fiction weaponry, conspicuous consumption—and let us experience them again as if in some spectacular sound and light show, as fantasy, as entertainment, at one step removed.

Because Reagan never left the Dream Life, he truly understood the power of Rambo and Dirty Harry, the importance of watching network

TV and being able to drop the name of Vanna White. The right stuff could move him to tears. He embodied the power of denial. He was our Teflon smile button. Facts *are* stupid things, and Reagan's conviction was such that it began to shape reality—as if in obedience to the drama of his narrative, the media began to fold back on itself.

Beginning with John Hinckley's providential assassination attempt, Reagan's reign was a succession of tawdry spectaculars. Effacing popular memory of the 1982 recession, his first term brought *E.T.*, The Downing of KAL 007, The Conquest of Grenada, and the climactic road show "New Morning in America." Somewhat rockier, Reagan II included a few media events beyond administration control: Bitburg was quickly succeeded by *Rambo*, Bombing Gaddhafi, and the Statue of Liberty Show; Iran-Contra subsumed by Ollie-mania (itself a debased remake of *Mr. Smith Goes to Washington*) and erased with the Moscow Summit.

If the theme of Reagan I was the menace of the Evil Empire, the theme of Reagan II, developed in collaboration with Mikhail Gorbachev, was *Friendly Persuasion*, if not *Butch Cassidy and the Sundance Kid*—the two movies that seemed most on the presidential mind during the ultimate summit. [Reagan screened *Butch Cassidy* at Camp David several weekends before the Moscow Summit, where he presented Gorbachev with a videocassette of *Friendly Persuasion*.]*

And then, from early 1983 on, there was the overarching dream of Star Wars—a fantasy so poignantly regressive and mind-boggling in its cost that it made the Pharaoh's tombs seem like hovels for the homeless. Star Wars was the supreme metaphor: defense by mirrors, security through special effects. It was Reagan's visionary attempt to extend the magic bubble to include everyone—even, he would claim while debating Walter Mondale, those pesky Russians.

---

* Set during the Civil War and notable for casting Gary Cooper as a devout Quaker, *Friendly Persuasion* had been adapted by Michael Wilson from Jessamyn West's novel. Because Wilson was blacklisted, his name could not appear in the movie's credits, despite its Oscar nomination for best adapted screenplay. Although nominated in several other categories, the movie failed to win any Oscars; it did, however, receive the Palme d'Or at the 1957 Cannes Film Festival.

It's been said that a great star resolves two conflicting images. Thus, Marilyn Monroe embodied sex and innocence, and Elvis Presley seemed simultaneously black and white. John Wayne appeared at once brutal and chivalrous. Madonna (like Shirley Temple before her) shows us hard work as constant play. Bruce Springsteen registers both Democrat and Republican, but Ronald Reagan incorporates so many contradictions we couldn't even begin to list them.

2. One-Eyed Jacks

Democracy is no longer lived, but is increasingly represented.

—TIMOTHY LUKE, "Televisual Democracy
and the Politics of Charisma"

American politics is the most refined of vicarious thrills. Our presidential election is the World Series, the network sweeps, Oscar night, *Wheel of Fortune*, Nintendo, and the Super Bowl rolled, commercials and all, into one endless orgy of navel-gazing and self-congratulation. The process creates a vortex of attention—the whole planet is watching the American public watch and define itself in the fun-house mirror of public opinion. It's fun. It's America. We should have known Big Brother would appear as a flag-waving Bozo the Clown.

With the controlled spontaneity of Reaganmania, the 1984 campaign played presidential politics as blockbuster entertainment—a parade of larger-than-life symbols and titillating fantasies, snappy buzzwords, and phantom opponents. It was too tacky to be true, too entertaining to ignore. The spectacle was made to be televised and watched, if at all, with a willing suspension of disbelief, and then shaken off the morning after the election, the way a dogged rationalist might dismiss a puzzling dream or assert as meaningless the idiot sitcom that had only just before held him spellbound. It might work twice, but perhaps not precisely the same way.

Thus, Reagan's first legacy was the 1988 campaign, or rather the 1988 meta-campaign—a triumph of formalism in which the coverage (or spin) given the events easily overshadowed the events themselves. Now the media not only treated the campaign as a production, a succession of photo opportunities, a continually moving movie set, it also described it as such. But where was their star? Compared to him, the candidates were hopeless dwarfs and wimps. As virtually their first assignment, both Vice President George Bush and Governor Michael Dukakis—or rather, their ectoplasmic forms—had to prove themselves "presidential." Both were Reagan disciples (as were key supporting players Jesse Jackson and Mikhail Gorbachev).

But despite the shamelessly Reaganesque spectacle of the Democratic convention, Dukakis was a rank amateur. The Duke intentionally left his positions vague, put the emphasis on his personality, and sought parallels between himself and John F. Kennedy—not fully realizing that Reagan, with his cost-free strategy of national greatness, had coopted Kennedy long ago.

With this pathetic attempt at voodoo Reaganism, Dukakis was unable to define himself. "Bush must present a new master plan that will resolve the accumulated contradictions and keep the essence of Reaganism," Andrew Kopkind wrote in *The Nation* last August. No problem, dude. If it ain't broke . . . After an initial fake left, "Bush" ran a rerun of 1984, stressing the emotional issues of crime, drugs, gun control, abortion, the environment, and patriotism against a carefully selected succession of backdrops. A theme was determined, floated, and played until its legs gave out. First the pledge, then Willie Horton's furlough . . .

The 1984 campaign had been no less choreographed, but "Bush" was, of course, far cruder than the model. Trained by Reagan's '84 debate coach Roger Ailes, and working from a script, the docile vice president managed to learn the John Wayne trick of speaking slowly and using his jaw to work key phrases, breaking a sentence if necessary to pause for applause. The endless repetition of toughness—"I am not going to let him get away with that"—ultimately gave "Bush" a patina of toughness. The continual Pavlovian deployment of the flag gave him the familiarity of a trademark. Similarly, although the candidate's junior partner Dan Quayle was hopefully floated as the new Robert Redford, his main purpose was to make "Bush" look paternal by comparison.*

Meanwhile, Bush's handlers assured sympathetic pundits that the

---

* As a young law student in Indiana, Quayle had, in fact, been inspired by Redford's performance in *The Candidate* to enter politics.

candidate's bark was the worst of his soundbite. A man's gotta do what a man's gotta do—whatever it takes. Could "Bush" fill Reagan's shoes as national symbol-maker? Could he be "the heart, the soul, the conscience of America"? The electorate recognized the script, but the man played good cop/bad cop so clumsily that his handlers finally decided to explain their strategy in the press. The *New York Times* dutifully reported that

> Mr. Bush's image-makers—Mr. Ailes, Mr. Atwater and James A. Baker 3rd, the campaign chairman—blended a Clint Eastwood image and dialogue with Mr. Bush's conventional Ivy League personality, producing a quiet guy with a steel core, willing to do and say what it takes to win the election. At the same time Peggy Noonan, Mr. Bush's speechwriter, analyzed his personality and wrote speeches playing to what she called the candidate's "Gary Cooper" side—an appealing individualist, a man who may be occasionally bumbling and inarticulate.

As early as September 10 (or as late as four years after 1984 established the outer limits of tele-democratic hoopla), the *Washington Post* declared, "Bush Gaining in Battle of TV Images." Why not? He was merely recirculating the ones that had worked so well for his boss. By the time the *Times* had cautiously pronounced "The Medium Is the Election," *Time* featured not one but two meta-campaign covers: "Battle of the Handlers" and "1988, You're No 1960: Myth, Memory and the Politics of Personality." Media self-consciousness was now part of the act.

Accordingly, both the Republican and Democratic advertising strategies came in for unprecedented formalist analysis. (Ironically, the Dukakis spot that attempted to go to the electronic interpersonal by attacking his opponent's packaging came in for the greatest criticism. Players play, commentator comment: showbiz rules.) Thus, Quayle was explained in terms of *The Candidate*, "Bush" ran against Dennis Hopper by boasting he helped to change America from a society that flocked to *Easy Rider* to one that exalted *Dirty Harry*, and Dukakis revealed more about himself by praising *The Seduction of Joe Tynan*—a movie about the corruption of power in which liberal senator Alan Alda is undone by his extramarital affair with the charming labor lawyer Meryl Streep. [The movie, directed by Jerry Schatzberg, opened during the summer of 1979; even Jimmy Carter knew enough not to screen it at the White House.]

No wonder the first hero who popped into George Bush's mind was Jaime Escalante, the heroic math teacher and subject of the movie *Stand and Deliver* [screened at Camp David on April 16, 1988]. On the eve of the final debate, with Bush out campaigning alongside Chuck Norris (as he had, that week, appeared with tough guys Arnold Schwarzenegger, Tom Selleck, and Charlton Heston), the *Times'* "Campaign Trail" column turned to showbiz in four out of four items: In the first, it was remarked that Lloyd Bentsen's "You're no Jack Kennedy" line had made him a "star." In the second, James Baker III was compared to Claude Rains in *Casablanca*. The third reiterated the vice president's appropriation of the Bobby McFerrin song "Don't Worry, Be Happy," the last—a plant—had the "new" Dukakis emerging as "the Milton Berle of American politics."

Faux pas, that last one. Truly, Dukakis's discomfort in the Dream Life never failed to astonish. His habitual expression was of Mr. Before in some antediluvian antacid commercial. Even so, one minute into the second debate, CNN newsman Bernard Shaw made the Duke a fantastic present—asking the governor if he would still oppose the death penalty if his wife, Kitty, were raped and murdered. Providentially, Shaw gave Dukakis the opportunity to play Charles Bronson in *Death Wish*. With one question he did more for Dukakis than any of his handlers. He created a scenario and offered the candidate an image. The Duke had only to live up to his nickname, to accept the role of a tough little ethnic— imagine himself the liberal college professor savage enough (in his fantasies and ours) to go on a revengeful murder spree after his family is butchered—and be president.*

The whole world was watching. Who was Dukakis, really? Or rather, who was Dukakis fakely? Could he be tough and tender, twinkly and

---

* *Death Wish* opened in late July 1974 as the House Judiciary Committee met to consider President Nixon's impeachment. According to Sidney Blumenthal, Dukakis had actually been prepped by his handlers to answer a question on crime and failed to deliver the answer he had rehearsed.

bellicose, like our reigning poster boy and Great White Father? Dukakis's inability to distinguish his death wish from ours was as conclusive as Gary Hart's fatal attraction. For the first time, the networks and news-weeklies declared the utterly forgettable "Bush" the winner.

3. Happy Trails
Politics is just like show business. You need a big opening. Then you coast for a while. Then you need a big finish.

—RONALD REAGAN, 1966

For want of a scenario, George Bush won the privilege of playing Herbert Hoover to Reagan's Calvin Coolidge. As late as October 1986, polls showed that Reagan was considered the greatest president since FDR. But the drug was wearing off. The bungled Daniloff "spy" swap, the Reykjavik summit meeting confusion, the loss of the Senate, the Iran-Contra revelations, the partial erasure of *Rambo* by *Platoon* precipitated a 23 percent drop in the President's approval rating, the steepest fall in modern times. Why then this tacit agreement to let him ride into the sunset, to have his happy ending—something that hadn't been granted a president in 28 years? [Or longer—perhaps since Coolidge.]

Just as Disneyland brought cartoons to life, Reaganland transformed America into its own ideal image—America as theme park and TV spectacular. Reaganland enables us to see and appreciate America as a symbolic representation. Where once we had the Western, now there is only this. Reagan lives in Reaganland and sincerely believes in its values. We're the visitors who pretend to believe—so long as the Muzak is playing, the crowd control works, and the robots run.*

There is a sense in which the Vietnam War was a massive public relations stunt, designed to convince the rest of the world of American

---

* Reaganland was a superior, virtual-reality version of New York's long-vanished, ill-fated, brick-and-mortar Freedomland U.S.A., a sort of public movie set in which fantasy was highly regulated. Plastic Indians crouched in the bushes and costumed pirates patrolled the periphery of Little Old New York. San Francisco quaked and Chicago burned every half hour as extras staged a gunfight on the main street of a scaled-down Western town.

might and resolve. Reaganism was a further refinement—predicated on the needs of a superpower to create images that will convince *itself* that it is the greatest power on earth. It is the power of positive thinking, the faith that allows Roger Rabbit to dash off a cliff and jog on thin air, and it worked, at least in the short run. The stock market crashes, yet the confidence game goes on. A Biblical seven years of borrowing transform the United States from the world's leading creditor to the world's greatest debtor, and no one looks down.

As the 1988 campaign swung into its final stages, Reagan's popularity rose, and voters were reported increasingly optimistic about the state of the nation. "He Isn't Running, but He's Winning," the *New York Times* noted the day after Dukakis self-destructed in the second debate. For lack of anything else, Reagan saw the election as a referendum on himself. Introduced at a Texas rodeo as "the grandest cowboy of them all," he told the crowd that "what you are really choosing is more than a slate of candidates, it's a vision of America, a dream we share."

Reagan isn't just our movie, we are his: *America, the Movie*. It's *Who Framed Roger Rabbit* and we're Bob Hoskins in Toontown—real people wandering around a delirious mental landscape of special effects, feelgood fantasies, militarist spectacles, endless remakes. It's expensive— productive assets sold off to underwrite the personal consumption that keeps jobs intact, profits high, and the fantasy going—but who would have imagined the spectacle of decay would be so mesmerizing? Pollution makes for the best sunsets. As America declines, its myth grows more potent, its self-absorption increasingly hypnotic.

Hooray for Hollywood! Live the Dream! Reagan reminded us that we are the movie the whole world watches.

"The Cold War is over," the former president proclaimed, flying away from Washington on Air Force One on Inauguration Day. As the Cold War was declared to be finished, so ended a long episode in the history of American entertainment.

Ronald Reagan changed the nature of American democracy. His was the triumph of public relations. Casting government as a political enemy and himself as the hero of the last and greatest Hollywood blockbuster, he told a wonderful story in which Communism was consigned to history's dustbin and America was again number one (the rich were richer than ever). But the Reagan movie did not end in January 1989, at least in the Dream Life.

EPILOGUE:
REMAKE MY DAY

The Berlin Wall fell in late November 1989. In the Dream Life, the Cold War was over in June with the Polish election, in which the victorious Solidarity slate successfully identified itself with the image of Gary Cooper in *High Noon*—appropriating the most celebrated example of an extinct genre and a favorite movie of American presidents, as well as an allegory readable as both anti- and anti-anti-Communist.

In any case, it was Ronald Reagan's successor George H. W. Bush who presided over the breaching of the Wall; the New Year's Day 1992 dissolution of the Soviet Union; the creation of the so-called New World Order; and the publication of Francis Fukuyama's infamous essay "The End of History"—by which the writer meant the culmination of liberal democracy—which first appeared, with a question mark in the title, during the summer of 1989. Indeed, in the absence of Communism, nativist Republicans and evangelical Christians were the first to turn on liberal democracy, advancing the so-called culture war announced by the 1988 attack on *The Last Temptation of Christ*.

It was also Richard Nixon's onetime CIA director, Bush, who in December 1989 closed the book on the Iran-Contra Deal (the Democrats having failed to capitalize on his involvement) with America's first post–Cold War foreign intervention, invading Panama and deposing his former CIA asset General Manuel Noriega. Most significantly, it was Bush who, in January 1991, orchestrated Operation Desert Storm—a long-awaited and expensive antidote to the Vietnam War that, in attacking another former asset Saddam Hussein, fired the opening salvo in what would be a decades-long conflict with and within the Muslim world.*

---

* Although the Iraqi dictator Saddam Hussein, a U.S. client throughout the Iraq-Iran War, had been assured that the U.S. had no interest in supporting Kuwait against Iraqi

In the aftermath of Desert Storm, Bush achieved a popularity beyond any enjoyed by President Reagan, and also far more evanescent. The Hollywood movies released during Bush's administration were largely a pallid postscript to the Reagan era, with sequels to *Ghostbusters*, *Gremlins*, *The Terminator*, and *Back to the Future* as well as the fifth installment of *Rocky*—a melancholy devolution in which, cheated by junk-bond artists, Rocky and his wife Adrian sink back into the swamp. There may be no more pathetic an image of the Dream dispelled than this couple, Cinderellas no more, dressed in their old clothes (including her glasses), wandering through the mean streets of the old neighborhood. Pre-Reagan America!

Ambitions were low. Only a handful of Hollywood movies even attempted to address their historical moment. Spike Lee's *Do the Right Thing* was one; Ridley Scott's female buddy film *Thelma and Louise* was another. Kevin Costner's clumsy *Dances with Wolves* was a deliberate throwback—not just an attempt to revive the Western but the first time since *Reds* that an apparent liberal, albeit in actuality a Bush-supporting Republican, thought to cast himself as a Hollywood Freedom Fighter.

Dances with Wolves won an Oscar and was attacked by cultural conservatives, but it was far surpassed as a movie by Clint Eastwood's terminal Western, *Unforgiven*. Eastwood and Oliver Stone were now Hollywood's two leading filmmakers—one right-wing and the other left-wing. Stone continued to revisit the Sixties with *Born on the Fourth of July*, *The Doors*, and, most significantly, *JFK*. Had the latter film been made in 1988, it would have capped this account of Cold War cinema; released three years later in December 1991, *JFK* surely played some small part in helping forty-six-year-old Arkansas governor Bill Clinton get to the White House. Reminding America of the original Star-Pol, the last heroic Democrat elected president, and the historical trauma that helped precipitate the Sixties, the movie at the very least provided a flashback to the formative collective experience of Clinton's generation.*

Bush was brought down in 1992 by the inevitable post-Reagan recession, as well as the Savings and Loan crisis that began under Reagan, with the

---

claims, Bush reversed himself, reportedly on the advice of British prime minister Margaret Thatcher, who told him that the Falklands War had helped keep her in office.

* The uncanny film clip of avid sixteen-year-old Bill Clinton eagerly shaking hands with JFK was the campaign's key image.

third-party candidacy of H. Ross Perot ensuring the election of the first baby boom—which is to say the first rock 'n' roll—president. Clinton, the onetime New Left fellow traveler, also fulfilled Reagan's mandate. He cut welfare, reduced government, and balanced the budget. (Indeed, after Clinton's 1994 State of the Union address, cranky Reagan accused him of stealing his material.)

The first president since Calvin Coolidge without anything resembling military experience, Clinton further buried Vietnam and made friends with the Russians, or at least bon vivant Boris Yeltsin. Clinton was pleased to be nicknamed Elvis and considered by some, most famously the novelist Toni Morrison, to be an honorary black man. His wife Hillary Rodham, a self-described feminist, would eventually run twice for president, but that's another story—call it the Boomerography.*

Reigning as entertainer-in-chief over a period of relative peace and prosperity during which the Internet began its inexorable move toward redefining the Dream Life, as well as American democracy, Clinton was succeeded by a second Bush who, essentially ignorant and ill-served by his advisers, embarked on disastrous, destabilizing wars in Iraq and the Soviet graveyard, Afghanistan. Disaster films, which made a comeback under Clinton, were briefly stalled by the actual, highly cinematic disaster of 9/11 and then revived, in concert with new digital technology, as comic book movies—the key genre of twenty-first-century Hollywood.

The Panic of 2008 opened the door for Illinois senator Barack Obama, perhaps the least likely president since Abraham Lincoln, whose victory over Arizona senator John McCain all but ensured that an authentic Viet-vet would never occupy the White House. As an African American, Obama had a greater impact on popular culture than either Bush. But a Clinton restoration in the form of America's first female president was thwarted in 2016 by the surprise victory of Obama's antithesis, the real estate magnate, television star, and masterful self-promoter Donald J. Trump.

---

* Deprived of their ultimate leading man and the moral universe of the Cold War, the Hollywood movies of the 1990s were far less compelling than those of the previous decade. Still, Clinton, like John F. Kennedy, inspired a number of political thrillers—and one notable media critique, Barry Levinson's 1997 *Wag the Dog.*

Reagan Nostalgia

In 1994, the year that Quentin Tarantino's *Pulp Fiction* won the Palme d'or at the Cannes Film Festival, a few days before the midterm election in which the Republican party, led by Georgia representative Newt Gingrich and running on the promise of a "Contract with America," retook the House of Representatives, Ronald Reagan acknowledged that he was suffering from Alzheimer's disease. With a touching handwritten two-page letter, his final communiqué, the former president vanished from the public sphere.*

Reagan's lost memory turned out to be America's. Having left the White House on a wave of goodwill (despite popular dissatisfaction with his policies) and generally regarded by historians as a slightly better-than-average president (on par with Jimmy Carter and George H. W. Bush), Reagan was elevated to a realm beyond criticism. Like the forever young king of Camelot, he was now a creature of legend.

Reagan remained in a state of suspended animation for Bill Clinton's first term, but after Clinton's reelection in 1996, his star rose again. In early 1997, Grover Norquist's Americans for Tax Reform initiated the "Ronald Reagan Legacy Project," a sub-rosa campaign to rename Washington National Airport (as well as highways and government facilities across the nation) in Reagan's honor. The revelation of Clinton's tawdry sexual activities gave Reagan's presumed propriety additional luster. "The pumping up of Reagan and the taking down of Clinton seemed to draw oxygen from each other in 1998," the journalist Will Bunch notes in his account of Reagan's posthumous career, *Tear Down This Myth.*†

Washington National renamed, Reagan partisans moved to add his visage to Mount Rushmore and put it on the ten-dollar bill. George W. Bush

---

* Reagan's main concern was the perception of his legacy. His last political statement appears to be a criticism of Oliver North's claim, during his 1994 senatorial campaign, that Reagan was fully aware of the Iran-Contra Deal.

† A year after Reagan left office, a *Boston Globe* poll put his popularity at 59 percent, three points lower than Jimmy Carter's 63 percent, but slightly higher than the 53 percent approval rating that, according to the Gallup poll, Reagan averaged while in office. Other presidents' average approval ratings, according to Gallup, were Gerald Ford's 47 percent, Carter's 45.5 percent, George Bush's 61 percent, Bill Clinton's 55 percent, George W. Bush's 49 percent, and Barack Obama's 48 percent, placing Reagan below his two immediate successors.

ran for president in 2000 not as his father's son but Reagan's heir. *The Reagans*, a CBS miniseries scheduled for late 2003, was taken as a Hollywood campaign to smear Reagan's reputation, not least because the former president was played by James Brolin, then married to the prominent Clinton supporter Barbra Streisand; it was also suspected that the telefilm would give Reagan insufficient credit for saving the economy and ending the Cold War. Radio talk shows and cable news commentators were mobilized. The conservative Media Research Center called on advertisers to vet the script. Internet response was orchestrated through BoycottCBS.com. The head of the Republican National Committee demanded that CBS identify the program's fictional elements. Responding to pressure, in what the network president Leslie Moonves termed "a moral call," given the show's "liberal political agenda" and "unfair" treatment of the Reagans, CBS announced that the completed film would be substantively reedited before bouncing it down to their premium-cable affiliate, Showtime.*

Finally telecast on November 30, *The Reagans* suggested a less salacious episode of *Dynasty*, with the Australian actress Judy Davis giving a flavorsome impersonation of Nancy Reagan. The *New York Times* reviewer Alessandra Stanley described it as "a domestic drama about a loving couple beset by Hollywood agents, Republican backers, scheming advisers and, most of all, their angry, needy children." Although the show did not lack for glamour, it seemed deficient in gravitas—the Reagan presidency as just another schlocky made-for-TV movie. Indeed, Stanley suggested that it was *The Reagans*' mise-en-scène that was most likely to offend Reagan partisans: "Shot mostly in darkly lit interiors and small, enclosed spaces like hospital rooms, elevators and the presidential bedroom, the film denies Mr. Reagan the Mount Rushmore–John Ford grandeur that his image-makers worked so hard to project." That would be provided less than seven months later, with Reagan's death and funeral in June 2004.

The first presidential full state funeral in Washington, DC, since Lyndon Johnson's in 1973, Reagan's was more splendiferous than JFK's—a six-day

---

* The Moonves critique was as cynical as it was craven. A project begun at ABC in 1999, *The Reagans* was initially considered too soft and inoffensive; in taking over the production, CBS intended it to be "highly controversial."

memorial, with events in California as well as Washington, available live in its entirety to network and cable television. (Despite, or perhaps because of, the blanket coverage, cable news reported only a slight rise in viewership.) The pageant, code-named "Operation Serenade," had been decades in the works. Nancy Reagan began planning her husband's funeral after the failed assassination attempt in 1981, and continued to refine the details of the ultimately three-hundred-page plan every year since his illness was disclosed. She personally approved every particular, from the riderless black horse with her husband's boots placed backward in the stirrups, to the mourners waving fifty thousand mini–American flags, to the jet fighters zooming overhead in missing-man formation. JFK was to be eclipsed once more.

Reviewing the televised spectacle, Stanley thought the event "a sign that the country [was] hungry for a moment of unity and shared experience"— in other words, a replay of the imagined Reagan presidency. Such was the power of implanted memory that *Time* and *Newsweek* independently used the same identical portrait as the cover image for their commemorative issues—a 1980 close-up of the Stetson-wearing buckaroo candidate flashing a friendly grin. Operation Serenade had a political message as well: Ronnie le Cowboy was the man who won the Cold War and restored America's faith in itself.

The 2004 campaign stopped as Reagan upstaged his would-be heir. George W. Bush was in Normandy to commemorate D-Day's sixtieth anniversary when the former president died, thus ensuring that his remarks would be totally obliterated by continual replays of Reagan's 1984 now-classic D-Day address. While the Reagan Funeral surely did Bush's reelection campaign more good than harm, it also served to diminish his stature. By 2008, Republican history had been streamlined. Eisenhower was forgotten. Ford and the first Bush were inconsequential. Nixon and the second Bush were toxic. Reagan stood alone. In 2008, the four leading contenders for the Republican presidential nomination—former Arkansas governor Mike Huckabee, former Massachusetts governor Mitt Romney, Texas representative Ron Paul, and the eventual nominee John McCain—engaged in a televised debate at the Reagan Library competing to claim the sacred legacy.

Then, in 2016, a miracle occurred: An idea burst out of the darkness, a new sheriff appeared with a star on Hollywood Boulevard. Once again, a professional entertainer and polished salesman was elected president of the United States.*

Vulgar Reaganism

Donald Trump may be a product of Reaganism—a believer in both the gospel of glorified capitalism and elasticized truth as well as the use-value of self-celebrating patriotism—but he is not simply Reagan redux.

Trump is also a student of his generational cohort Bill Clinton, the president whose spouse he managed to defeat. For it was under Clinton that the distinctions between show business and hard news completely collapsed as an openly partisan section of media—right-wing talk radio and Fox News, launched in 1996—became a political opposition while the Internet emerged as a source of information and innuendo. Trump, like Clinton, is a Man of the Sixties and hence a veteran of the Orgy, with an appreciation for sexual license, a sense of life as a movie, and an even more megalomaniacal desire to project his personal fantasy on the screen. Before joining his father's real estate business, he had toyed with the idea of going to film school—a potential classmate of George Lucas or Martin Scorsese.

Reagan was Hollywood incarnate, a true believer in movie magic, the embodiment of happy endings and uncomplicated emotions, amusing anecdotes and conspicuous consumption, cornball patriotism and bombastic anti-Communism, cheerful bromides and a built-in production code designed to suppress any uncomfortable truth. Trump is something else. Although burnished by appearances in the tabloid press, on late-night TV, talk radio, primetime sitcoms, and parodic references in post-Reagan movies such as *Back to the Future Part II* (1989) and *Gremlins 2: The New Batch* (1990), as

---

* Less than six months after Reagan's death, Donald Trump's future adviser Steve Bannon released his documentary, *In the Face of Evil: Reagan's War in Word and Deed*, a Manichean recasting of the Reagan presidency as a crusade against Communism aka fascism, aka Islamic terrorism. "Ronald Reagan's praises are sung in an operatic documentary that rises to new heights, slipping the surly bonds of hagiography," the *New York Times* critic Ned Martel drily noted. "The Reagan biography is retold with maximum good guy-bad guy intensity and a manic dose of Hollywood histrionics, but with little film-making grace."

well as the cameo he demanded in *Home Alone 2* (1992) as the price for filming a scene in Trump Tower, he was spawned and nurtured by Hollywood's successors. Trump is a product of the cable news, talk radio, trash TV talk show, reality TV drama, social media Totality that, in the post–Cold War period, reshaped the nation's Dream Life.

"In postmodern culture, it's not TV as a mirror of society, but just the reverse: it's society as a mirror of television," Arthur Kroker had declared back in the Eighties. Didn't the Donald know it! A notable 1984 television commercial for cough medicine began with an actor from the popular soap opera *General Hospital* announcing, "I'm not a doctor but I play one on TV." That commercial, in a sense, is Trump's equivalent to *Stand Up and Cheer*—a source of revelation.

Reagan was a politician who built a career as a professional image. So too Trump. As an actor, Reagan intuitively grasped how a president (or a good Joe or action hero) is supposed to present himself. As a celebrity, Trump understood what it took to land on the front page of the *New York Post*. The only person with neither political nor military experience ever elected president, Trump was famous less for his actual real estate transactions than for a ghostwritten best-seller about real estate transactions, *The Art of the Deal*. As president, JFK became a brand; Trump already was one. This self-proclaimed billionaire made his fortune by licensing his name as an international trademark. Trump floated the idea of running for president as early as 1988 and explored the possibility of a third-party candidacy in 2000, but his ascension was an idea that almost no one, save the visionary himself, could claim to see coming.*

Having gone bankrupt numerous times, Trump made a comeback at the dawn of the twenty-first century and became a star with *The Apprentice* (NBC, 2004–7), the reality TV show that enabled him to play a gruff yet beneficent Daddy Warbucks. Shades of *The King of Comedy* and Rupert Pupkin: during the Obama administration, Trump was a regular guest on late night TV and

---

* Weirdly, Francis Fukuyama may have been one of the few. Fukuyama argued that, having defeated Communism and consequently in decline, liberal democracies might no longer be able to contain the individual's natural desire for what he called *thymia* (a desire for recognition). Capitalism's superficial celebrity culture was, he warned, prone to produce an outsized *megalothymia*, and hence likely to breed authoritarian narcissistic demagogues, citing as an example "a developer like Donald Trump."

Fox News, repeatedly advancing the lie that Obama had been born in Kenya and was thus not entitled to be president. In the hiatus between *The Apprentice* and its successor *The Celebrity Apprentice* (NBC, 2008–15) he sometimes appeared as a wrestler.*

Unlike Reagan or JFK, Trump grew up with television—not Hollywood's crafted scenarios but TV's "continuous, incoherent present," to use communications theorist Neil Postman's phrase. As a showman with experience promoting such carnivalesque events as beauty pageants and professional wrestling bouts, Trump is fluent in the principles of entertainment. However speciously, he promised abundance over scarcity and community over fragmentation. During the 2016 campaign, he contrasted his own energy to his rivals' exhaustion, posing the "honest" intensity of his racist innuendo and xenophobic rhetoric against their tired manipulation and thus further demonstrated an exciting freedom from constraint. Assimilating the logic of the blockbuster, Trump understood that publicity was more important than content. His campaign rallies were deemed to be newsworthy, broadcast live, and free of charge, on CNN.†

Trump's 2016 campaign was essentially an arena tour in which, not unlike the 1990s comedian Andrew Dice Clay, he performed a boorish, politically incorrect stand-up act. A demagogue of genius, Trump introduced the

---

* While some have seen a premonition of Trump in Mike Judge's lowbrow comedy *Idiocracy* (2006), a movie positing a moronic future in which a former wrestler is president and civilization collapses because crops are irrigated with a brain-destroying sports drink, Trump is also a synthesis of the two great movie demagogues of late 1976. One is *Network*'s rogue newscaster Howard Beale, who uses TV to articulate and organize dissent, telling viewers go to their windows and yell, "I'M AS MAD AS HELL, AND I'M NOT GOING TO TAKE THIS ANYMORE!" (That the movie impressed Trump may be gauged in his modeling *The Apprentice* boardroom after that in *Network*.) The other is Rocky or rather, *Rocky*, a movie that affected its original moviegoers viscerally: "They leave the theater beaming and boisterous, as if they'd won a door prize rather than parted with the price of a first-run ticket, and they volunteer ecstatic opinions of the film to the people waiting on line for the next show," as Frank Rich reported. Trump is only the latest of the countless American politicians who have used the *Rocky* theme as walk-on music.

† Not entirely oblivious to movies, Trump is said to regard Clint Eastwood as Hollywood's greatest star: "He and [his wife] Melania model their squints on Eastwood," according to his biographer Tim O'Brien. Eastwood's 1966 spaghetti Western triumph, *The Good, the Bad and the Ugly*, is one of Trump's five favorite films. It's striking that once elected he would turn on the universal 1990s action star Arnold Schwarzenegger who, no longer California's governor, succeeded Trump as the host of *Celebrity Apprentice* and was thus perceived as a rival.

wrestling trope that the match was fixed, conjuring imaginary enemies—Implacable Alien Others who were mainly immigrants, people of color, and the media that sustained him—while cultivating feuds and creating cartoon characters with insulting nicknames to serve as foils: Little Mario, Lyin' Ted, Crooked Hillary, Pocahontas.

Given his modest margin of victory in Pennsylvania or Michigan, it's possible Trump won the electoral vote because of his entertainment value. Some people thought him a hoot—not unlike the left-liberal cable programs, notably *The Daily Show* (Comedy Central, 1996–) and *The Colbert Report* (Comedy Central, 2005–14), that savaged George W. Bush and mocked the enemies of Barack Obama.*

A key text of the 2016 campaign, the film historian Charles Musser's *Politicking and Emergent Media: US Presidential Elections of the 1890s*, recounts four consecutive elections, analyzing their use of daily newspapers, projected slide shows, early cinema, and the phonograph. Republicans, who won three of the four, were invested in new media, both financially and strategically. The candidate most adroit in deploying new communications technology almost always prevailed.

Extrapolating forward from Musser's book, one can cite Roosevelt's successful use of radio and Eisenhower's pioneering TV commercials as well as his running mate Richard Nixon's televised mea culpa. Conventional wisdom has it that Kennedy's victory was secured by the appeal he projected during his televised debate with Nixon. Twenty years later, Reagan demonstrated a similar mastery to triumph over Jimmy Carter and Walter Mondale.

Bill Clinton was the first presidential candidate to grasp the significance of cable television, specifically MTV; Obama was the first to deploy social media, most importantly YouTube. Trump was and is defined by Twitter.

---

* Not that TV did not feature intimations of the 2016 election with a number of serious dramas or comedies showcasing crypto-Hillaries: *Veep* (HBO, 2012–19), in which, after five seasons, Julia Louis-Dreyfus lost the presidency; *Madam Secretary* (CBS, 2014–), Téa Leoni as a CIA analyst appointed secretary of state; *The Good Wife* (CBS, 2009–16), Julianna Margulies as a wronged political wife who ultimately runs for office herself; and even *Homeland* (Showtime, 2011–19), Claire Danes as the most mystical of CIA operatives. But what were these compared to *Celebrity Apprentice*?

His true innovation was the combination of TV entertainment and social media—something that any number of TV shows attempted by giving their fictional characters a social media presence.

Using the principles of reality TV and the power of Twitter, Trump was able to create the spectacle and almost immediately annotate it to an audience of fans. This powerful double spin offered a sense of community and transparency. *The Celebrity Apprentice* provided the template for Trump's presidency, with its props, stunts, and manufactured suspense. Each daily episode begins with a flurry of sound bites, delivered while Trump watches a Fox TV morning show that, knowing he is watching, delivers news items straight to him. The media then dutifully reports the tweets, which set each day's agenda as Trump creates his own distractions— pretending to consider policies that he will certainly reject, complaining that he is being hounded by a witch hunt, announcing plans to make a later announcement.

Reagan filled the national discourse with pleasing fantasies and a cheerful denial of the self-evident. His frequent untruths were typically reported as "misleading accounts," "misstatements" and "debatable assertions of fact." The public never seemed to mind—at least for his first five and a half years in office—and his aides maintained that these lies were made in service of a larger truth. Trump has thrived in a far shoddier information ecosystem that was already polluted with falsehoods and where his roustabout antics were taken for authenticity. In its way, *The Reagans* paved the way for a presidency as tawdry telefilm.

Trump lies so continuously—looking back on his campaign and first year in office, the press watchdog PolitiFact found 69 percent of his assertions to be false or mostly false—that his moments of truth are not taken seriously, as when, in 2000, he bragged, "It's very possible that I could be the first presidential candidate to run and make money on it." Distraction helps him even when it shouldn't. Scandals serve to divert attention from policies. Every day ends with Trump being ridiculed on late night TV. "In America, we are never denied the opportunity to amuse ourselves," Neil Postman wrote in 1985. "How delighted would be all the kings, czars, and führers of the past to know that censorship is not a necessity when all political discourse takes the form of a jest."

It Can Happen Here

Writing in late 2018, I cannot foresee how much longer the Trump show will last or how it will end, but I cannot imagine that the conclusion will be as happy as Reagan's. It is difficult to imagine Trump as the star of a sunny propaganda film like *A New Beginning*, although he might well be auditioning for the sequel to Steve Bannon's celebration of crusader Reagan, *In the Face of Evil.*

Hollywood was founded on the proposition that scenarios that are naturally hegemonic and usually reassuring will appeal to the largest possible audience. Conceived during the Great Depression, the Department of Amusement was given a mandate to constitute that audience. Some years later, the Hollywood Freedom Fighter cast himself as the star of an inspirational world-historical scenario. Reagan was the greatest of these, seamlessly merging the concept of "Freedom" with the gospel of "Entertainment." Unlike any of his predecessors, Trump has dispensed with unity, reassurance, and inspiration—not to mention good cheer. For him, the Department of Amusement is a megaphone for grievance and negativity. His insight is that when it comes to ratings, love and hate are identical. (It may be that Trump confuses his approval rating with television ratings: 40 percent is poor for a president but tremendous for a TV show.)

Reagan's movie was America—or rather, America as it imagined itself. Far less cornball, Trump's movie is Trump, as America imagines him. Reagan truly believed Hollywood's "noble intent" to reveal that "people everywhere share common dreams and emotions." Sincerely cornball, he reversed the process of disillusionment. In his rhetoric and scenarios, as in the films of George Lucas and Steven Spielberg and the fictional character Rocky, America's lost illusions were found, dusted off and deployed one last time. Reagan provided the nation with a new collective memory and a new representation—as well as a representative—of the national past. He was JFK Resurrected, the Duke without Nam, a cross between Dirty Harry and Indiana Jones, the Last of the Cowboys.

In addition to losing Reagan, America has lost the moral certainties of the Cold War (or the War in Vietnam). The Western vanished. The hegemony of network television and the grand illusion of Hollywood's (already lost) universality are gone. Photography has forfeited its truth claim. Even as

TV's virtual audience has become dispersed (and thus even more virtual), Hollywood's great stars are post-human Comic Book characters in fantastic, digitally contrived universes.*

As we enter the Age of Streaming, Artificial Intelligence, and Virtual Reality, it is scarcely insignificant that Trump appropriated Reagan's 1980 slogan, "Let's Make America Great Again" (albeit dropping the inclusive "let's"). Reagan invoked the imaginary Pax Americana of the Fifties. Trump invokes Reagan's now doubly imaginary Fifties, his Morning in America. As *Happy Days* became a real Fifties sitcom, so the lost reality of the Eisenhower era merged with its restoration, the Age of Reagan—the entrancing period of American self-absorption and patriotic solipsism.

Trump is a beneficiary of Reagan-nostalgia, which is to say, a nostalgia that is nostalgic for nostalgia itself—a Dream Life that, no longer Norman Mailer's "subterranean river of untapped, ferocious, lonely, and romantic desires," has been rationalized as something more stunted and primal, no longer Hollywood but Trump's Florida resort Mar-a-Lago, an imaginary gated community where, to paraphrase Hannah Arendt, everything seems possible and nothing is true.†

---

* While Reagan can easily be construed as a superhero (Ronbo!), Trump is more easily conceived, and perhaps admired, as a supervillain: a braggadocious plutocrat avidly looting the world's resources for his own personal gain, or a tabloid monster who would have amused the art-punk denizens of Club 57.

† Writing at the dawn of the Cold War, Arendt maintained that "the result of a consistent and total substitution of lies for factual truth is not that the lie will now be accepted as truth and truth be defamed as a lie, but that the sense by which we take our bearings in the real world—and the category of truth versus falsehood is among the mental means to this end—is being destroyed."

ACKNOWLEDGMENTS

In addition to pieces originally published in the *Village Voice*, I have reworked and integrated some later writing. An early version of Chapter 1 was published in *The Last Great American Picture Show* (Amsterdam University Press, 2004) and parts of Chapter 2 appear in *When the Movies Mattered: The New Hollywood Revisited* (Cornell University Press, 2019). Some material on *Gremlins* in Chapter 4 is adapted from my contribution to the Austrian Film Museum's 2013 monograph on Joe Dante; that on *The Last Temptation of Christ* draws upon an entry in the Jewish Museum catalog *Entertaining America: Jews, Movies, and Broadcasting* (Princeton University Press, 2003) as well as an article appearing in *The Forward* in 2004.

A version of the introduction was delivered as the 2014 Kracauer lecture at the Goethe-University, Frankfurt am Main; parts of the epilogue were incorporated in a presentation given in 2018 at the National School of Decorative Arts (Paris) in conjunction with the project "Politics of Distraction." I am grateful in every case for the opportunity to develop my ideas while working on a larger undertaking. In addition, like an industrious magpie, I have taken bits and pieces from articles published over the years under my byline in *Artforum, Film Comment, The Forward*, the *Los Angeles Times*, the *New York Times*, and the *Virginia Literary Quarterly*.

As important to the book as my writing was the Seminar in Current Cinema that I had the pleasure of teaching for twenty-odd summers at New York University, as well as the various undergraduate film history courses I gave at the Cooper Union during this time. In a general sense, the *Found Illusions* trilogy—which began germinating in the late 1980s—is a product of these classes. Most of my research was done at the Museum of Modern Art Study Center and the Lincoln Center Library for the Performing Arts in New York City; the Margaret Herrick Library in Beverly Hills; and the Ronald Reagan Presidential Library and Museum in Simi Valley. I also enjoyed access to three outstanding university libraries, Columbia, Harvard and NYU.

Of the many books that I read or consulted, Sidney Blumenthal's corrosive *Pledging Allegiance: The Last Campaign of the Cold War,* Lou Cannon's awe-inspiring *President Reagan: The Role of a Lifetime,* Lloyd deMause's provocative *Reagan's America,* Susan Jeffords's pioneering *Hard Bodies: Hollywood Masculinity in the Reagan Era,* David Marc's shrewd and hilarious *Comic Visions: Television Comedy and American Culture,* Garry Wills's brilliant *Reagan's America* and, of course, *The Reagan Diaries* were always at hand. So was the historic winter 1986 double issue of *Movie* that first published Andrew Britton's remarkable essay "Blissing Out: The Politics of Reaganite Entertainment."

My thanks to Andy Hsiao, who rescued the manuscript of *The Dream Life* and brought it to The New Press, to Sarah Fan, who skillfully edited *An Army of Phantoms,* and to Carl Bromley, who enthusiastically took on the final volume, as well as to copy-editor Brian Baughan. My agent Jim Rutman was a supportive presence throughout. Art Spiegelman gave me the gift of a wonderful cover illustration. I benefited from discussions with my friends Dan Czitrom, Dave Kehr, and especially the late Mel Gordon, my most supportively stimulating reader. All but the first of the interpolated *Village Voice* pieces were encouraged, edited, and improved by the marvelously perceptive Karen Durbin.

My beloved helpmeet Shelley Hoberman was as always a steadying presence. The writing of *Make My Day* coincided with the birth of our four grandchildren, Julian, Izidore, Caleb, and Elena, to whom this book is dedicated.

SOURCES

Abbreviations

AMPAS = Margaret Herrick Library, Academy of Motion Picture Arts and Sciences, Beverly Hills, CA

LAT = *Los Angeles Times*

NYT = *New York Times*

RRPL = Ronald Reagan Presidential Library, Simi Valley, CA

TRD = *The Reagan Diaries*, ed. Douglas Brinkley (New York: HarperCollins, 2007)

VV = *Village Voice*

WP = *Washington Post*

Introduction: The Department of Amusement

FN: Valenti to Deaver letter (2/4/81), RRPL.

Stand Up and Cheer! (1934)

Dyer, "Entertainment and Utopia," *Movie* #24 (Spring 1977), 3; David Platt, "What a Racket," *New Theatre* (June 1934), 19.

Benedict Anderson, *Imagined Communities: Reflections on the Origin and Spread of Nationalism* (London: Verso, 1983), passim.

FN: Anne Edwards, *Early Reagan* (New York: William Morrow, 1987), 128–9.

"Where Were You in '62" (or August 1973)?

Gerald Clarke, "The Meaning of Nostalgia," *Time* (5/3/71), 7; Dale Pollock, *Skywalking: The Life and Films of George Lucas, the creator of Star Wars* (New York: Ballantine Books, 1983), 113.

Pollock op. cit. 15; Tom Wolfe, *The Electric Kool-Aid Acid Test* (New York: Bantam Books, 1969), 34; Pollock op. cit. 50, 64, 66; Pauline Kael, "Un-People," *Reeling* (New York: Warner Books, 1977), 268.

Jameson, *Postmodernism or, The Cultural Logic of Late Capitalism* (Durham, NC: Duke University Press, 1991), 19; Baudrillard, *Simulacra and Simulation* (Ann

Arbor MI: University of Michigan Press, 1995), 45; "The Nifty Fifties," *Life* (6/12/72), 40; "Back to the '50s," *Newsweek* (10/16/72); Richard R. Lingeman, "There Was Another Fifties," *NYT Magazine* (6/17/73).

Jameson op. cit. 25; Kracauer, "The Group as Bearer of Ideas," *The Mass Ornament* (Cambridge MA: Harvard University Press, 1995), 143f; John J. O'Connor, "'Happy Days' and 'Chopper One' Prove Familiar Fare as A.B.C. Entries," *NYT* (1/17/74); Cyclops, "It Wasn't All Ponytails," *NYT* (2/10/74); Les Brown, "Pre-color TV Era Enjoying Revival," *NYT* (1/23/75); Donald Lyons, "Flaws in the Iris: The Private Eye in the Seventies," *Film Comment* (July/August 1993); David Marc, *Comic Visions: Television Comedy and American Culture* 2nd edition (Malden, MA: Blackwell Publishers, 1997), 177.

FN: Jacques Ellul, *Propaganda: The Formation of Men's Attitudes* (New York: Vintage Books, 1973), 64ff.

Found Illusions

Horkheimer and Adorno, *Dialectic of Enlightenment* (New York: Seabury Press, 1972), 144; Ellul op. cit. 87; Fred Pfeil, *Another Tale to Tell: Politics and Narrative in Postmodern Culture* (London: Verso, 1990), 111.

I. *Nashville* Contra *Jaws*, 1975

"Indochina: The Anatomy of a Debacle," *Time* (4/13/75); Wood, *Hollywood from Vietnam to Reagan* (New York: Columbia University Press, 1986), 29; Sontag, "The Imagination of Disaster," *Against Interpretation and Other Essays* (New York: Dell, 1966), 21; Horkheimer and Adorno op. cit. 158; *Time* (6/10/74), 158.

Kael, "On the Future of Movies," *Reeling* op. cit. 427; Nora Sayre, "Earthquake," *NYT* (11/16/74); Irwin Allen in Herbert J. Gans, "Only the Stars Survive," *Social Policy* (Jan/Feb 1975) v5 #5, 51.

FN: Allen in Gans op. cit.

Watergate Unplugged

Carl Gottlieb, *The Jaws Log* (New York: Dell, 1975), 177; "making it up as we go along" in David Halpern, "At Sea with Steven Spielberg," *Take One* (Mar–Apr 1974), 10; Reston, "Lingering Tragedy," *NYT* (9/25/74); Edith Blake, *The Making of the Movie Jaws* (New York: Ballantine, 1975), 116; Kopechne visit, *NYT* (5/16/74); "Settlement Is Reported with Kopechne Parents," *NYT* (7/12/74); Robert Sherrill, "Chappaquiddick Plus 5," *NYT Magazine* (7/14/74); William Shannon, "The Kennedy Problem," *NYT* (8/18/74); Reston op. cit.; Kael, "Coming: *Nashville*," *Reeling* op. cit. 591; Ted Morgan, "Sharks," *NYT Magazine* (4/21/74), 10–11ff; Turan, "Jaws," *The Progressive* (July 1975).

"Smoking dope and having good parties" in "From the Heartland," *Time* (6/16/75);

Spielberg in Chris Holdenfield, "The Sky Is Full of Questions," *Rolling Stone* (1/26/78), 35; Julia Phillips, *You'll Never Eat Lunch in This Town Again* (New York: Random House, 1991), 140; "Altman Surveys 'Nashville' and Sees 'Instant' America," *NYT* (6/13/75); Kael, "Coming: *Nashville*," op. cit. 593; "Summer of the Sharks," *Time* (6/23/75); "A Strong but Risky Show of Force," *Time* (5/26/75); *Newsweek* (5/26/75); Sidey, "An Old-Fashioned Kind of Crisis," *Time* (5/26/75).

FN: "Strong but Risky," *Time* (5/26/75) op. cit.

The Spirit of '56, Twenty Years Later

Tewkesbury, "Introduction," *Nashville* (New York: Bantam, 1976), unpaginated.

Wicker, "Nashville—Dark Perceptions in a Country-Music Comedy," *NYT* (6/15/75); Mazzocco, "Letter from Nashville," *New York Review of Books*; Marcus, "Ragtime and Nashville: Failure-of-America Fad," *VV* (8/4/75); David Brudnoy, "Their Town," *National Review* (8/15/75); "Nixon Plays Piano on Wife's Birthday at Grand Ole Opry," *NYT* (3/17/74); Bill Hance, "'Nashville' Premiere Churns Sour Reaction," *Nashville Banner* (8/9/75).

Robert Hatch, "Films," *Nation* (7/5/75); Wicker op. cit.; Brudnoy op. cit.; Reagan and Howard Phillips in Jules Witcover, *Marathon: The Pursuit of the Presidency 1972-1976* (Viking, New York: 1977), 46–47; Kevin Phillips, "Nashville Candidate: Has Fiction Become Fact in '76 Race?," *TV Guide* (2/21–27/76).

FN: Chilton Williamson, Jr., "Nashville Sound," *Harper's* (Sept 1975), 78. FN: "Denver to Star in New 'Mr. Smith,'" *NYT* (12/1/74)

The Entertainment Machine

Horkheimer and Adorno op. cit. 134; Carl Gottlieb op. cit. 17.

Kurt Vonnegut, Jr. "Nashville," *Vogue* (October 1975), 103; "directing the audience with an electric cattle prod," Richard Combs, "Primal Screen: An interview with Steven Spielberg," *Sight and Sound* (Spring 1977).

"I took the Mafia out of it," *Take One* op. cit.; *Time* (7/28/75); *NYT* (07/16/75) "Swimmers More Timid," *NYT* (7/16/75).

Time (6/23/75) op. cit.; Stephen Farber, "Jaws and Bug—The Only Difference Is Hype," *NYT* (8/24/75); *Newsweek* (7/28/75); Vonnegut op. cit.; *Boston Phoenix* (6/4/74); "Jaws should never have been made" in *Time* (6/23/75) op. cit.; Gottlieb op. cit. 115.

FN: "I wanted to do *Jaws* for hostile reasons" in *Time* (6/23/75) op. cit. 44. FN: Eco, *Travels in Hyperreality* (San Diego: Harcourt Brace Jovanovich, 1986), 57.

They Love Us in Hiroshima!

Nixon to Altman inquiring how to get a "cassette" copy of *Nashville*, www.reddit .com/r/movies/comments/62g73u/a_letter_from_richard_nixon_to_robert _altman; Carl Gottlieb op. cit. 144.

Time (6/23/75) op. cit.; Howard Whitman, "Dynamism + Dior = Hiroshima + 30," *NYT* (2/16/75).

FN: Les Brown, "'Jaws' Played to 80 Million on ABC," *NYT* (11/7/79).

II. Born Again in the U.S.A., 1976–80

Canby, "Redford a C.I.A. Eccentric in 'Three Days of Condor,'" *NYT* (9/25/75); Berman, *On the Town: One Hundred Years of Spectacle in Times Square* (New York: Random House, 2006), 187; Phillips, *You'll Never Eat Lunch in This Town Again* op. cit. 212; Reagan in Rick Perlstein, *The Invisible Bridge: The Fall of Nixon and the Rise of Reagan* (New York: Simon and Schuster, 2014), 516; Phillips op. cit. 210.

Patrick Anderson, "A Peanut Farmer for President" *NYT Magazine* (12/14/75); Safire, "Night of the Center Right," *NYT* (2/26/76).

FN: McGilligan, *Clint: The Life and Legend* (New York: St. Martin's Press, 2002), 266. FN: Stuart Byron, "Second Annual Grosses Gloss," *Film Comment* (Mar/Apr 1977), 35.

Jimmy Carter's *Rocky* Road

"one of the smartest men" in James T. Wootenmarch, "Carter's Drive from Obscurity to Front," *NYT* (3/15/76); Eleanor Coppola, *Notes on the Making of Apocalypse Now* (New York: Limelight Editions, 1991), 27; "almost evangelical" in "Contrast in Appeal Shown by Carter and Humphrey," *NYT* (4/28/76); Coppola op. cit. 51; "If I become president" in Benjamin Breen, "Dear Space Aliens: Hello! Love, Jimmy Carter," www.slate.com/human-interest/2013/10/jimmy-carter-the-president-s-letter-on-the-voyager-probe.html; Mailer, "The Search for Jimmy Carter," *NYT* (9/26/76).

Davis Shear, *Philadelphia Sunday Bulletin* Entertainment/Arts (12/19/76), 1, 2; Frank Rich, "'Rocky' Hits a Nerve," *NY Post* (12/4/76), 22; Flatley quoted in Stuart Byron, "Rocky and His Friends, *Film Comment* (Jan–Feb 1977), 37; Pete Hamill, "Rocky KOs Movie Biz," *VV* (11/8/76), 12; *Time* (11/15/78); Stallone in Judy Klemesrud, "'Rocky Isn't Based on Me,' Says Stallone, 'But We Both Went the Distance,'" *NYT* (11/28/76); Beth Gillin Pombeiro, *Philadelphia Inquirer* Arts & Leisure (11/21/76), 1-H; Simon, "Stallone's Ring of Truth," *New York* (11/29/76).

FN: Richard Reeves, "Lots of footwork, no footnotes," *NYT Book Review* (4/18/76).

The Next *Next Voice You Hear*

Canby, "Cynical Cinema Is Chic," *NYT* (11/21/76); Kael "Stallone and Stahr," *When the Lights Go Down* (New York: Holt, Rhinehart and Winston, 1980), 213; Rich, *NY Post* (12/4/76) op. cit. 22.

Ernest Schier, "The Hollywood Movie Hero Has Returned," *Philadelphia Bulletin* (1/9/77); Miller, *Seeing Through Movies* (New York: Pantheon Books, 1990), 216;

Canby, "'Rocky,' Pure 30's Make-Believe," *NYT* (11/22/76); Rich, *NY Post* (12/4/76) op. cit.; Kael, "Stallone and Stahr" op. cit. 213; Maslin, "Knockout," *Newsweek* (11/29/76), 113; "I knew Carter was going to win" in Gillin Pombeiro op. cit. 6-H; Flaherty, "The First Three Rocky Movies Were Nothing but White Wish Fulfillment, *Film Comment* (July–Aug 1982).

Variety (5/25/77); Coppola in Steve Daly, "Behind the Scenes of 'The Phantom Menace,'" *Entertainment Weekly* (3/26/99); Lucas in Bill Moyers, "Of Myth and Men," *Time* (4/18/99); *Skywalking* op. cit. 157, see also J. Hoberman, "The Force Will Always Be with Us," *VV* (5/12/99), 48; Clancy Sigal, "Anodyne," *The Spectator* (10/24/1977), 34; Frank Allnutt, *The Force of Star Wars* (Van Nuys CA: Bible Voice, Inc.), 168; Spielberg in Jerzy Kosinski, "Close Encounter with Spielberg," *Newsweek* (11/21/77), 98; Kauffmann, "Epiphany," *New Republic* (12/10/77), 20; *Today's Student* in John Shelton Lawrence and Robert Jewett, *The Myth of the American Superhero* (Grand Rapids, MI: Eerdmans, 2002), 349; Westerbeck, "Keeping in Touch," *Commonweal* (3/17/77), 179.

Tom Zito, "Zooming In from the Beyond for a Successor to 'Jaws' . . ." *WP* (8/11/76), B3; Jack Kroll, "The UFO's Are Coming," *Newsweek* (11/21/77), 88; Frank Rich, "The Aliens Are Coming!," *Time* (11/7/77), 102; Westerbeck op. cit.; Haskell, "The Dumbest Story Ever Told," *New York* (12/5/77), 143; Rich, *Time* op. cit. 103.

Warga, "The Film That Watergate Got Off the Ground," *LAT* (1/30/77), S36; Gregg Kilday, "The Space Shot as a Sham," *LAT* (10/13/76), F9; Benedict Nightingale "'What If a Mars Landing Were Faked?' Asks Peter Hyams," *NYT* (5/28/78), 11; Champlin, "The Making of a Movie-Movie," *LAT* View (7/14/78); Hyams in NYT (5/28/78) op. cit. 22.

FN: Stallone in *NYT* (11/28/76). FN: Phillips op. cit. 139. Chris Hodenfield, "The Sky Is Full of Questions!!," *Rolling Stone* (1/26/78). FN: Hodenfield op. cit. FN: French, "Space Flight to Nowhere," *The Observer* (1/14/79), 17. Alex Beam, "Capricorn One, Two, Three," *Boston Globe* (5/10/11).

Disc-O-pocalypse Now

Kael, "Nirvana," *When the Lights Go Down* op. cit. 376; Sarris, *VV* (12/26/77); *Variety* (12/14/77); Rich, *Time* (12/9/77); Buckley, "Tribal Rites of Our New Society," *NY Post* (4/6/78).

Denby, "A Man of Honor," *New York* (9/4/78), 88; Biskind, *Easy Riders, Raging Bulls: How the Sex-Drugs-and-Rock 'n' Roll Generation Saved Hollywood* (New York: Simon and Schuster, 1998), 368; H. Bruce Franklin, *M.I.A. or Mythmaking in America* (Chicago: Lawrence Hill Books, 1992), 134; Canby, *NYT* (12/15/78); Kael, "The God-Bless-America Symphony," *When the Lights Go Down* op. cit. 518.

"We were all asleep" in Charles Freund, "Pods Over San Francisco," *Film Comment*

(Jan–Feb 1979); Sarris, "Peas in a Pod," *VV* (12/25/78), 46; Kael, "Pods," *When the Lights Go Down* op. cit. 523–24.

Coppola 40th birthday in Biskind op. cit. 373; "Izvestia Assails Oscar for 'The Deer Hunter,'" *NYT* (4/12/79).

Milius and Lucas in Pollock op. cit. 140; Coppola in Joe Brown, "Hearts of Darkness: A Filmmaker's Apocalypse," *WP* (1/17/92); Kauffmann in Jon Lewis, *Whom God Wishes to Destroy: Francis Coppola and the New Hollywood* (Durham NC: Duke University Press, 1995), 51.

FN: Nadia Khomami, "Disco's Saturday Night Fiction, *The Guardian* (6/26/2016). FN: Kathleen Belew's *Bring the War Home: The White Power Movement and Paramilitary America* (Cambridge: Harvard University Press, 2018), 56f, 140f. FN: 29th Berlin International Film Festival Yearbook, www.berlinale.de/en /archiv/jahresarchive/1979/01_jahresblatt_1979/01_Jahresblatt_1979.html.

Spielberg Strikes Out and *The Empire Strikes Back*

McBride, *Steven Spielberg: A Biography* (New York: Simon and Schuster, 1997), 300; "I'm scared" in "Animal House Goes to War," *Time* (4/16/79), 97; "utter horror" and "total conceptual disaster" in Chris Hodenfield, "'1941': Bombs Away!," *Rolling Stone* (1/24/80), 37; Stuart Byron, "Expensively Made in U.S.A.," *Village Voice* (8/13/79), 50.

"I'll spend the rest of my life disowning this picture," "From the first day," "kids will see similarities" in Bill Davidson, "Will '1941' Make Spielberg a Billion-Dollar Baby," *NYT* (12/9/79); "Making a movie, any movie, is like fighting a hand-to-hand war" in Hodenfield, *Rolling Stone* (1/24/80) op. cit. 42; "I opened up the letter" in ibid. 42; McBride op. cit. 131n; earlier version of *1941* screenplay, ibid. 302; Farber, "Nuts!," *New West* (1/14/80), 59; Sragow and Champlin in McBride op. cit. 309; Canby, *NYT* (12/14/79).

O'Conner in Edwin Diamond and Stephen Bates, *The Spot: The Rise of Political Advertising on Television* (Cambridge MA: MIT Press, 1988), 280f; "For Reagan, the Stump Is a Stage," Clyde Haberman, *NY Post* [clipping nd]; Maslin, *NYT* (5/23/80); Maslin, *NYT* (6/11/80).

Variety (5/9/80); Grenier, "Celebrating Defeat," *Commentary* (August 1980), 58; Fred Hauptfuhrer and Karen Peterson, "Up Front," *People* (6/9/80), 38; "Text of Reagan's Speech Accepting the Republicans' Nomination; Economy, Defense, Energy 'Trust Me' Government Pattern for Nation," *NYT* (7/18/80), 8.

III. Bad Trips, 1981–82

FN: Garry Wills, *Reagan's America* (New York: Penguin Books, 1988), 206–7. FN: Michael Rogin, *Ronald Reagan, the Movie and Other Episodes in Political Demonology* (Berkeley CA: University of California Press), 24; David Platt, "Warners 'This Is the Army' Is a Terrific War Musical Full of Fun and Vigor," *Daily Worker* (8/-/43). FN: Rogin op. cit. 38; *NYT* (4/5/52). FN: Kathleen Sharp, *Mr. and Mrs. Hollywood: Edie and Lew Wasserman and Their Entertainment Empire* (New York: Carroll and Graf, 2003), 79–80. FN: Kathleen Hall Jamieson, *Packaging the Presidency: Third Edition* (New York: Oxford University Press, 1996), 407. FN: Tuchman papers, AMPAS. FN: Mark Weinberg, *Movie Nights with the Reagans: A Memoir* (New York: Simon and Schuster, 2018), 109.

The Time Is Now

Carter's "meanness" in Jamieson op. cit. 410.
Canby, *NYT* (11/18/80).
FN: Kael, "Stallone and Stahr" op. cit. 215.

Being There with Ronald Reagan

Lynn Rosellini, "Glittering Festivities Usher In Reagan Era," *NYT* (1/21/81); Hinckley material drawn from "President Ronald Reagan Assassination Attempt—John Hinckley FBI Files," www.paperlessarchives.com/reagan_assassination_attempt.html; Aaron Latham, "The Dark Side of the American Dream," *Rolling Stone* (8/5/82); Douglas Linder, "The Trial of John W. Hinckley, Jr.," http://www.law.umkc.edu/faculty/projects/ftrials/hinckley/hinckleyaccount.htmil; and Donald Cupps, "John W. Hinckley, Jr: A Case of Narcissistic Personality Disorder," *Pastoral Psychology* 62 (2013); New Year's Eve monologue in Lindner op. cit.; "a fantasy of shooting up Congress" in Latham op. cit.

Lloyd deMause, *Reagan's America* (New York: Creative Roots, 1984), 13; "Ask Travis" in Daniel Schorr, "Hinckley: Media Freak," *NYT* (5/10/82); Schrader in radio interview, "Fresh Air" (Philadelphia: WHYY, 8/30/2017), also Mahita Gajanan, "What to Know About John Hinckley Jr.," *Time* (7/27/16).

Allen, *VV* (12/24/79); Rich, *Time* (1/14/80); Goodman, *LAT* (3/27/80); Jack Rosenthal, "Being There," *NYT* (7/22/80); Wills, *Baltimore Sun* (4/9/82); "Reagan's Sources" (letter), *NYT* (2/20/83); Howell Raines, "Political Drama Surrounds the First Speech Since Attack," *NYT* (4/29/81); deMause op. cit. 15; "Iron Man Reagan," *NY Post* (3/21/81); D'Amato in *NY Post* (4/29/81).

FN: deMause op. cit. 11–13.

Raiders, *Reds*, and the Return of the Hollywood Freedom Fighter

TRD, 24; "By Raiding Hollywood Lore and His Childhood Fantasies, Steven Spielberg Rediscovers an Ark That's Pure Gold," *People* (7/20/81); *Variety* (6/1/81); "Slam! Bang! A Movie Movie," *Time* (6/15/81); Kauffmann, "Old Ark, New Covenant," *New Republic* (7/4–11/81); "My films are closer to amusement-park rides," *Time* (6/15/81) op. cit.

McBride op. cit. 312; Canby, *NYT* (6/12/81); Leogrande and Reed, *Daily News* (6/12/81); Hootkins in John Baxter, *Steven Spielberg* (New York: Harper Collins, 1996), 211; "If I could be a dream figure" in McBride op. cit. 312; "I was the Indiana Jones behind the camera" in ibid. 322; Tomasulo, "Mr. Jones Goes to Washington: Myth and Religion in Raiders of the Lost Ark," *Quarterly Review of Film Studies* v7 #4 (Fall 1982), 332.

Kael, "The Devil in the Flesh," *Taking It All In* (New York: Holt, Rinehart, Winston, 1984), 269; *TRD*, 46, 50; William Greider, "The Education of David Stockman," *The Atlantic* (December 1982).

Variety (12/2/81); Denby, "Badge of Courage, *New York* (12/14/81); Kauffmann, "Warren Beatty's Triumph," *New Republic* (12/16/81); Kehr, "Historical Present," *Chicago Reader* (12/11/81); Canby, "Film View: Why 'Reds' Succeeds and 'Ragtime' Doesn't," *NYT* Arts & Leisure (12/6/81); Lerner, "Reed: A Red-Blooded Revolutionary," *NY Post* [MoMA clipping nd]; Geng, "Radical Cheekbones," *Soho Weekly News* (12/8/81); Simon, "To Russia, with Love," *National Review* (1/22/82); Sarris, *VV*; Podhoretz "Seeing Reds," *Harper's* (Feb 1982), 75–76.

Beatty in Chris Nashawaty, "Warren Beatty in His Unlikely Friendship with Ronald Reagan," *Entertainment Weekly* (11/11/16); "Washington Talk," *NYT* (12/8/81), A4; Podhoretz op. cit. 76; Denby, *New York* (12/14/81) op. cit.; *Barron's* cited in "Reds Is Coming," *The Tattler* (March 1982); McDonald in "Required Reading," *NYT* (12/28/81); Phillips and Irvine in "President Lends Prestige to Beatty's 'Reds' Film," *Human Events* (12/19/81); Buckley, "On Seeing Reds," *WP* (1/21/82); "Some blamed the deputy chief of staff," Kitty Kelley, *Nancy Reagan: The Unauthorized Biography* (New York: Simon and Schuster, 1991), 398; Podhoretz op. cit. 76.

FN: Wilson in Hoberman, *An Army of Phantoms: American Movies and the Making of the Cold War* (New York: The New Press, 2011), 263n. FN: Weinberg op. cit. 41ff. FN: Pikser, interview, New York City (1/3/2018).

Noisy Ghosts

Scorsese in J. Hoberman, "King of Outsiders," *VV* (2/15/83); *TRD* 69; "Reagan Seems Confused on Vietnam's History," *NYT* (2/19/82); *TRD*, 74; Kelley op. cit. 373; *TRD*, 75–76.

Clarens, "Barbarians Now," *Film Comment* (May–June 1982), 26; Milius ran the set in mock-military fashion in *US* (7/20/82); *Mad* (December 1982); Denby, *New York* (5/24/82); "Claim Conan Best Ever in Germany," *Daily Variety* (9/8/82); Wood, *From Vietnam to Reagan* op. cit. 172; Rickey, "Conan and the Reaganauts," *VV* (5/18/82); *People* (6/7/82); Schwarzenegger in *NY Post* (6/7/82).

Eastwood to Reagan letter (4/15/82) and Reagan to Eastwood letter (5/7/82) #82057 RRPL; Weinberger in *People* (6/28/82); *Variety* (6/16/82); Canby, *NYT* (6/18/82);

Denby, *New York* (6/28/18); Richard Grenier, "Summertime Visions," *Commentary* (August 1982), 66; Kehr, "Vanishing Point," *Chicago Reader* [MoMA files nd].

TRD, 90; "Night Time" treatment (3/31/80), AMPAS.

Canby, *NYT* (6/4/82); Denby, "Night Moves," *New York* (6/7/82); *Variety* (5/19/82); David Ehrenstein, "The Hollow Horror of Spielberg's *Poltergeist*," *LA Reader* (6/4/82); Jon Carroll, "Ghosts from San Rafael," *San Francisco*, 44; Spielberg in *Time* (5/31/82); "Nancy Reagan was crying" in "Director Steven Spielberg Takes the Wraps Off E.T., Revealing His Secrets at Last," *People* (8/23/82), 81, see also Open Minds: UFO News and Investigations (6/6/11), www.openminds.tv /spielberg-confirms-reagan-705/10057.

FN: Kelley op. cit. 372. FN: *TRD*, 88.

The Whatsit of the Year: *E.T.* or *Blade Runner*?

"Talk of the Town," *New Yorker* (7/19/82), 24; deMause op. cit. 86; Reed quoted in Mason Wiley and Damien Bona, *Inside Oscar* (New York: Ballantine Books, 1986), 616; "Falling asleep in your lounge chair" in Todd McCarthy, "Sand Castles," *Film Comment* (May–June 1982), 54; Kael, "The Pure and the Impure," *Taking It All In* op. cit. 348; Will, *Newsweek* (7/19/82), 76; "a broad-based story" in David Breskin, "Steven Spielberg: The Rolling Stone Interview," *Rolling Stone* (10/24/85); Barthes, *Mythologies* (New York: Hill and Wang, 1972), 153; *TRD*, 100.

Don Steinberg, "The Curse of 'Blade Runner,'" *Premiere* (October 1991); Denby, *New York* (6/28/82), 54; Kael, "Baby, the Rain Must Fall," *Taking It All In* op. cit. 365; Sragow in J. Hoberman, *The Magic Hour: Film at Fin de Siècle* (Philadelphia: Temple University Press, 2003), 18; Stephen Schiff, "The Crock of the New," *Boston Phoenix* (6/29/82), 12; Grenier, "Summertime Visions" op. cit. 67f; Eco, "*Casablanca*: Cult Movies and Intertextual Collage," *Travels in Hyperreality* (San Diego: Harcourt Brace Jovanovich, 1986), 208; *L.A. 2000* in Mike Davis, *Ecology of Fear: Los Angeles and the Imagination of Disaster* (New York: Vintage, 1999), 359; Peter Wollen, "Delirious Projections," *Sight and Sound* (August 1992), 26; "Making the Everyday Seem Unique," *Time* (1/3/83), 41.

Drawing *First Blood*

O'Connor, "TV: Vietnam Veterans, U.S. Crimes and Prison," *NYT* (7/15/82), C22; Carhart in Christopher Buckley, "The Wall," *Esquire* (September 1985), 66; other critics in Marita Sturken, "The Wall, the Screen, and the Image," *Representations* 35 (Summer 1991), 122; Wolfe "Art Disputes War: The Battle of the Vietnam Memorial," *WP* (10/13/82), B4. Price in Buckley, "The Wall" op. cit. 66.

"Five Novels," *NYT* (6/18/72); *Variety* (10/27/82); Reed, "Violence & Gore Galore as Sly Draws 'First Blood,'" *NY Post* (10/22/82); Ebert, "Stallone Does the Unlikely," *Chicago Sun-Times* (10/22/82).

TRD, 114, 115; "Private Raid on Laos Reported," *NYT* (2/1/83); Richard E. Meyer and Mark Gladstone, "Eastwood Told Reagan of Planned POW Raid," *LAT* (2/25/83). See also H. Bruce Franklin, *Vietnam and Other American Fantasies* (Amherst: University of Massachusetts Press, 2000), 189–90.

FN: Kelley op. cit. 373. FN: Franklin, *M.I.A., or, Mythmaking in America* op. cit. 54. FN: Seth Rosenfeld, *Subversives: The FBI's War on Student Radicals, and Reagan's Rise to Power* (New York: Farrar, Strauss and Giroux, 2012), 494. FN: Jerry Lembcke, *The Spitting Image: Myth, Memory, and the Legacy of Vietnam* (New York: New York University Press, 1998), 78.

IV. "I Ain't Afraid of No Ghost!," 1983–84

"visibly alarmed" in *NYT* (2/15/83).

Kroker and Cook, *The Postmodern Scene: Excremental Culture and Hyper-Aesthetics* (New York: St. Martin's Press, 1986), 268; Ellul op. cit. 175.

Dyer op. cit. 177; *WP* (1/16/83); deMause op. cit. 127.

FN: Shapiro in Peter W. Kaplan, "Why the Rich Rule the TV Roost," *NYT* (4/7/85). FN: Schroeder in "At Its 50th Birthday, Teflon Still as Slick as Ever," *LAT* (4/5/88). FN: Greil Marcus, "Speaker to Speaker," *Artforum* (Nov 1985). FN: Kael, "Jokers," *Taking It All in* op. cit. 461. FN: Kael, "Anybody Home?," *State of the Art* (New York: E.P. Dutton, 1985), 24.

"Star Wars," *WarGames*, and Yuppies

TRD, 134; *TRD*, 135; Joan Didion, *Salvador* (New York: Simon and Schuster, 1983), 19; deMause op. cit. 137; *TRD*, 140.

Anderson to Dever [sic] letter (4/25/83), #101224, RRPL; *WP* (5/25/83); Gary Arnold, *WP* (5/22/83); Canby, *NYT* (5/25/83); *Variety* (5/11/83); Denby, *New York* (6/6/83); Sarris, *VV* (6/7/83); Lou Cannon, "President Goes to the Movies, Skips New Hampshire for Now," *WP* (6/13/83); "'WarGames' Is a Blast at the Box Office, but a Bomb at the Pentagon," *People* (8/15/83).

Time (7/18/83); *Inquiry* (July 1983); Maslin, *NYT* (8/5/83); Denby, "Supply-Side Hero," *New York* (8/22/83); new ending, Dana Harris, "At 20, 'Risky' Is Still Frisky," *Variety* (6/18/01), 54; Julie Salamon, "The Comex on Screen: Zooming Into the Futures," *Wall Street Journal* (8/5/83), 21; "Rich Man, Poor Man, Beggarman, Twit," *Newsweek* (6/20/83); Schickel, "Down the Tubes, Up the Ladder," *Time* (6/13/83); Denby, *New York* (6/27/83), 58; Denby, "Supply-Side Hero" op. cit.; Maslin, *NYT* (6/8/83); Sarris, *VV* (6/21/83), 49.

Dave Kehr, "Saluting the Sixties," *Chicago* (October 1983), 140; Rex Reed, *NY Post* (9/23/83).

FN: deMause op. cit. 137. FN: "Reagan Presses Call for Antimissile Plan Before Space Group," *NYT* (3/30/85). FN: Rogin op. cit. 2; Wills, *Reagan's America* op.

cit. 427; Cannon op. cit. 290–91. FN: Hoberman, "War Bond," *VV* (6/21/83). FN: "FBI 'WarGames' Raid Nets 10 Whiz Kids," *NY Post* (10/14/83); Scott Brown, "Wargames: A Look Back at the Film That Turned Geeks and Phreaks into Stars," *Wired* (July 2008). FN: Belew, *Bring the War Home* op. cit. 104. FN: Alison Mitchell, "Clinton Has $10 Million Wish for Birthday Bash," *NYT* (8/19/96).

The Day After the Conquest of Grenada

Maslin, "Daniel, A Question of Justice," (8/26/83); Kael, "Sex and Politics," *State of the Art* op. cit. 43; Michael Blowen, "Filmmakers Staunchly Defend Their Daniel," *Boston Globe* (9/18/83).

Seymour M. Hersh, *"The Target Is Destroyed": What Really Happened to Flight 007 and What America Knew About It* (New York: Vintage, 1987), passim; Patrick Leigh Fermor, *The Traveler's Tree: A Journey Through the Caribbean Islands* (New York: New York Review Books, 2011), 184; "thoroughly planned crisis" in *The Progressive* (January 1984); "We blew them away" in *WP* (11/6/83); "most popular invasion since *E.T.*" in *WP* (11/3/83); "Reagan's Youthful Boomlet," *Time* (10/8/84).

Bob Woodward, *Veil: The Secret Wars of the CIA 1981–1987* (New York: Simon and Schuster, 1987), 294–96; Nate Jones (ed.), *Able Archer 83* (New York: The New Press, 2016), passim. Stoddard in Steven Church, *The Day After the Day After* (New York: Soft Skull Press, 2010), 59; "ABC Film Depicting Consequences of Nuclear Attack Stirring Debate," *NYT* (10/6/83); Wick to Reagan memo (10/7/83) #16780655, RRPL; *TRD*, 185–86; Senior Staff Meeting Action Items (11/18/83) #185361, RRPL; "Administration Mounts Drive to Counter Atom War Film," *NYT* (11/19/83); *TRD*, 199; *Chicago Tribune* (11/20/83); John Corry, "'The Day After': TV as a Rallying Cry," *NYT* (11/20/83); "Concrete Barriers Installed at White House Gate," *NYT* (12/4/83).

Denby, "The Last Angry Men," *New York* (1/16/84); Bregman in Enrique Fernández, "Scarface Died for My Sins," *VV* (12/20/83); Corliss, "Say Good Night to the Bad Guy," *Time* (12/5/83), 96; Sarris, "Pacino's Cuban Capone Comes a Cropper," *VV* (12/13/83).

Kael, "Vanity, Vainglory, and Lowlife," *State of the Art* op. cit. 119; Aljean Harmetz, "2 Holiday Movies Turn Into Surprise Successes," *NYT* (2/13/84).

FN: Elida Moreno, "Panama's Noriega: CIA Spy Turned Drug-Running Dictator," *Reuters World News* (5/30/17), https://www.reuters.com/article/us-panama -noriega-obituary/panamas-noriega-cia-spy-turned-drug-running-dictator -idUSKBN18Q0NW. FN: See Stephen Rebello, "The Resurrection of Tony Montana," *Playboy* (December 2011), 64ff.

The Right Stuff at the Wrong Time

Cuomo and Glenn in Jack W. Germond and Jules Witcover, *Wake Us When It's*

Over: Presidential Politics of 1984 (New York: Macmillan, 1985), 105–6; Diamond and Bates op. cit. 18; *Variety* (2/27/63); *Hollywood Reporter* (2/27/63); Rick Lyman, "Why a Movie Might Alter John Glenn's Presidential Race," *Philadelphia Inquirer* (7/17/83).

Howell Raines, "Politics: For Glenn, 'The Right Stuff' Seems to Be Right," *NYT* (9/21/83); Curtis Wilkie, "Film Could Be 'The Right Stuff' for Glenn," *Boston Globe* (10/17/83); Winkler in "From Hero to Candidate," *Time* (10/3/83), 59; Kaufman in Raines, "Politics: Hart's Tactics, Askew's Train and Film Anxieties," *NYT* (10/19/83); "Glenn Meets the Dream Machine," *Newsweek* (10/3/83), 36.

Ansen, "A Movie with All the Right Stuff," ibid. 41, 43; Schickel. "Saga of a Magnificent Seven," *Time* (10/3/83), 57; Raines, *NYT* (9/21/83) op. cit.; *Boston Globe* (10/17/83); Kaufman to Dingilian (10/26/83), *The Right Stuff* file, AMPAS; *TRD*, 214.

John Corry, "TV: Coverage of Hart," *NYT* (3/16/84); Steven V. Roberts, "Hart Taps a Generation of Young Professionals," *NYT* (3/18/84); Mudd interview, Germond and Witcover op. cit. 199; Caddell to Hart, ibid. 134; Hedrick Smith, "U.S. Latin Force in Place If Needed, Officials Report," *NYT* (4/23/84), 1.

Bruce Bawer, "My Turn: Ronald Reagan as Indiana Jones," *Newsweek* (8/27/84).

Lou Cannon, *President Reagan: The Role of a Lifetime* (New York: Simon and Schuster, 1991), 485–86.

FN: Aljean Harmetz, "Right Stuff, Wrong Results," *NYT* (3/7/84). FN: "Hart Taps," *NYT* (3/18/84).

We begin bombing in five minutes . . . who you gonna call?

David Chute, "Dante's Inferno," *Film Comment* (June 1984), 23; Scott Rosenberg, *Boston Phoenix* [nd]; Canby, "'Gremlins,' Kiddie Gore," *NYT* (6/8/84).

Chute op. cit. 26–27; "Gremlins Promo Biggest in Warner Bros. History," *Variety* (6/6/84); "High Hopes for 'Gremlins' Merchandise," *Variety* (6/27/84); Janet Maslin, "Why Gremlins' Audiences Emitted Sound of 'Aaah!,'" *NYT* (5/25/84); Andrew Britton, "The Politics of Reaganite Entertainment," *Movie* 31/32 (Winter 1986), 3.

Pfeil, *Another Tale to Tell* op. cit. 111; Stephen M. Silverman, "'Ghostbusters' Is Plum Logo," *NY Post* (7/31/84); "Variations of 'No Ghost' Are Coming On Like Gangbusters," *NYT* (10/12/84).

TDR, 249.

Peter Bart, "Doing It McVeigh's Way," *Variety* (6/16–22/97); Elizabeth Kastor, "The Night of 'Red Dawn,'" *WP* (8/9/84); *Variety* (8/8/84); "Newly Patriotic Crowds Cheer Rabble-Rousing Film," Jan Cherubin, "A 'Red (White and Blue) Dawn,'"

LA Herald Examiner Style section (8/15/84); Roger Simon, "'Red Dawn': All's Right with War," *Chicago Sun-Times* (8/16/84); Susan Vigilante, "The Russians Are Coming," *Policy Review* (Winter 1985), 90–91.

Germond and Witcover op. cit. 430; *Variety* (8/29/84); Oran P. Smith to Ronald Reagan (8/30/84), #246188, RRPL.

Francis X. Clines, "Reporter's Notebook: Few Blacks in Reagan Crowds," *NYT* (9/8/84); Clines, "Reagan Plays His Campaign Song at Country Music's Capital," *NYT* (9/16/84); "is that really me?" in Peter W. Kaplan, "The Man Behind the Ferraro Ad," *NYT* (3/7/85); Germond and Witcover op. cit. 549; "The media will notice" in *Letters of the Century 1900–1999*, ed. Lisa Grunwald and Stephen J. Adler (New York: Random House, 2008), 587.

FN: Dante in McBride op. cit. 340. FN: Stan Hart, "Grimlins," *Mad* (Sept 1984). FN: Silverman, *NY Post* (7/31/84) op. cit.; "'Ghostbusters' Overcomes Short Prod. Sked to Smash Results," *Variety* (6/27/84); Gitlin, "The Medium: Down the Tubes," *Seeing Through Movies*, ed. Mark Crispin Miller (New York: Pantheon Books, 1990), 16. FN: Bernard Avishai, "Orwell and the English Language," *1984 Revisited: Totalitarianism in Our Century*, ed. Irving Howe (New York: Harper & Row, 1983), 67. FN: Kopkind, *Nation* (9/15/84), 25.

Stars & Hype Forever

FN: "The Best Conservative Movies," *National Review* (2/9/09). FN: Graham Yost, "Journals: Belushi of the Spirits," *Film Comment* (May/June 1984).

V. Forward into the Past, 1985–86

Champlin, "Rewards of Reassurance: Big Votes, Large Grosses," *LAT* Calendar (11/8/84); Richard Corliss, "Box-Office Brawn," *Time* (12/24/90); Collins, "Pumping Arnold," *Rolling Stone* (1/17/85); *TRD*, 74.

Jane Gross, "Mourning 6 Million Jews," *NYT* (4/18/85), 13; *NYT* (4/19/85), 1. *TRD*, 315.

Hendrik Hertzberg, "Notes and Comments," *New Yorker* (5/27/85), 27–28; Haines, "'What Kind of War?': An Analysis of the Vietnam Veterans Memorial," *Critical Studies in Mass Communication* (March 1986), 10; See Joshua Hammer, "Cashing In on Vietnam," *Newsweek* (1/16/89), 38–39; Stallone in Richard Zoglin, "An Outbreak of Rambomania," *Time* (6/24/85).

Bernard Weinraub "President Accuses 5 'Outlaw States' of World Terror," *NYT* (7/9/85).

FN: *Variety* (10/31/84); "Schwarzenegger Wanted Title Role," *NYT* (11/9/84). FN: Corliss, "Box-Office Brawn" op. cit. FN: Reagan and Shamir, see Cannon op. cit. 486–87. FN: Berman, "Rambo: From Counter-Culture to Contra," *Telos* (Summer

1985), 144. FN: Collins, "The Rolling Stone Interview: Sylvester Stallone," *Rolling Stone* (12/9/85), 166.

Happy Daze

Jack Rosenthal, "The Endless Fifties," *NYT* (1/3/82), A22; Wills, *Reagan's America* op. cit. 459; Richard Zoglin, "Cosby, Inc." *Time* (9/28/87), 56; Marc, *Comic Visions* op. cit. 181.

Hard Bodies op. cit. 70; Spielberg in *Back to the Future* production notes (1985); Universal executive in McBride op. cit. 385; Marc op. cit. 182; *Reagan's America* op. cit. 460; David Haglund, "Reagan's Favorite Sitcom," Slate.com (3/2/2007).

Life (July 1985); *TRD*, 343; *TRD*, 351; Weinberg op. cit. 223; Canby, "Is Action or Politics the Real Attraction?," *NYT* Arts and Leisure (9/29/85).

FN: Marty, "Looking Backward Into the Future," *NYT* (2/6/75); Weinberg op. cit. 148. FN: Hoberman, "Spielbergism and Its Discontents," *VV* (7/9/85). FN: Weinberg op. cit. 151.

Top Ray-Gun

Rovin cited in Canby *NYT* (12/8/85); *Newsweek* (12/23/85); Philip Taubman, "Soviet Pans 'Rocky' and 'Rambo' Films," *NYT* (1/4/86); "War-nography," *NYT* (1/8/86); Buchanan to Daniels memo (4/7/86) with handwritten reply (4/10/86) #390394, RRPL; "I was a teenage Rambo," *Variety* (1/22/86); *TRD*, 36; *TRD*, 401; *TRD*, 405.

Stone in Patrick Goldstein, "'Salvador'—Drawing a Bead on a Dirty War," *LAT* (12/1/85); Denby, *New York* (3/24/86); Brooks, *Washington Times* Insight (4/28/85); Kehr, "The Left Stuff," *Chicago Reader* (4/25/86), 12.

Bruckheimer in Tom Shone, *Blockbuster: How Hollywood Learned to Stop Worrying and Love the Summer* (New York: Free Press, 2004), 174; Rappaport, "Vietnam: The Thousand Plateaus," *The 60s Without Apology*, ed. Sohnya Sayres, Anders Stephanson, Stanley Aronowitz, and Frederic Jameson (Minneapolis: University of Minnesota Press, 1984), 141; "Top Gun Boosting Service Sign-Ups," *LAT* (6/5/86).

Denby, "Poison," *New York* (6/9/86); Philip Taubman "Russians Strike Back with a Rambo of Their Own," *NYT* (7/24/86).

FN: Weintraub to Peter Roussel, Office of the Press Secretary letter (12/2/85) and Roberts to Fielding memo (12/12/85) #369455, RRPL. FN: Cockburn, "Superfiend," *The Nation* (4/26/86), 576–77. FN: Canby, "Inside 'Cobra' May Dwell a Pussycat," *NYT* Arts and Leisure (6/1/86). FN: See J. Hoberman, "The Self-Made Man," *VV* (2/12/91), 53–54, and "Nietzsche's Boy," *Sight and Sound* (Sept 1991), 22–25.

In Dreams: *Blue Velvet* and the New AmericanArama

Lance Morrow, "Yankee Doodle Magic: What Makes Reagan So Remarkably Popular a President?," *Time* (8/7/86).

James, *NYT* (8/14/86); *Variety* (9/3/86); Aljean Harmetz, "River's Edge' Defies Experts' Expectations," *NYT* (6/6/87); Denby, *New York* (5/18/87), 91.

Baudrillard, *America* (New York: Verso, 1988), 114, 31, 2, 51, 104.

"Probing the Depths of Evil," *Christian Century* (1/7–14/87), 5; Simon, "Neat Trick," *National Review* (11/7/86), 54; Ebert, *Chicago Sun-Times* (9/19/86); Hampton, "David Lynch's Secret History of the United States," *Film Comment* (May–June 1993), 40; Joseph Breen to Jack L. Warner letter (4/22/41), AMPAS *Kings Row* file.

Cannon op. cit. 61.

TRD, 448; *TRD*, 449; *TRD*, 450; *TRD*, 452.

FN: "The Reagan Hangover," *New Republic* (10/13/86), 7, 10. FN: "The boy is an idealist" in *L'Ecran fantastique* 76 (Jan 1987). FN: *TRD*, 445. FN: *Comics Journal* 116 (July 1987). FN: Redford in Hoberman, *The Dream Life* (New York: The New Press, 2003), 350.

Platoon Time (from *Heartbreak Ridge* to *Hamburger Hill*)

"mean and hostile," Patrick McGilligan, *Clint: The Life and Legend* (New York: St. Martin's Press, 2002), 400; Zaenger, "Recycled Plot Is a Heartbreak, All Right," *Fort Wayne News-Sentinel* (12/9/86), 5F; Sims to Manes (11/18/86) and Eastwood to Sims (11/19/86), FOIA request RRPL; "Marines Withdraw Support for 'Ridge,'" *Variety* (7/3/86).

Kehr, "Eastwood Takes Risk and Wins," *Chicago Tribune* (12/5/86); Kael "The Good, the So-So, and the Ugly," *Hooked* (New York: E.P. Dutton, 1989), 246–47; Jack Mathews, "Hollywood Steps on a Gold Mine," *LA Times*, January 25th Calendar; Fonda in ibid.; Podhoretz, "Platoon Sullies Vietnam Veterans," *Washington Times* Insight (1/19/87), 65.

Drew, *New Yorker* (3/30/87); Peter J. Boyer, "Is It Prime Time for Vietnam?," *NYT* Arts & Leisure (8/2/86), 1, 16; Denby, "Without a Whisper of Doubt," *New York* (9/14/87), 108; Canby, *NYT* (3/27/87); Denby, "Flea-Bagged," *New York* (4/13/87); Kauffmann, "Hanoi and Elsewhere," *New Republic* (4/18/87); repeatedly defended, see *Human Events* (7/11/87), 7; Timothy Egan, "Veterans Returning to Vietnam to End a Haunting," *NYT* (1/24/89).

FN: Lee Siegel, "Vets in Battle over Clint Film's Accuracy," *NY Post* (7/3/86). FN: Cockburn, "Afterglow: All the President's Men," *The Nation* (4/4/87), 422. FN: Carabatsos in Jay Carr, "Taking the Politics out of Vietnam," *Boston Globe* (8/26/87), 29; Carabatsos in Jay Sharbutt, *LAT* (2/9/85). FN: *Variety* (6/17/87); Maslin, *NYT* (6/12/87); Juliann Garey, "Beefy Boys," *VV* (6/23/87). FN: *Newsweek* (1/16/89) op. cit.

Ishtar, Moment of Truth

TRD, 496; Ebert, *Chicago Sun Times* (5/15/87); Biskind, "Madness in Morocco: The Road to Ishtar," *Vanity Fair* (February 2010).

Reagan 700 Club interview, *Spiritual Warfare: The Politics of the Christian Right* (Boston, MA: South End Press, 1989), 76–77; Bob Drogin, "After High Hopes for Mission, He Found 'Rug Merchants': McFarlane Quickly Disillusioned in Iran," *LAT* (2/28/87).

Harmetz, "Elaine May's 'Ishtar': A $51 Million Film in Trouble," *NYT* (5/19/87); Sarris, "The Buddy Syndrome," *VV* (6/23/87); "Blind Camels, Idiot Execs, and 5 Other *Ishtar* Revelations from Director Elaine May," *Movieline* (5/18/2011); *TRD*, 499.

FN: Sylbert in Biskind op. cit. FN: *Movieline* op. cit.

VI. Once upon a Time in the Eighties, 1987–88

"Friends Say Oliver North Is Taking It Like a Soldier," *NYT* (11/30/86); Dowd, "Iran Contra Hearings: The Non-Audience and the Audience; for the 'Can Do' Colonel, Admissions, No Apology," *NYT* (7/8/87); Dowd, ". . . As Books and Movies Are Hatching Apace," *NYT* (12/19/86); "Ollie-Oop!," *People* (7/27/87); Rickey, "Right Out of 'Mr. Smith,'" *Philadelphia Inquirer* (7/13/87); Denby, "Ollie North, the Movie," *New Republic* (8/3/87).

Edelstein, "Heavy Metal," *VV* (7/21/87), 58; Verhoeven in Brian Cronenworth, "Man of Iron," *American Film* (October 1987), 35. Babbitt in Dennis Lythgoe, "Joke-Tellers: When It Comes to Wit, Politicians Have High Standards to Follow," *Desert News* (6/3/88); Douglas in J. Hoberman, "Victim Victorious: Well-Fed Yuppie Michael Douglas Leads the Charge for Resentful White Men," *VV* (3/7/95), 32.

FN: Shales, "The Ollie Finale," *Washington Post* (7/15/87). FN: William E. Schmidt, "As Oliver North's Story Fades, 'People Are Ready for a New Controversy,'" *NYT* (8/7/87); "North Souvenirs Draw Few Takers," *NYT* (9/13/87).

The Crash

"If suddenly the earth's civilizations" in Robert Service, *The End of the Cold War 1985–1991* (New York: PublicAffairs, 2015), 287; "I've often wondered" in Sean Wilentz, *The Age of Reagan: A History 1974–2008* (New York: HarperCollins, 2008), 262; see also Cannon op. cit. 59–60; "a younger son I never knew I had" in Rogin op. cit. 16; "Bush Battles the 'Wimp Factor,'" *Newsweek* (10/19/87); David S. Broder and David Hoffman, "Bush Deflects Attacks During GOP Debate," *WP* (10/29/87); David S. Broder, "Round 1 Goes to George Bush," *WP* (10/30/87).

Richard J. Meislin, "The Market Turmoil: A Far-Ranging Impact: Yuppies' Last Rites Readied," *NYT* (10/21/87), D14; Lee A. Daniels, "After the Fall: Will the Yuppies Rise Again?," *NYT* (11/2/87); Hertzberg, "The Short Happy Life of the American Yuppie," *Esquire* (February 1988), 102; Bunch, 95; "Iacocca Disavows 1988 Race," *NYT* (12/29/86); Fox Butterfield, "Trump Turns Down Democrats' Dinner," *NYT* (11/24/87); Fox Butterfield, "Trump Hints of Dreams Beyond Building," *NYT* (10/5/87); Geraldine Fabrikant, "Wall Street Reviews 'Wall Street,'" *NYT* (12/10/87); *Newsday* and *Washington Post* in J. Hoberman, "Gordon Gekko May Be a Problem for Mitt Romney," *LAT* (4/15/12); "*Wall Street* as a *Scarface* of Business," *Oliver Stone's USA: Film, History, and Controversy*, ed. Robert Brent Toplin (Lawrence, KS: University Press of Kansas, 2000), 233; Edelstein, "Raiders of the Lost Market," *VV* Film Supplement (December 1987), 30; "drunken Wall Street broker" in Michael Cieply, "Film's Wall Street Predator to Make a Comeback," *NYT* (5/5/2007); Douglas in Hoberman, "Victim Victorious" op. cit. 32.

FN: Alex Cox, *X Films: The True Confessions of a Radical Filmmaker* (Berkeley CA: Soft Skull Press, 2008). FN: Hoberman, "Gordon Gekko May Be a Problem" op. cit.

Roger Rabbit's Last Temptation: "Read My Lips"

Bill Barol, "The Eighties Are Over," *Newsweek* (1/4/88), 40; Sidney Blumenthal, *Pledging Allegiance: The Last Campaign of the Cold War* (New York: Harper Perennial, 1991), 155; Peter J. Boyer, "Rather's Questioning of Bush Sets Off Shouting on Live Broadcast," *NYT* (1/26/88); Julie Johnson, "Dole Confronts Bush in Senate; Voices Anger at Criticism of Wife," *NYT* (2/5/88); Mimi Avins, "The Secret of Sly's Excess: Rambo 3," *Premiere* (June 1988), 54.

J. Hoberman, "With God, and the Constitution, on His Side: A 1988 Film Anticipated 'The Passion of the Christ' and Puts It in a Discomfiting Light," *The Forward* (2/20/2004), 11–12, see also J. Hoberman and Jeffrey Shandler, *Entertaining America: Jews, Movies, and Broadcasting* (Princeton NJ: Princeton University Press, 2003), 72.

FN: Rosenbaum, "Who Framed Roger Rabbit?" *Film Quarterly* (Fall 1988), 36. FN: Hoberman, "With God" op. cit. FN: ibid.; Blumenthal op. cit. 269.

Running on Empty, They Live Again

Maslin, *NYT* (5/8/87); Rainer, "River's Edge," *Premiere* (July/August 1987); Edelstein, "Night of the Toking Dead," *VV* (5/12/87), 65; "It's just too bad" in Hoberman, *The Dream Life* op. cit. 388–89.

E.J. Dionne Jr., "Poll Shows Bush Sets Agenda for Principal Election Issues," *NYT* (9/14/88); *TRD*, 648; Dowd, "For Bush on the Campaign Trail, the Style Is First

Sour, Then Sweet," *NYT* (10/12/88), 1; "can't even pronounce his name" in "Country Singers Stand by Their Man," *NYT* (9/29/88); Gerald M. Boyd, "Proud to Run with Quayle, Bush Says," *NYT* (8/23/88); "Story on Mrs. Dukakis Is Denied by Campaign," *NYT* (8/26/88); Michael Oreskes, "2 Hopefuls Sharpen Debate Weapons," *NYT* (9/19/88); "time to unleash our one-liners?" in *New Yorker* (10/10/87), 108; *Time* (10/3/88); Gerald M. Boyd, "Bush, Fighting Back Glee, Vows Tough Battle to End," *NYT* (10/15/88); Maureen Dowd, "Bush Boasts of Turnaround from 'Easy Rider' Society," *NYT* (10/7/88), B7; "Novelty Makers Fear Post-Reagan Era," *NYT* (11/3/88); "Reagan Sees Election as Referendum on Him," *NYT* (11/6/88).

Michael Oreskes, "TV's Role in '88: The Medium Is the Election," *NYT* (10/30/88), 1; Beale, "Horrors! Yuppies vs. the Homeless," *Philadelphia Daily News* (11/8/88); Matthew Flamm, "Yuppie Bodysnatcher," *NY Post* (11/2/87), 27; Zizek, "Through the Glasses Darkly," *In These Times* (November 2008), 42.

FN: Canby, "Film View: Into the Dark Heartland," *NYT* Arts & Leisure (6/13/87), 23. FN: "Patty Hearst is today" in J. Hoberman, "Believe It or Not," *Artforum* (December 1988). FN: Blumenthal op. cit. 262. FN: Marsha Kinder, "Back to the Future in the 80s with Fathers & Sons, Supermen & PeeWees, Gorillas & Toons," *Film Quarterly* (Summer 1989). FN: Pickrell, UCLA *Daily Bruin* (11/3/88). FN: Zizek op. cit. 42–43.

Morning After in America

"cold war is over" in Blumenthal op. cit. 323.

FN: Quayle inspired by *The Candidate* in Hoberman, *The Dream Life* op. cit. 356n. FN: Blumenthal op. cit. 308–9.

Epilogue: Remake My Day

FN: Michael Miner, "When Thatcher and George H.W. Bush Discussed the Iraqi Invasion of Kuwait," *Chicago Reader* (4/11/13).

Reagan Nostalgia

Will Bunch, *Tear Down This Myth: The Right-Wing Distortion of the Reagan Legacy* (New York: Free Press, 2010), 159; "Shifting 'Reagans' to Cable Has CBS Facing New Critics," *NYT* (11/2/03), A1; Alessandra Stanley, "What Hatchet Job? Reagan Movie Is Run of the Mill," *NYT* (11/30/03); Alessandra Stanley, "A Pageant Over 2 Decades in the Making," *NYT* (6/10/04).

FN: Bunch op. cit. 98. FN: "Shifting 'Reagans,'" *NYT* (11/2/03) op. cit.

Vulgar Reaganism

Trump and film school, Maureen Dowd, "The Don and His Badfellas," *NYT* (7/29/18); Charles Ventura, "Matt Damon: Trump Required Cameos for Movies

Filmed in His Buildings," *USA Today* (9/2/2017); Kroker and Cook, *The Postmodern Scene* op. cit. 268; Neil Postman, *Amusing Ourselves to Death: Public Discourse in the Age of Show Business* (New York: Viking, 1985), 137.

Peter Baker, "Trump and the Truth: A President Test His Own Credibility," *NYT* (3/17/18); Philip Bump, "Trump Once Figured He'd Be the First Person to Make Money Running for President. He Didn't," *WP* (6/27/17); Postman op. cit. 141.

FN: Ned Martel, "Ronald Reagan, in Black and White," *NYT* (10/29/04). FN: https://aeon.co/essays/was-francis-fukuyama-the-first-man-to-see-trump-coming. FN: James Poniewozik, "A Well-Wrought Stage Helps Bolster Trump," *NYT* (1/26/18). FN: "Trump and Eastwood in Dowd," *NYT* (7/29/18) op. cit.

It Can Happen Here

FN: Hannah Arendt, *The Origins of Totalitarianism* (New York: Harcourt, 1973), 382.

INDEX

ABOUT THE AUTHOR

J. Hoberman's books include *The Dream Life: Movies, Media, and the Mythology of the Sixties* and *An Army of Phantoms: American Movies and the Making of the Cold War* (both from The New Press). He has written for *Artforum*, *The Nation*, the *New York Review of Books*, and the *New York Times*. For over thirty years, he was a film critic for the *Village Voice*. He lives in New York.

PUBLISHING IN THE PUBLIC INTEREST

Thank you for reading this book published by The New Press. The New Press is a nonprofit, public interest publisher. New Press books and authors play a crucial role in sparking conversations about the key political and social issues of our day.

We hope you enjoyed this book and that you will stay in touch with The New Press. Here are a few ways to stay up to date with our books, events, and the issues we cover:

- Sign up at www.thenewpress.com/subscribe to receive updates on New Press authors and issues and to be notified about local events
- Like us on Facebook: www.facebook.com/newpressbooks
- Follow us on Twitter: www.twitter.com/thenewpress

Please consider buying New Press books for yourself; for friends and family; or to donate to schools, libraries, community centers, prison libraries, and other organizations involved with the issues our authors write about.

The New Press is a 501(c)(3) nonprofit organization. You can also support our work with a tax-deductible gift by visiting www.thenewpress.com/donate.